STORY AND ART BY
RUMIKO TAKAHASHI

CONTENTS

THE STORY THUS FAR

Long ago, in the "Warring States" era of Japan's Muromachi period, dog-like half demon Inuyasha attempted to steal the Shikon Jewel—or "Jewel of Four Souls"—from a village. The village priestess, Kikyo, put a stop to his thievery with an enchanted arrow. Pinned to a tree, Inuyasha fell into a deep sleep, while mortally wounded Kikyo took the jewel with her into her funeral pyre. Years passed...

In the present day, Kagome, a Japanese high school girl, is pulled down into a well and transported into the past. There she discovers trapped Inuyasha—and frees him.

When the Shikon Jewel mysteriously reappears, demons attack. In the ensuing battle, the jewel *shatters*!

Now Inuyasha is bound to Kagome with a powerful spell, and the grudging companions must battle to reclaim the shattered shards of the Shikon Jewel to keep them out of evil hands...

LAST VOLUME Kagome shoots Naraku and exorcises him. As Hitomiko dies, she reveals that Kagome's priestess powers have been blocked from birth!

Naraku inhabits the evil aspect of the Jewel, Magatsuhi. Lightning shoots from Sesshomaru's empty left sleeve and destroys Magatsuhi's physical body. Suddenly, Sesshomaru grows both a new left arm and a new blade—Bakusaiga! Totosai explains that his new sword proves he has finally surpassed his father. Now...where did Naraku go?!

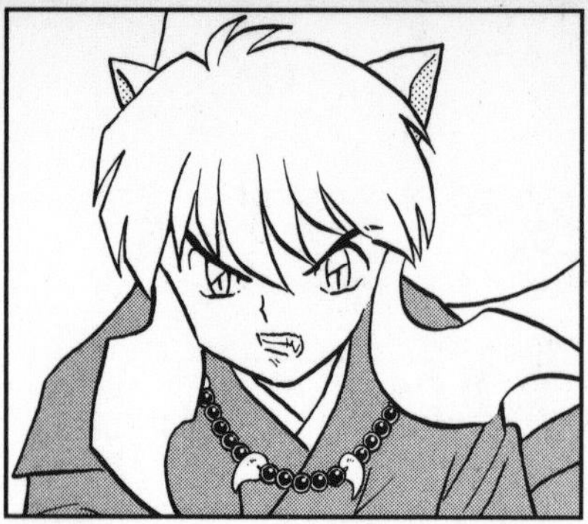

INUYASHA
Half-demon hybrid, son of a human mother and demon father. His necklace is enchanted, allowing Kagome to control him with a word.

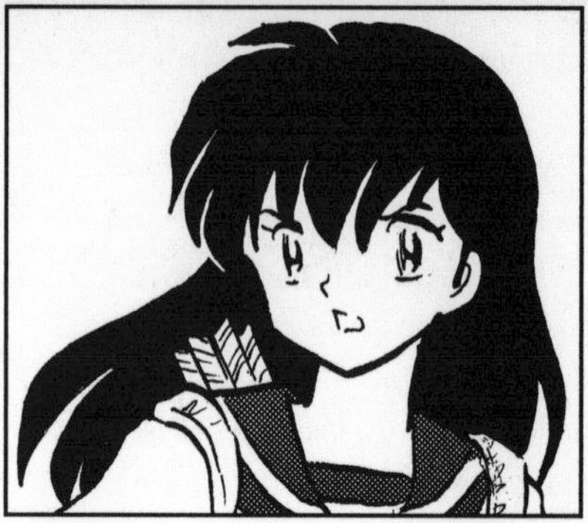

KAGOME
Modern-day Japanese schoolgirl who can travel back and forth between the past and present through an enchanted well.

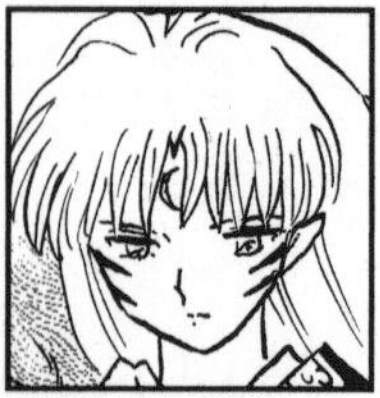

SESSHOMARU
Inuyasha's pure-blood demon half brother. They have the same demon father. Sesshomaru covets the sword left to Inuyasha by their father.

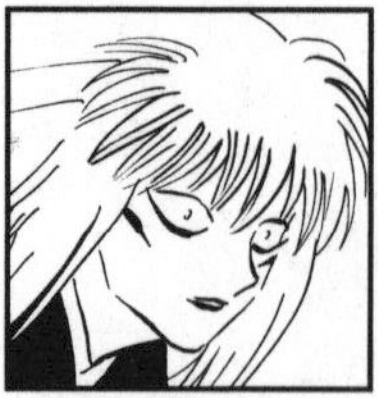

MAGATSUHI
A monstrous demon who dwells inside the Shikon Jewel but can sometimes escape to wreak havoc on everyone.

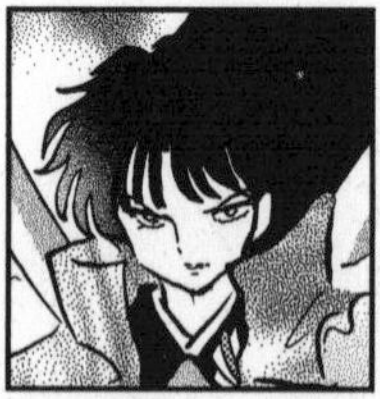

NARAKU
Enigmatic demon mastermind behind the miseries of nearly everyone in the story. He has the power to create multiple incarnations of himself from his body.

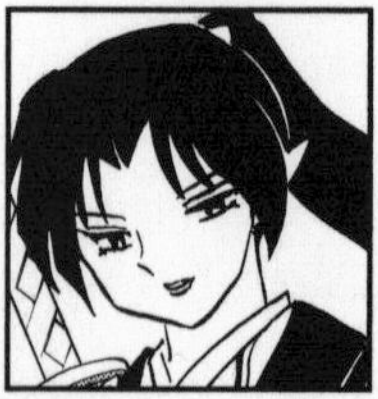

BYAKUYA
A powerful sorcerer and master of illusions created by Naraku.

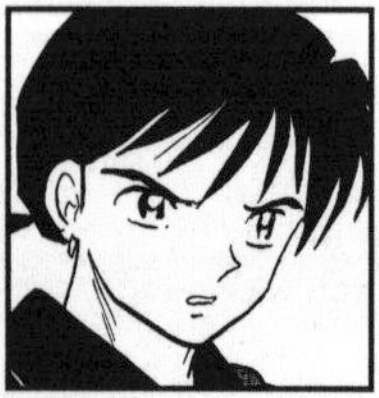

MIROKU
A Buddhist monk cursed with a mystical "Wind Tunnel" imbedded in his hand that both functions as a weapon and is slowly killing him.

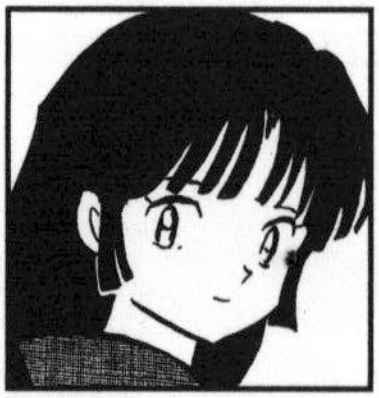

SANGO
A demon slayer from the village where the Shikon Jewel originated.

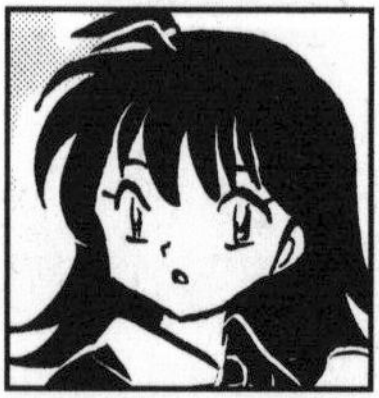

RIN
An orphaned girl devoted to Sesshomaru. He once resurrected her with Tenseiga. She brings out the best in him.

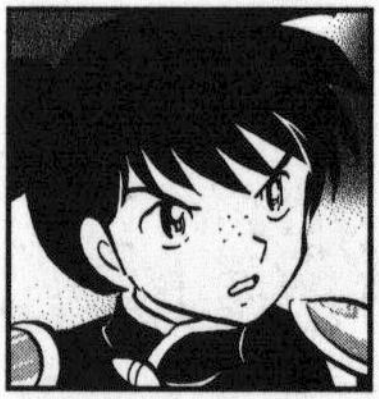

KOHAKU
Kohaku performed Naraku's dirty work for him and is trying to redeem himself.

SCROLL 1

MAGATSUHI'S SHADE

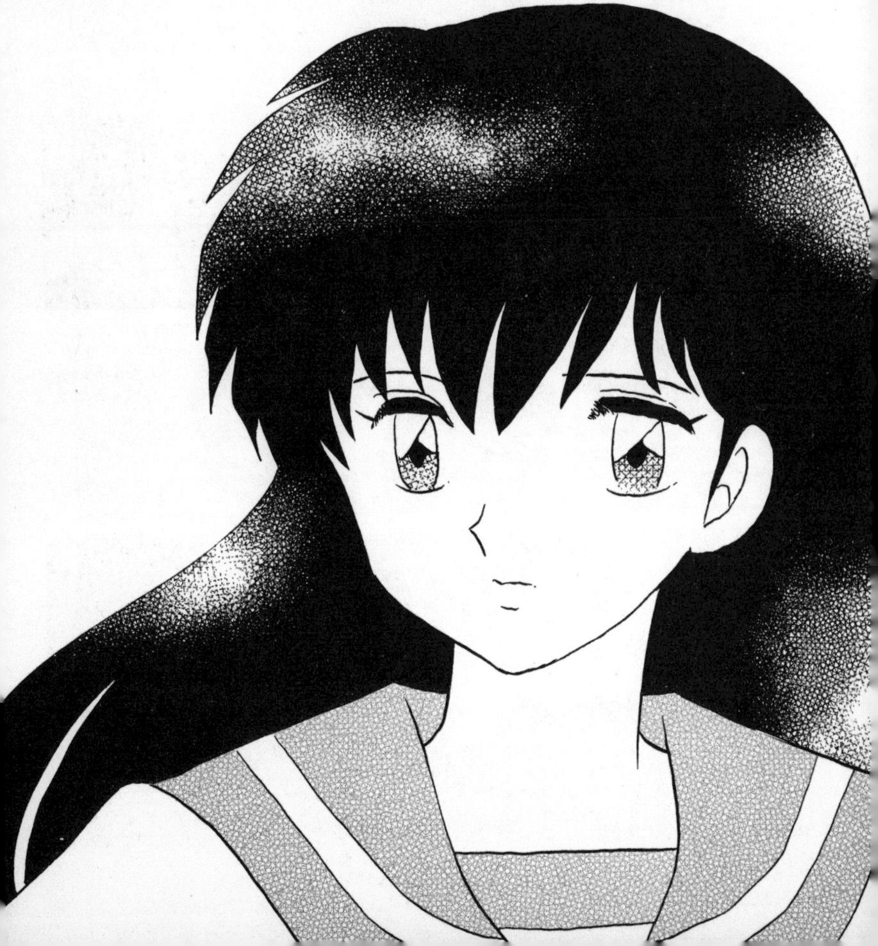

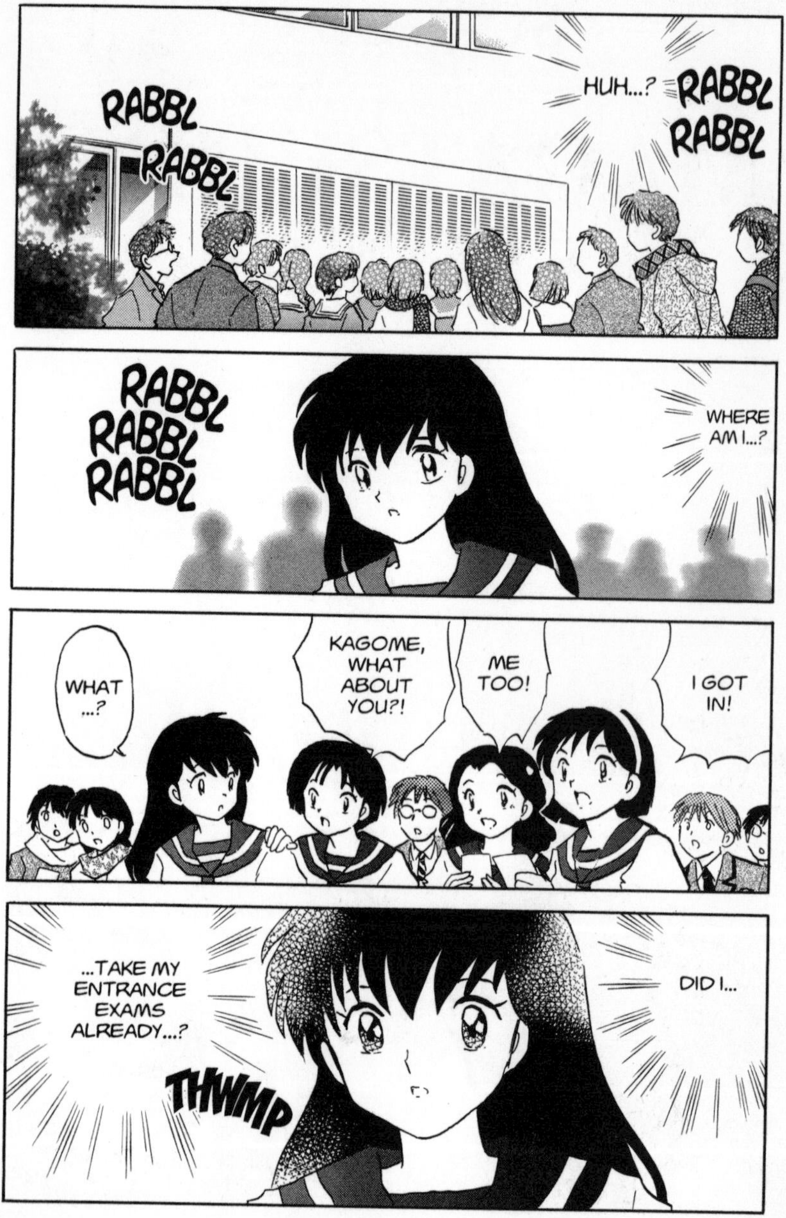
RABBL RABBL
HUH...?
RABBL RABBL
WHERE AM I...?
RABBL RABBL RABBL
I GOT IN!
ME TOO!
KAGOME, WHAT ABOUT YOU?!
WHAT ...?
DID I...
...TAKE MY ENTRANCE EXAMS ALREADY...?
THWMP

OH...

RIGHT.

WHAT ABOUT YOU, KAGOME...?

YES!! WE ALL MADE IT!

THWMP THWMP

YADDA

WEEEE

2	70	108	146	174	200	233
3	7	109	147	177	1	236
4	7	110	149	178	202	237
5	76	112	150	181	203	238

WHAT?

WHAT...?

NO!!

VWTH!

I...

...FAILED...

RR RK

IT'S NOT LISTED?!

MY EXAM NUMBER...

7

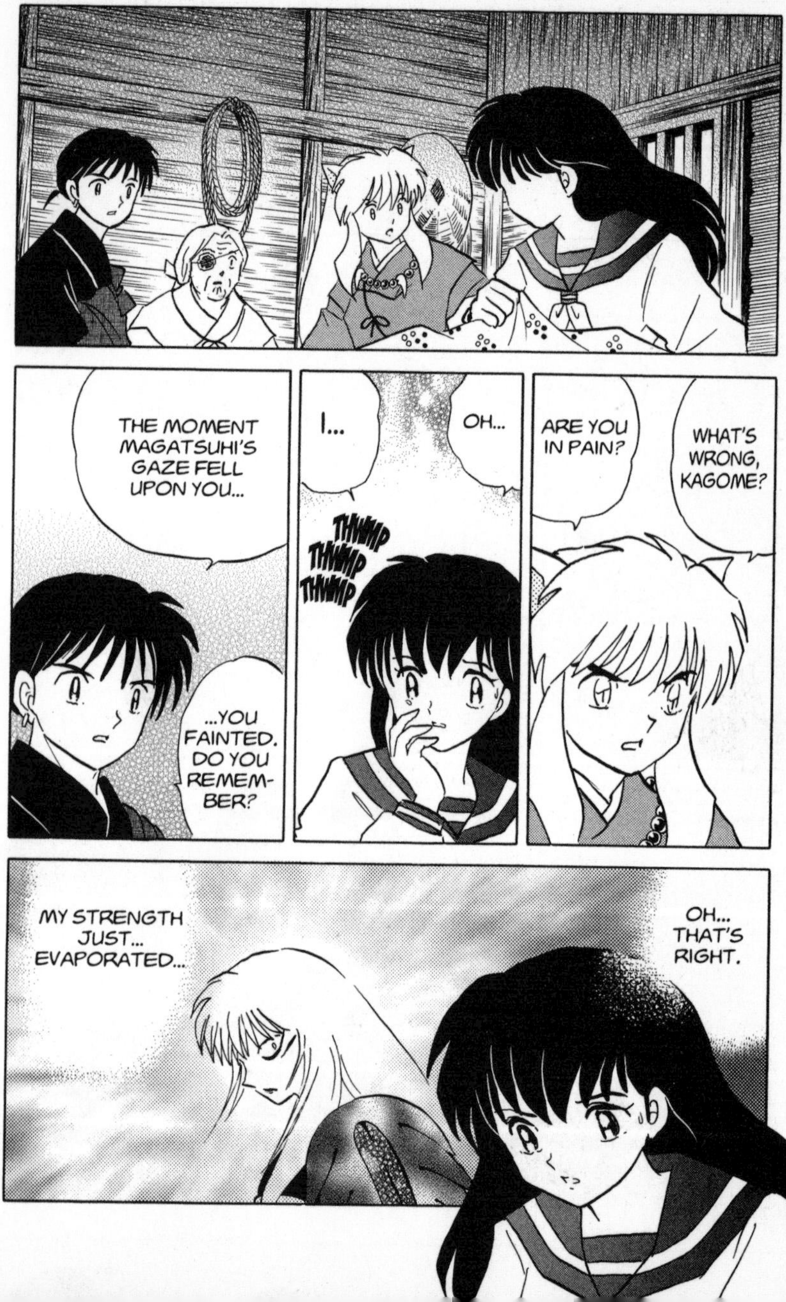
WHAT'S WRONG, KAGOME?
ARE YOU IN PAIN?
OH...
I...
THWMP THWMP THWMP
THE MOMENT MAGATSUHI'S GAZE FELL UPON YOU...
...YOU FAINTED. DO YOU REMEMBER?
OH... THAT'S RIGHT.
MY STRENGTH JUST... EVAPORATED...

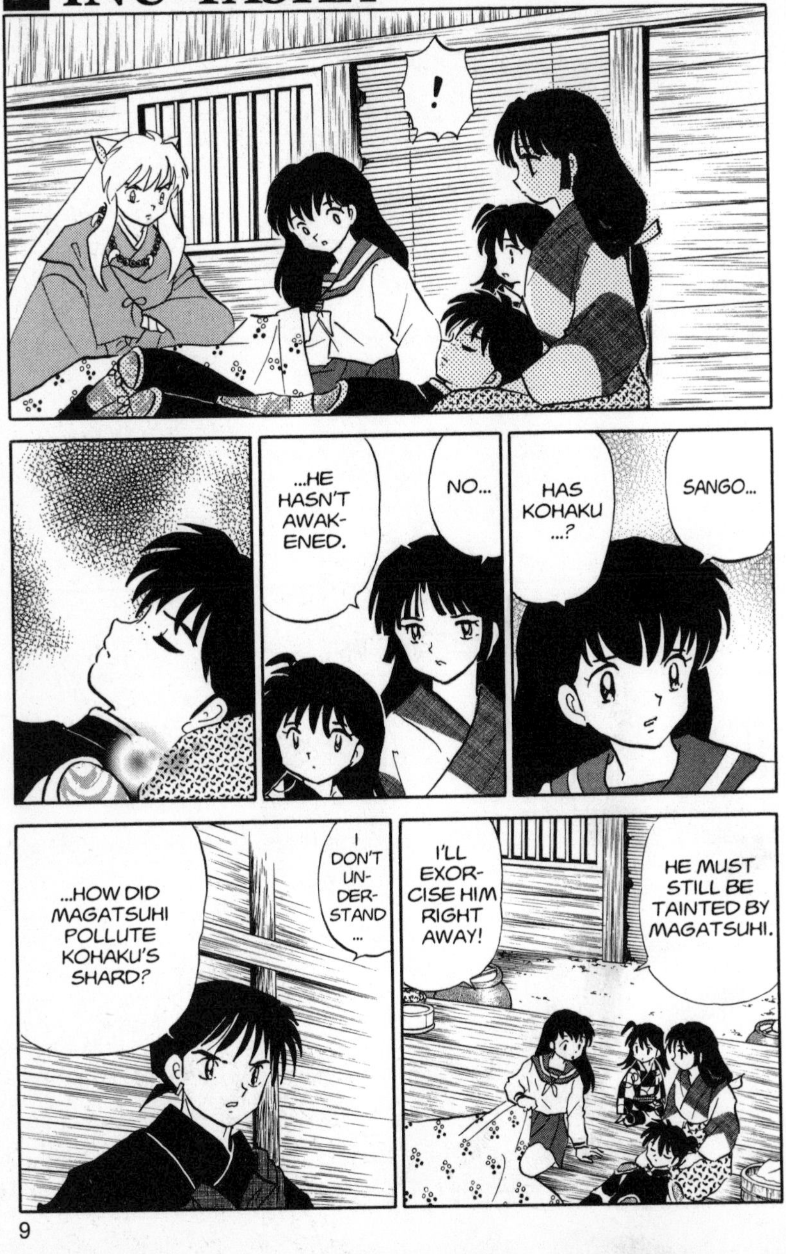
!
SANGO...
HAS KOHAKU ...?
NO...
...HE HASN'T AWAK-ENED.
HE MUST STILL BE TAINTED BY MAGATSUHI.
I'LL EXOR-CISE HIM RIGHT AWAY!
I DON'T UN-DER-STAND ...
...HOW DID MAGATSUHI POLLUTE KOHAKU'S SHARD?

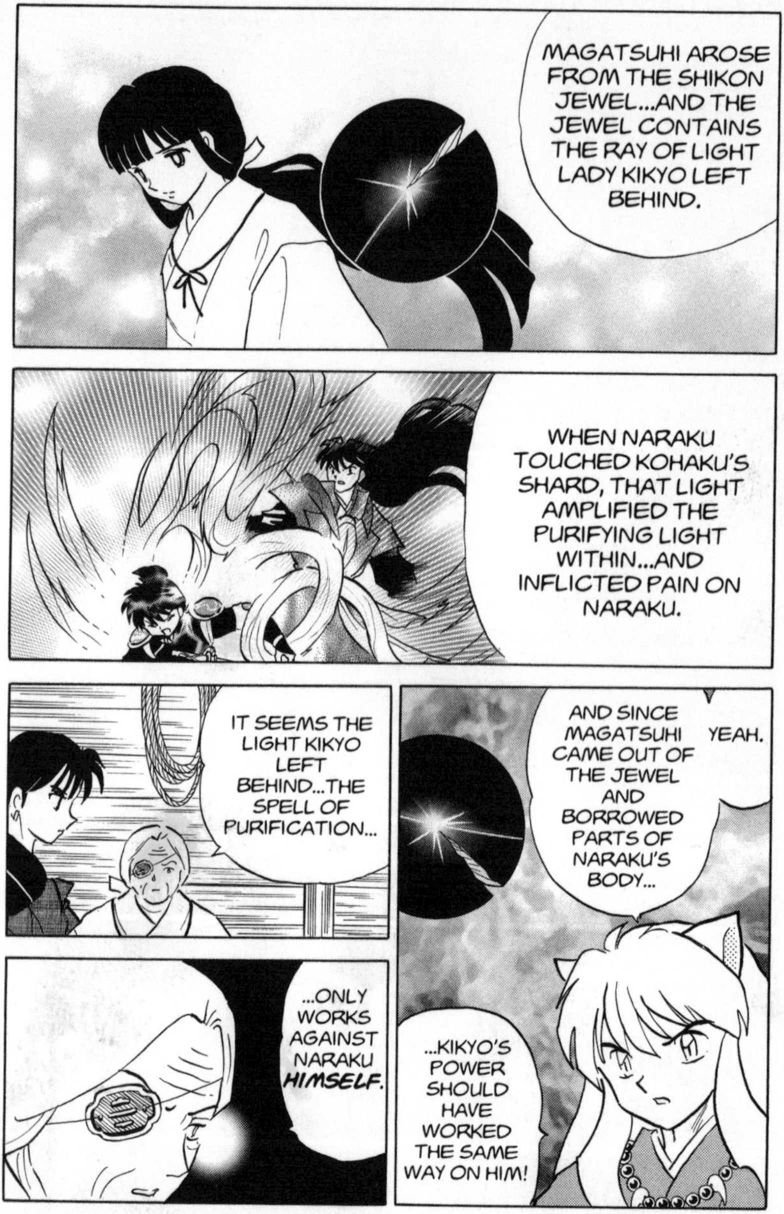
MAGATSUHI AROSE FROM THE SHIKON JEWEL...AND THE JEWEL CONTAINS THE RAY OF LIGHT LADY KIKYO LEFT BEHIND.
WHEN NARAKU TOUCHED KOHAKU'S SHARD, THAT LIGHT AMPLIFIED THE PURIFYING LIGHT WITHIN...AND INFLICTED PAIN ON NARAKU.
YEAH.
AND SINCE MAGATSUHI CAME OUT OF THE JEWEL AND BORROWED PARTS OF NARAKU'S BODY...
...KIKYO'S POWER SHOULD HAVE WORKED THE SAME WAY ON HIM!
IT SEEMS THE LIGHT KIKYO LEFT BEHIND...THE SPELL OF PURIFICATION...
...ONLY WORKS AGAINST NARAKU **HIMSELF**.

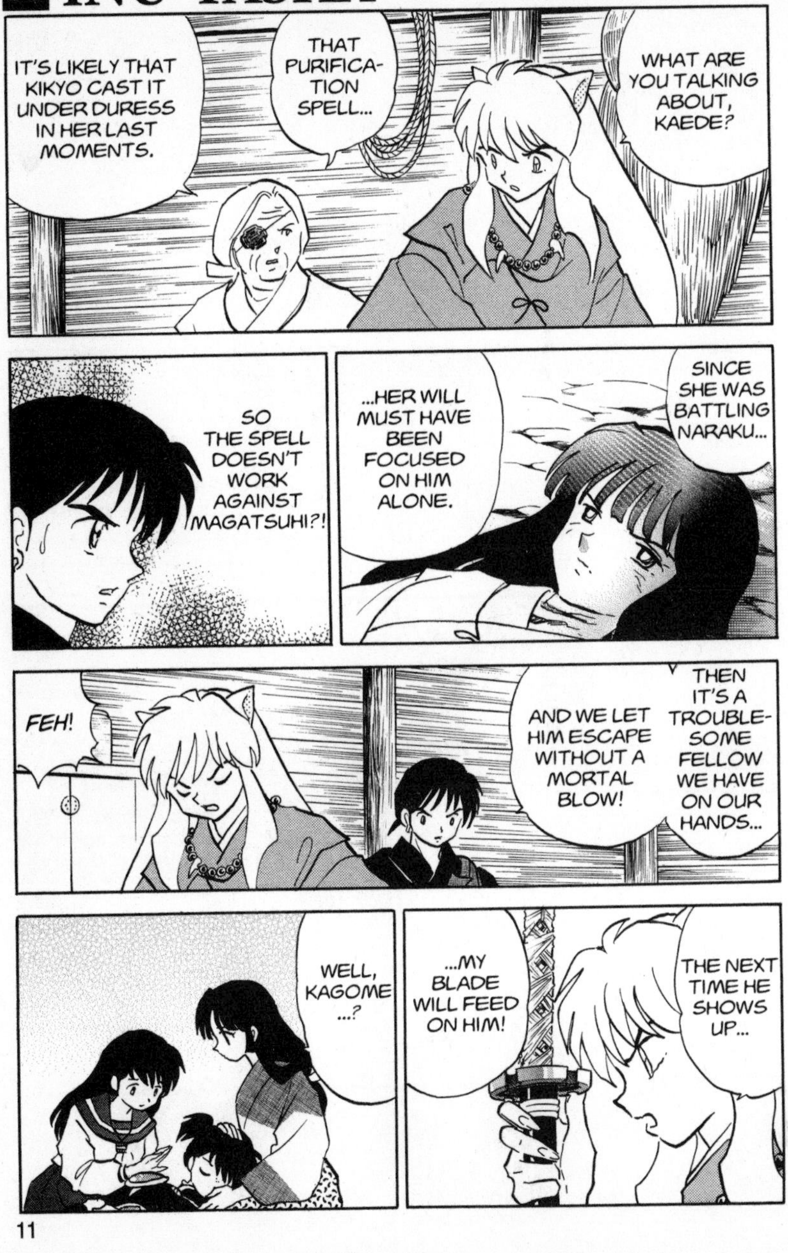
WHAT ARE YOU TALKING ABOUT, KAEDE?
THAT PURIFICATION SPELL...
IT'S LIKELY THAT KIKYO CAST IT UNDER DURESS IN HER LAST MOMENTS.
SINCE SHE WAS BATTLING NARAKU...
...HER WILL MUST HAVE BEEN FOCUSED ON HIM ALONE.
SO THE SPELL DOESN'T WORK AGAINST MAGATSUHI?!
THEN IT'S A TROUBLESOME FELLOW WE HAVE ON OUR HANDS...
AND WE LET HIM ESCAPE WITHOUT A MORTAL BLOW!
FEH!
THE NEXT TIME HE SHOWS UP...
...MY BLADE WILL FEED ON HIM!
WELL, KAGOME ...?

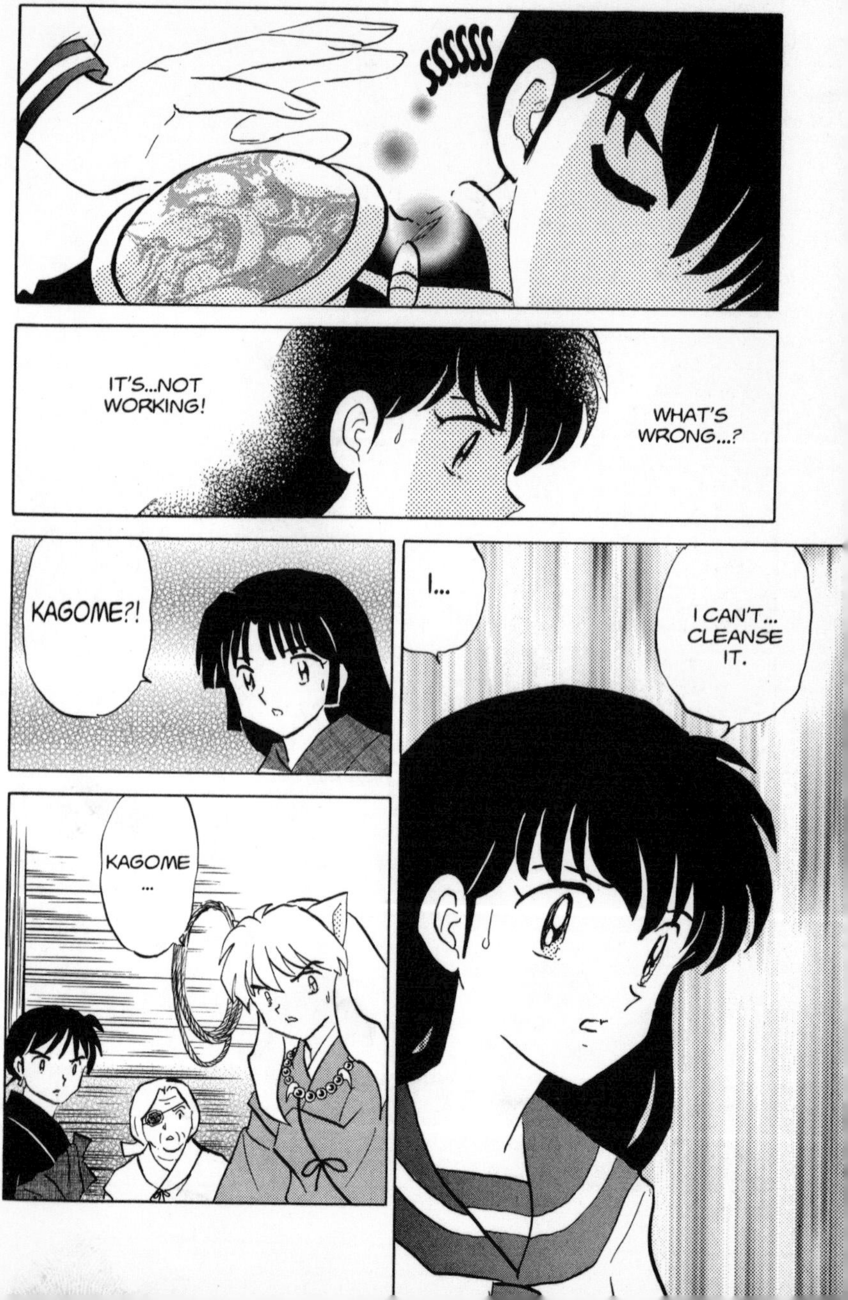
SSSSSS
IT'S...NOT WORKING!
WHAT'S WRONG...?
I...
I CAN'T... CLEANSE IT.
KAGOME?!
KAGOME ...

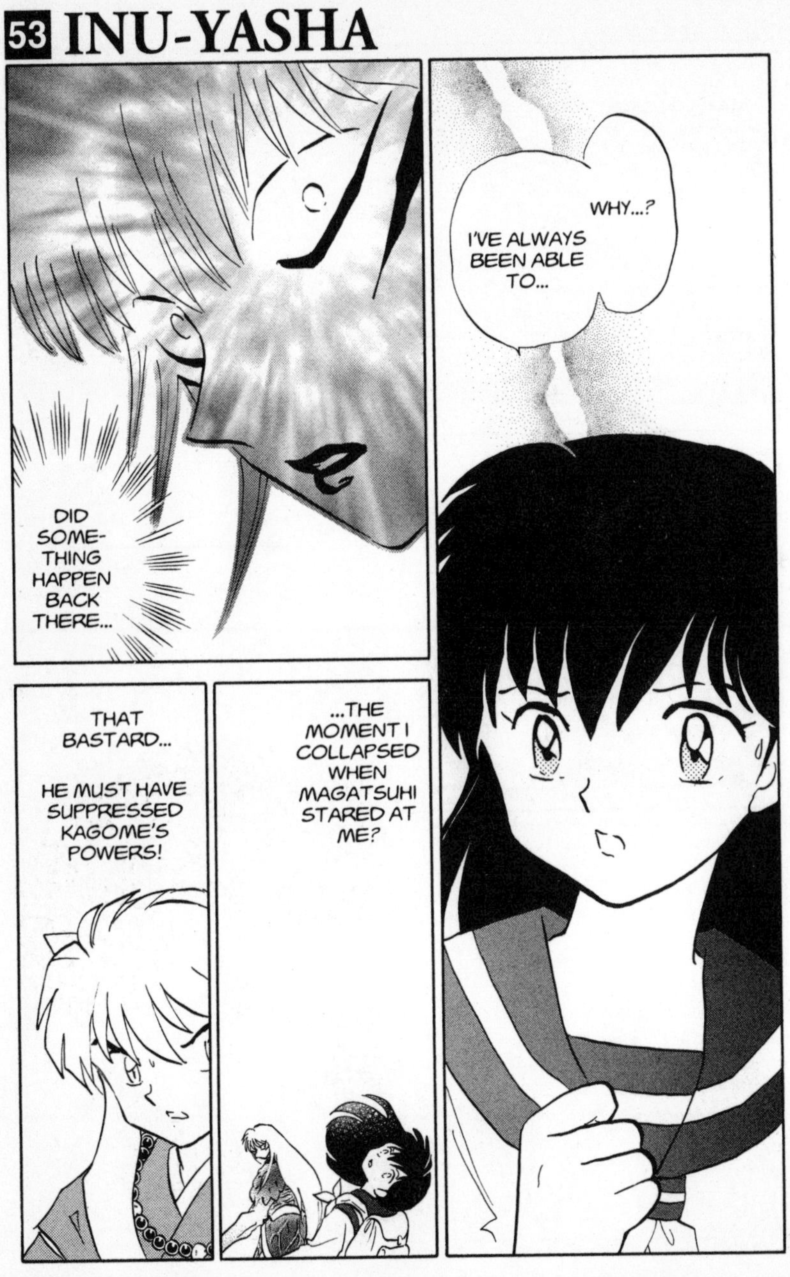
WHY...?
I'VE ALWAYS BEEN ABLE TO...
DID SOME-THING HAPPEN BACK THERE...
...THE MOMENT I COLLAPSED WHEN MAGATSUHI STARED AT ME?
THAT BASTARD...
HE MUST HAVE SUPPRESSED KAGOME'S POWERS!

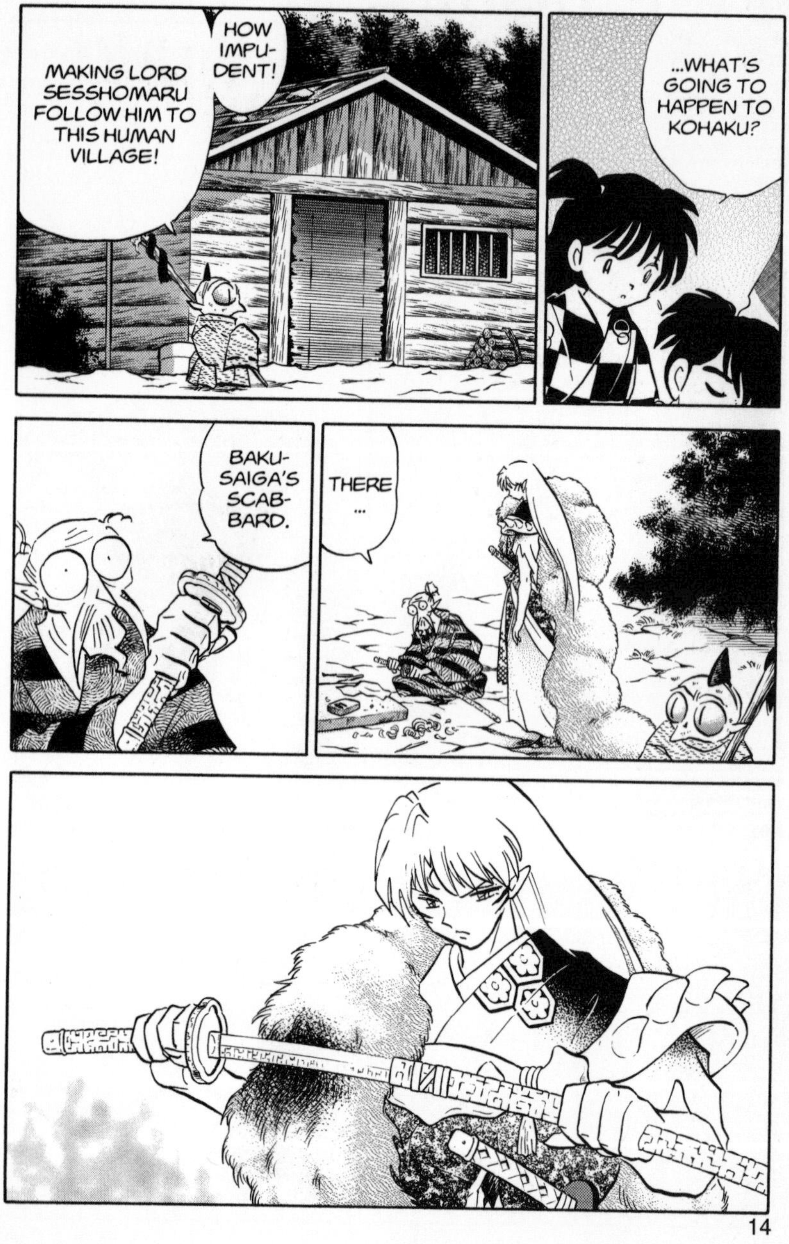
...WHAT'S GOING TO HAPPEN TO KOHAKU?
HOW IMPU-DENT!
MAKING LORD SESSHOMARU FOLLOW HIM TO THIS HUMAN VILLAGE!
THERE ...
BAKU-SAIGA'S SCAB-BARD.

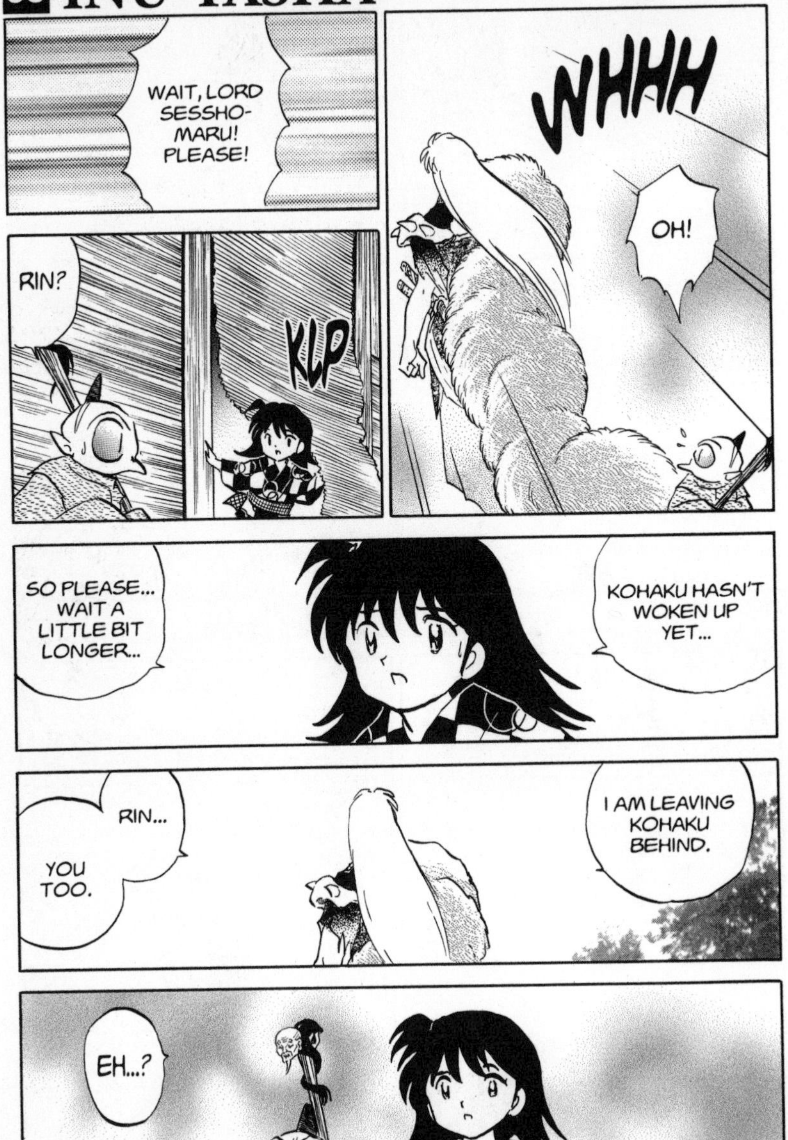
WHHH
OH!
WAIT, LORD SESSHOMARU! PLEASE!
KLP
RIN?
KOHAKU HASN'T WOKEN UP YET...
SO PLEASE... WAIT A LITTLE BIT LONGER...
I AM LEAVING KOHAKU BEHIND.
RIN... YOU TOO.
EH...?

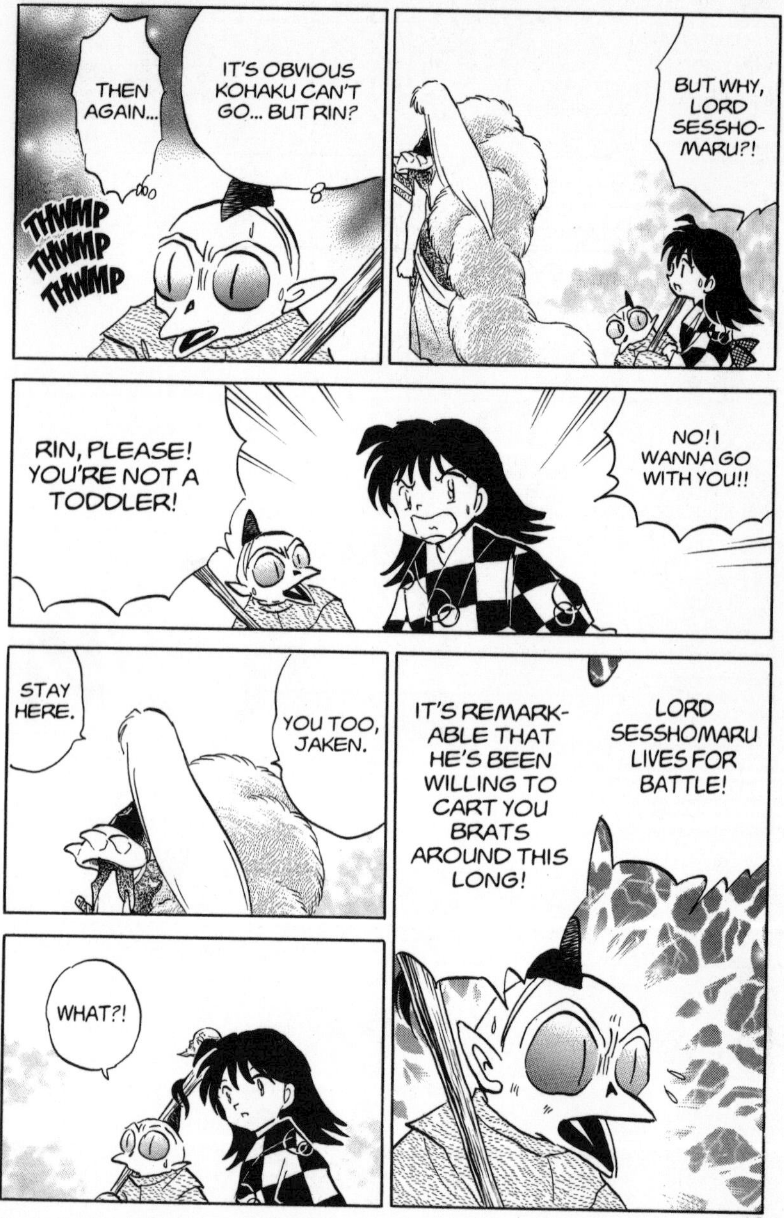
BUT WHY, LORD SESSHO-MARU?!
IT'S OBVIOUS KOHAKU CAN'T GO... BUT RIN?
THEN AGAIN...
THWMP THWMP THWMP
NO! I WANNA GO WITH YOU!!
RIN, PLEASE! YOU'RE NOT A TODDLER!
LORD SESSHOMARU LIVES FOR BATTLE!
IT'S REMARK-ABLE THAT HE'S BEEN WILLING TO CART YOU BRATS AROUND THIS LONG!
YOU TOO, JAKEN.
STAY HERE.
WHAT?!

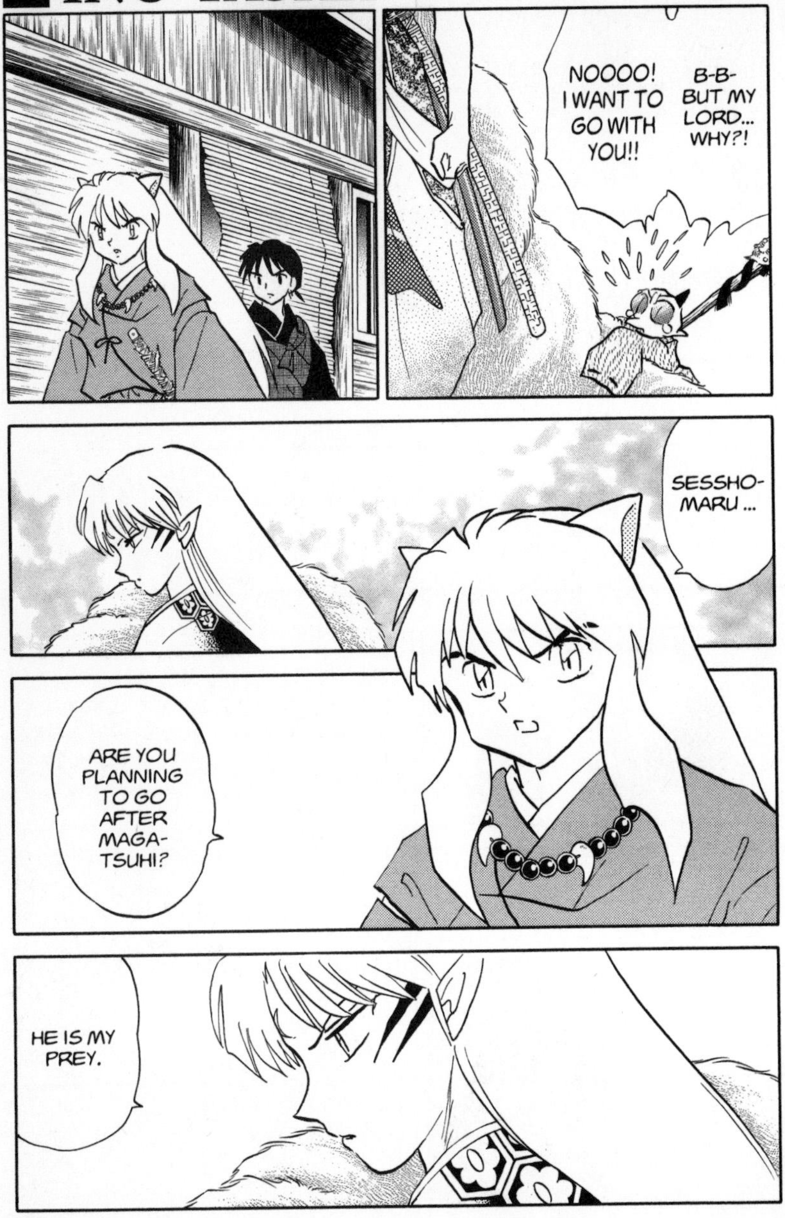
B-B- BUT MY LORD... WHY?!
NOOOO! I WANT TO GO WITH YOU!!
SESSHO- MARU...
ARE YOU PLANNING TO GO AFTER MAGA- TSUHI?
HE IS MY PREY.

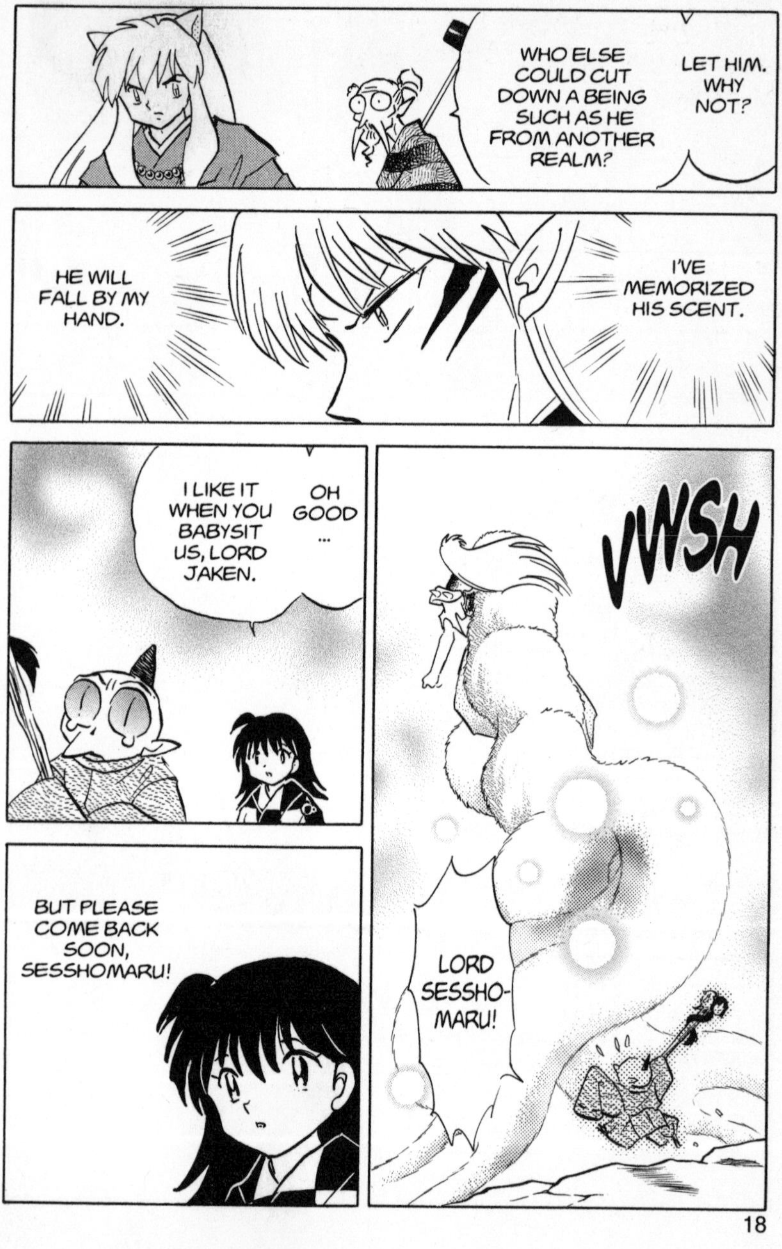
LET HIM. WHY NOT?
WHO ELSE COULD CUT DOWN A BEING SUCH AS HE FROM ANOTHER REALM?
I'VE MEMORIZED HIS SCENT.
HE WILL FALL BY MY HAND.
VVNSH
LORD SESSHO-MARU!
OH GOOD ...
I LIKE IT WHEN YOU BABYSIT US, LORD JAKEN.
BUT PLEASE COME BACK SOON, SESSHOMARU!

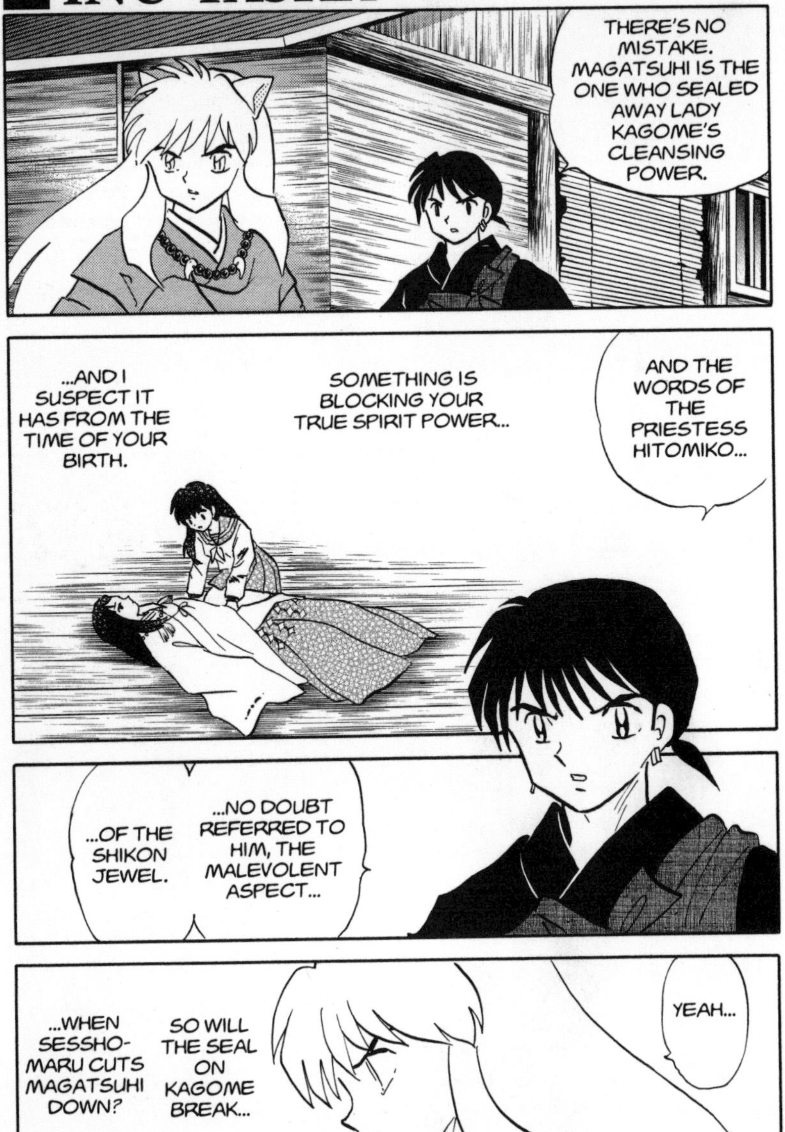
THERE'S NO MISTAKE. MAGATSUHI IS THE ONE WHO SEALED AWAY LADY KAGOME'S CLEANSING POWER.
AND THE WORDS OF THE PRIESTESS HITOMIKO...
SOMETHING IS BLOCKING YOUR TRUE SPIRIT POWER...
...AND I SUSPECT IT HAS FROM THE TIME OF YOUR BIRTH.
...NO DOUBT REFERRED TO HIM, THE MALEVOLENT ASPECT...
...OF THE SHIKON JEWEL.
YEAH...
SO WILL THE SEAL ON KAGOME BREAK...
...WHEN SESSHO-MARU CUTS MAGATSUHI DOWN?

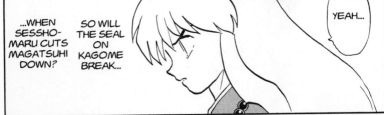

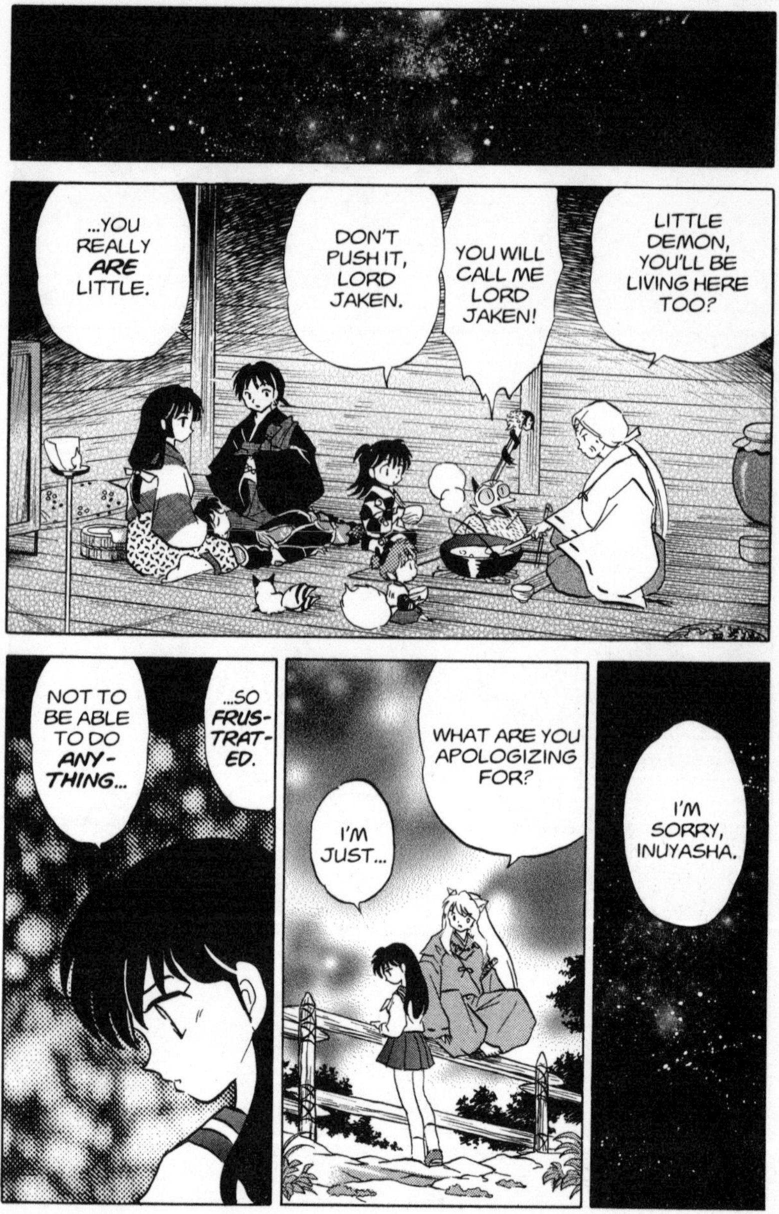
LITTLE DEMON, YOU'LL BE LIVING HERE TOO?
YOU WILL CALL ME LORD JAKEN!
DON'T PUSH IT, LORD JAKEN.
...YOU REALLY *ARE* LITTLE.
I'M SORRY, INUYASHA.
WHAT ARE YOU APOLOGIZING FOR?
I'M JUST...
...SO *FRUSTRATED*.
NOT TO BE ABLE TO DO *ANYTHING*...

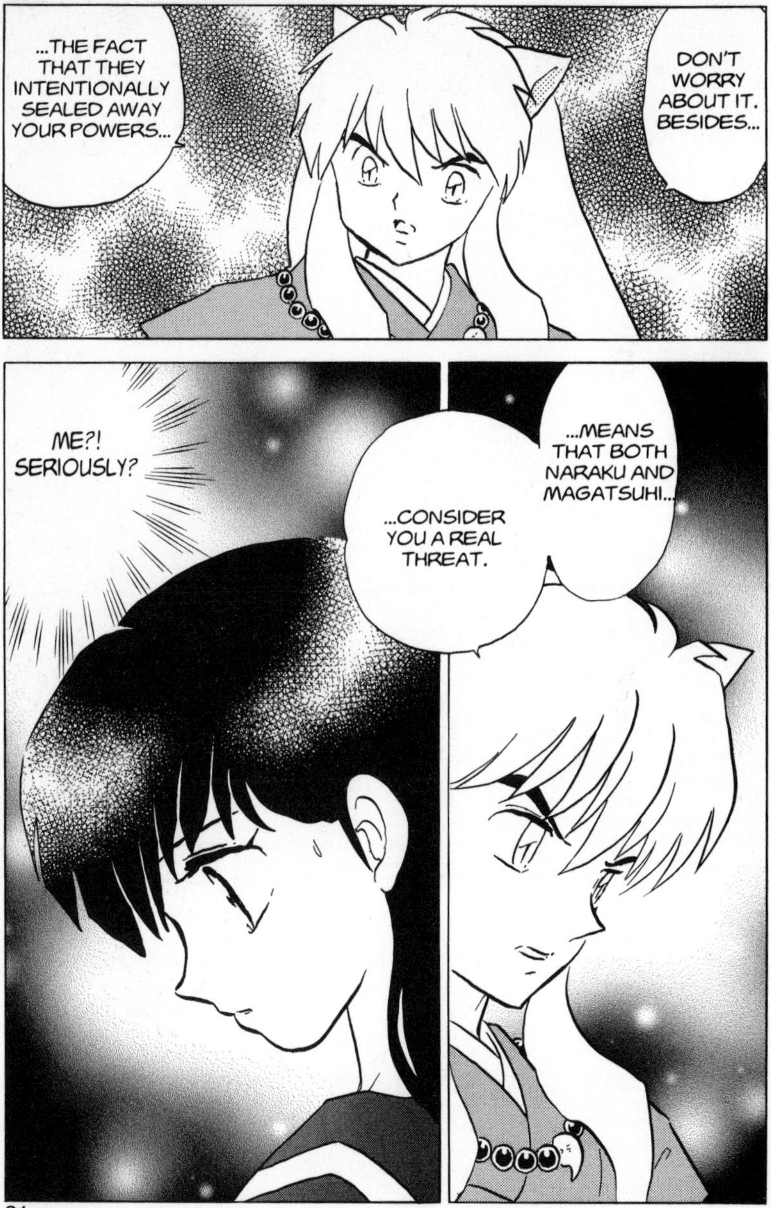
DON'T WORRY ABOUT IT. BESIDES...
...THE FACT THAT THEY INTENTIONALLY SEALED AWAY YOUR POWERS...
...MEANS THAT BOTH NARAKU AND MAGATSUHI...
...CONSIDER YOU A REAL THREAT.
ME?! SERIOUSLY?

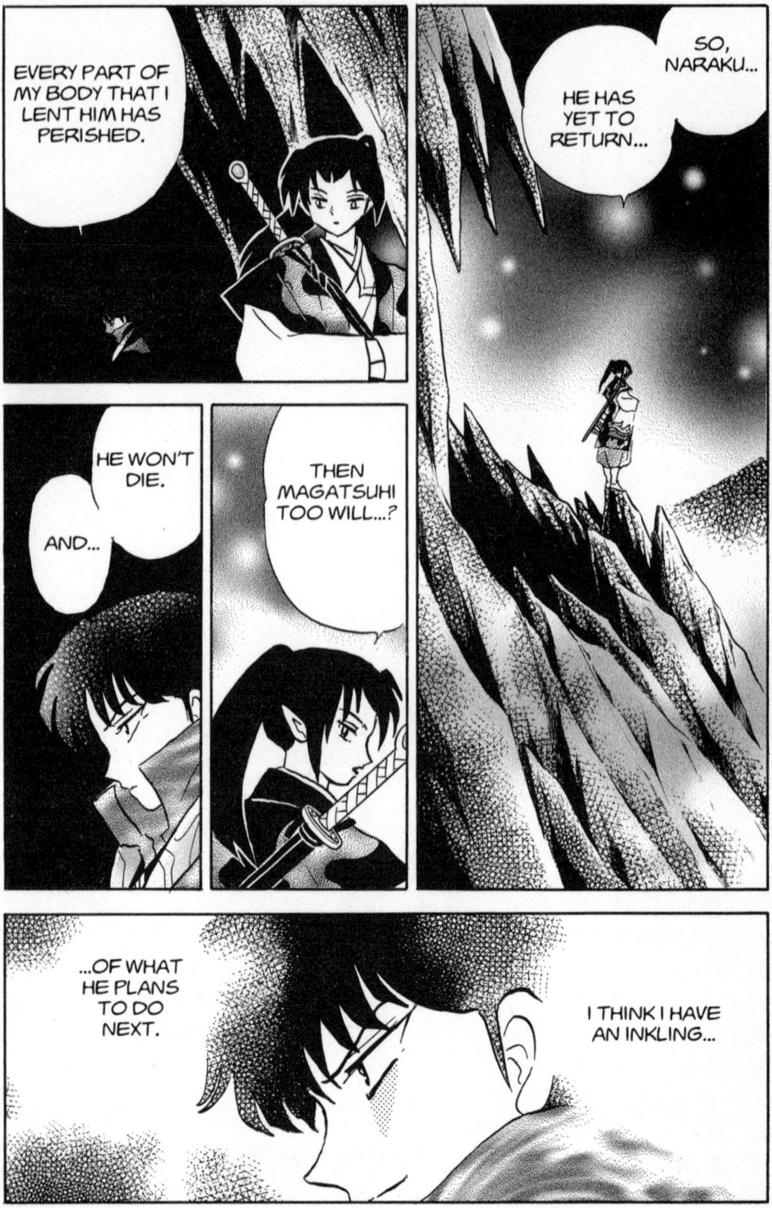
SO, NARAKU...
HE HAS YET TO RETURN...
EVERY PART OF MY BODY THAT I LENT HIM HAS PERISHED.
THEN MAGATSUHI TOO WILL...?
HE WON'T DIE.
AND...
I THINK I HAVE AN INKLING...
...OF WHAT HE PLANS TO DO NEXT.

SCROLL 2

THE DAY OF DAYS

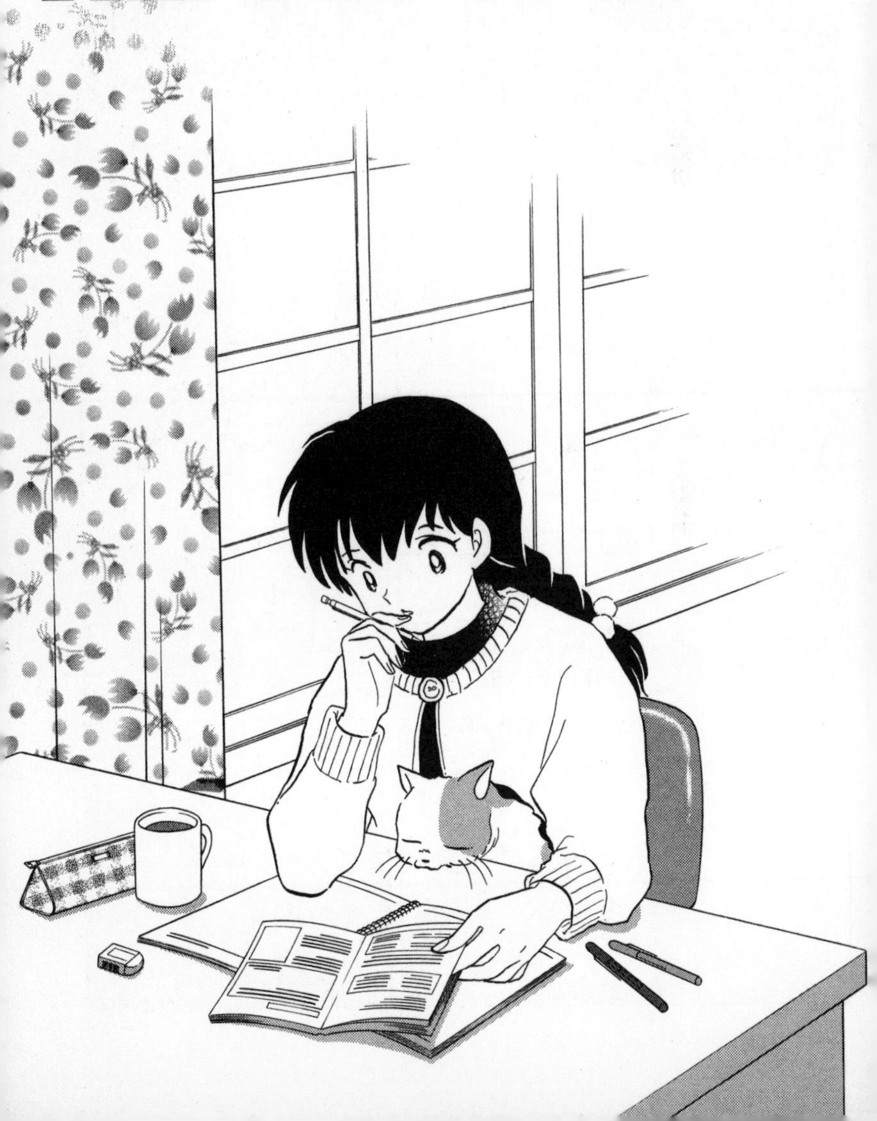

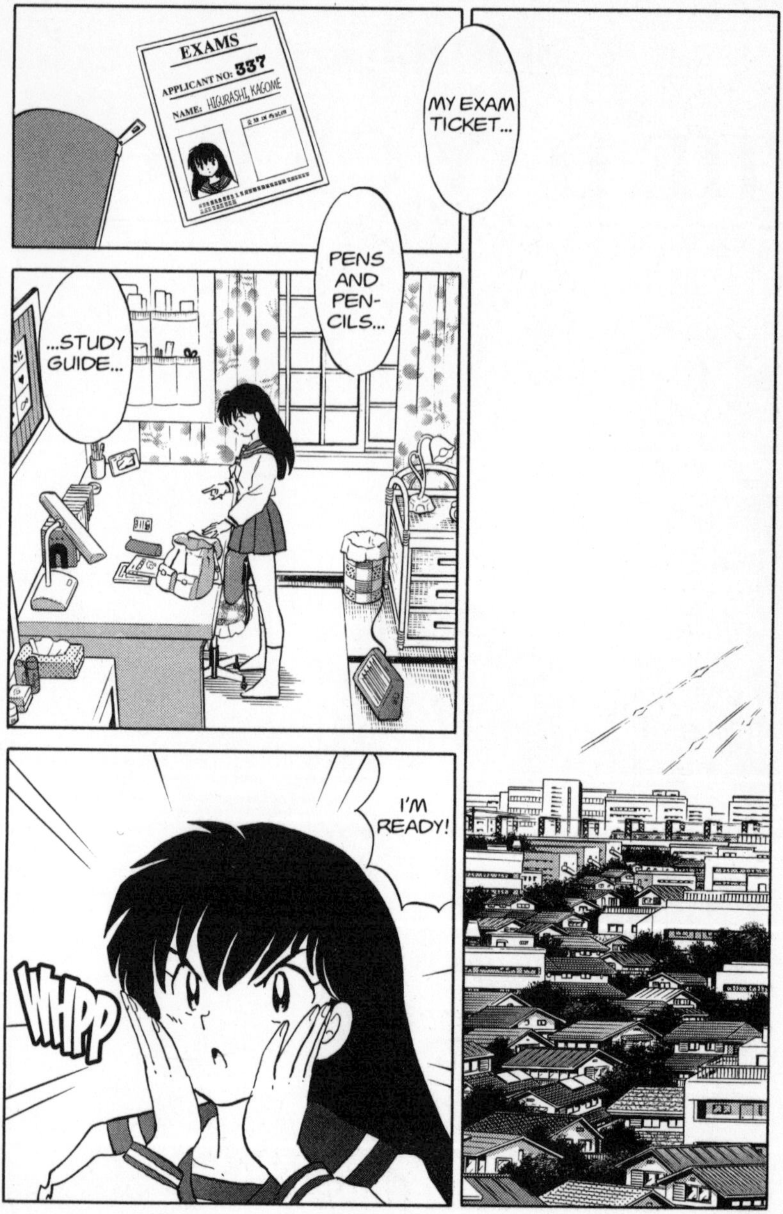
MY EXAM TICKET...
EXAMS
APPLICANT NO: 337
NAME: HIGURASHI, KAGOME
PENS AND PEN-CILS...
...STUDY GUIDE...
I'M READY!
WHPP

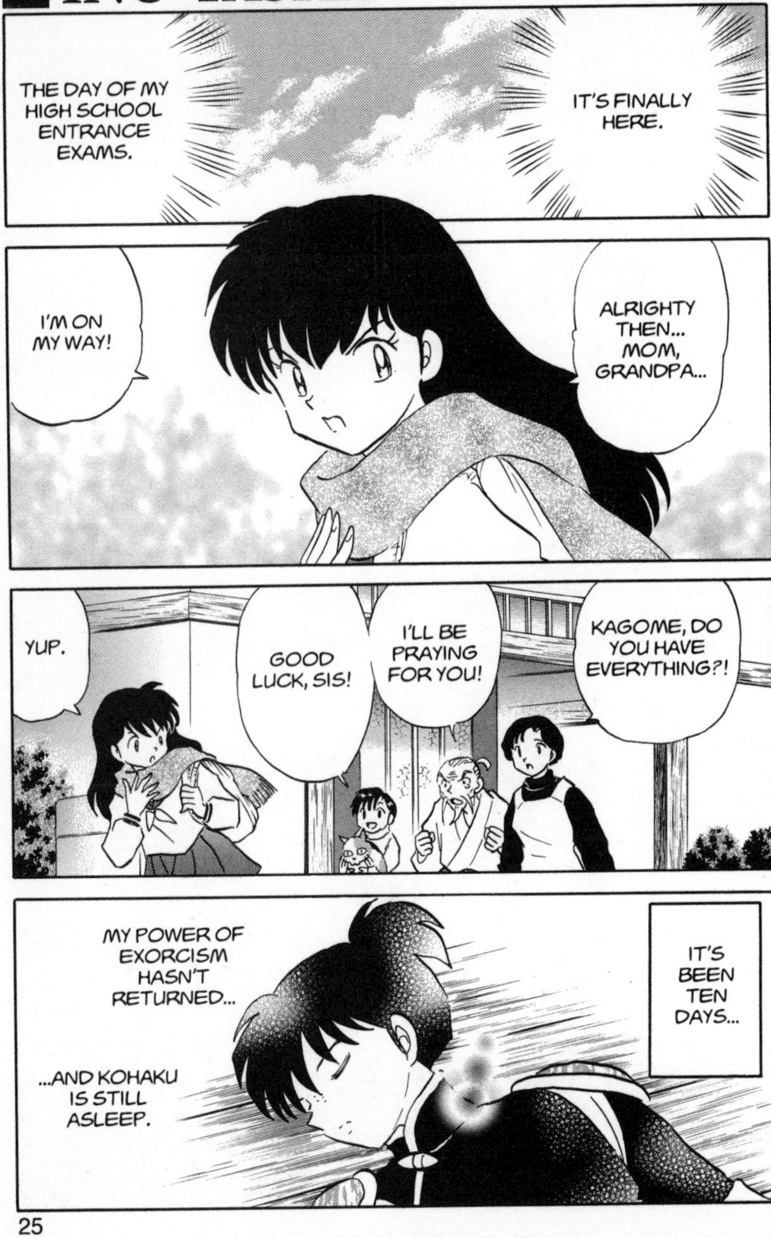
IT'S FINALLY HERE.
THE DAY OF MY HIGH SCHOOL ENTRANCE EXAMS.
ALRIGHTY THEN... MOM, GRANDPA...
I'M ON MY WAY!
KAGOME, DO YOU HAVE EVERYTHING?!
I'LL BE PRAYING FOR YOU!
GOOD LUCK, SIS!
YUP.
IT'S BEEN TEN DAYS...
MY POWER OF EXORCISM HASN'T RETURNED...
...AND KOHAKU IS STILL ASLEEP.

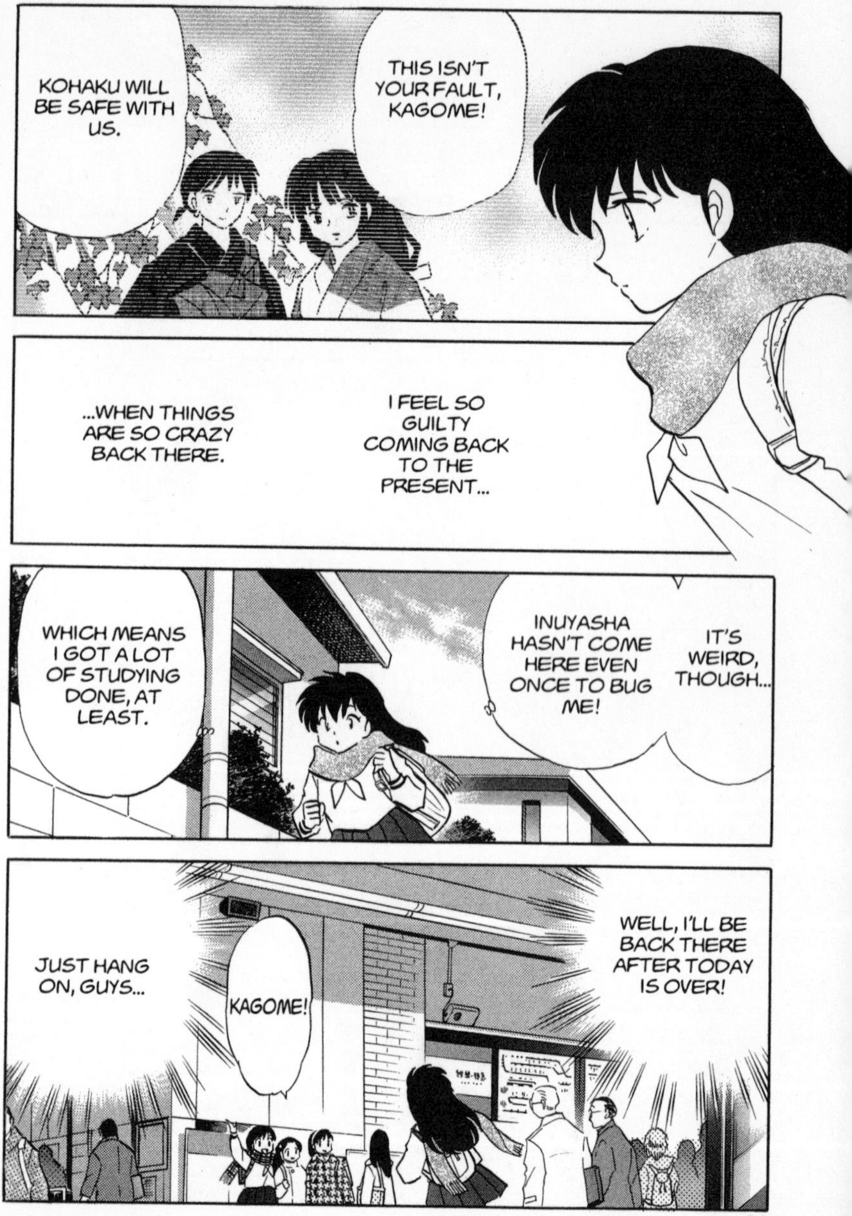
THIS ISN'T YOUR FAULT, KAGOME!
KOHAKU WILL BE SAFE WITH US.
I FEEL SO GUILTY COMING BACK TO THE PRESENT...
...WHEN THINGS ARE SO CRAZY BACK THERE.
IT'S WEIRD, THOUGH...
INUYASHA HASN'T COME HERE EVEN ONCE TO BUG ME!
WHICH MEANS I GOT A LOT OF STUDYING DONE, AT LEAST.
WELL, I'LL BE BACK THERE AFTER TODAY IS OVER!
KAGOME!
JUST HANG ON, GUYS...

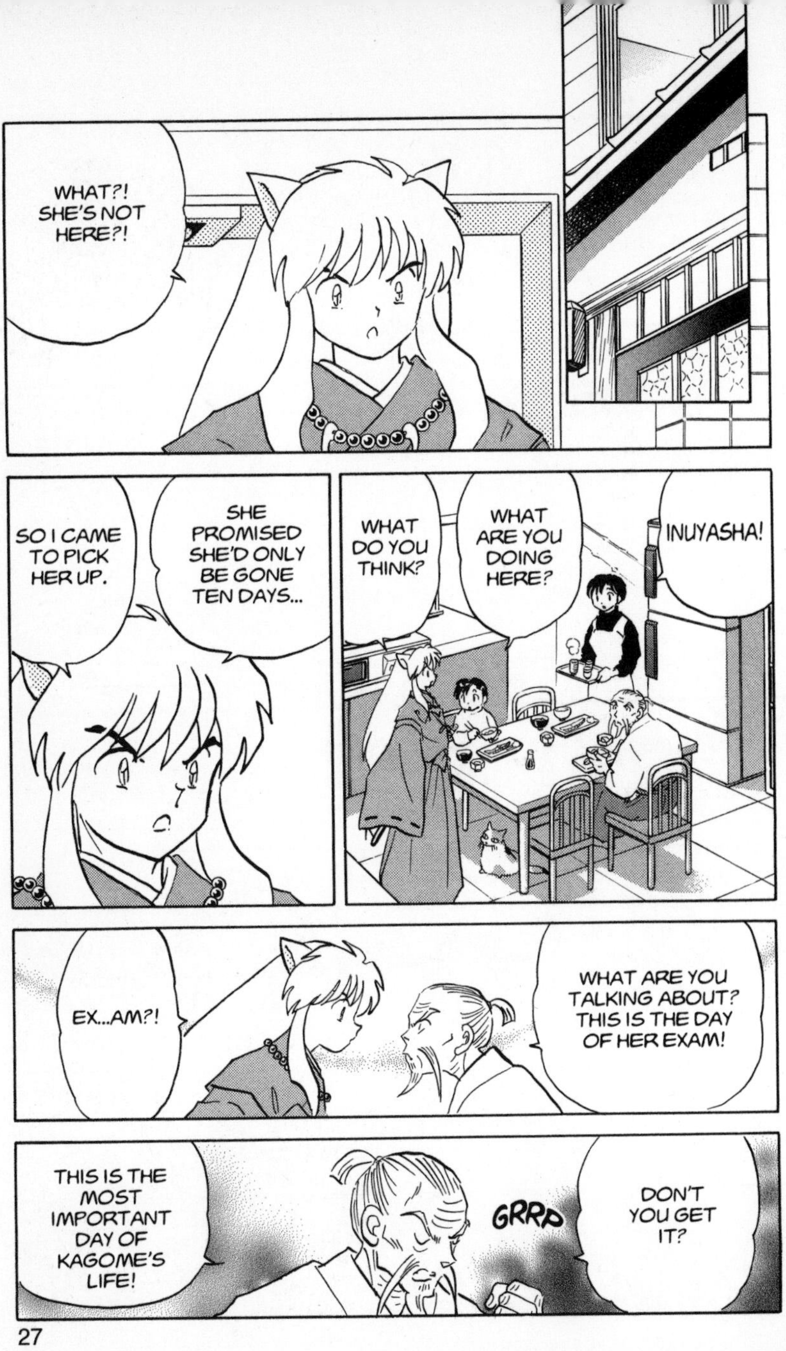
WHAT?! SHE'S NOT HERE?!
INUYASHA!
WHAT ARE YOU DOING HERE?
WHAT DO YOU THINK?
SHE PROMISED SHE'D ONLY BE GONE TEN DAYS...
SO I CAME TO PICK HER UP.
WHAT ARE YOU TALKING ABOUT? THIS IS THE DAY OF HER EXAM!
EX...AM?!
DON'T YOU GET IT?
GRRP
THIS IS THE MOST IMPORTANT DAY OF KAGOME'S LIFE!

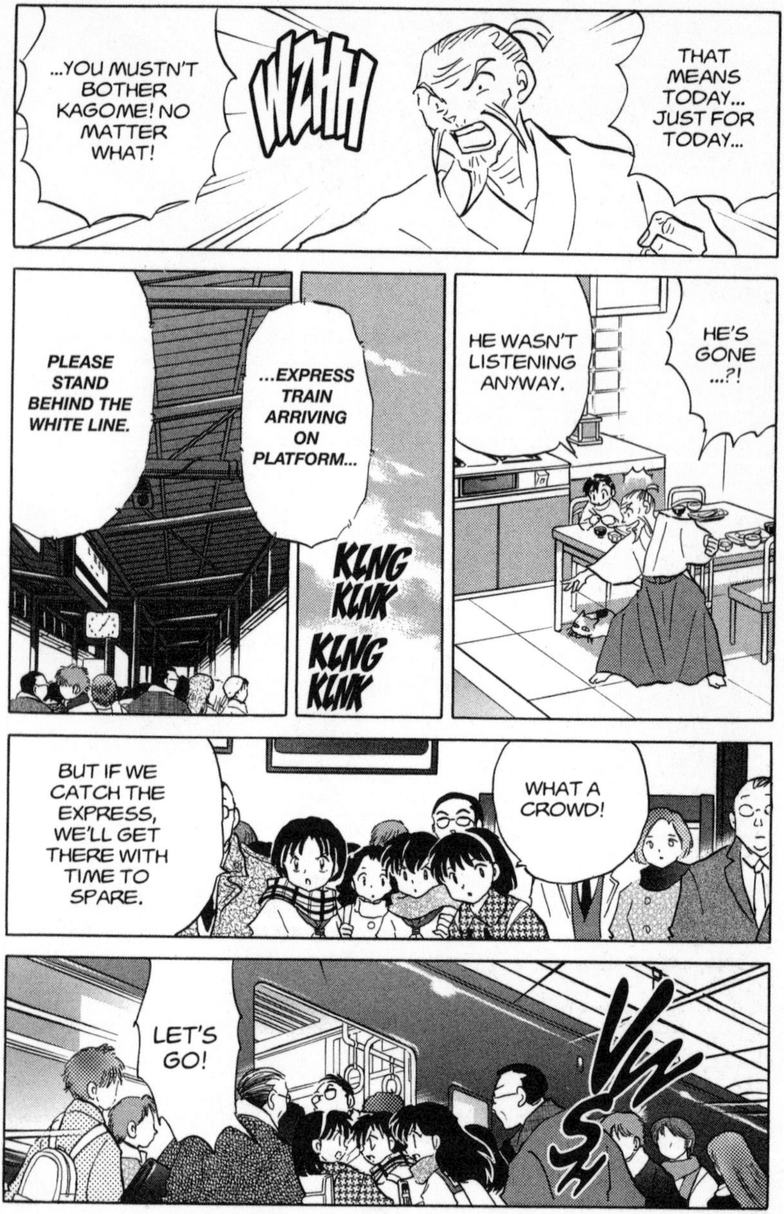
THAT MEANS TODAY... JUST FOR TODAY...
WZHHH
...YOU MUSTN'T BOTHER KAGOME! NO MATTER WHAT!
HE'S GONE ...?!
HE WASN'T LISTENING ANYWAY.
...EXPRESS TRAIN ARRIVING ON PLATFORM...
KLNG KLNK
KLNG KLNK
PLEASE STAND BEHIND THE WHITE LINE.
WHAT A CROWD!
BUT IF WE CATCH THE EXPRESS, WE'LL GET THERE WITH TIME TO SPARE.
VWSH
LET'S GO!

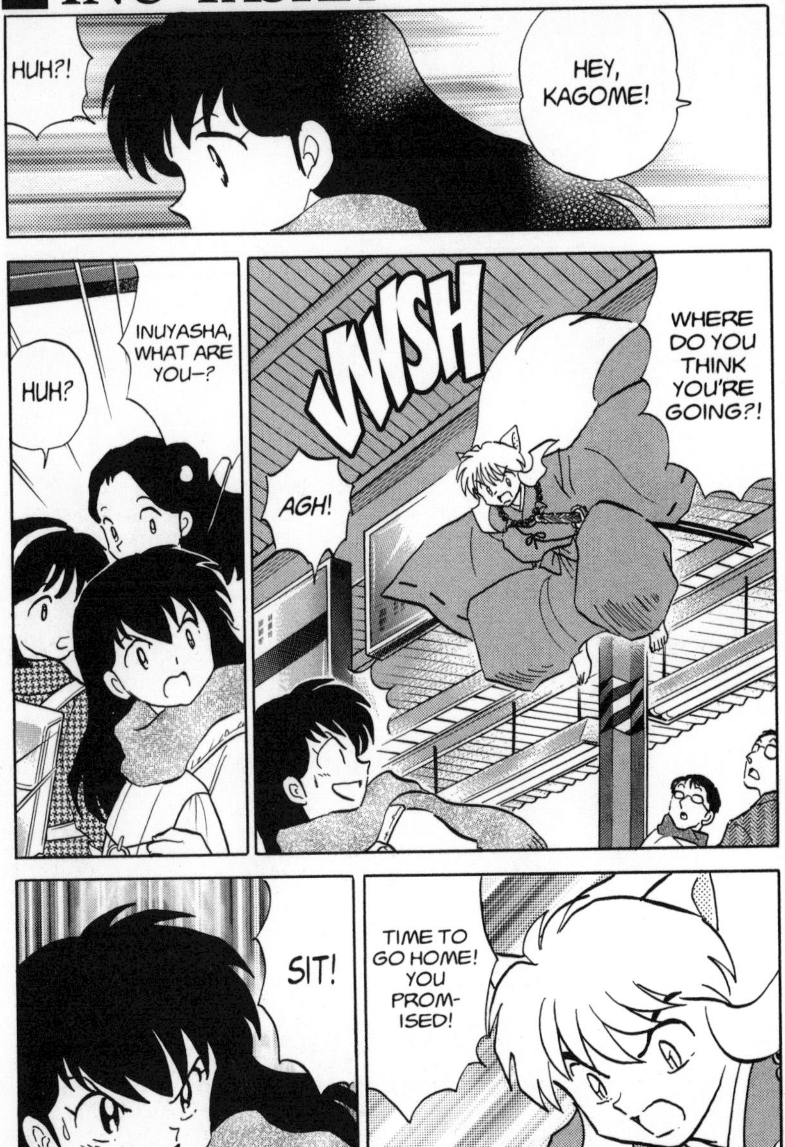
HEY, KAGOME!
HUH?!
WHERE DO YOU THINK YOU'RE GOING?!
VWSH
AGH!
INUYASHA, WHAT ARE YOU–?
HUH?
TIME TO GO HOME! YOU PROM-ISED!
SIT!

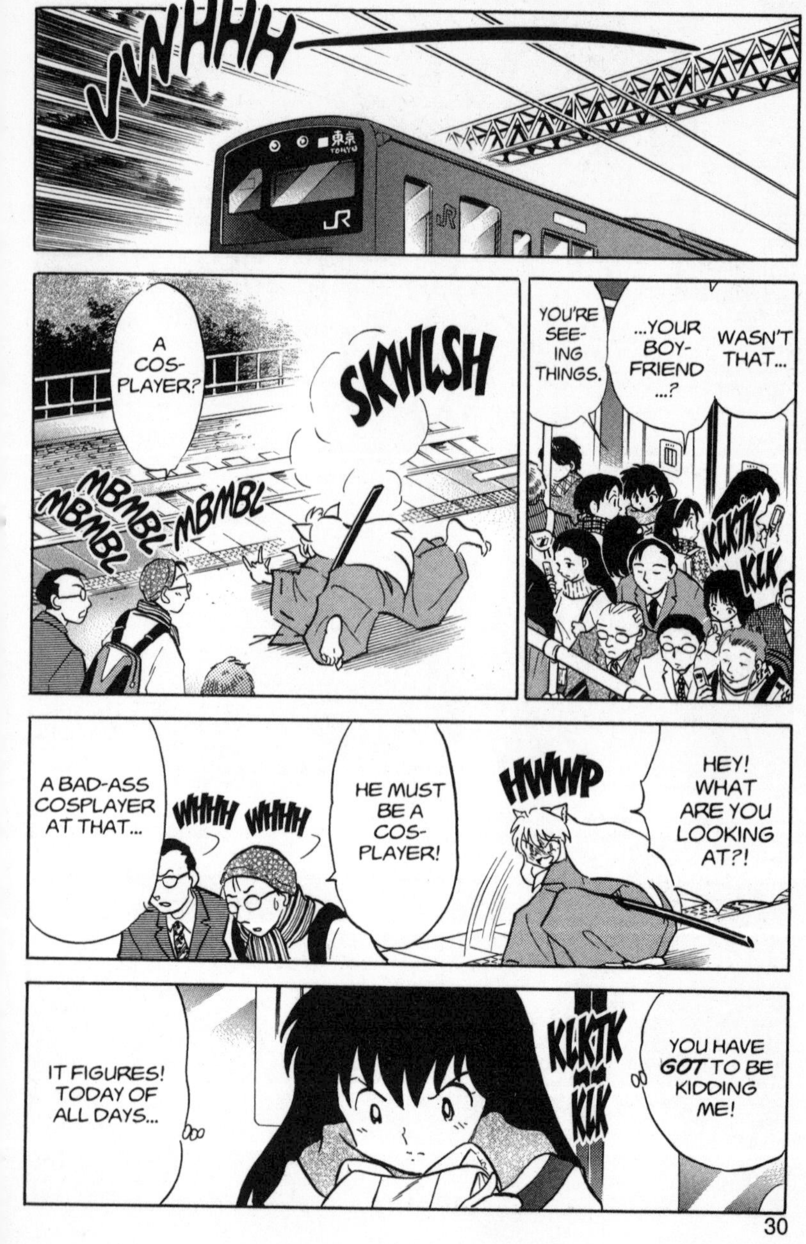
VWHHHH
WASN'T THAT...
...YOUR BOY-FRIEND ...?
YOU'RE SEE-ING THINGS.
KLKTK KLK
SKWLSH
A COS-PLAYER?
MBMBL MBMBL
MBMBL
HEY! WHAT ARE YOU LOOKING AT?!
HWWP
HE MUST BE A COS-PLAYER!
WHHH WHHH
A BAD-ASS COSPLAYER AT THAT...
YOU HAVE **GOT** TO BE KIDDING ME!
KLKTK KLK
IT FIGURES! TODAY OF ALL DAYS...

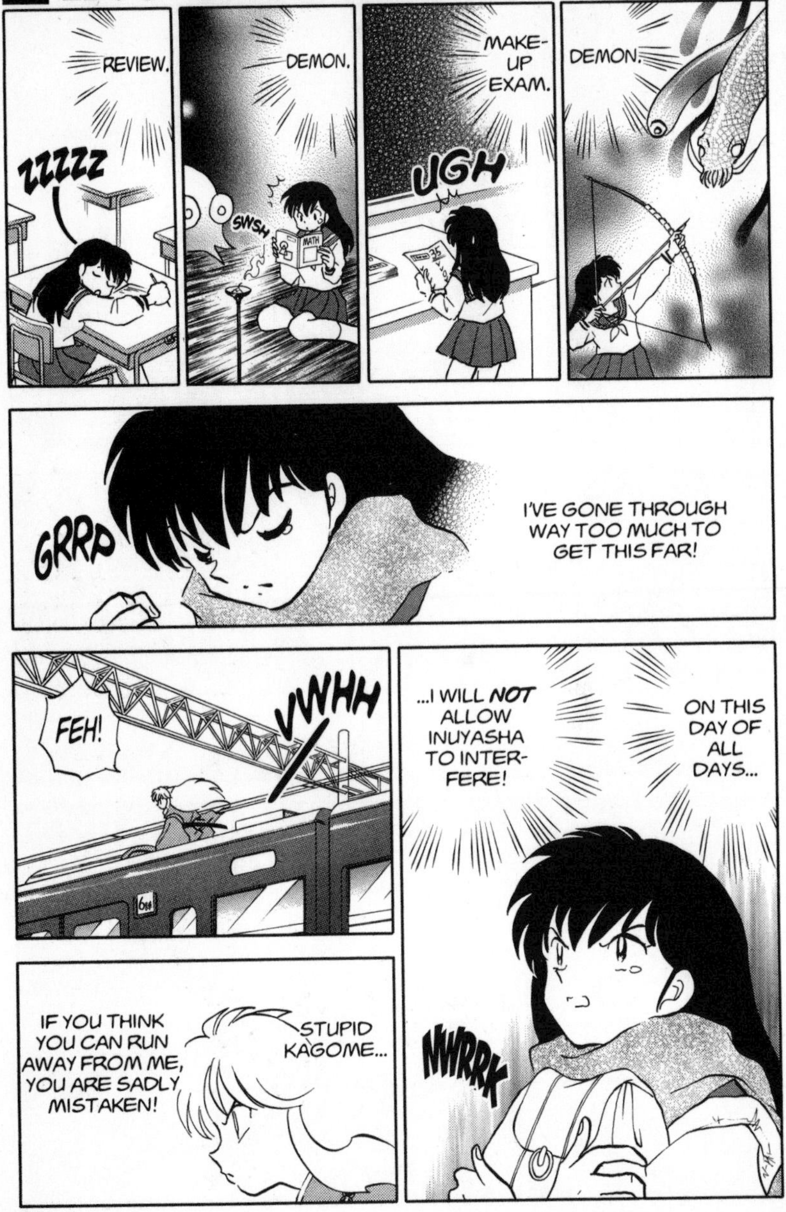
DEMON.
MAKE-UP EXAM.
UGH
DEMON.
SWSH
MATH
REVIEW.
ZZZZZ
I'VE GONE THROUGH WAY TOO MUCH TO GET THIS FAR!
GRRP
ON THIS DAY OF ALL DAYS...
...I WILL *NOT* ALLOW INUYASHA TO INTER-FERE!
NWRRK
VWHH
FEH!
STUPID KAGOME...
IF YOU THINK YOU CAN RUN AWAY FROM ME, YOU ARE SADLY MISTAKEN!

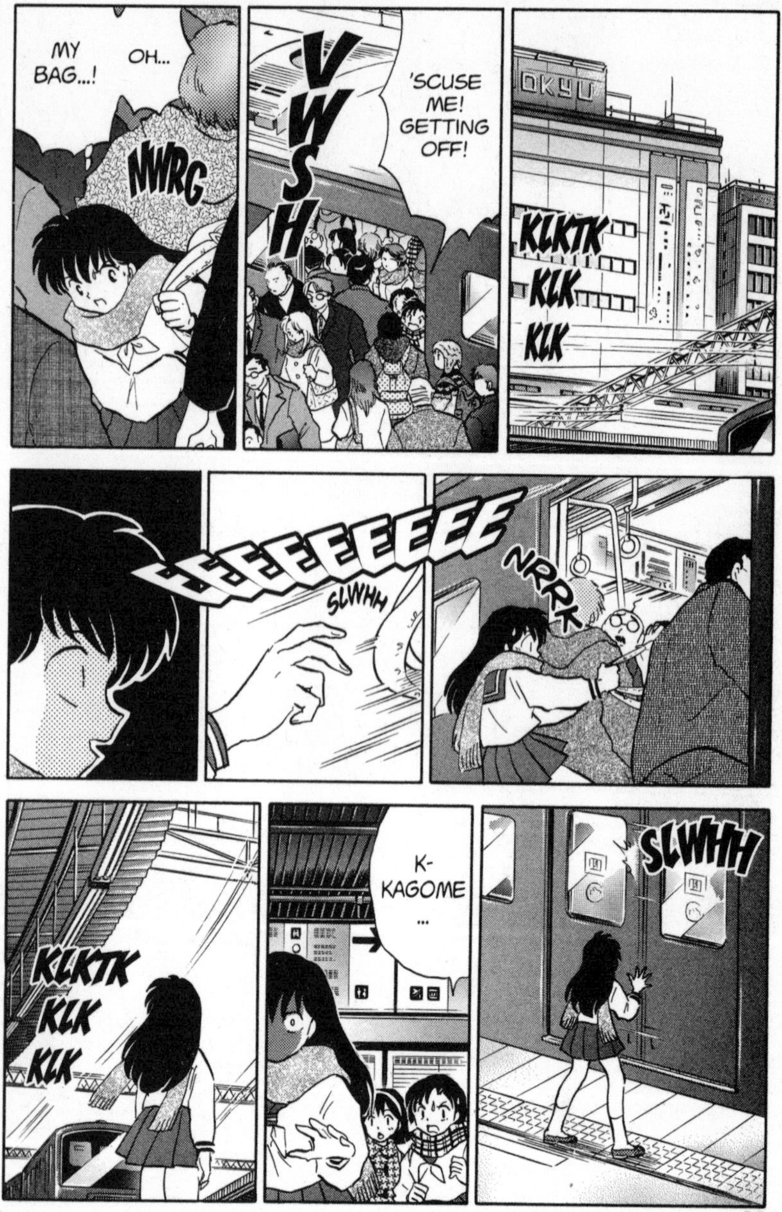
OKYU
KLKTK KLK KLK
VWSH
'SCUSE ME! GETTING OFF!
OH...
MY BAG...!
NWRG
NRRK
EEEEEEEE
SLWHH
SLWHH
K-KAGOME ...
KLKTK KLK KLK

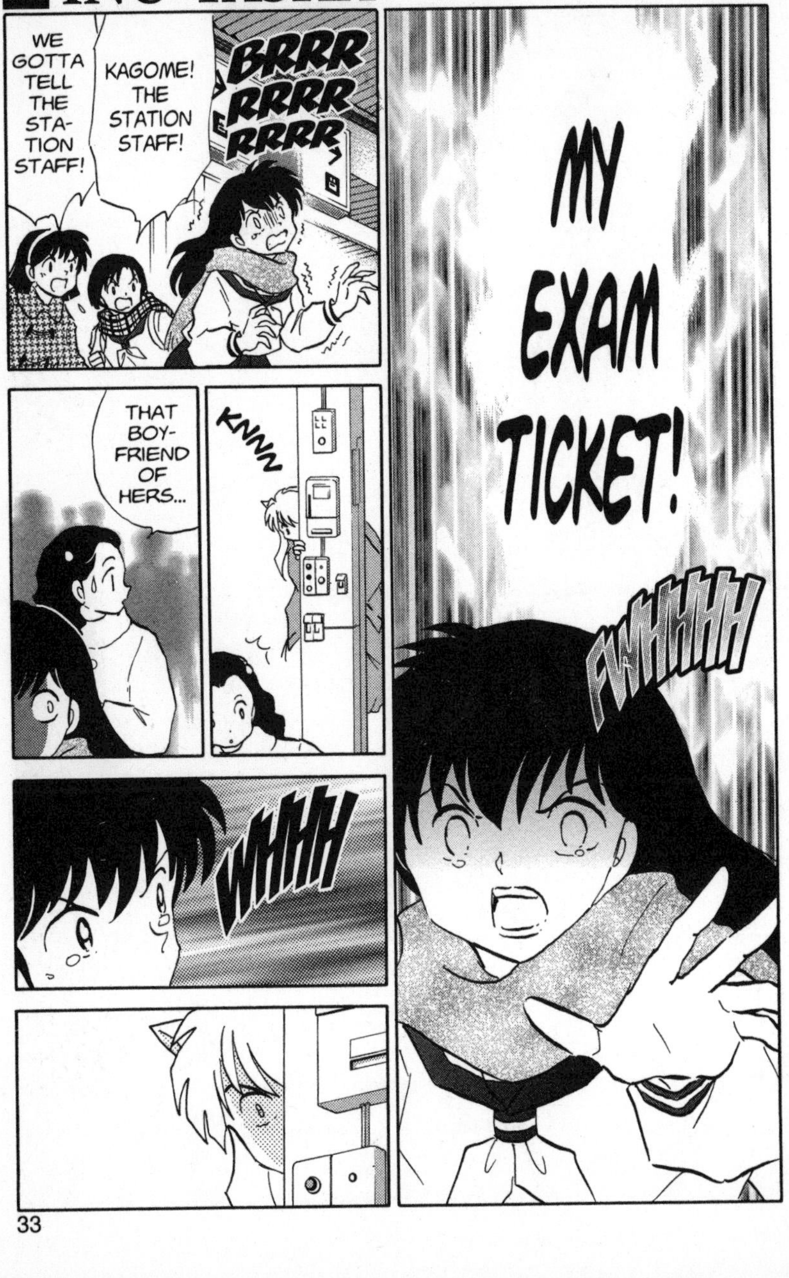
MY EXAM TICKET!
FWHHHHH
BRRRR RRRRR RRRRR
KAGOME! THE STATION STAFF!
WE GOTTA TELL THE STA-TION STAFF!
KNNN
THAT BOY-FRIEND OF HERS...
WHHH

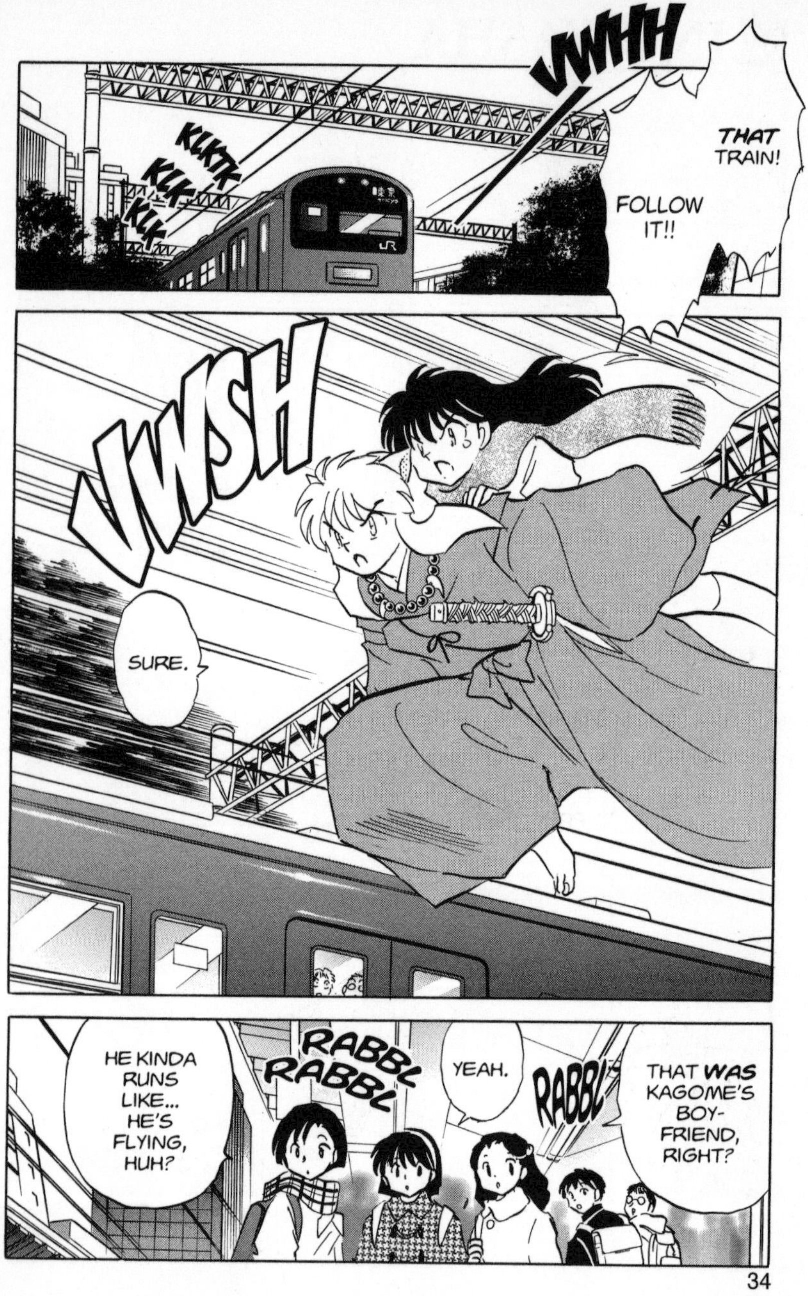
THAT TRAIN!
FOLLOW IT!!
VWHH
KLKTK KLK KLK
VWSH
SURE.
THAT WAS KAGOME'S BOY-FRIEND, RIGHT?
RABBL
YEAH.
RABBL RABBL
HE KINDA RUNS LIKE... HE'S FLYING, HUH?

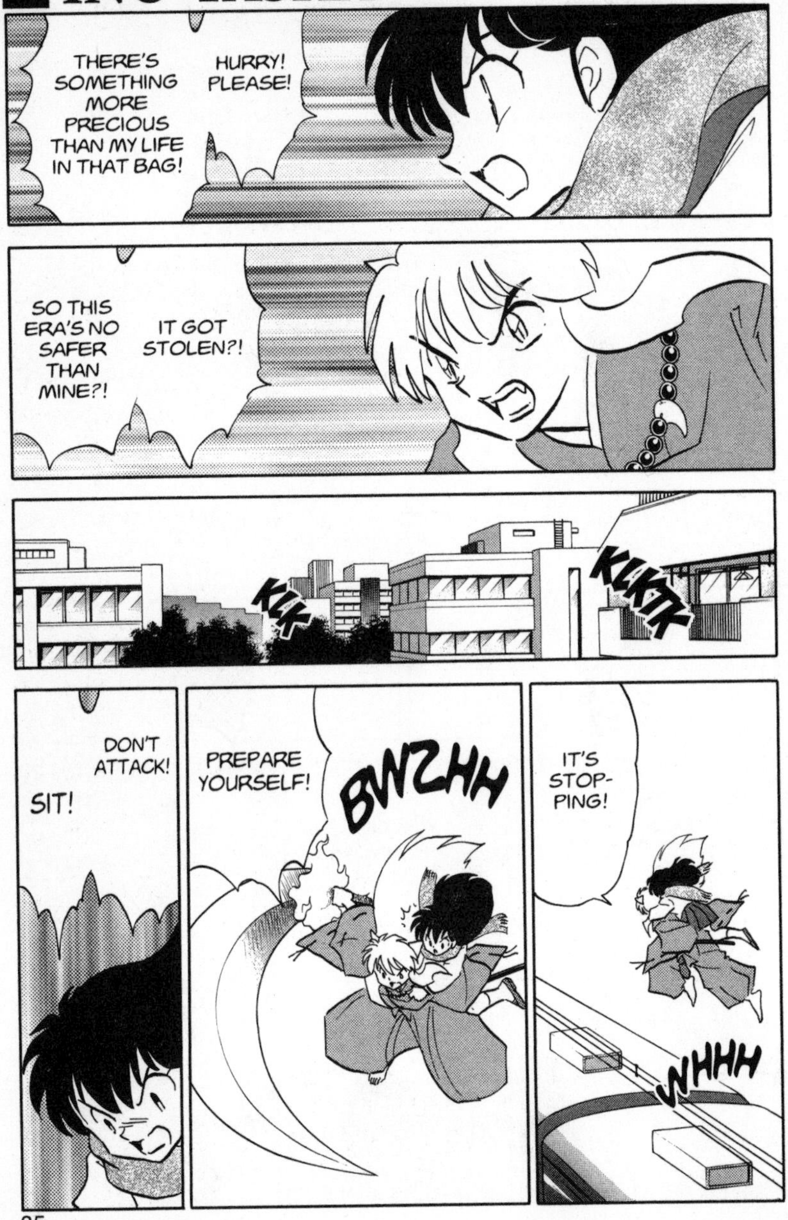
HURRY! PLEASE!
THERE'S SOMETHING MORE PRECIOUS THAN MY LIFE IN THAT BAG!
IT GOT STOLEN?!
SO THIS ERA'S NO SAFER THAN MINE?!
KIKIK
KIK
IT'S STOP-PING!
WHHH
BWZHH
PREPARE YOURSELF!
DON'T ATTACK!
SIT!

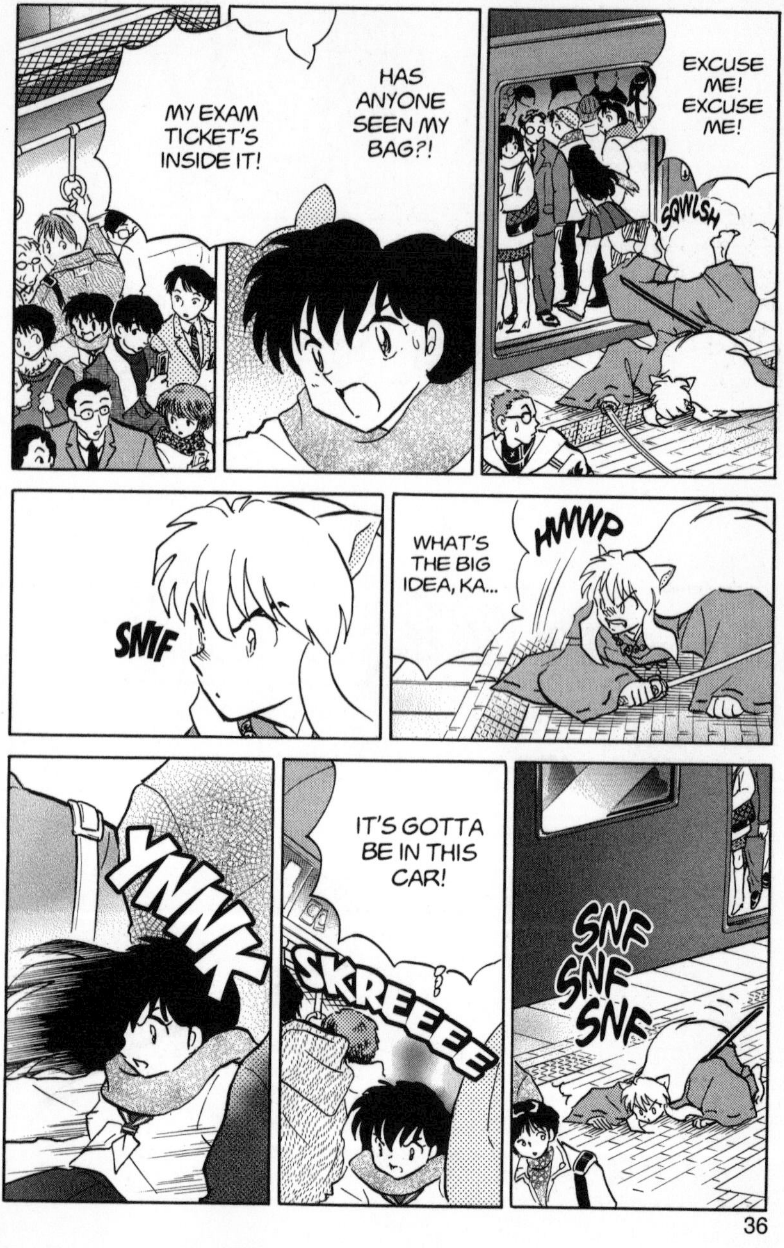
EXCUSE ME! EXCUSE ME!
SQWLSH
HAS ANYONE SEEN MY BAG?!
MY EXAM TICKET'S INSIDE IT!
HWWP
WHAT'S THE BIG IDEA, KA...
SNIF
SNF SNF SNF
IT'S GOTTA BE IN THIS CAR!
SKREEEEE
YNNK

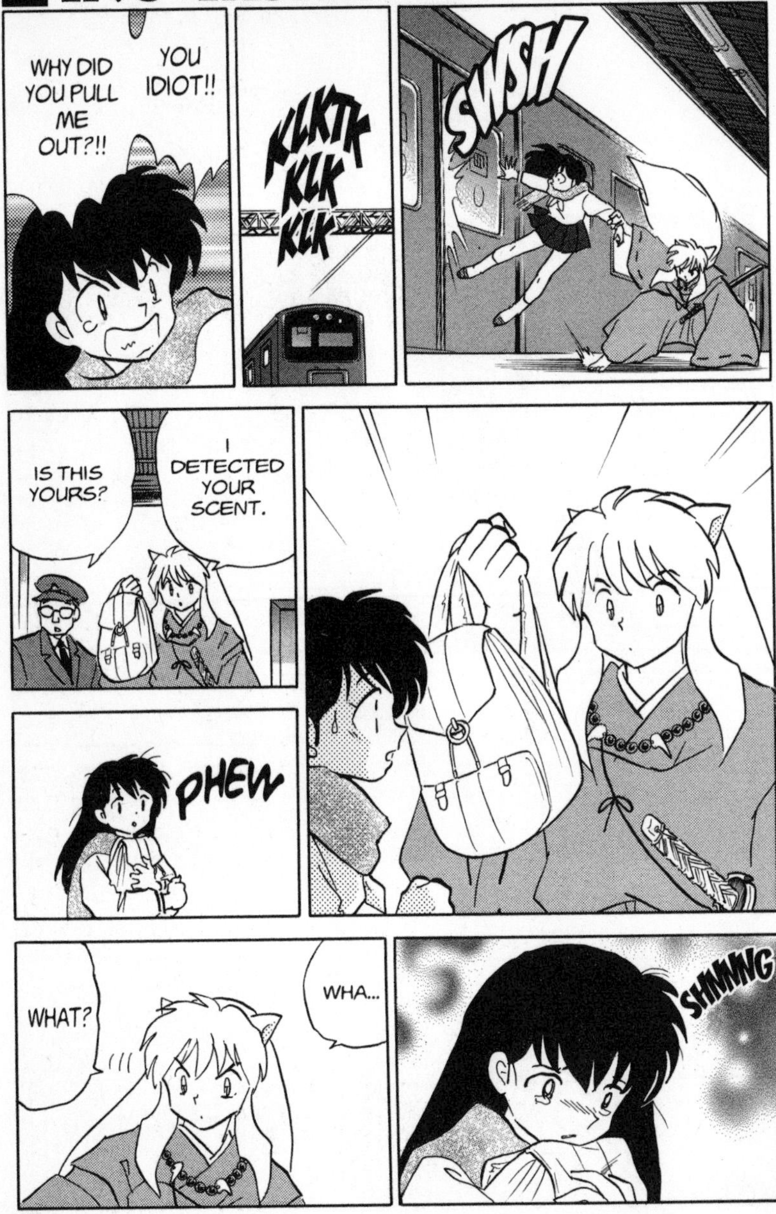
SWSH
KLKTIK KLK KLK
YOU IDIOT!!
WHY DID YOU PULL ME OUT?!!
I DETECTED YOUR SCENT.
IS THIS YOURS?
PHEW
SHNNNG
WHA...
WHAT?

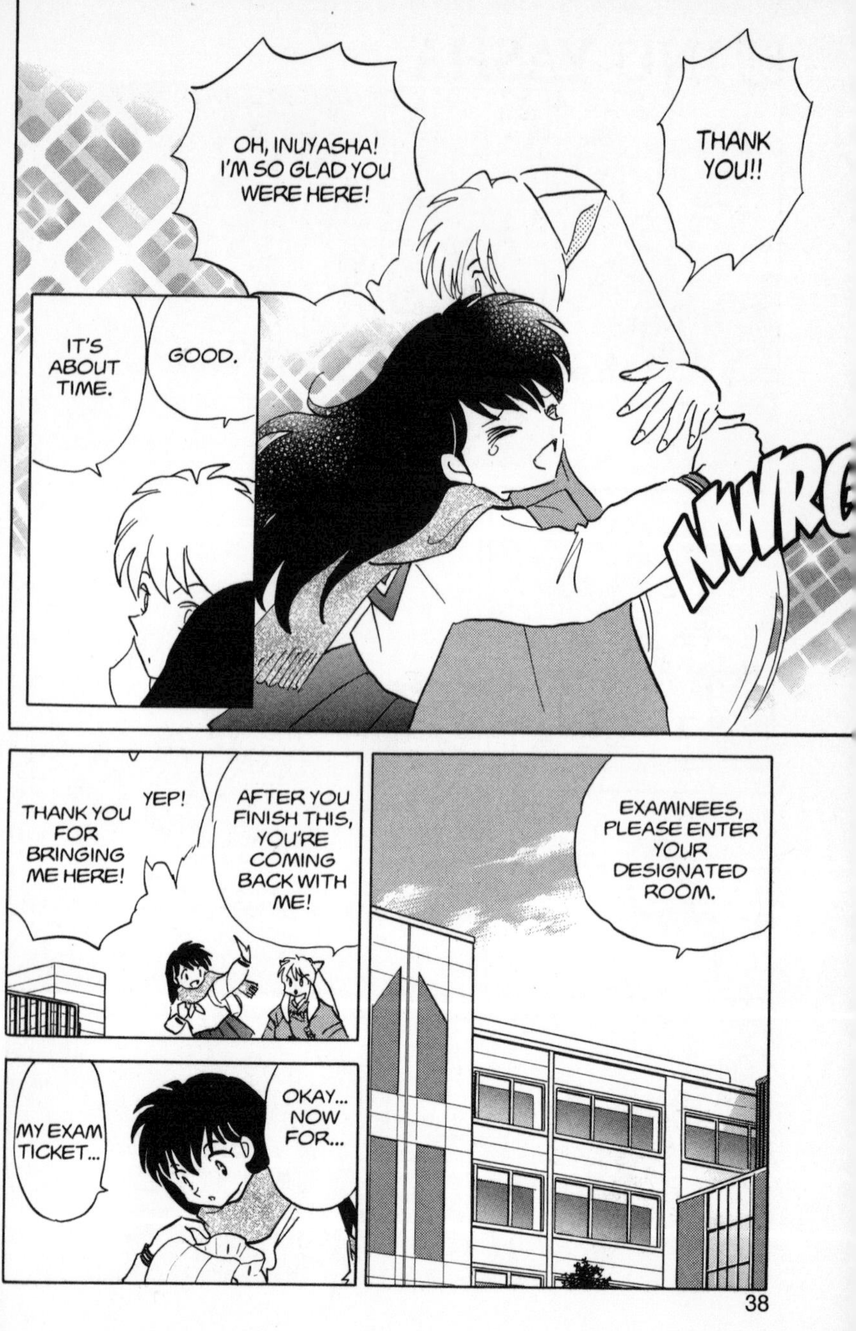
THANK YOU!!
OH, INUYASHA! I'M SO GLAD YOU WERE HERE!
NWRG
GOOD.
IT'S ABOUT TIME.
EXAMINEES, PLEASE ENTER YOUR DESIGNATED ROOM.
AFTER YOU FINISH THIS, YOU'RE COMING BACK WITH ME!
YEP!
THANK YOU FOR BRINGING ME HERE!
OKAY... NOW FOR...
MY EXAM TICKET...

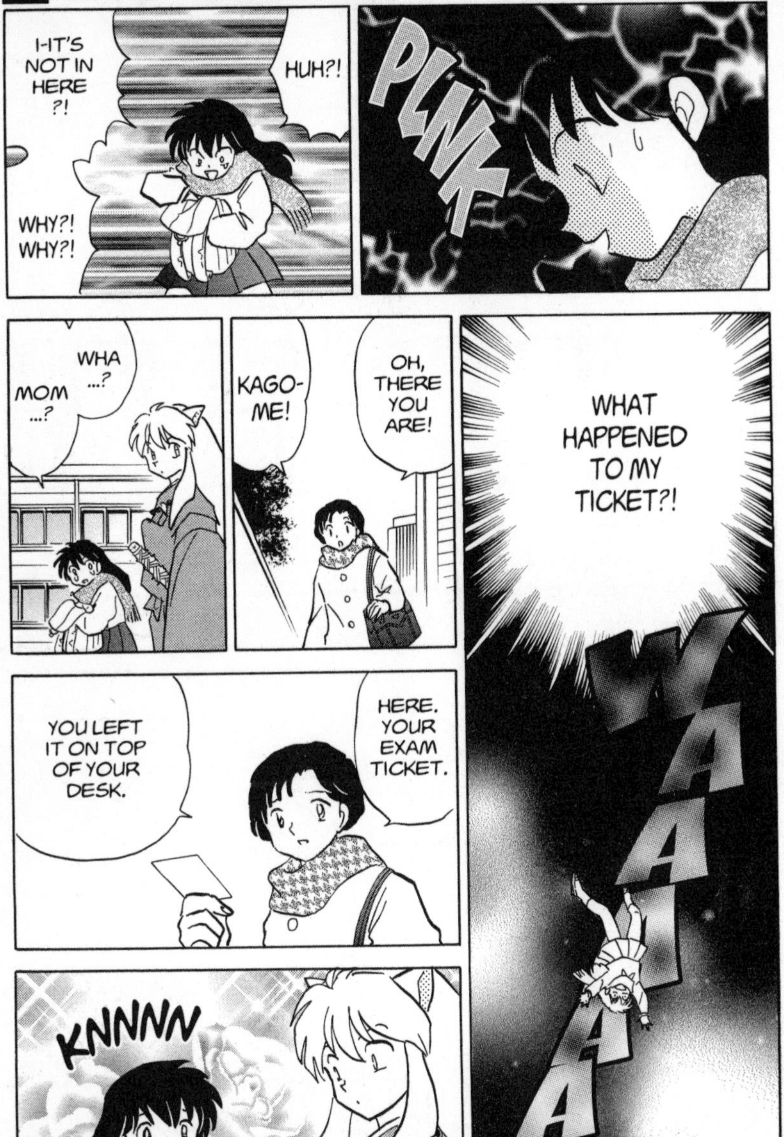
PLINK
HUH?!
I-IT'S NOT IN HERE ?!
WHY?! WHY?!
WHAT HAPPENED TO MY TICKET?!
WAAAAAAA
OH, THERE YOU ARE!
KAGO-ME!
WHA ...?
MOM ...?
HERE. YOUR EXAM TICKET.
YOU LEFT IT ON TOP OF YOUR DESK.
KNNNN

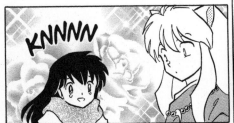

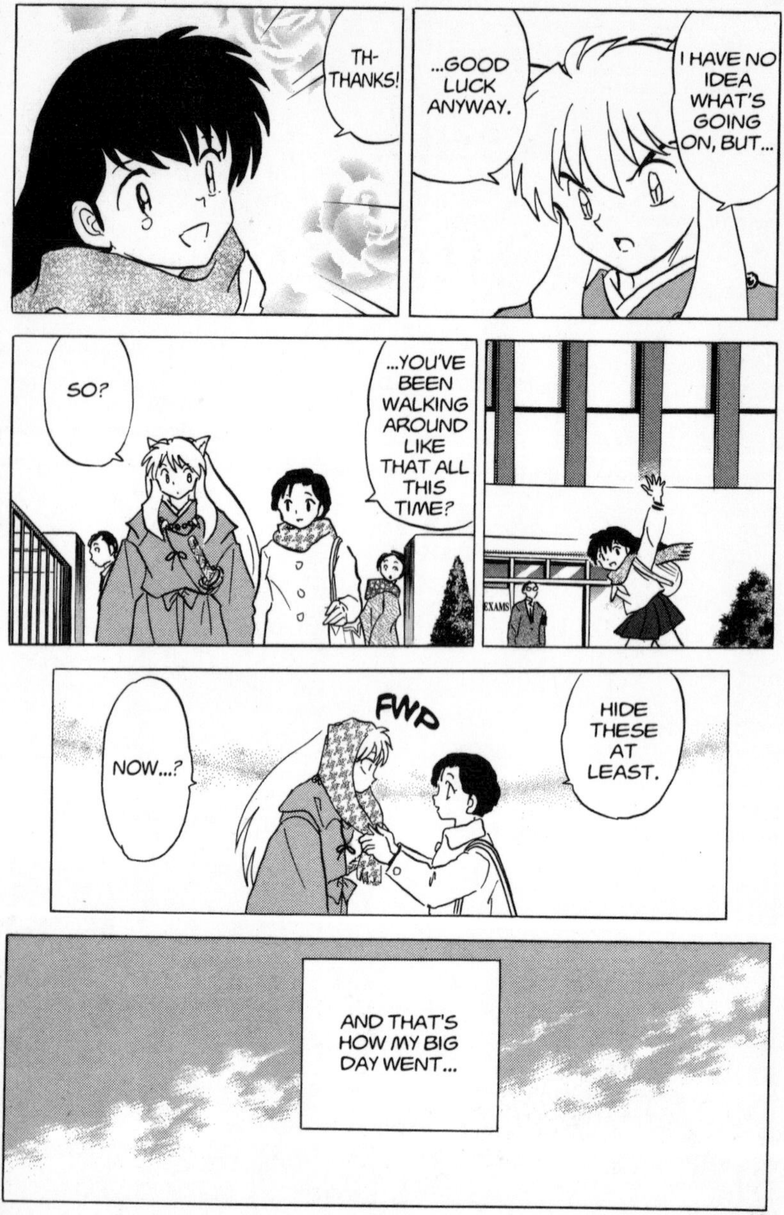
I HAVE NO IDEA WHAT'S GOING ON, BUT...
...GOOD LUCK ANYWAY.
TH- THANKS!
EXAMS
...YOU'VE BEEN WALKING AROUND LIKE THAT ALL THIS TIME?
SO?
HIDE THESE AT LEAST.
FWP
NOW...?
AND THAT'S HOW MY BIG DAY WENT...

SCROLL 3

THE SHADOW

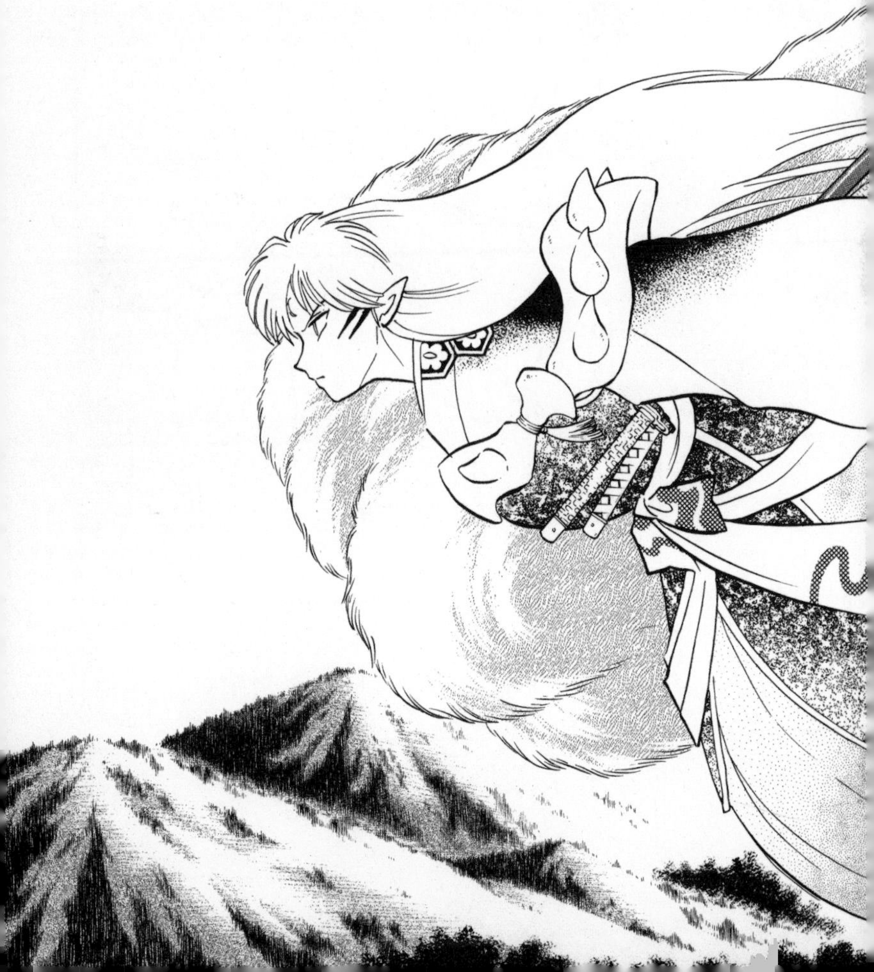

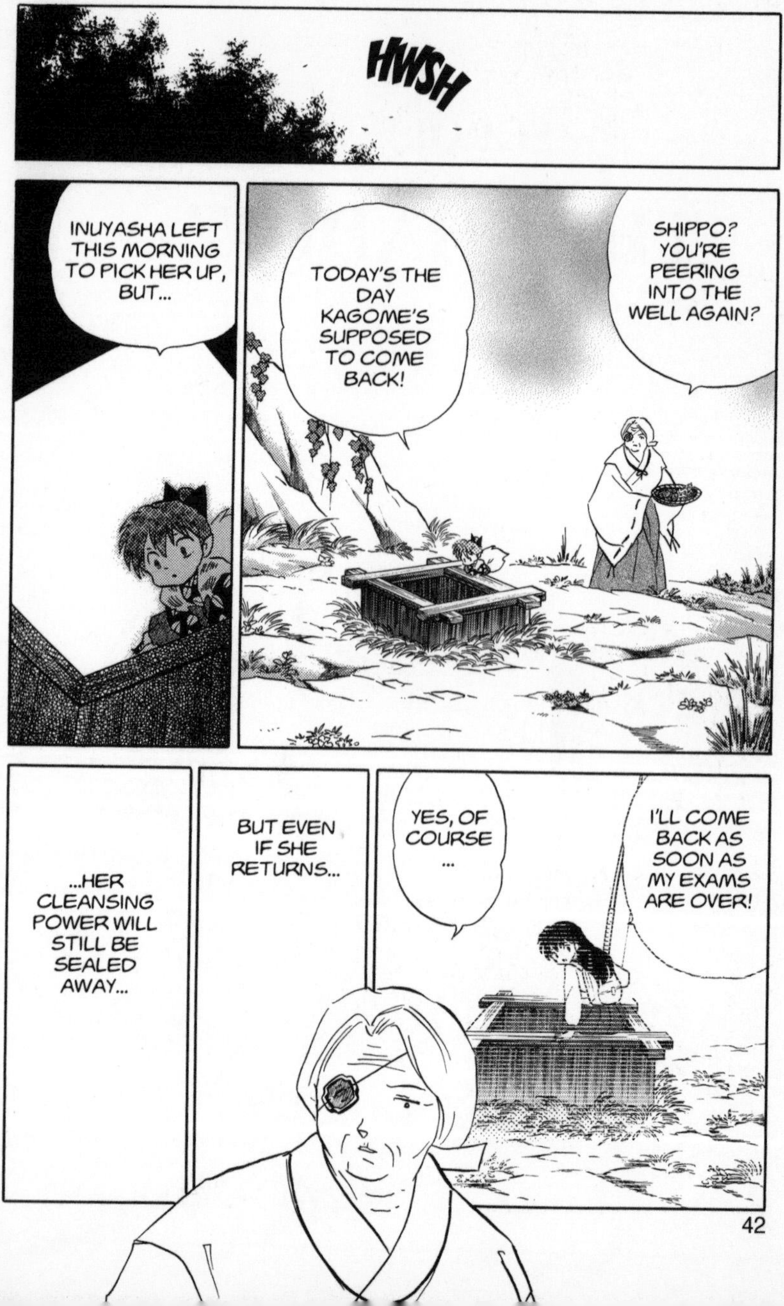
HWSH
SHIPPO? YOU'RE PEERING INTO THE WELL AGAIN?
TODAY'S THE DAY KAGOME'S SUPPOSED TO COME BACK!
INUYASHA LEFT THIS MORNING TO PICK HER UP, BUT...
I'LL COME BACK AS SOON AS MY EXAMS ARE OVER!
YES, OF COURSE ...
BUT EVEN IF SHE RETURNS...
...HER CLEANSING POWER WILL STILL BE SEALED AWAY...

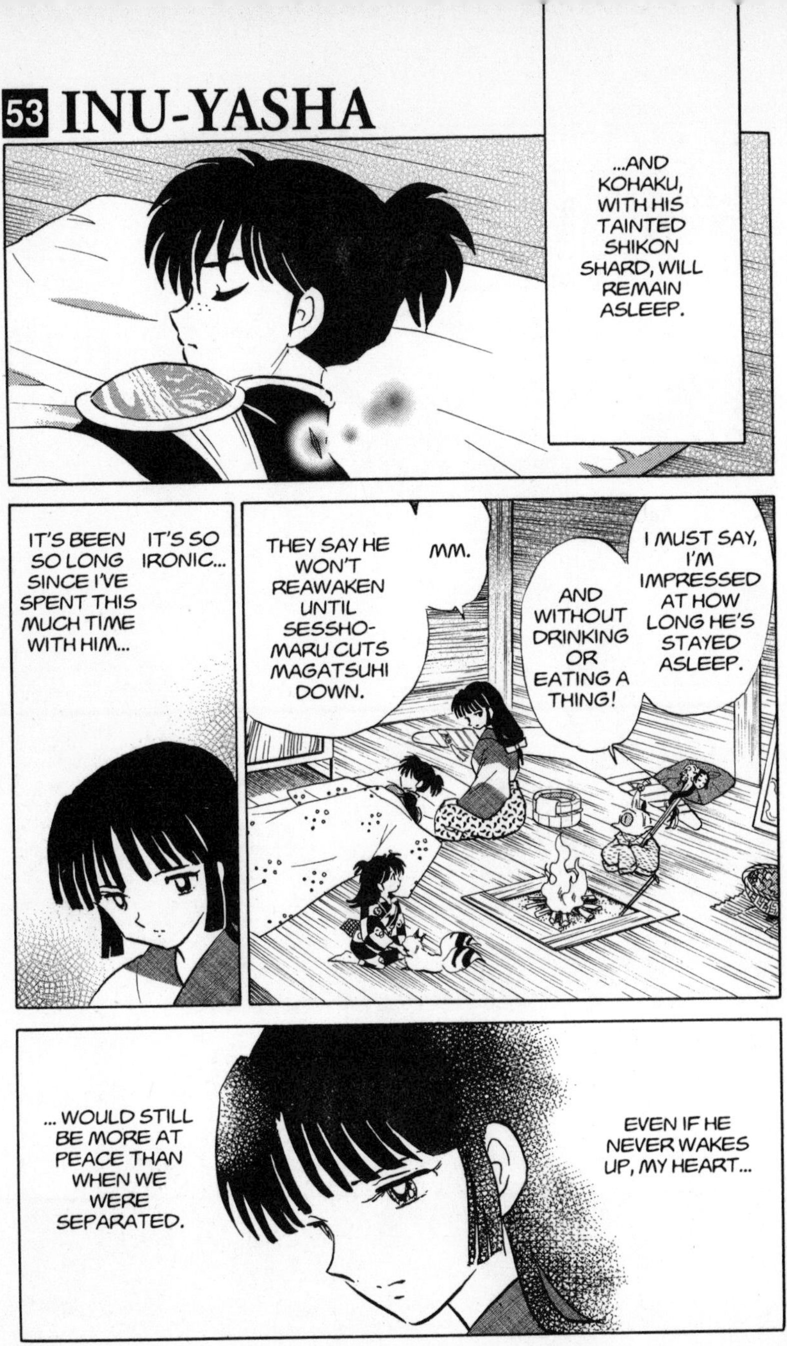
...AND KOHAKU, WITH HIS TAINTED SHIKON SHARD, WILL REMAIN ASLEEP.
I MUST SAY, I'M IMPRESSED AT HOW LONG HE'S STAYED ASLEEP.
AND WITHOUT DRINKING OR EATING A THING!
MM.
THEY SAY HE WON'T REAWAKEN UNTIL SESSHO-MARU CUTS MAGATSUHI DOWN.
IT'S SO IRONIC...
IT'S BEEN SO LONG SINCE I'VE SPENT THIS MUCH TIME WITH HIM...
EVEN IF HE NEVER WAKES UP, MY HEART...
... WOULD STILL BE MORE AT PEACE THAN WHEN WE WERE SEPARATED.

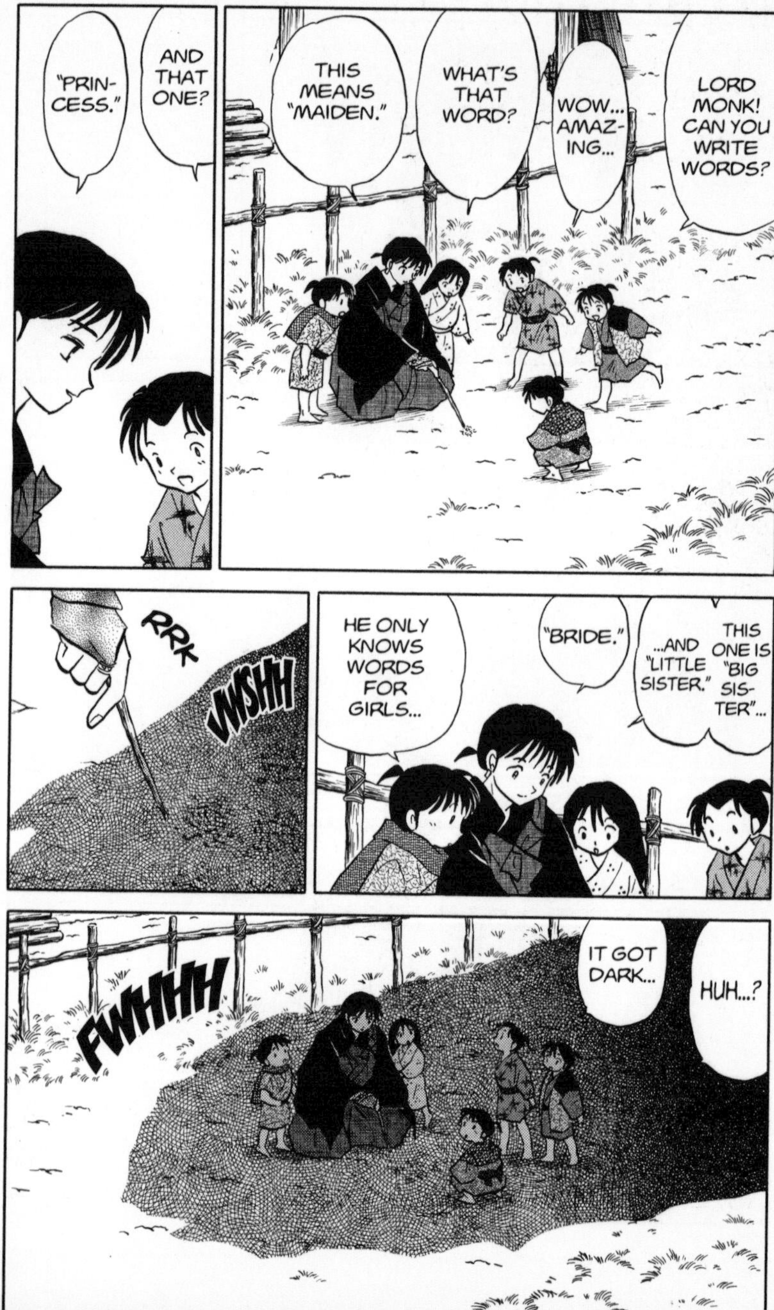
LORD MONK! CAN YOU WRITE WORDS?
WOW... AMAZ-ING...
WHAT'S THAT WORD?
THIS MEANS "MAIDEN."
AND THAT ONE?
"PRIN-CESS."
THIS ONE IS "BIG SIS-TER"...
...AND "LITTLE SISTER."
"BRIDE."
HE ONLY KNOWS WORDS FOR GIRLS...
RRK
WSHH
HUH...?
IT GOT DARK...
FWHHHH

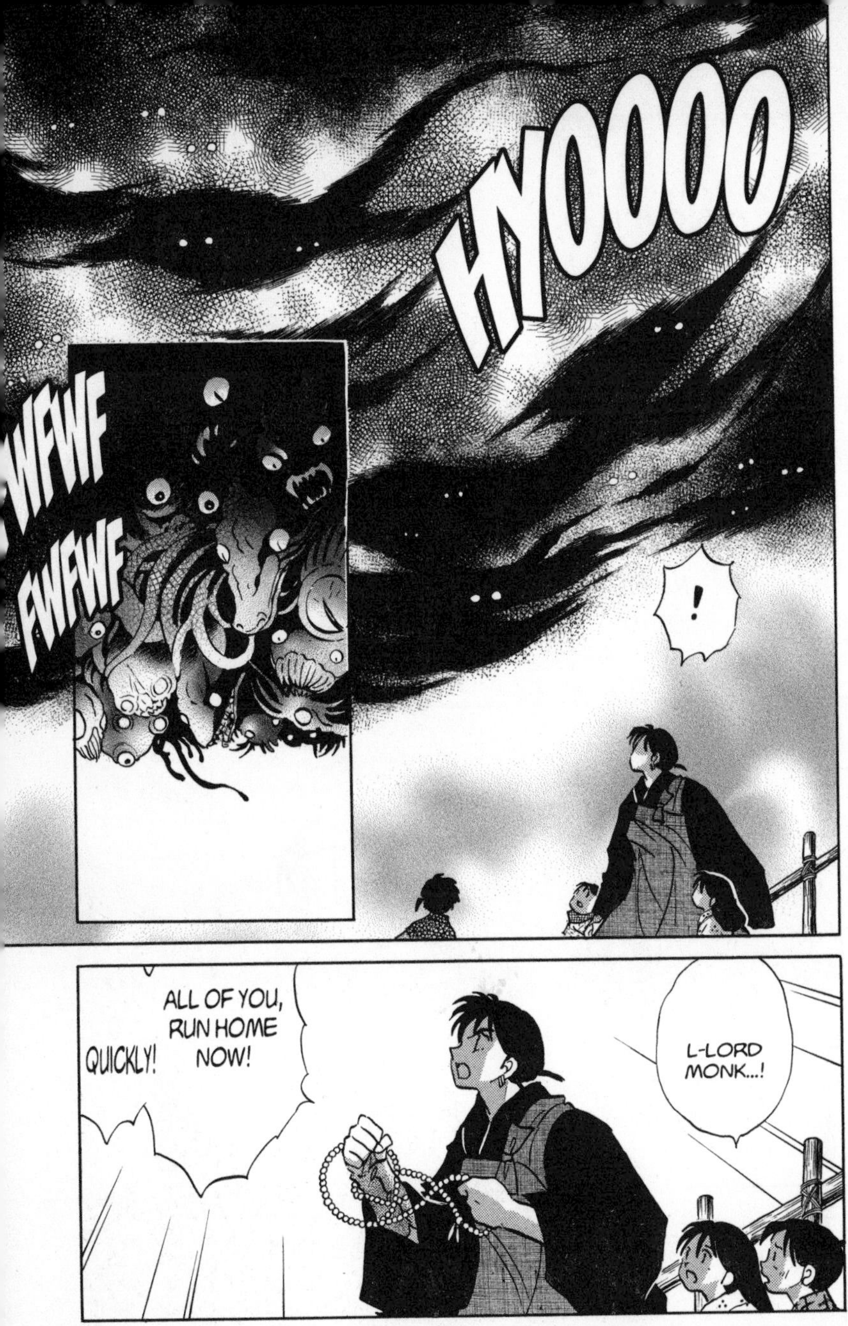
HYOOOO
!
WFWF FWFWF
L-LORD MONK...!
ALL OF YOU, RUN HOME NOW!
QUICKLY!

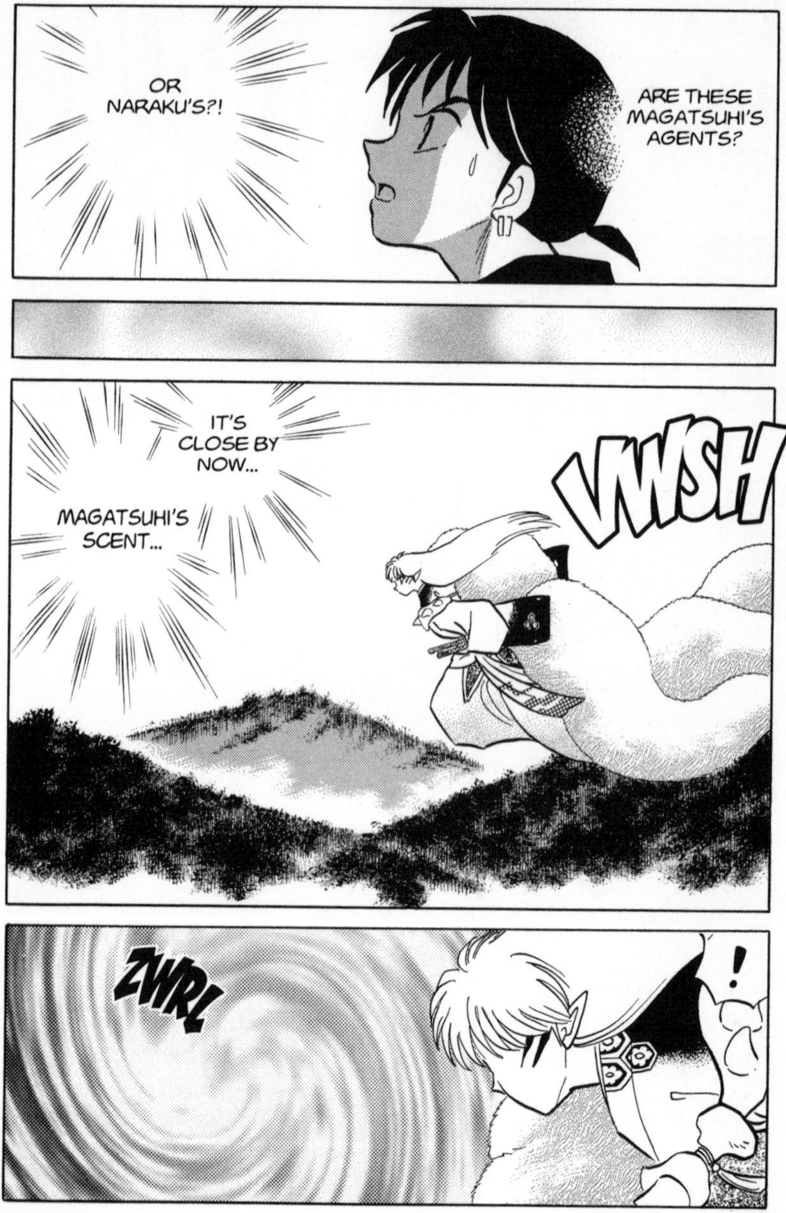

ARE THESE MAGATSUHI'S AGENTS?
OR NARAKU'S?!
VWSH
IT'S CLOSE BY NOW...
MAGATSUHI'S SCENT...
!
ZWRL

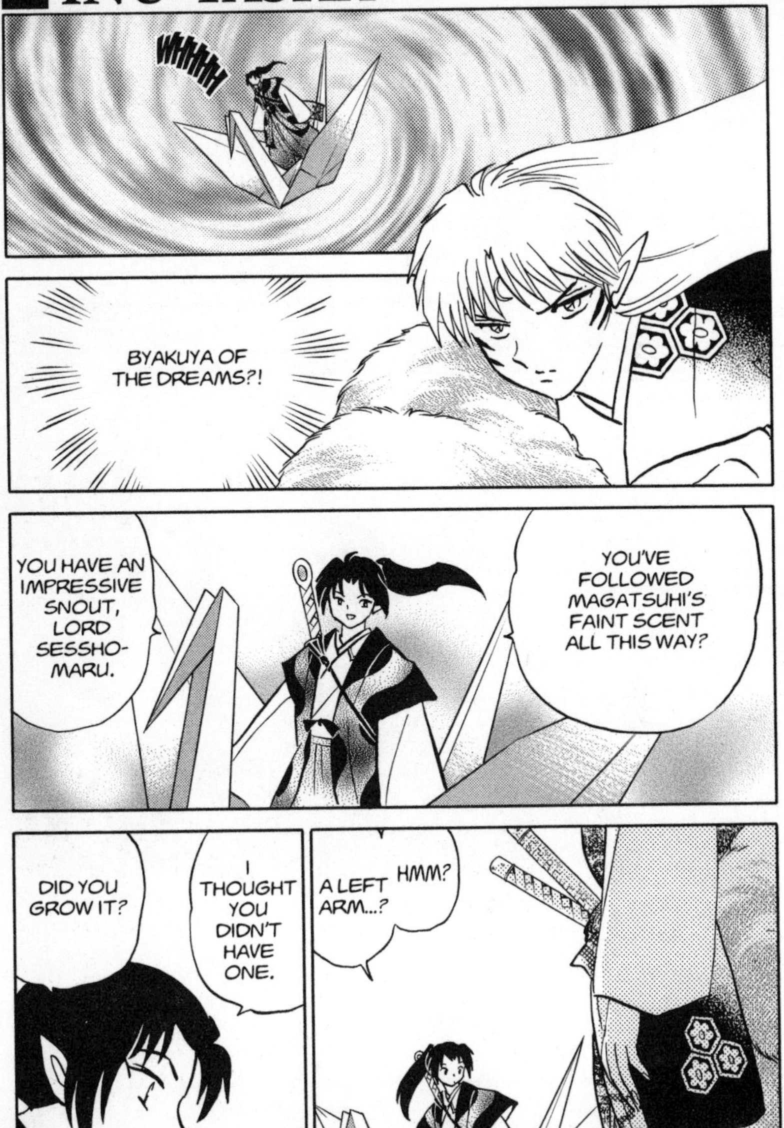
WHHHHH
BYAKUYA OF THE DREAMS?!
YOU'VE FOLLOWED MAGATSUHI'S FAINT SCENT ALL THIS WAY?
YOU HAVE AN IMPRESSIVE SNOUT, LORD SESSHO-MARU.
HMM?
A LEFT ARM...?
I THOUGHT YOU DIDN'T HAVE ONE.
DID YOU GROW IT?

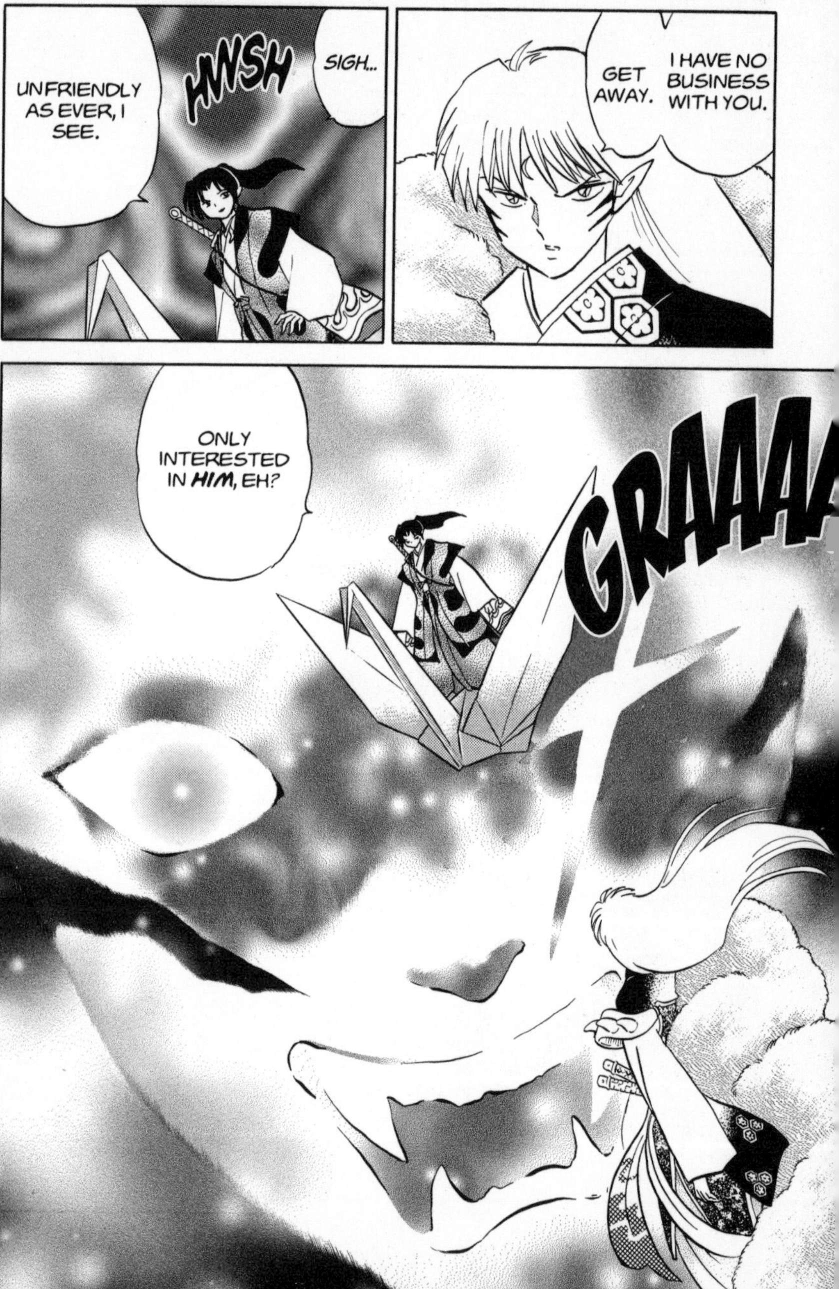
GET AWAY. I HAVE NO BUSINESS WITH YOU.
SIGH...
HWSH
UNFRIENDLY AS EVER, I SEE.
ONLY INTERESTED IN *HIM*, EH?
GRAAAA

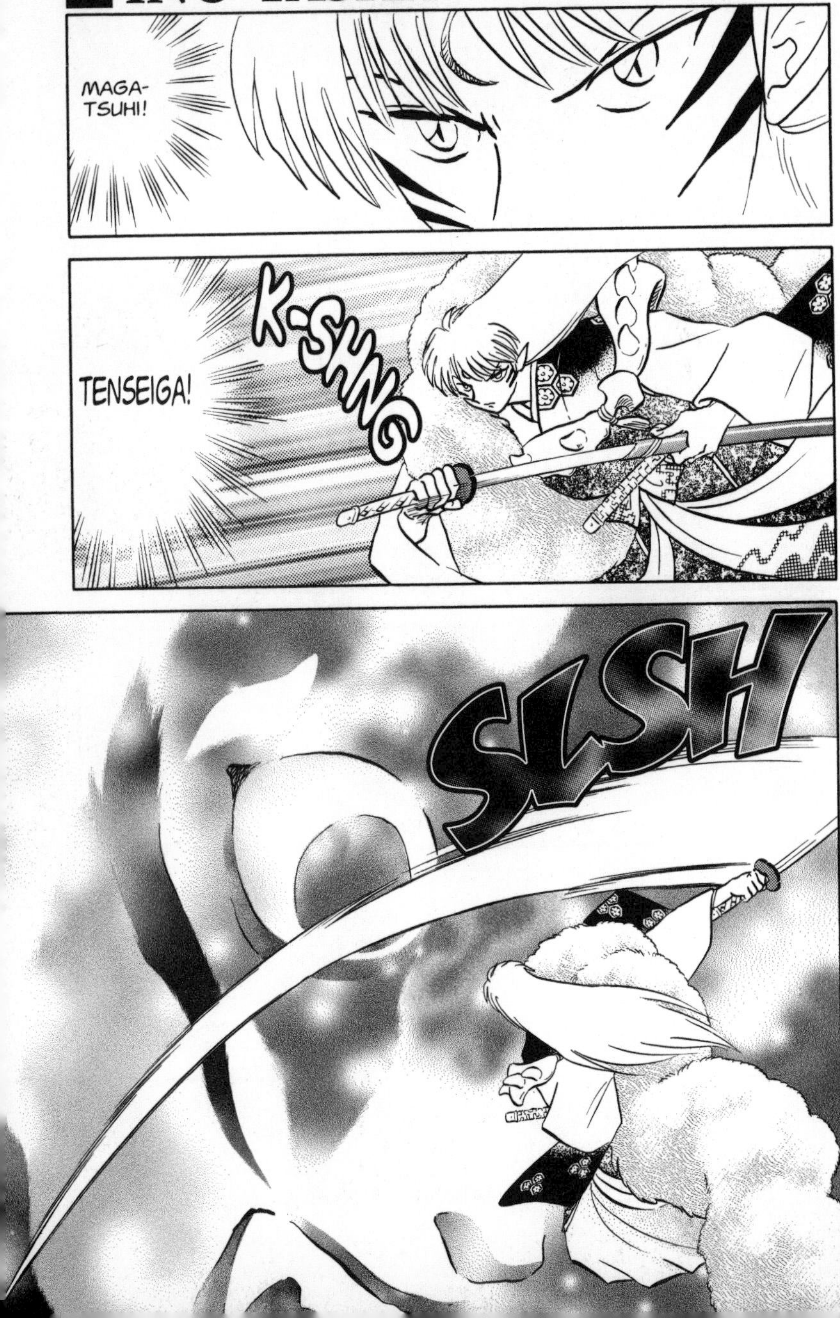
MAGA-
TSUHI!
K-SHING
TENSEIGA!
SLSH

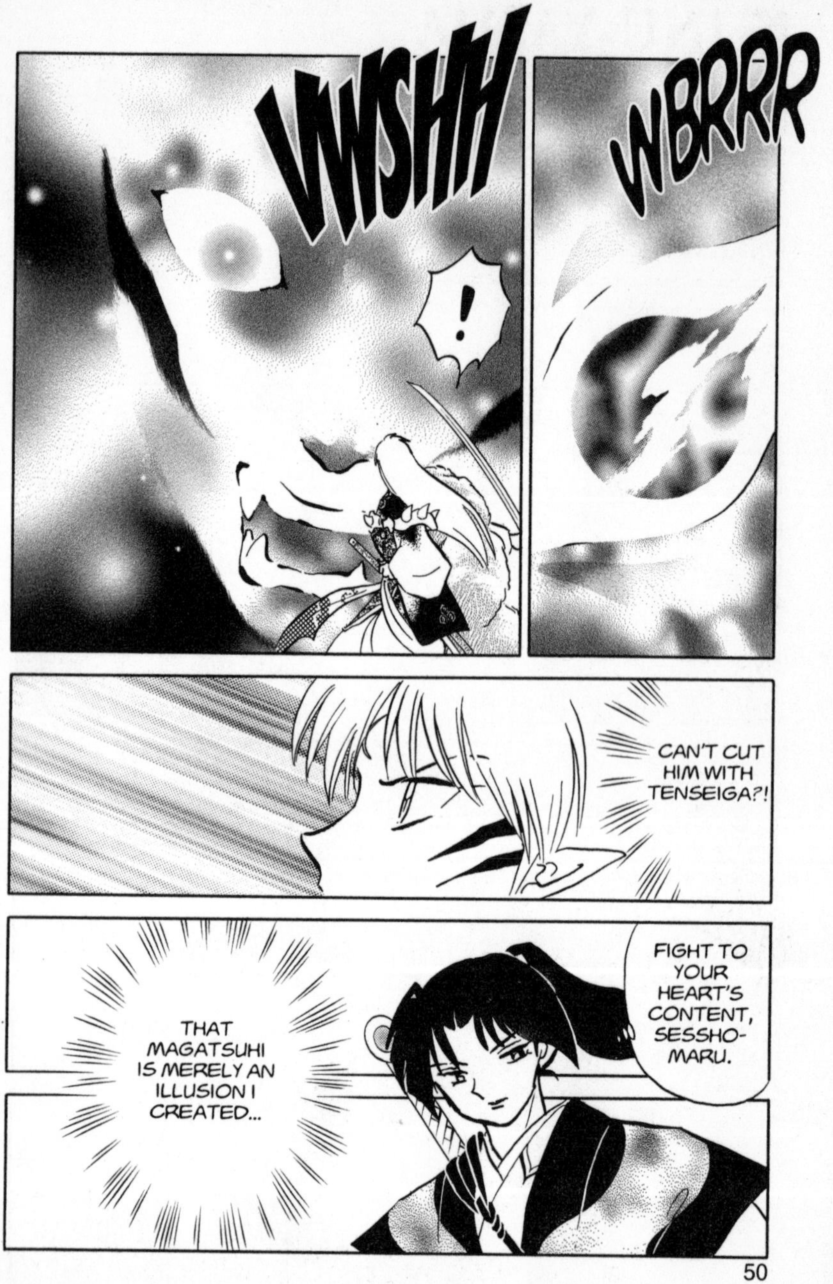
WBRRR
VWSHH
!
CAN'T CUT HIM WITH TENSEIGA?!
FIGHT TO YOUR HEART'S CONTENT, SESSHO-MARU.
THAT MAGATSUHI IS MERELY AN ILLUSION I CREATED...

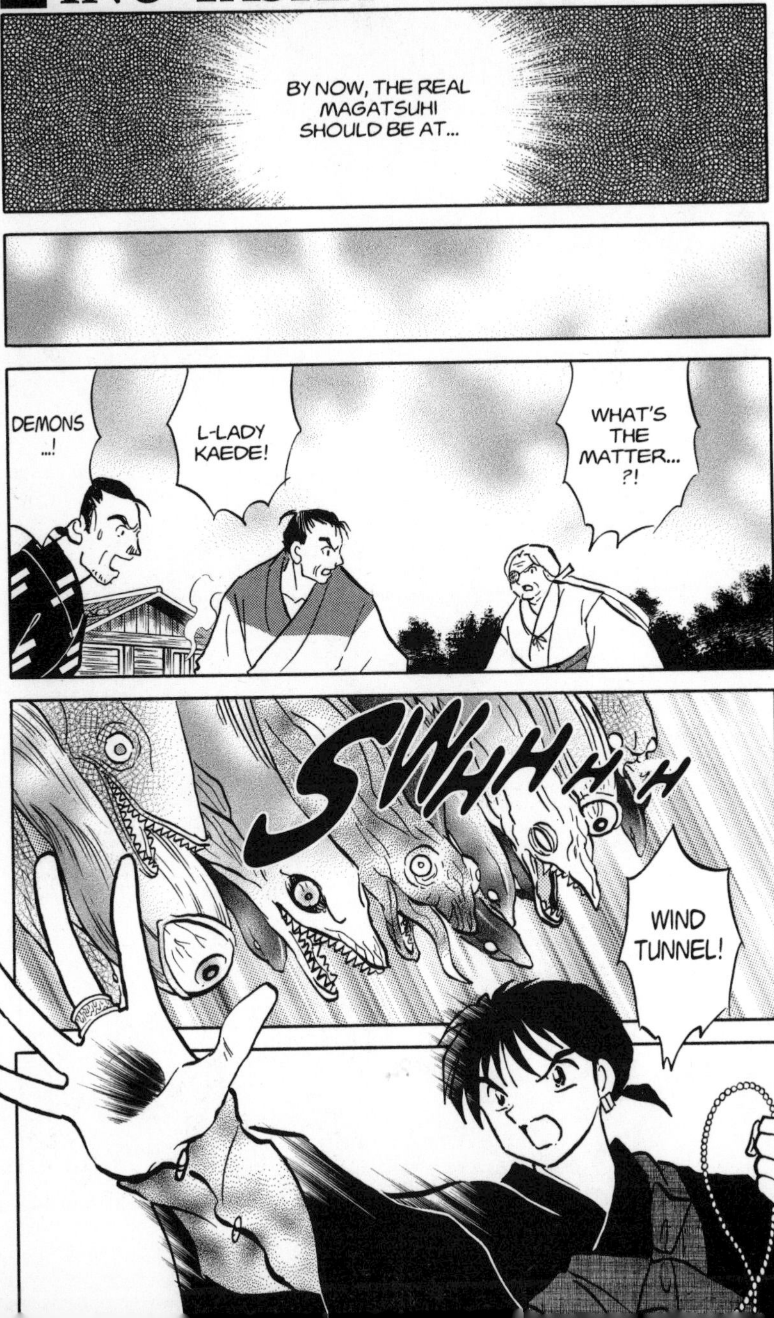
BY NOW, THE REAL MAGATSUHI SHOULD BE AT...
WHAT'S THE MATTER... ?!
L-LADY KAEDE!
DEMONS ...!
SWHHHH
WIND TUNNEL!

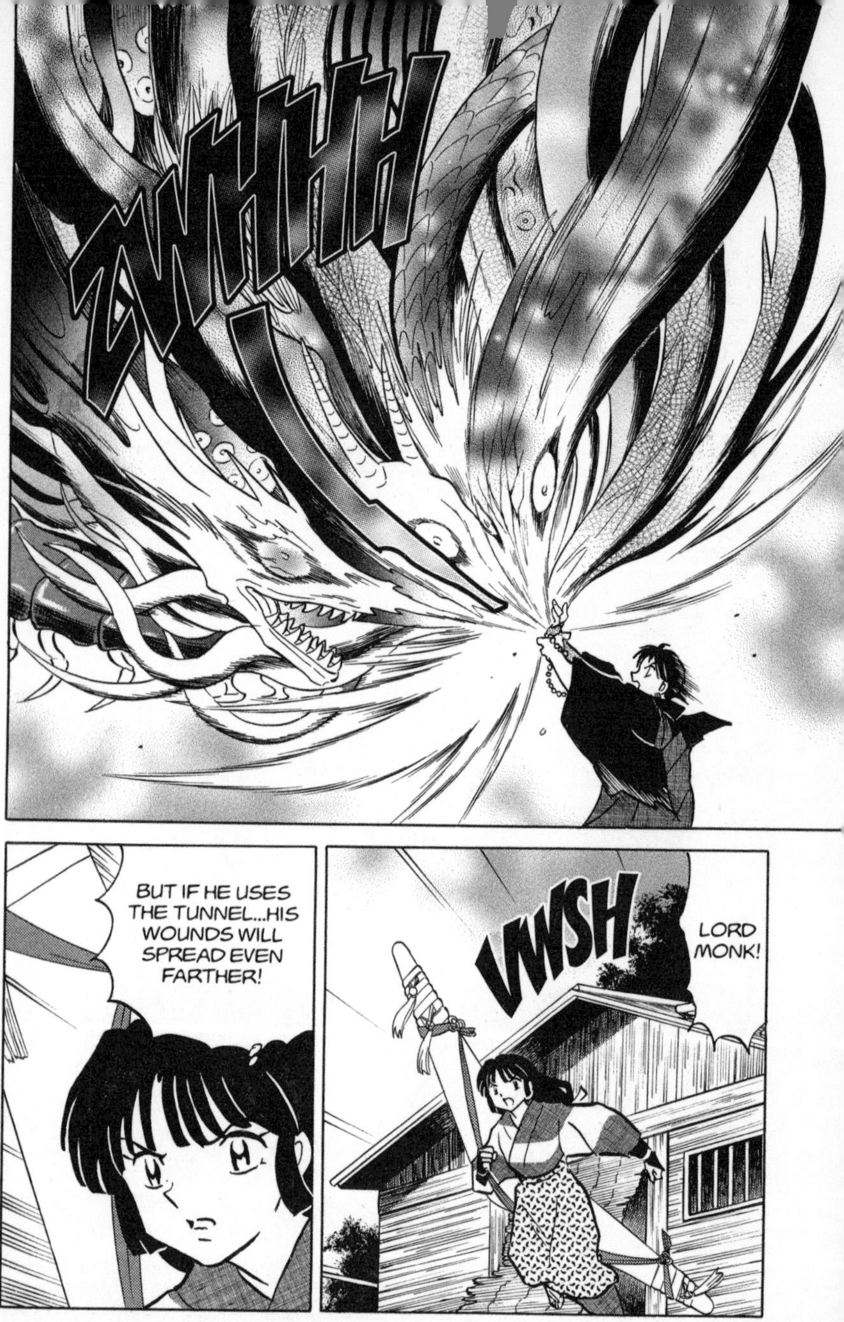
ZWHHHH
LORD MONK!
VWSH
BUT IF HE USES THE TUNNEL...HIS WOUNDS WILL SPREAD EVEN FARTHER!

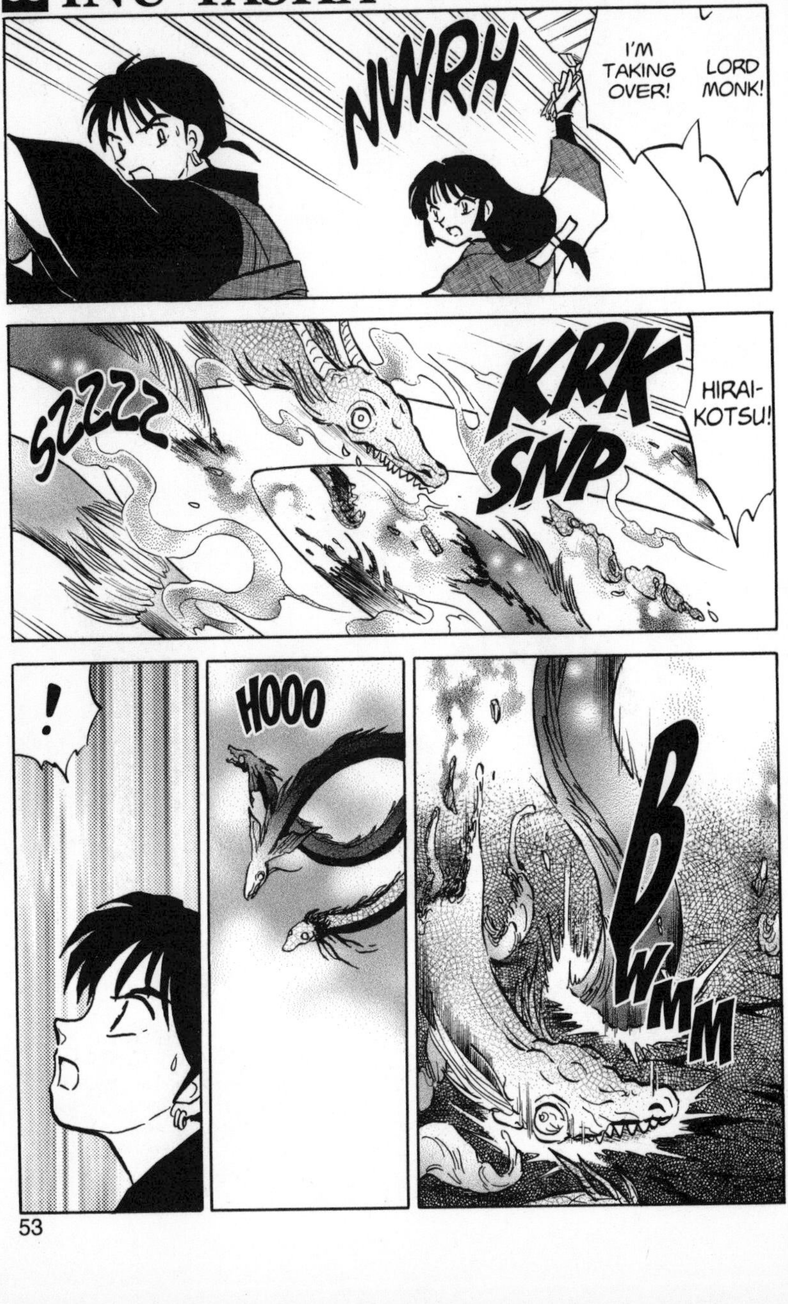
LORD MONK!
I'M TAKING OVER!
NWRH
HIRAI-KOTSU!
KRK SNP
SZZZZ
BWMM
HOOO
!

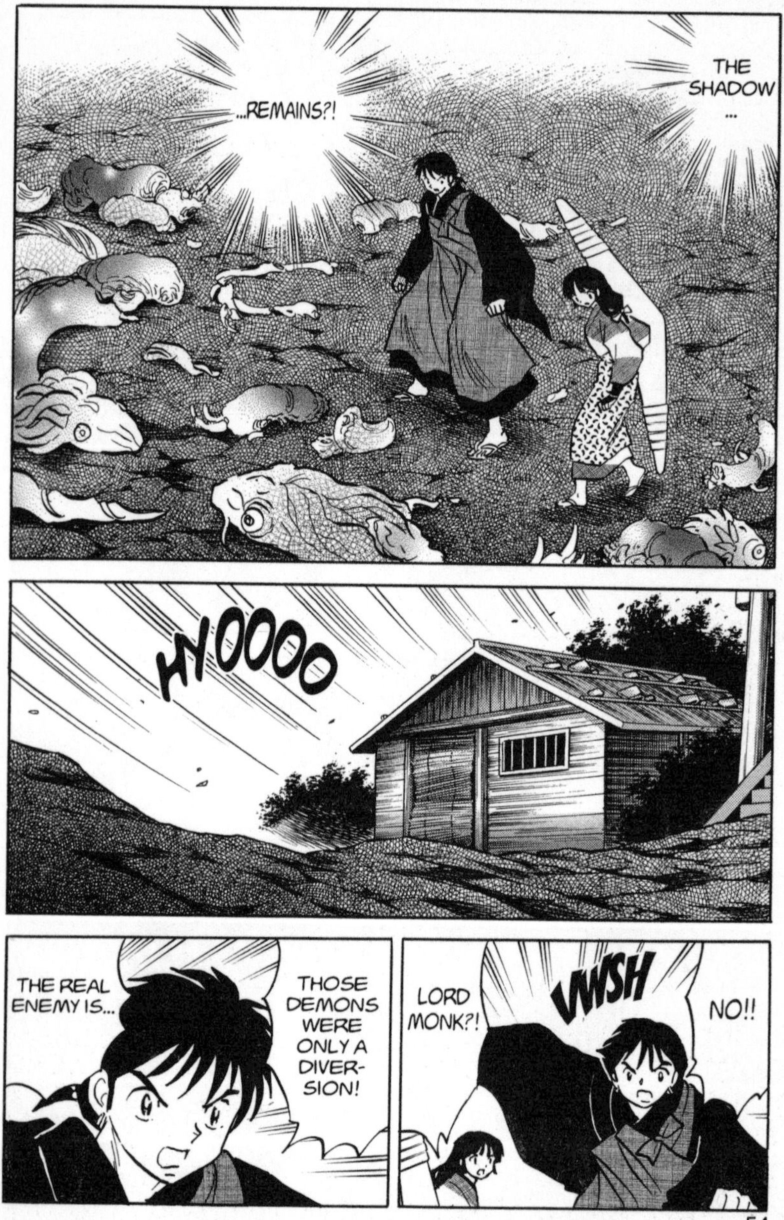
THE SHADOW ...
...REMAINS?!
HYOOOO
NO!!
VWSH
LORD MONK?!
THOSE DEMONS WERE ONLY A DIVER-SION!
THE REAL ENEMY IS...

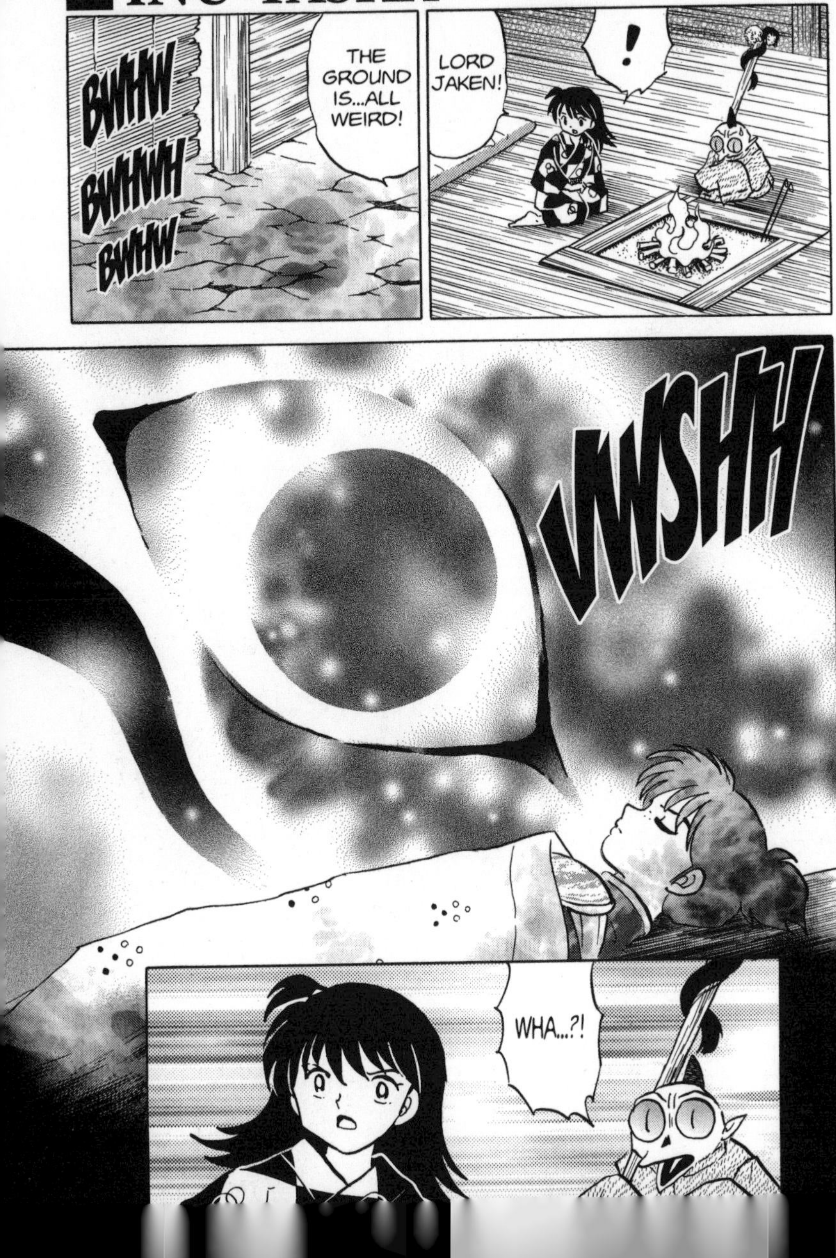
!
LORD JAKEN!
THE GROUND IS...ALL WEIRD!
BWHW
BWHWH
BWHW
VWSHH
WHA...?!

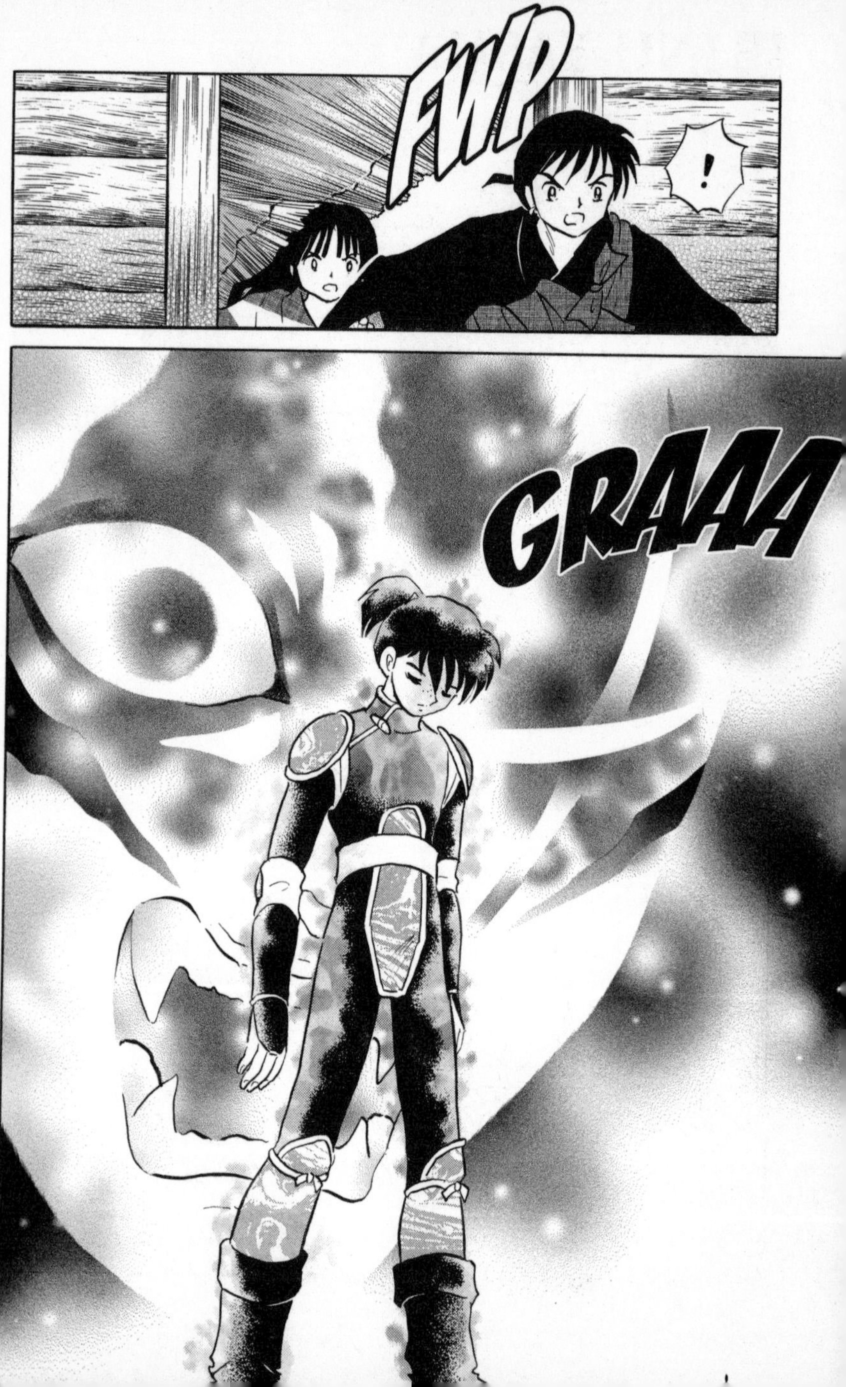
FWP
!
GRAAA

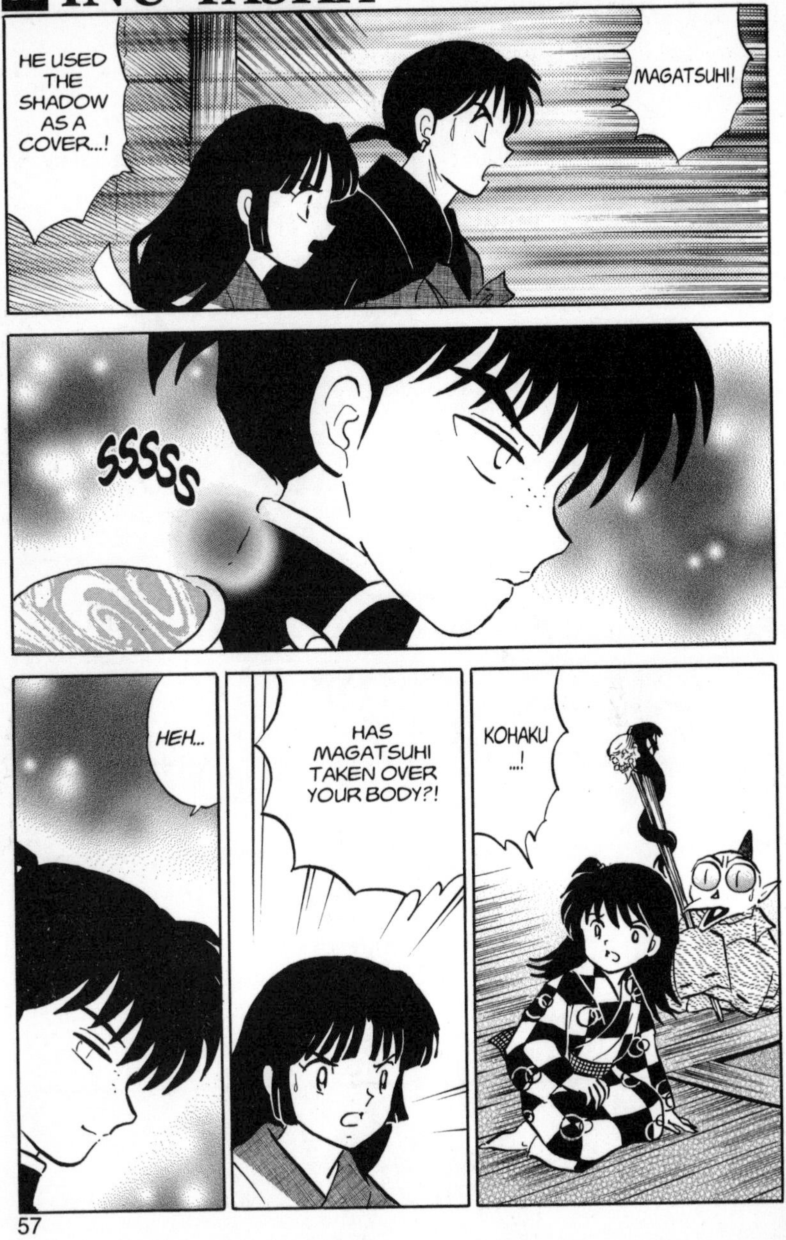
MAGATSUHI!
HE USED THE SHADOW AS A COVER...!
SSSSS
KOHAKU ...!
HAS MAGATSUHI TAKEN OVER YOUR BODY?!
HEH...

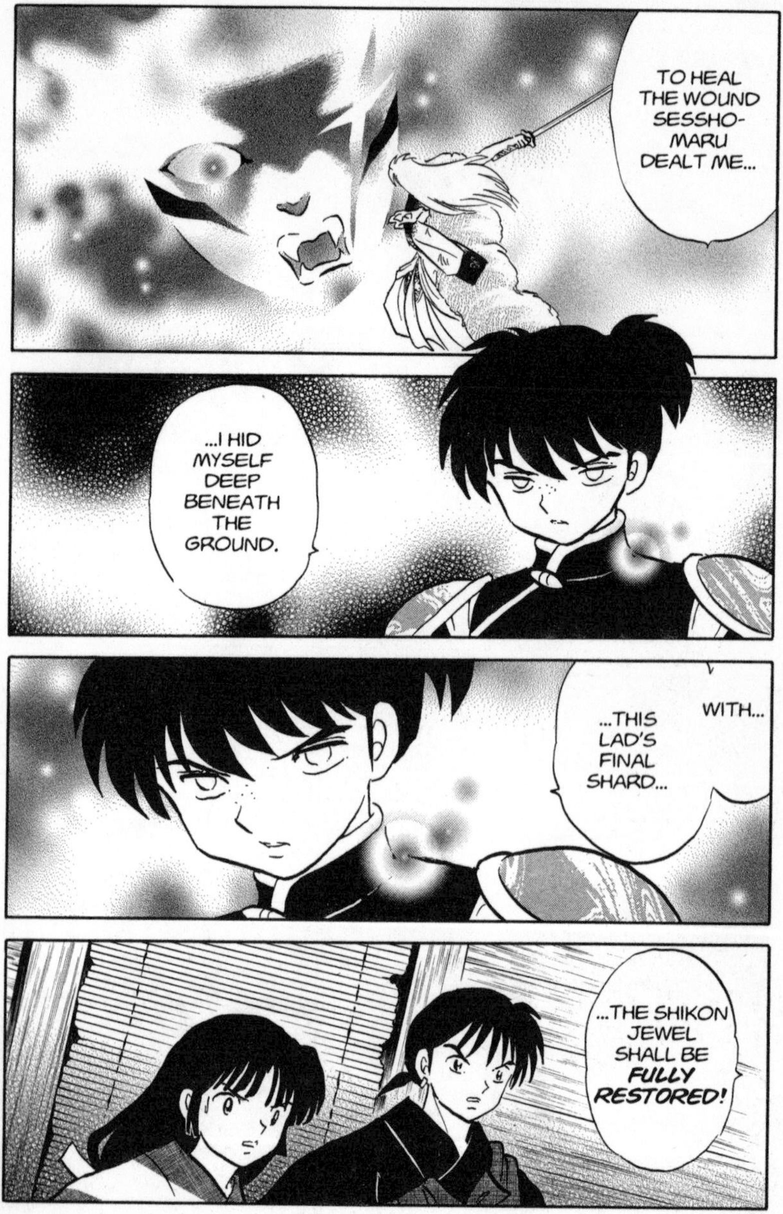
TO HEAL THE WOUND SESSHO-MARU DEALT ME...
...I HID MYSELF DEEP BENEATH THE GROUND.
WITH...
...THIS LAD'S FINAL SHARD...
...THE SHIKON JEWEL SHALL BE **FULLY RESTORED!**

SCROLL 4

POSSESSED

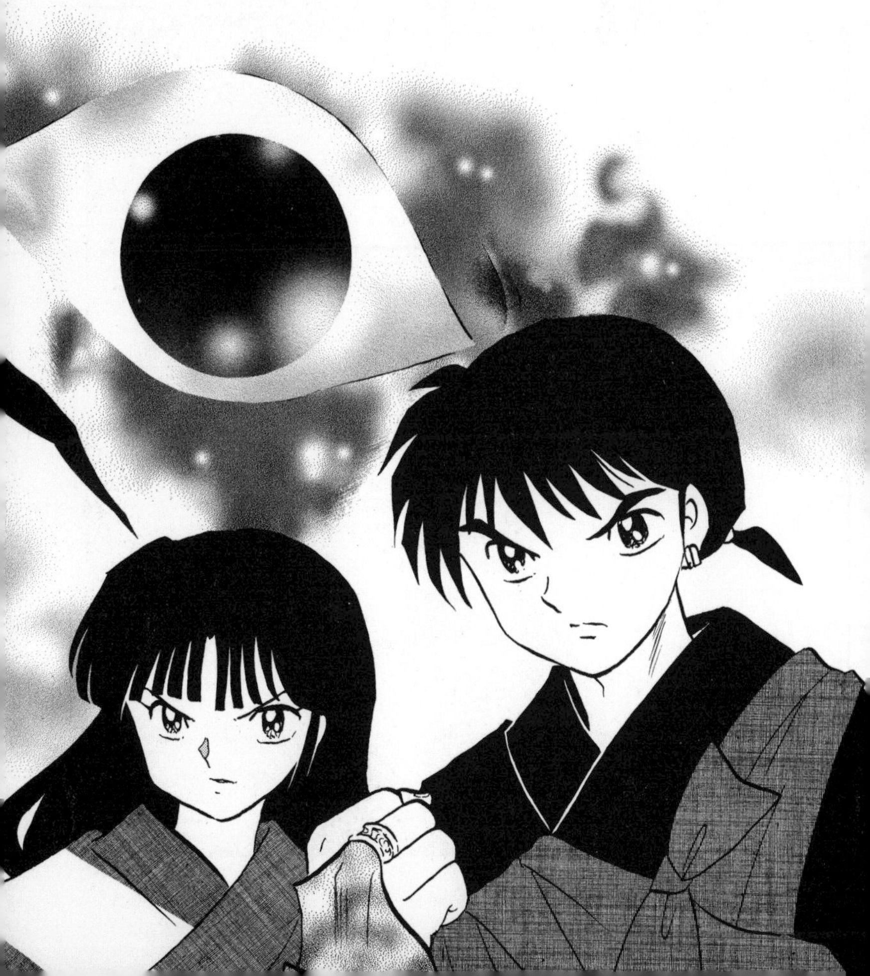

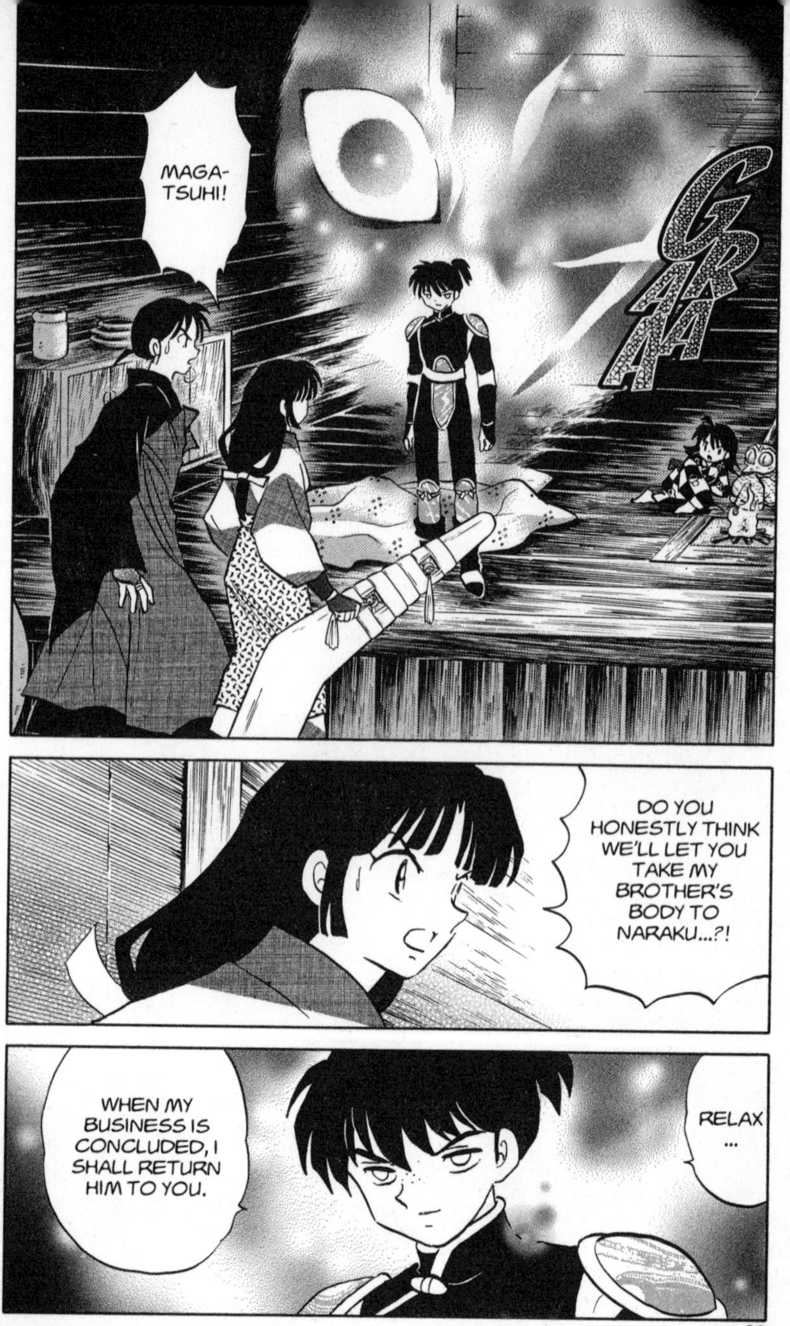
MAGA-
TSUHI!
GRAAA
DO YOU HONESTLY THINK WE'LL LET YOU TAKE MY BROTHER'S BODY TO NARAKU...?!
RELAX ...
WHEN MY BUSINESS IS CONCLUDED, I SHALL RETURN HIM TO YOU.

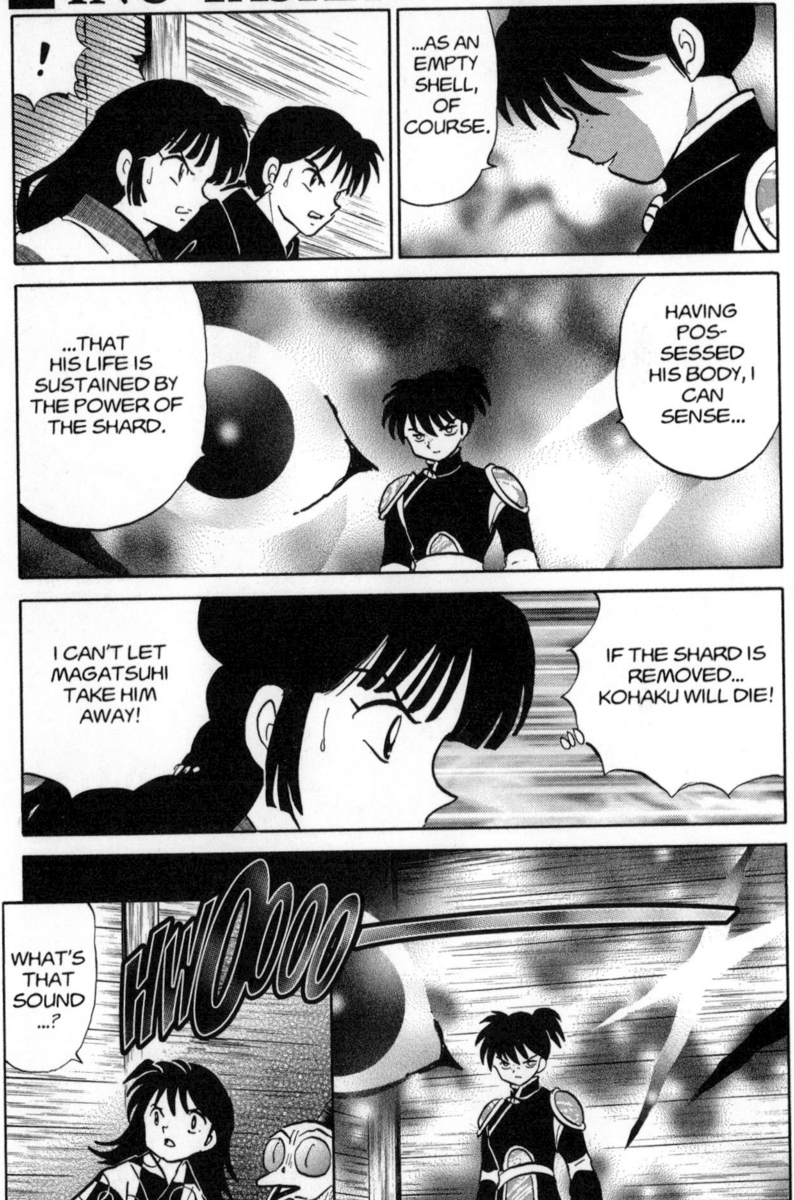
...AS AN EMPTY SHELL, OF COURSE.
!
HAVING POS-SESSED HIS BODY, I CAN SENSE...
...THAT HIS LIFE IS SUSTAINED BY THE POWER OF THE SHARD.
IF THE SHARD IS REMOVED... KOHAKU WILL DIE!
I CAN'T LET MAGATSUHI TAKE HIM AWAY!
HWOOOO
WHAT'S THAT SOUND...?

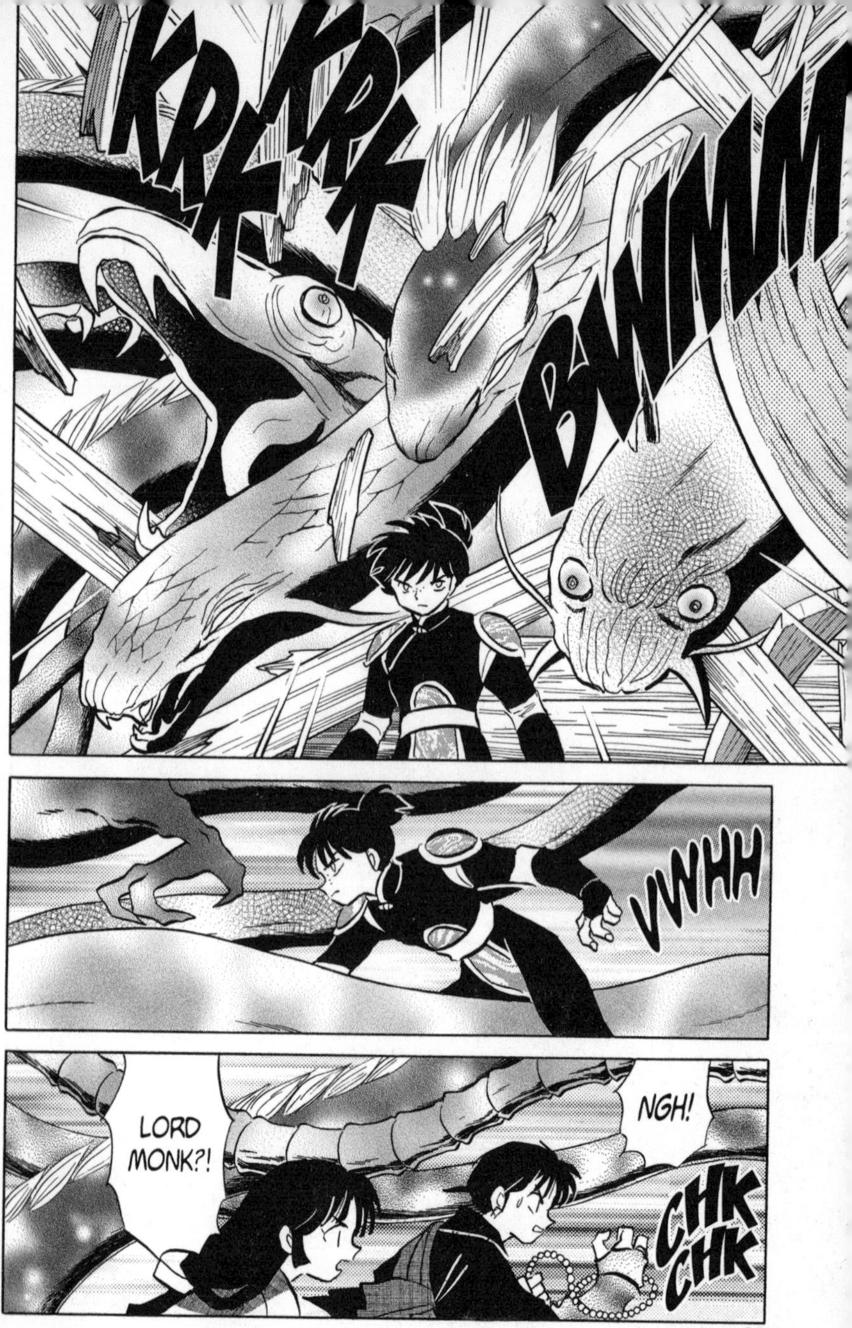
VWHH
NGH!
CHK CHK
LORD MONK?!

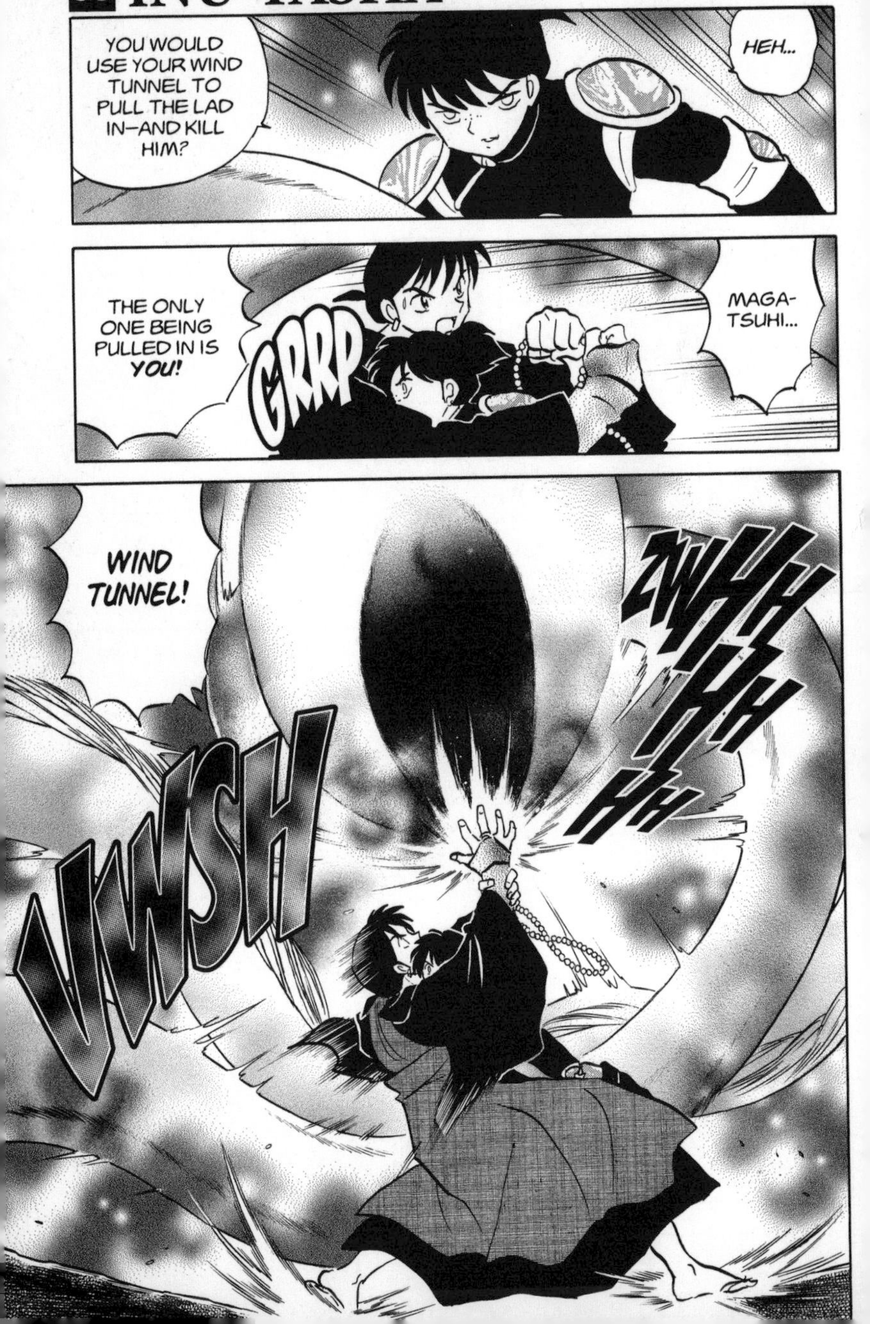
HEH...
YOU WOULD USE YOUR WIND TUNNEL TO PULL THE LAD IN—AND KILL HIM?
MAGA-TSUHI...
GRRP
THE ONLY ONE BEING PULLED IN IS *YOU!*
ZWHHHHHH
WIND TUNNEL!
VWSH

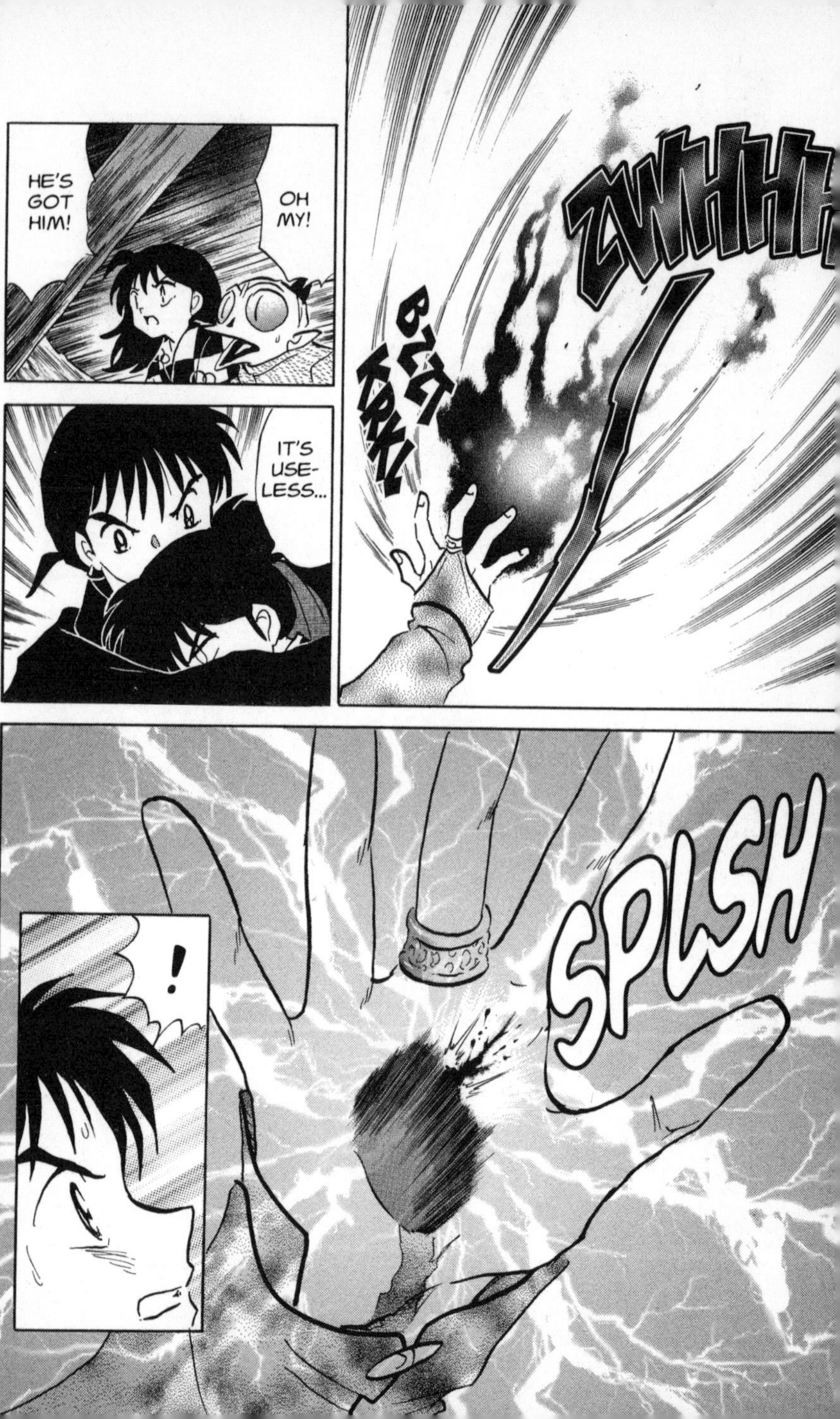
ZWHHHH
BZZT KRRKL
OH MY!
HE'S GOT HIM!
IT'S USE-LESS...
SPLSH
!

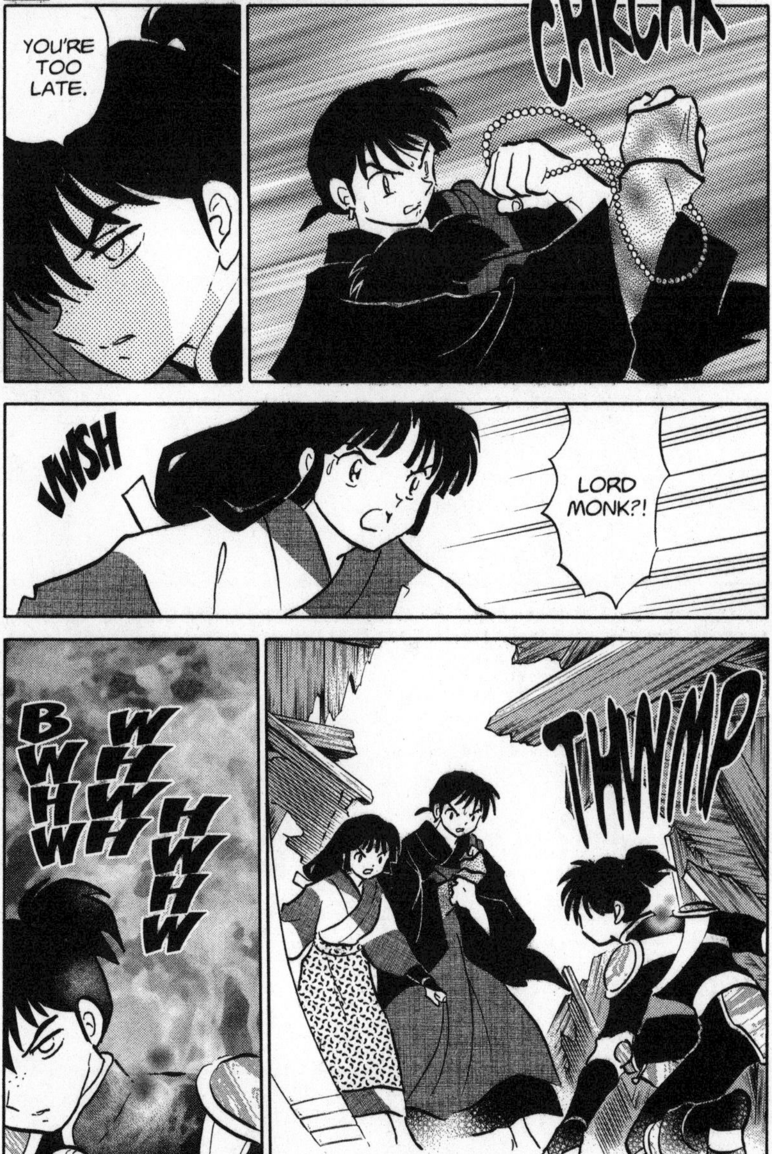
CHKCHK
YOU'RE TOO LATE.
LORD MONK?!
VWSH
THWMP
BWHW WHWH HWHW

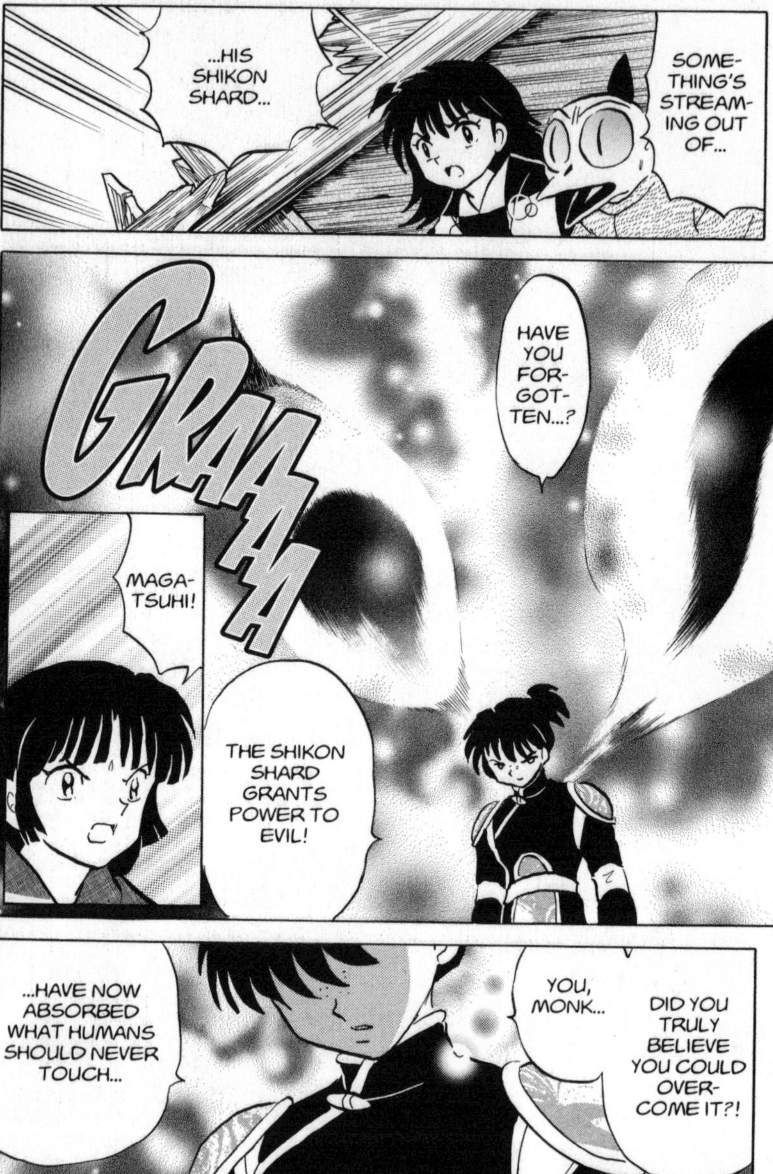
SOME-THING'S STREAM-ING OUT OF...
...HIS SHIKON SHARD...
HAVE YOU FOR-GOT-TEN...?
GRAAAA
THE SHIKON SHARD GRANTS POWER TO EVIL!
MAGA-TSUHI!
YOU, MONK...
...HAVE NOW ABSORBED WHAT HUMANS SHOULD NEVER TOUCH...
DID YOU TRULY BELIEVE YOU COULD OVER-COME IT?!

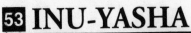

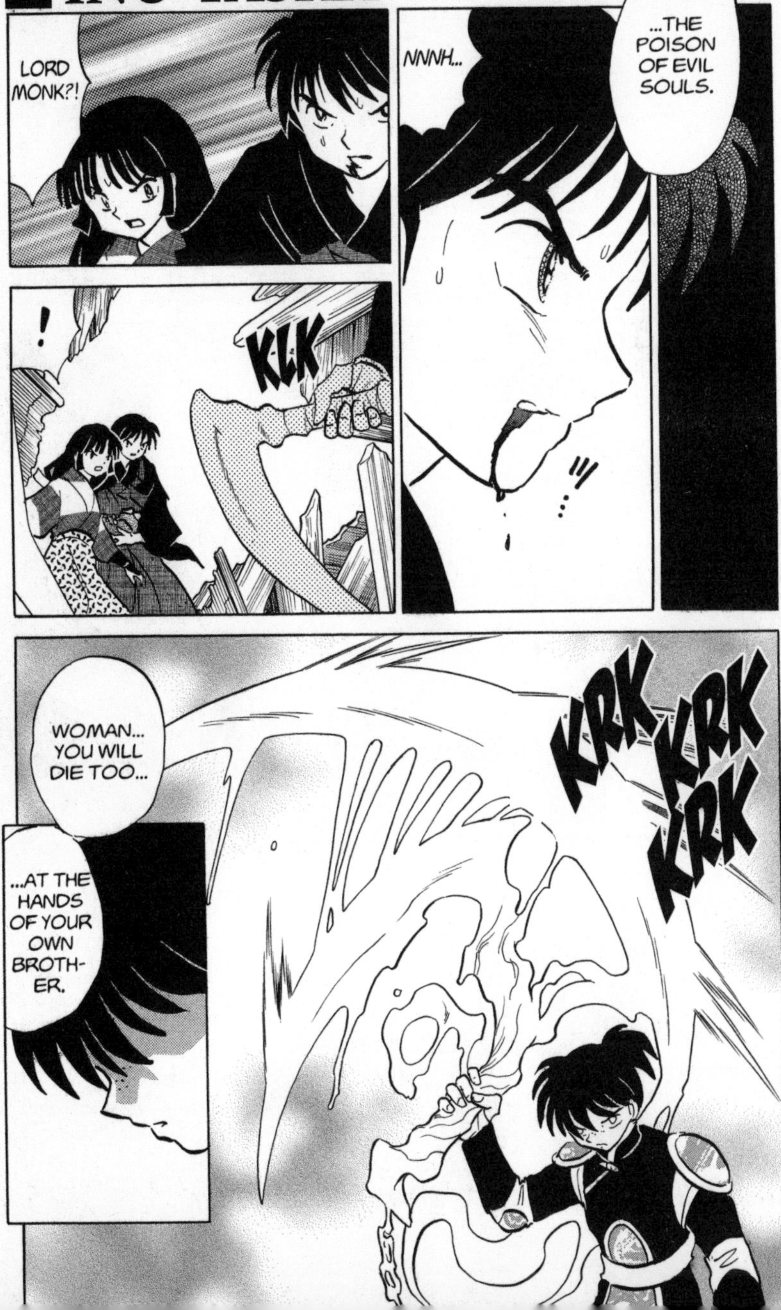
...THE POISON OF EVIL SOULS.
NNNH...
LORD MONK?!
KLK
!
KRK KRK KRK
WOMAN... YOU WILL DIE TOO...
...AT THE HANDS OF YOUR OWN BROTHER-ER.

KRK KRK KRK

RGH!

SZZZ

KRK

KOHAKU, STOP!

WSH

WPSH

JWH

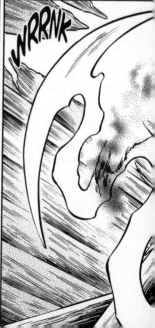

WRRNK

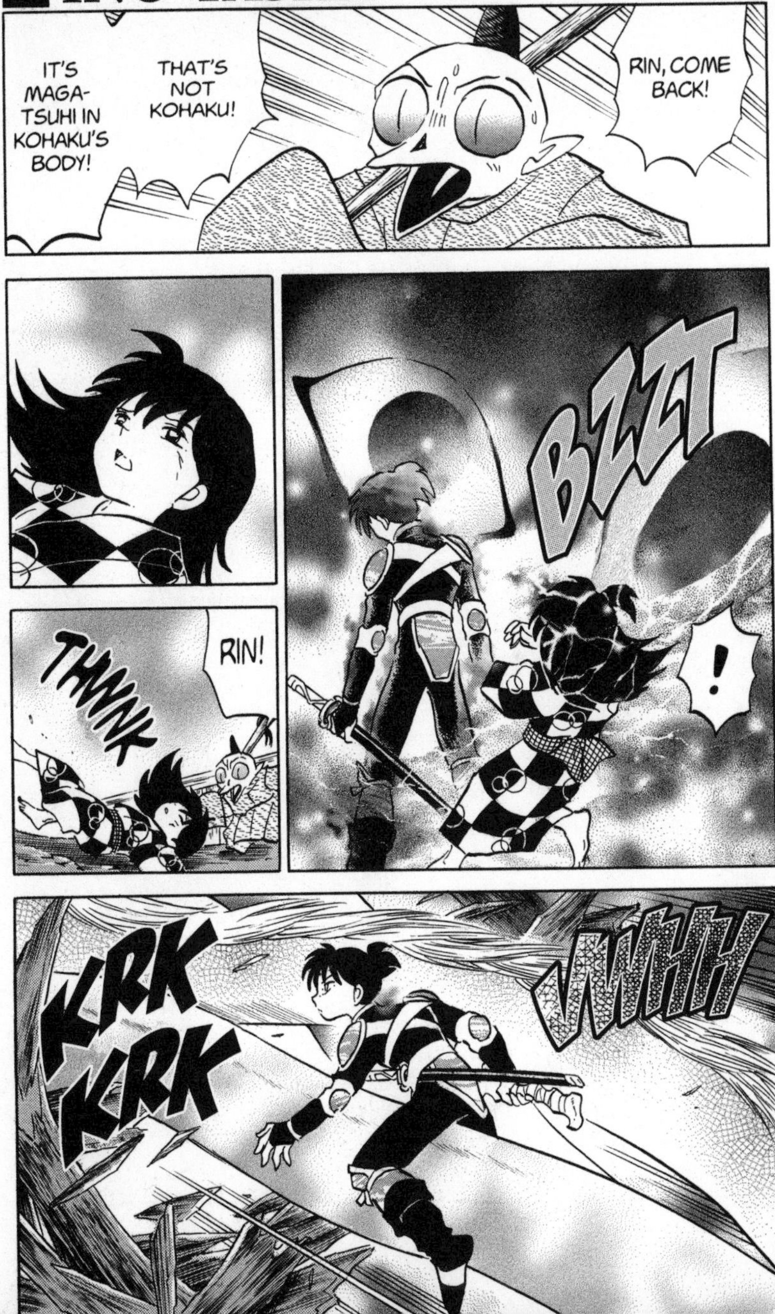
RIN, COME BACK!
THAT'S NOT KOHAKU!
IT'S MAGA-TSUHI IN KOHAKU'S BODY!
BZZT
!
RIN!
THWNK
JWHH
KRK KRK

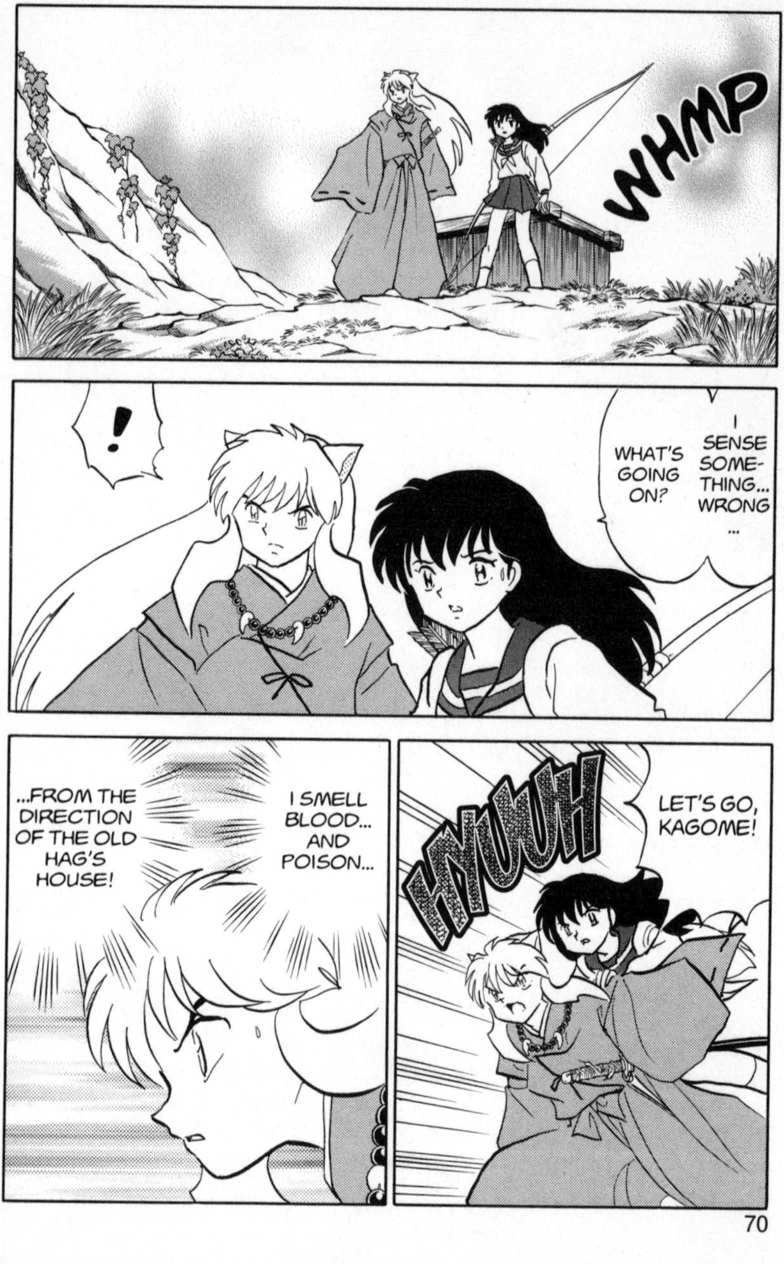
WHMP
I SENSE SOMETHING... WRONG ...
WHAT'S GOING ON?
!
LET'S GO, KAGOME!
HYUUH
I SMELL BLOOD... AND POISON...
...FROM THE DIRECTION OF THE OLD HAG'S HOUSE!

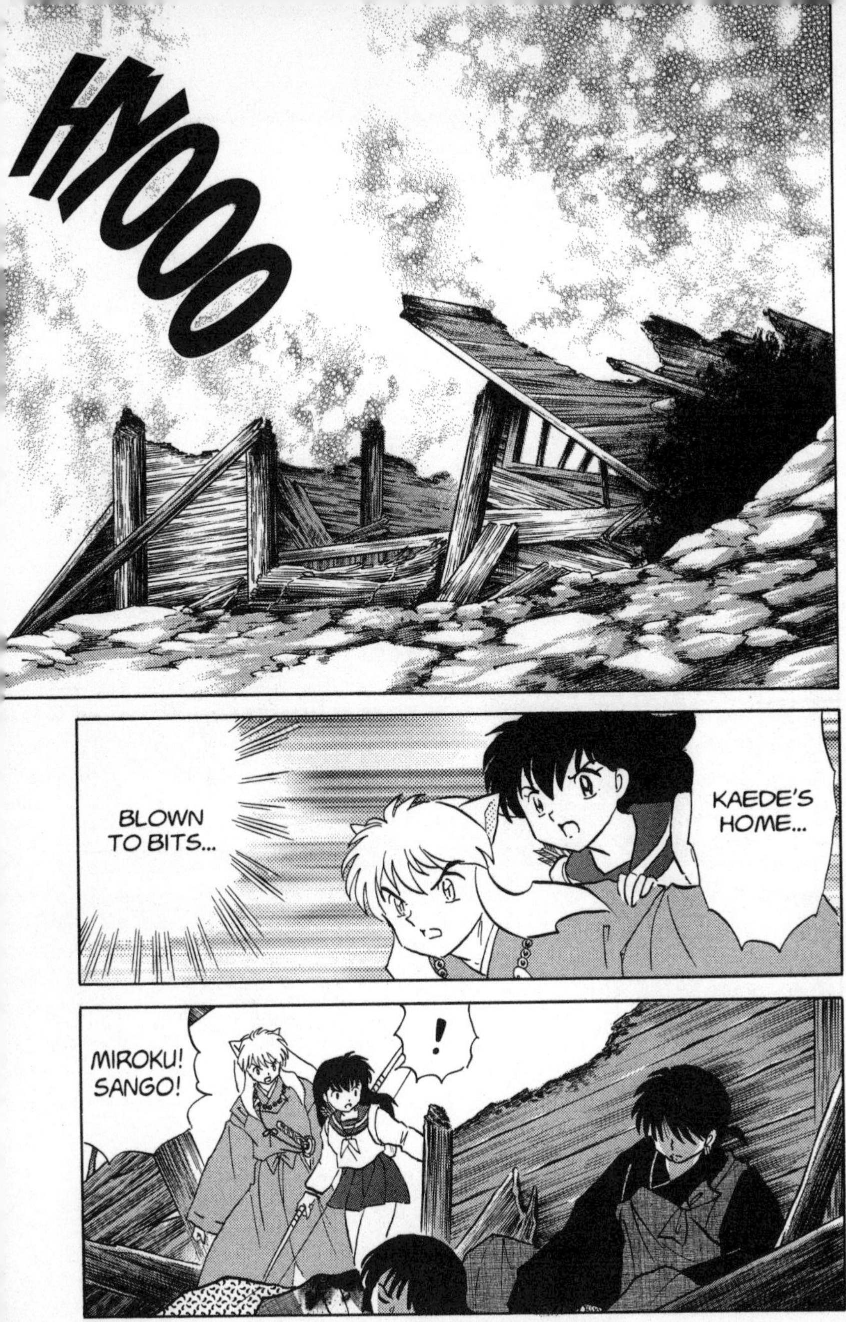
HYOOO
KAEDE'S HOME...
BLOWN TO BITS...
!
MIROKU! SANGO!

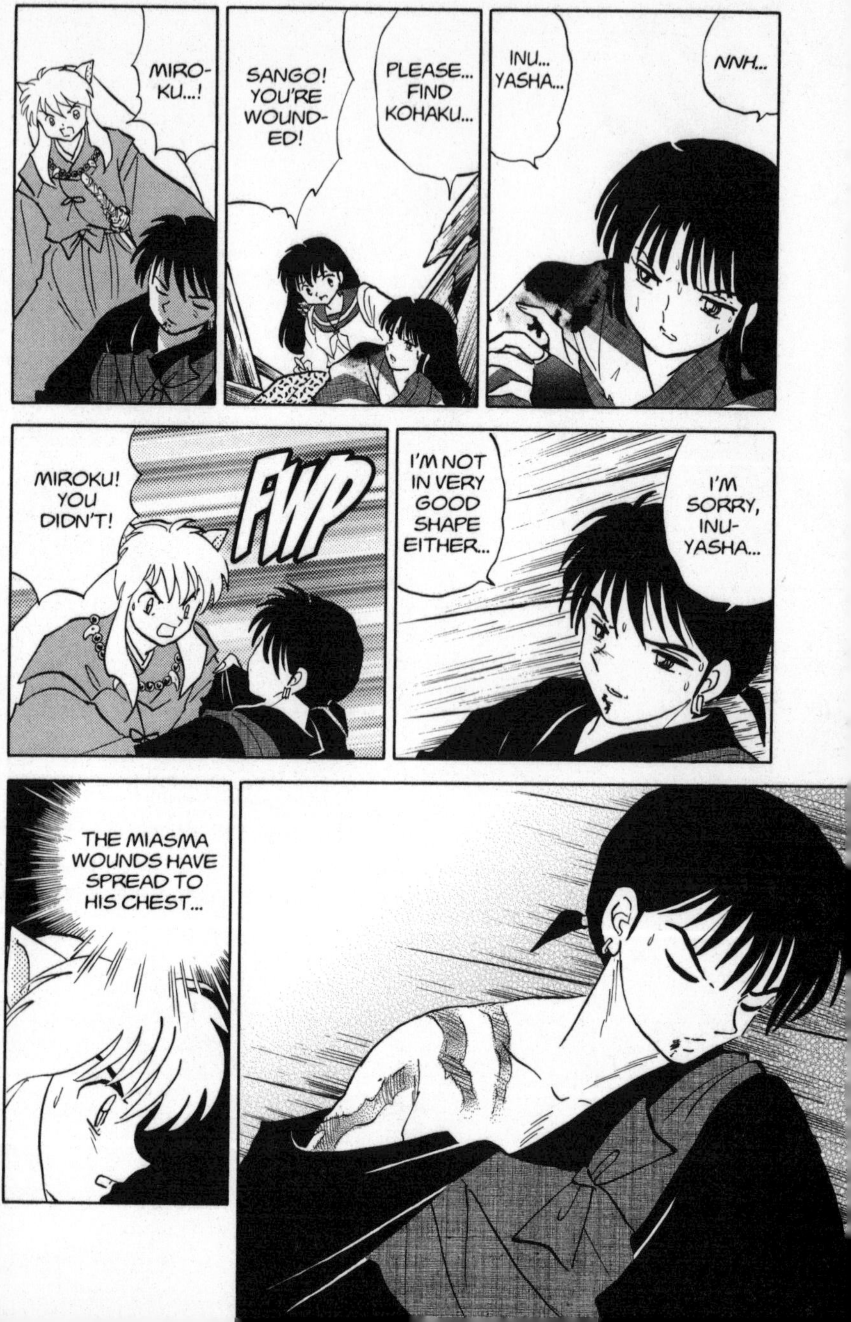
NNH...
INU... YASHA...
PLEASE... FIND KOHAKU...
SANGO! YOU'RE WOUND-ED!
MIRO-KU...!
I'M SORRY, INU-YASHA...
I'M NOT IN VERY GOOD SHAPE EITHER...
FWP
MIROKU! YOU DIDN'T!
THE MIASMA WOUNDS HAVE SPREAD TO HIS CHEST...

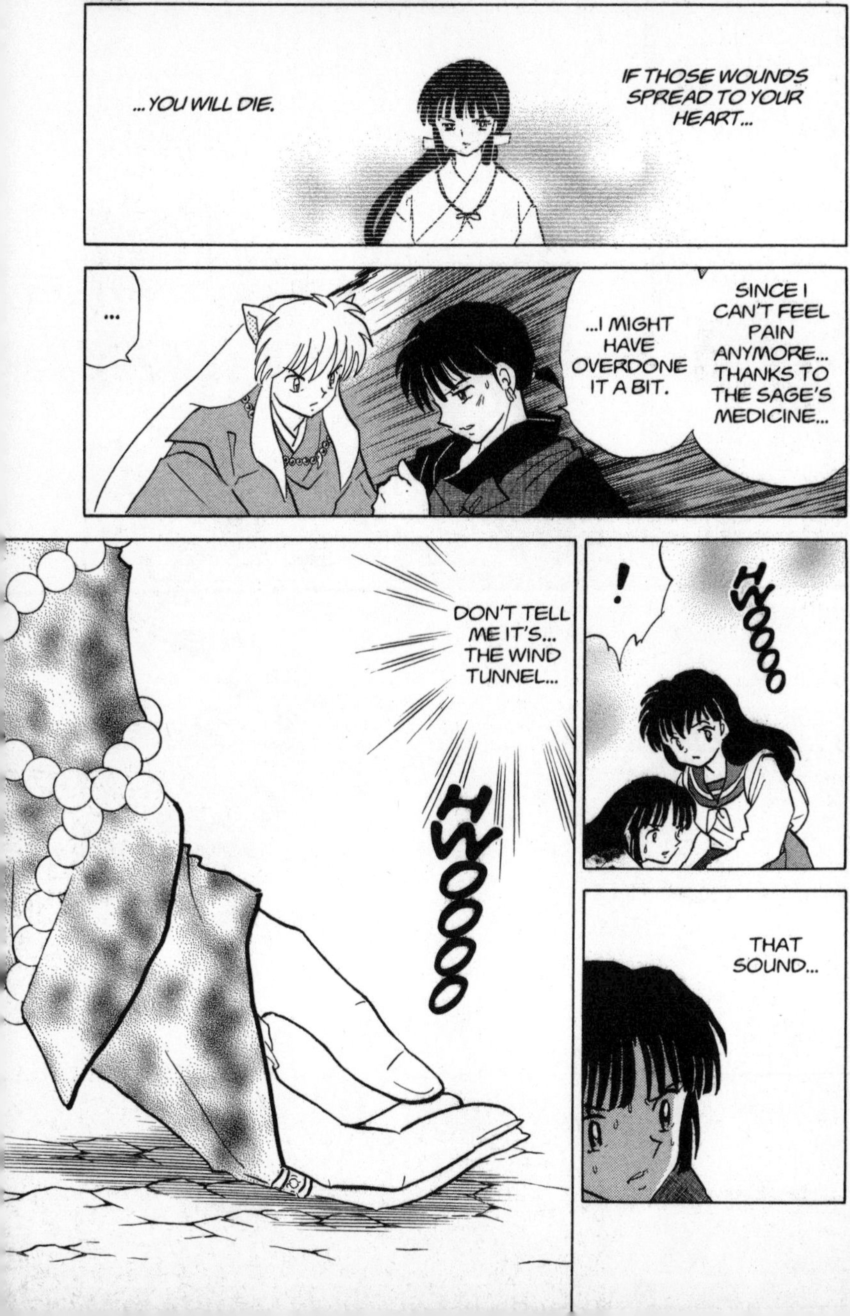
IF THOSE WOUNDS SPREAD TO YOUR HEART...
...YOU WILL DIE.
SINCE I CAN'T FEEL PAIN ANYMORE... THANKS TO THE SAGE'S MEDICINE...
...I MIGHT HAVE OVERDONE IT A BIT.
...
!
HWOOOO
THAT SOUND...
DON'T TELL ME IT'S... THE WIND TUNNEL...
HWOOOOO

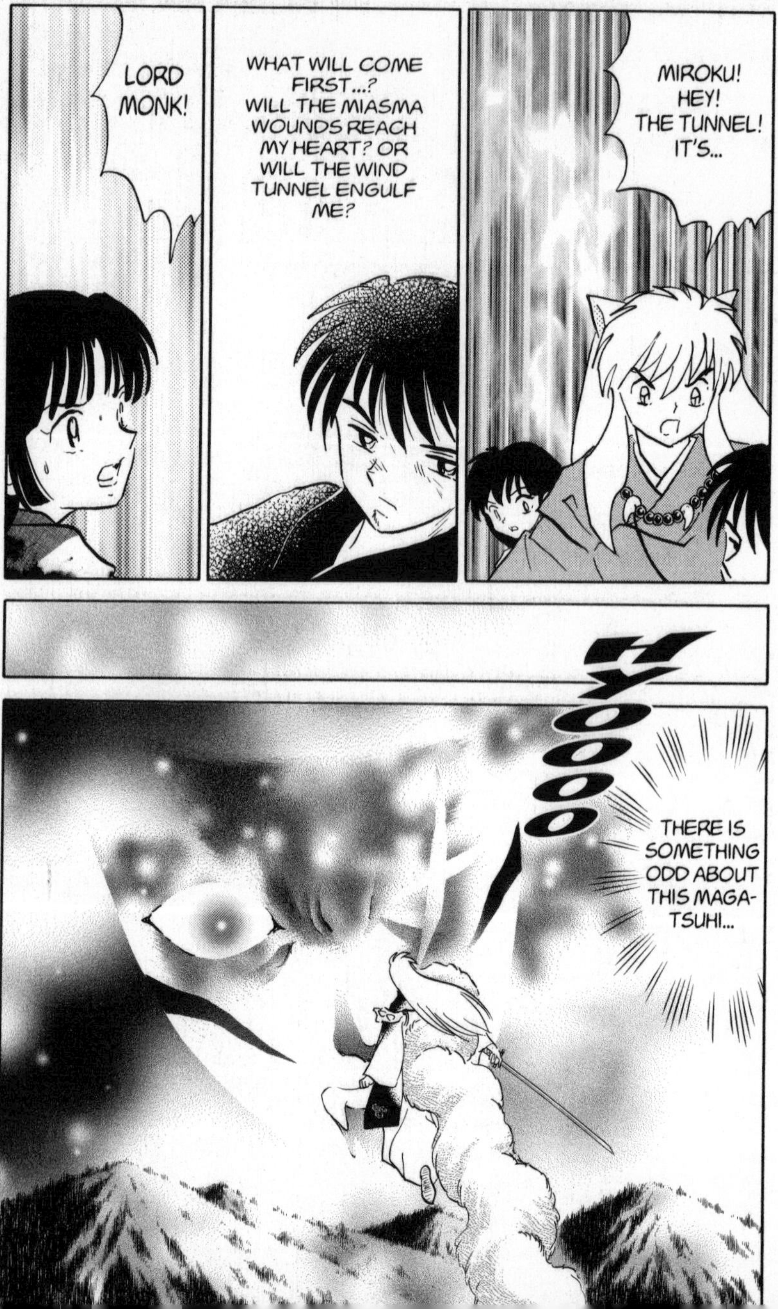
MIROKU! HEY! THE TUNNEL! IT'S...
WHAT WILL COME FIRST...? WILL THE MIASMA WOUNDS REACH MY HEART? OR WILL THE WIND TUNNEL ENGULF ME?
LORD MONK!
HYOOOOO
THERE IS SOMETHING ODD ABOUT THIS MAGA-TSUHI...

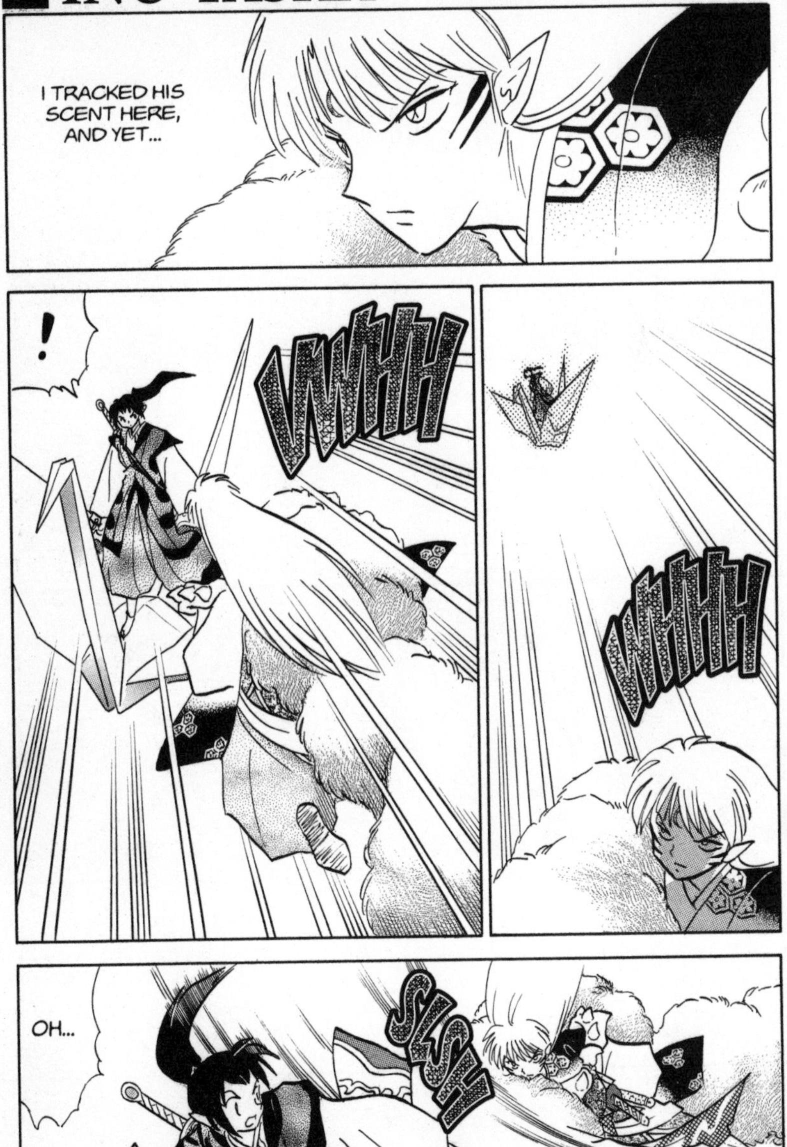
I TRACKED HIS SCENT HERE, AND YET...
WHHHH
!
WHHH
SWSH
OH...

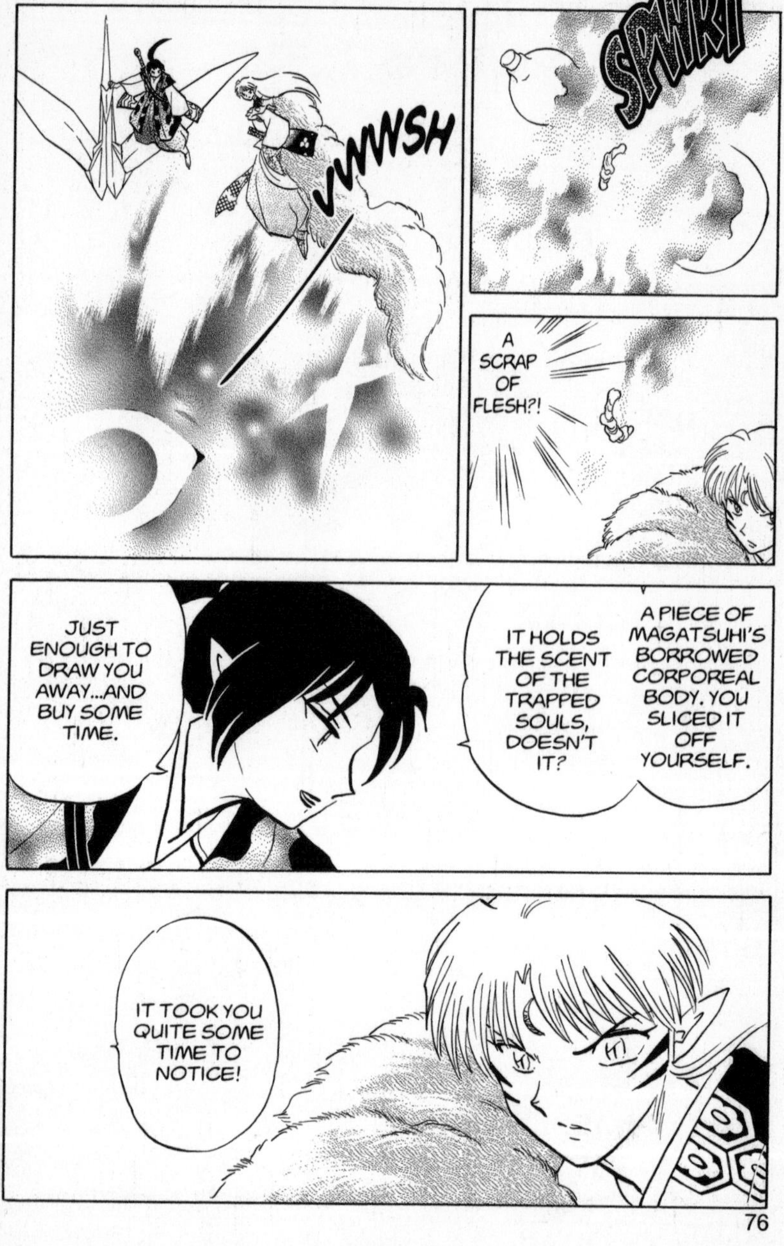
SPWRT
A SCRAP OF FLESH?!
VWWSH
A PIECE OF MAGATSUHI'S BORROWED CORPOREAL BODY. YOU SLICED IT OFF YOURSELF.
IT HOLDS THE SCENT OF THE TRAPPED SOULS, DOESN'T IT?
JUST ENOUGH TO DRAW YOU AWAY...AND BUY SOME TIME.
IT TOOK YOU QUITE SOME TIME TO NOTICE!

SCROLL 5

SANGO'S WISH

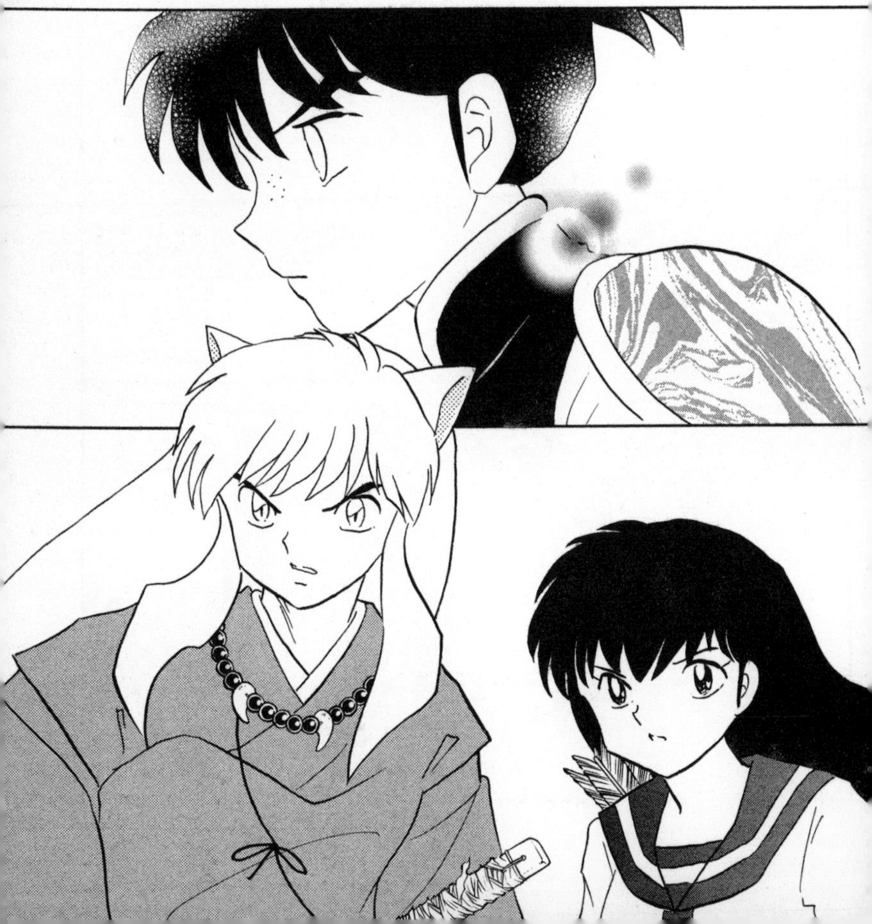

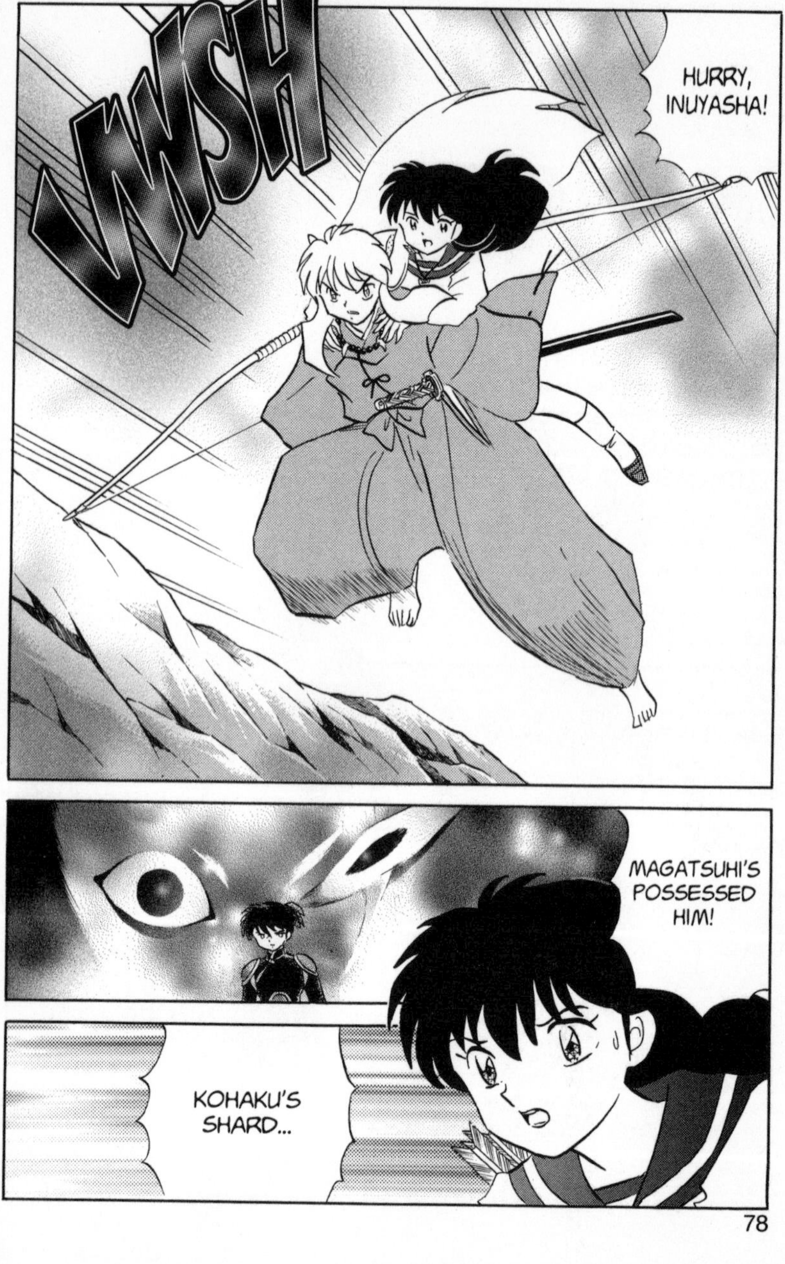
WHSH
HURRY, INUYASHA!
MAGATSUHI'S POSSESSED HIM!
KOHAKU'S SHARD...

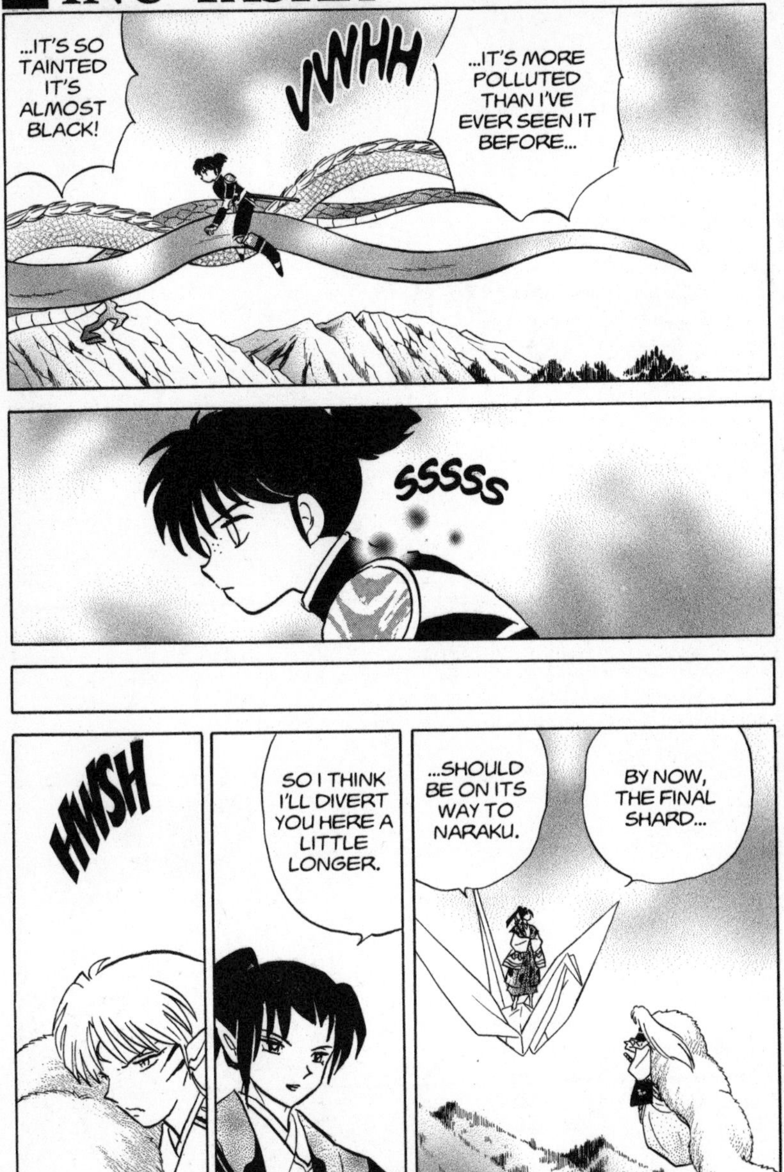
...IT'S MORE POLLUTED THAN I'VE EVER SEEN IT BEFORE...
VWHH
...IT'S SO TAINTED IT'S ALMOST BLACK!
SSSSS
BY NOW, THE FINAL SHARD...
...SHOULD BE ON ITS WAY TO NARAKU.
SO I THINK I'LL DIVERT YOU HERE A LITTLE LONGER.
HWSH

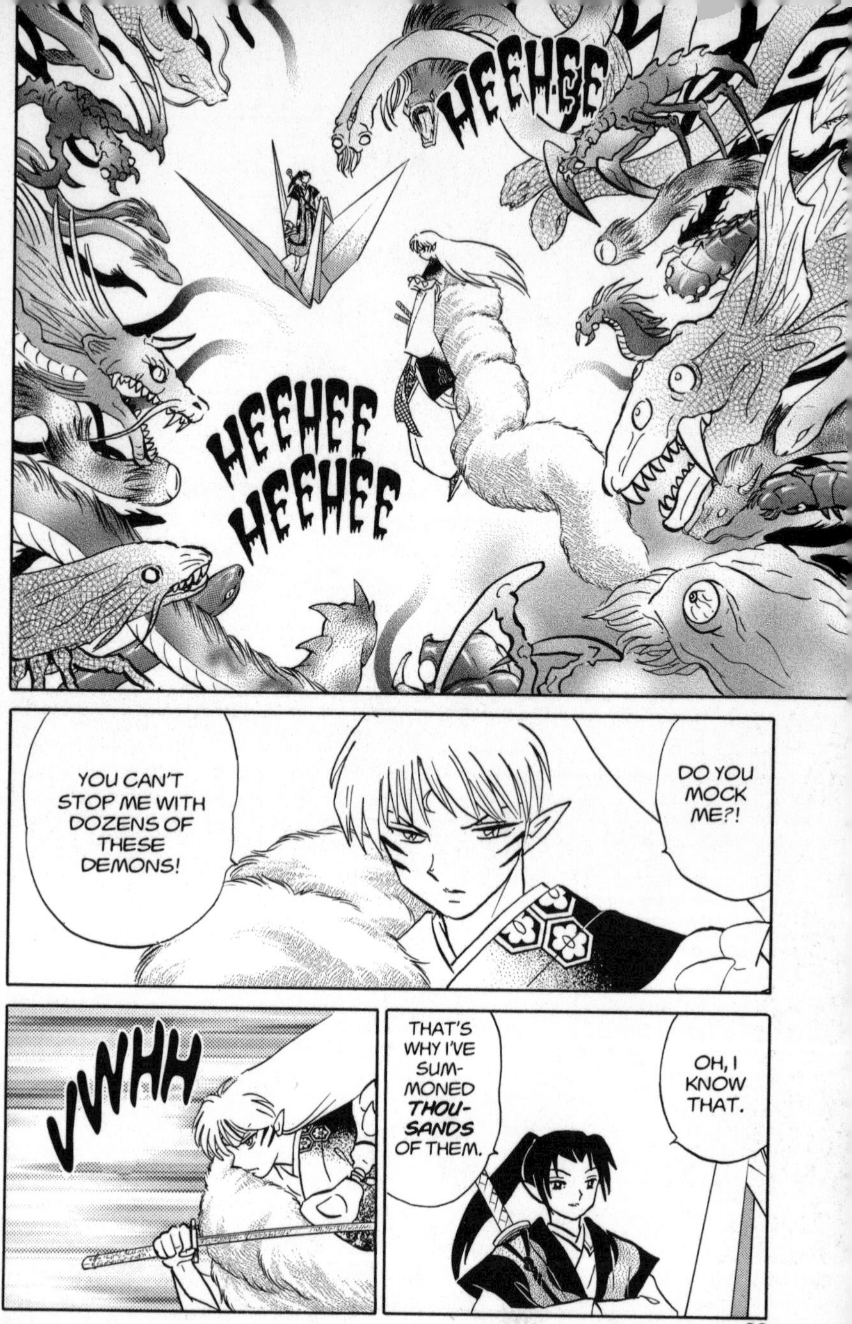
HEEHEE
HEEHEE HEEHEE
DO YOU MOCK ME?!
YOU CAN'T STOP ME WITH DOZENS OF THESE DEMONS!
OH, I KNOW THAT.
THAT'S WHY I'VE SUM-MONED ***THOU-SANDS*** OF THEM.
VWHH

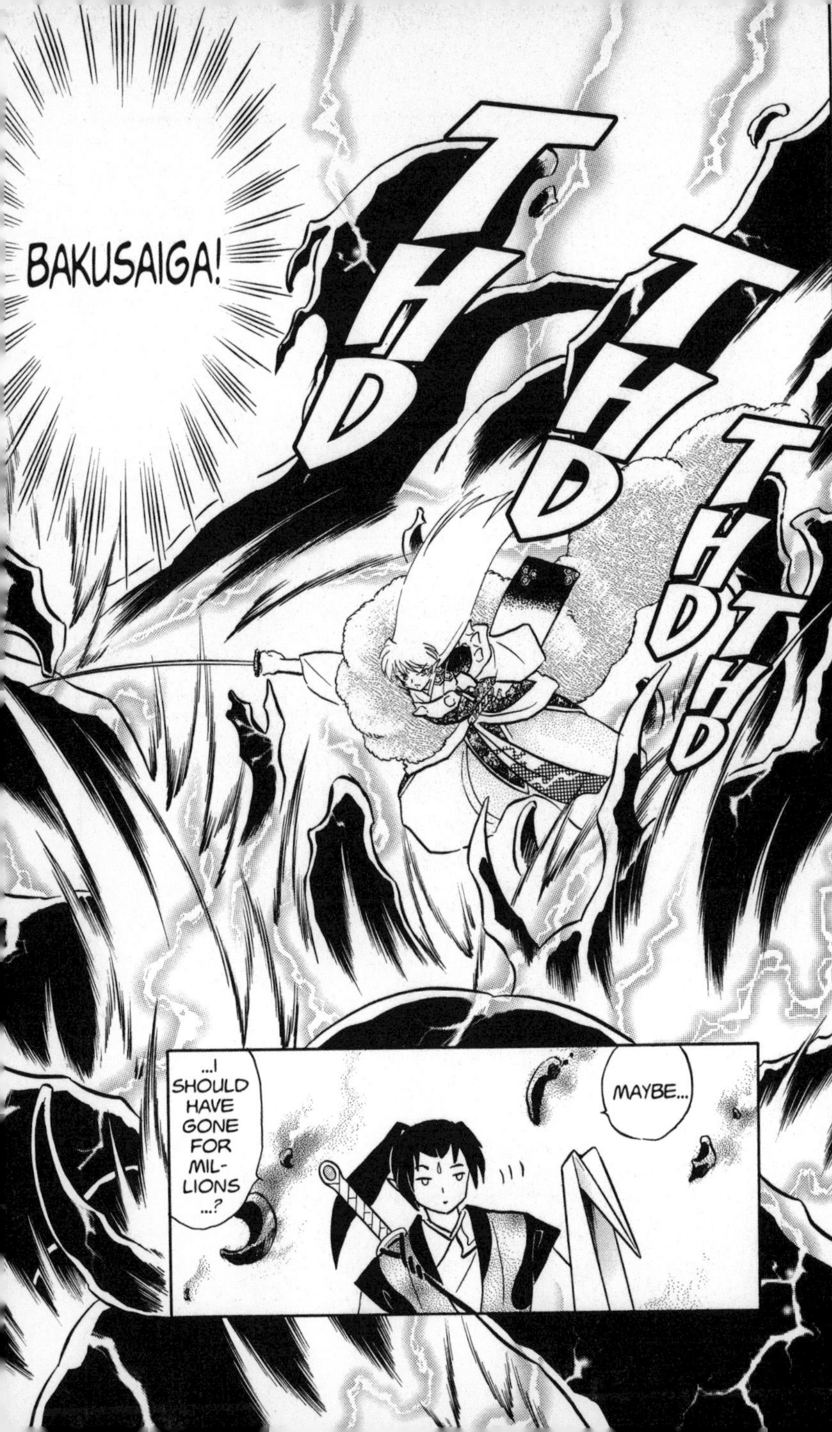
THD
THD
BAKUSAIGA!
THD
THD
MAYBE...
...I SHOULD HAVE GONE FOR MIL-LIONS ...?

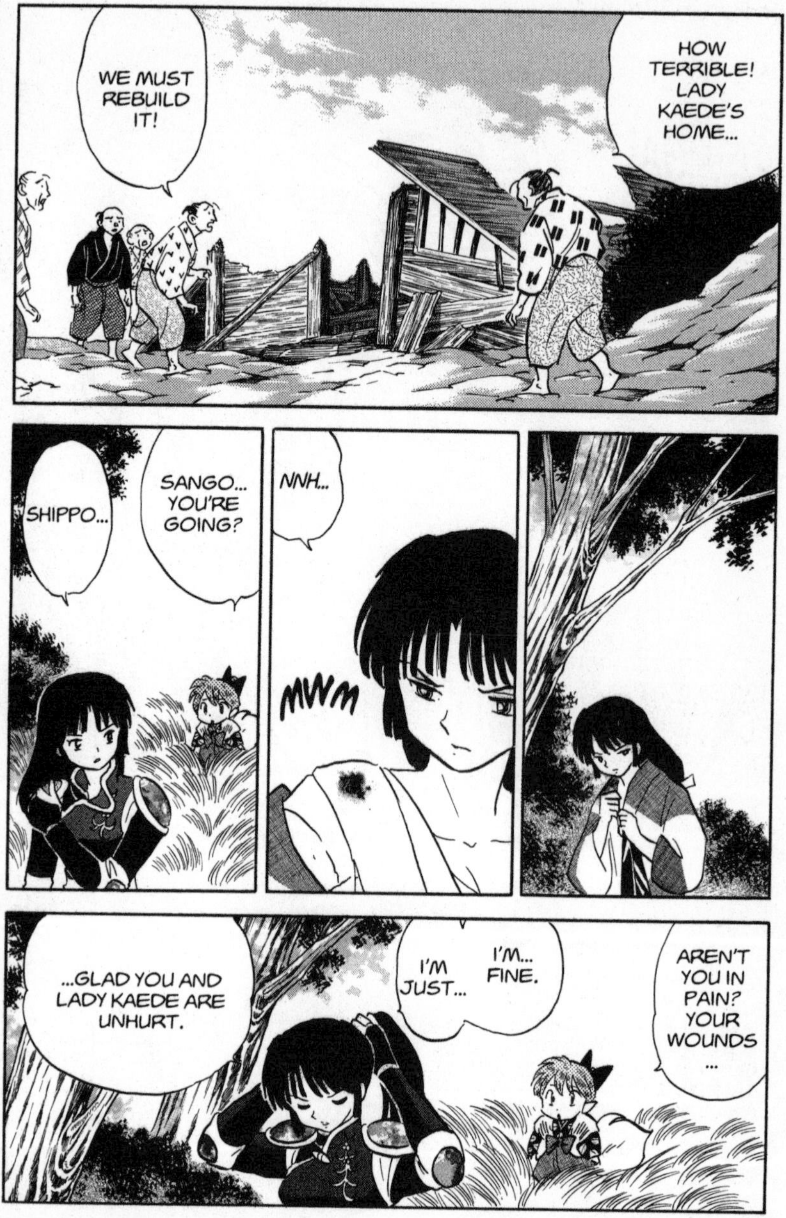
HOW TERRIBLE! LADY KAEDE'S HOME...
WE MUST REBUILD IT!
NNH...
MWM
SANGO... YOU'RE GOING?
SHIPPO...
AREN'T YOU IN PAIN? YOUR WOUNDS ...
I'M... FINE.
I'M JUST...
...GLAD YOU AND LADY KAEDE ARE UNHURT.

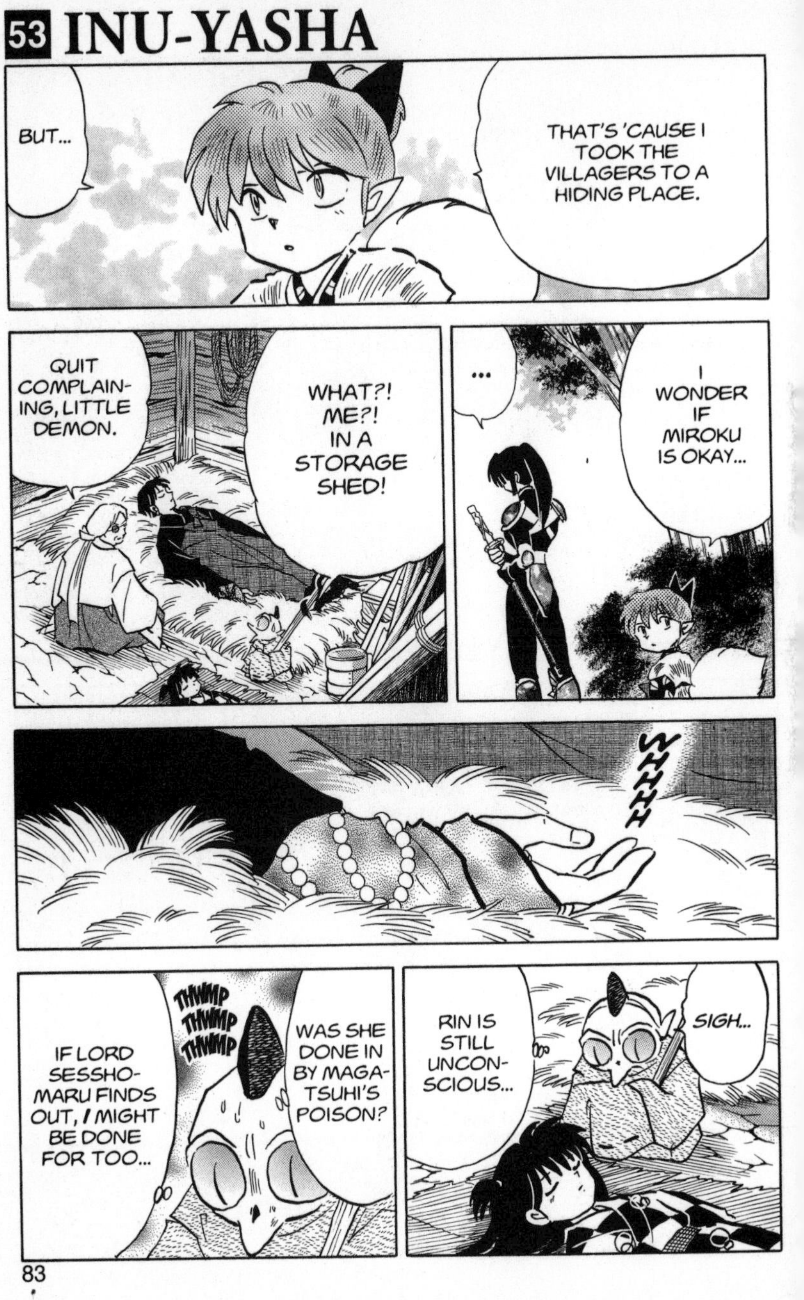
THAT'S 'CAUSE I TOOK THE VILLAGERS TO A HIDING PLACE.
BUT...
I WONDER IF MIROKU IS OKAY...
...
WHAT?! ME?! IN A STORAGE SHED!
QUIT COMPLAINING, LITTLE DEMON.
SIGH...
RIN IS STILL UNCONSCIOUS...
WAS SHE DONE IN BY MAGATSUHI'S POISON?
THWMP THWMP THWMP
IF LORD SESSHOMARU FINDS OUT, I MIGHT BE DONE FOR TOO...

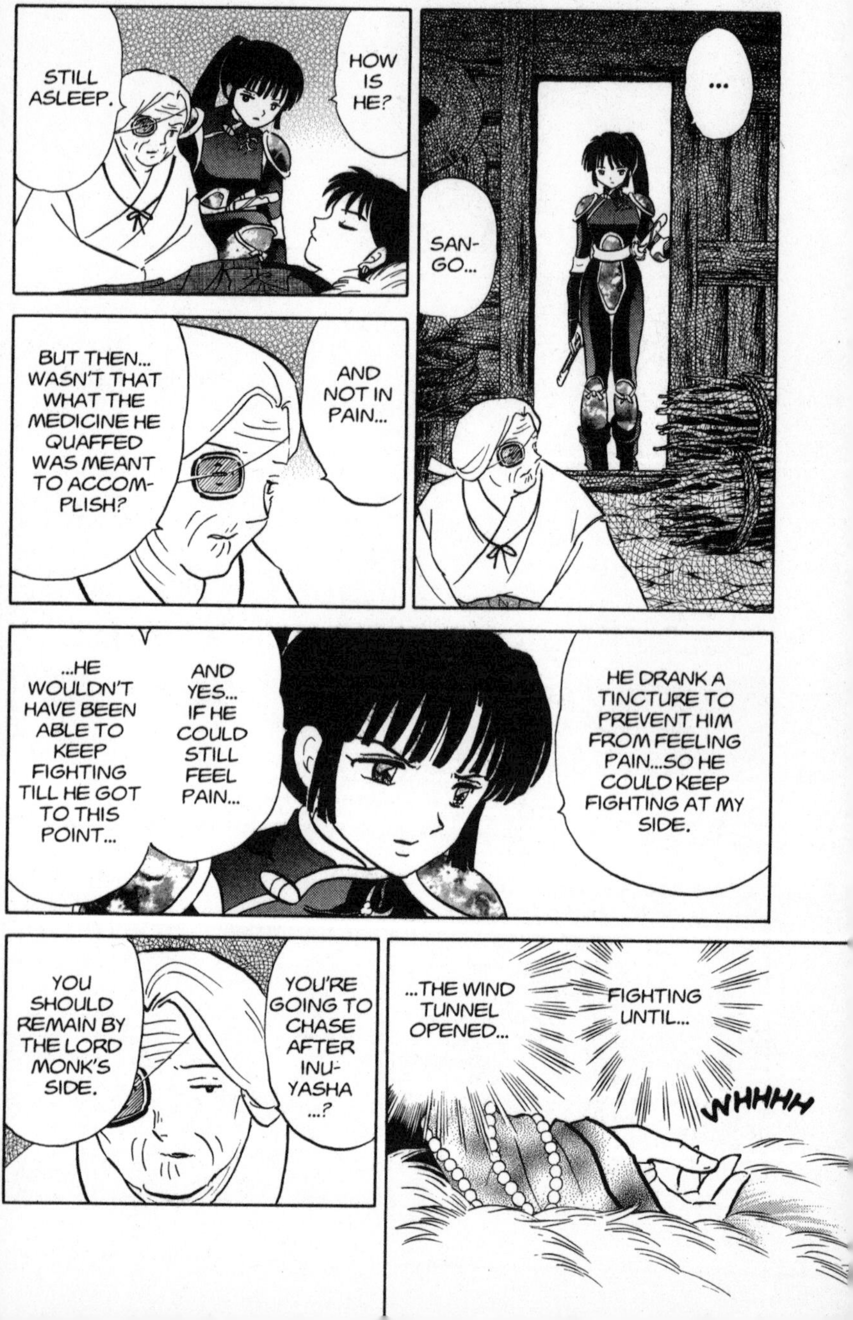
...
SANGO...
HOW IS HE?
STILL ASLEEP.
AND NOT IN PAIN...
BUT THEN... WASN'T THAT WHAT THE MEDICINE HE QUAFFED WAS MEANT TO ACCOMPLISH?
HE DRANK A TINCTURE TO PREVENT HIM FROM FEELING PAIN...SO HE COULD KEEP FIGHTING AT MY SIDE.
AND YES... IF HE COULD STILL FEEL PAIN...
...HE WOULDN'T HAVE BEEN ABLE TO KEEP FIGHTING TILL HE GOT TO THIS POINT...
FIGHTING UNTIL...
...THE WIND TUNNEL OPENED...
WHHHH
YOU'RE GOING TO CHASE AFTER INUYASHA ...?
YOU SHOULD REMAIN BY THE LORD MONK'S SIDE.

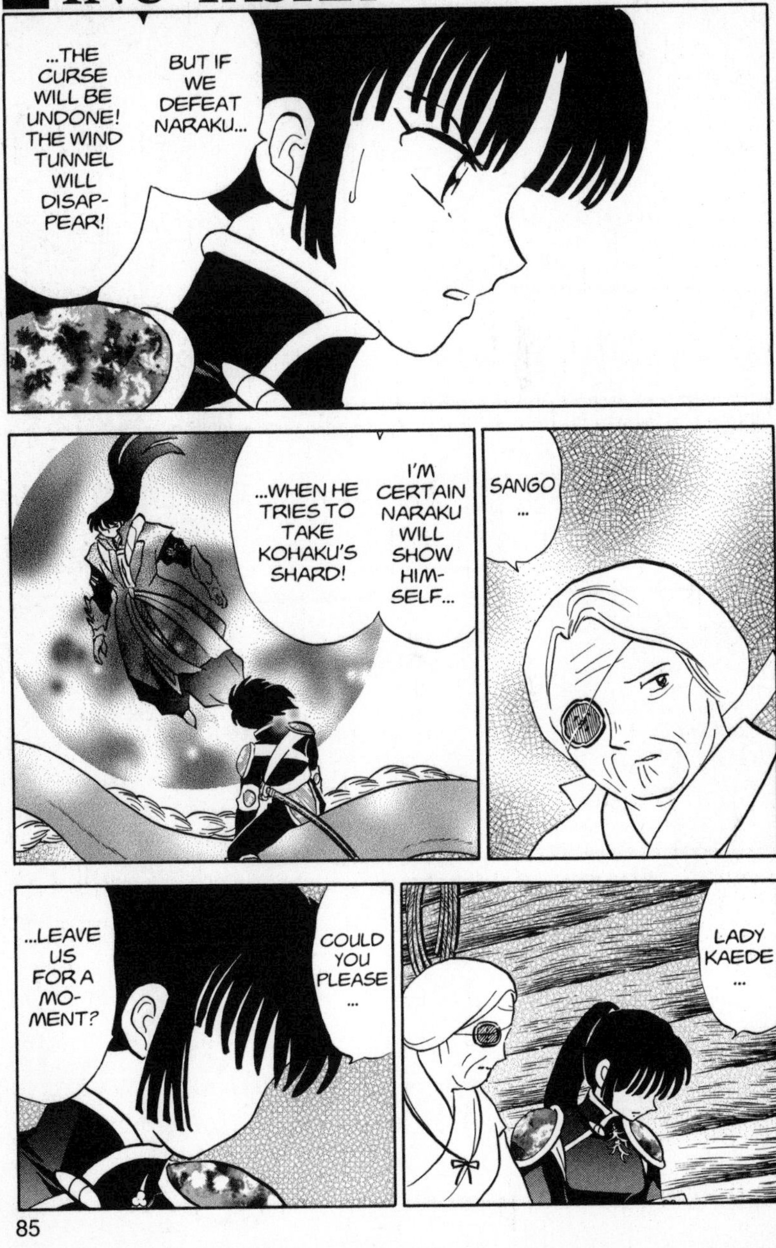
BUT IF WE DEFEAT NARAKU...
...THE CURSE WILL BE UNDONE! THE WIND TUNNEL WILL DISAP-PEAR!
SANGO ...
I'M CERTAIN NARAKU WILL SHOW HIM-SELF...
...WHEN HE TRIES TO TAKE KOHAKU'S SHARD!
LADY KAEDE ...
COULD YOU PLEASE ...
...LEAVE US FOR A MO-MENT?

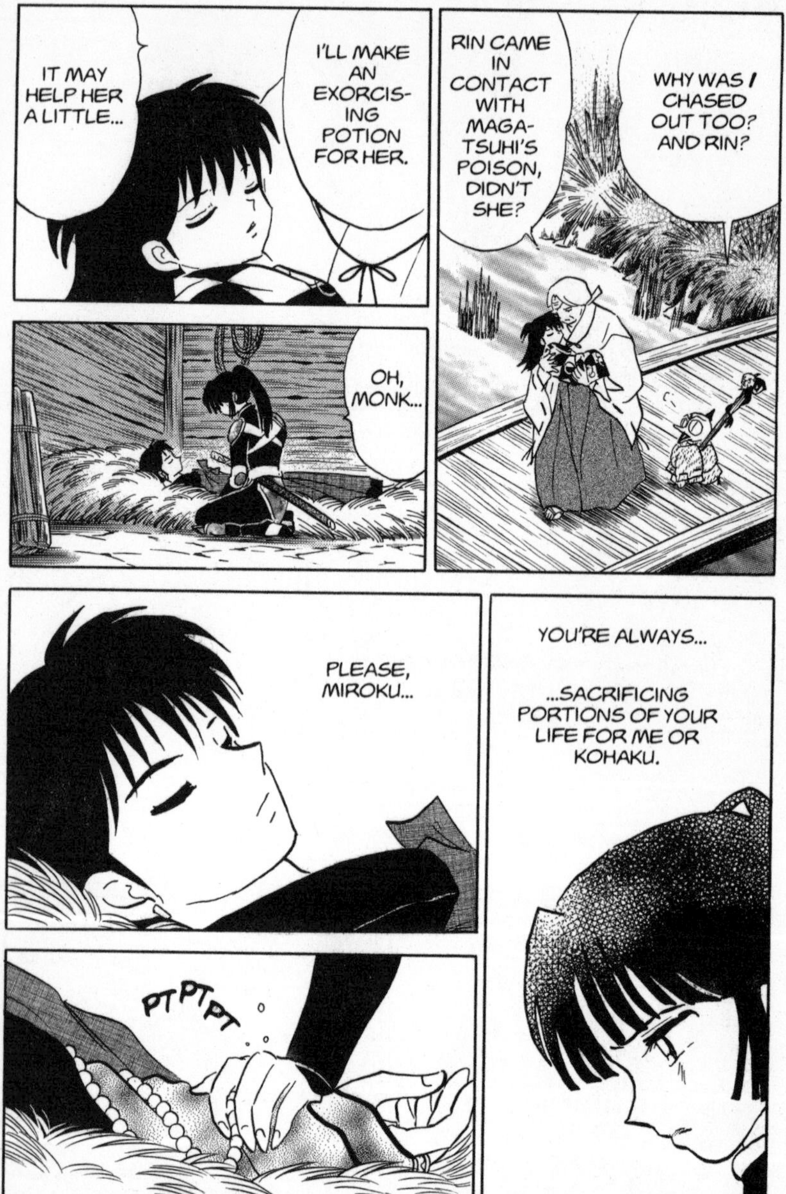
WHY WAS I CHASED OUT TOO? AND RIN?
RIN CAME IN CONTACT WITH MAGA-TSUHI'S POISON, DIDN'T SHE?
I'LL MAKE AN EXORCIS-ING POTION FOR HER.
IT MAY HELP HER A LITTLE...
OH, MONK...
YOU'RE ALWAYS...
...SACRIFICING PORTIONS OF YOUR LIFE FOR ME OR KOHAKU.
PLEASE, MIROKU...
PTPTPT

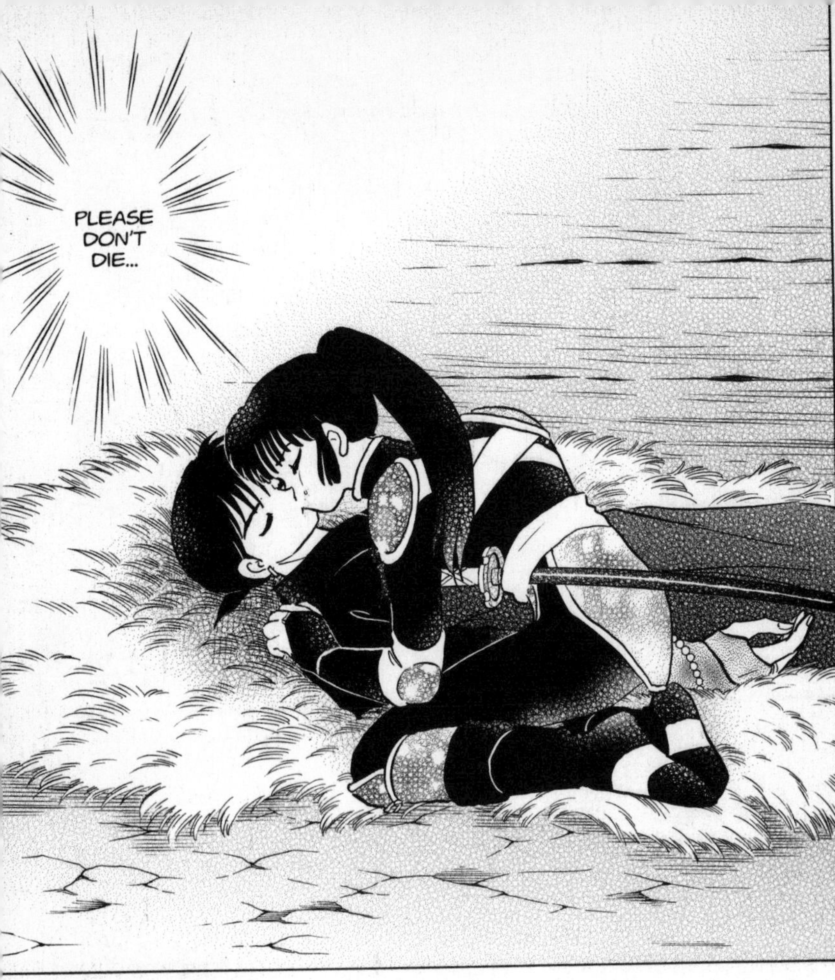
PLEASE DON'T DIE...

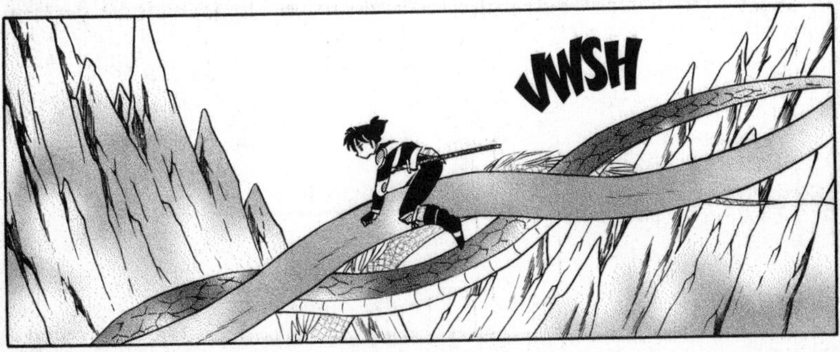
VWSH

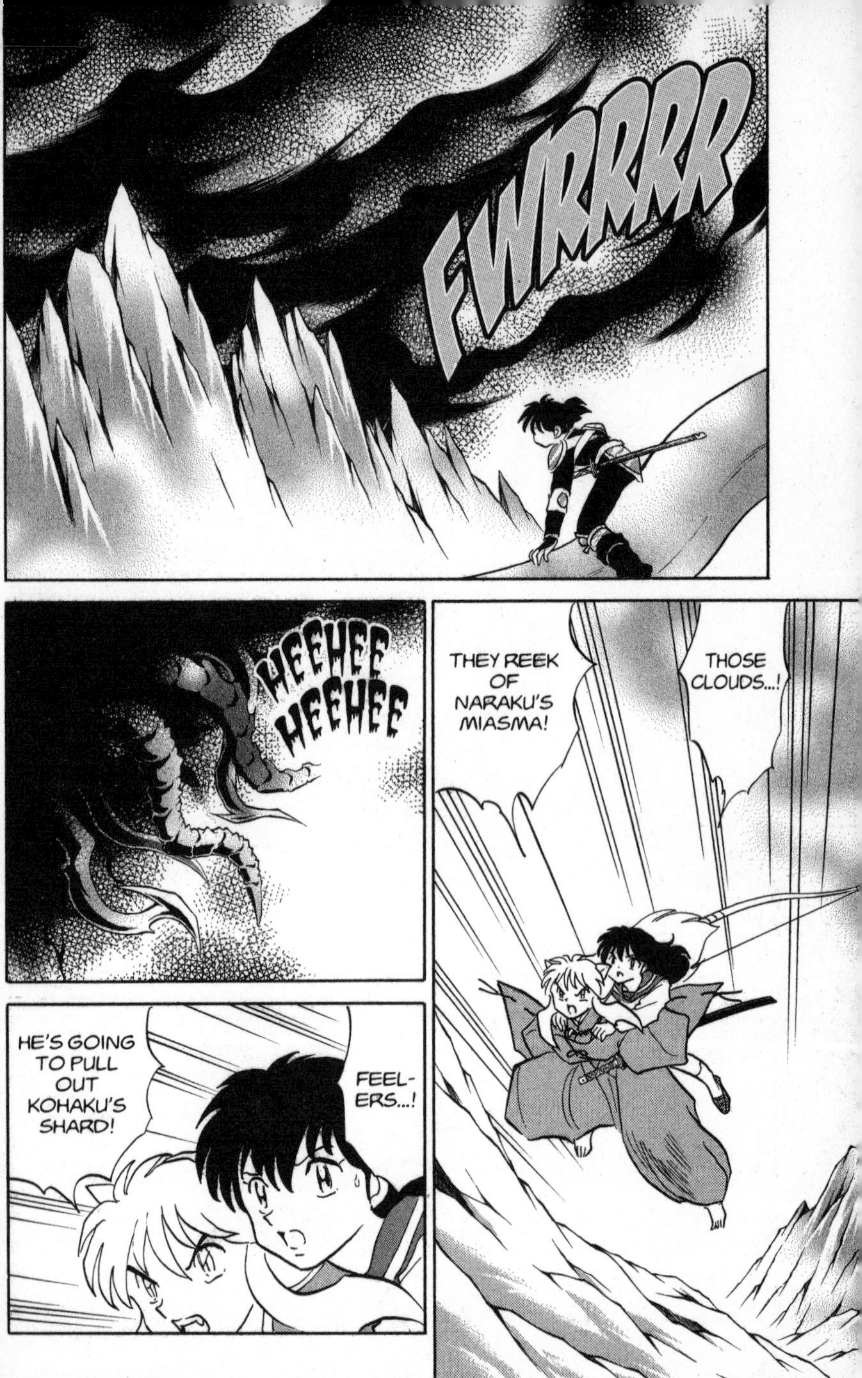
FWRRRR
THOSE CLOUDS...!
THEY REEK OF NARAKU'S MIASMA!
HEEHEE HEEHEE
FEEL-ERS...!
HE'S GOING TO PULL OUT KOHAKU'S SHARD!

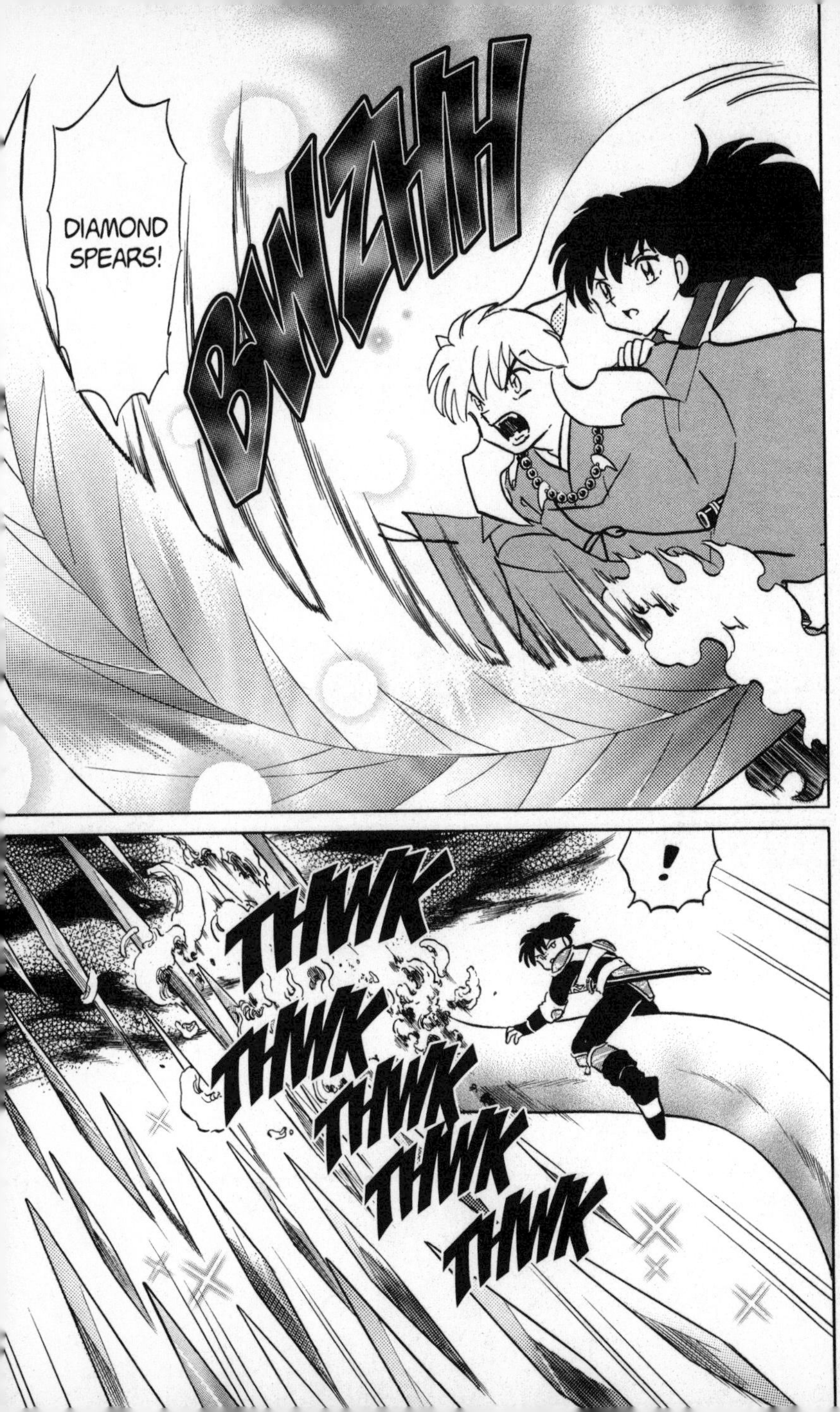
DIAMOND SPEARS!
BWZHH
!
THWK THWK THWK THWK THWK

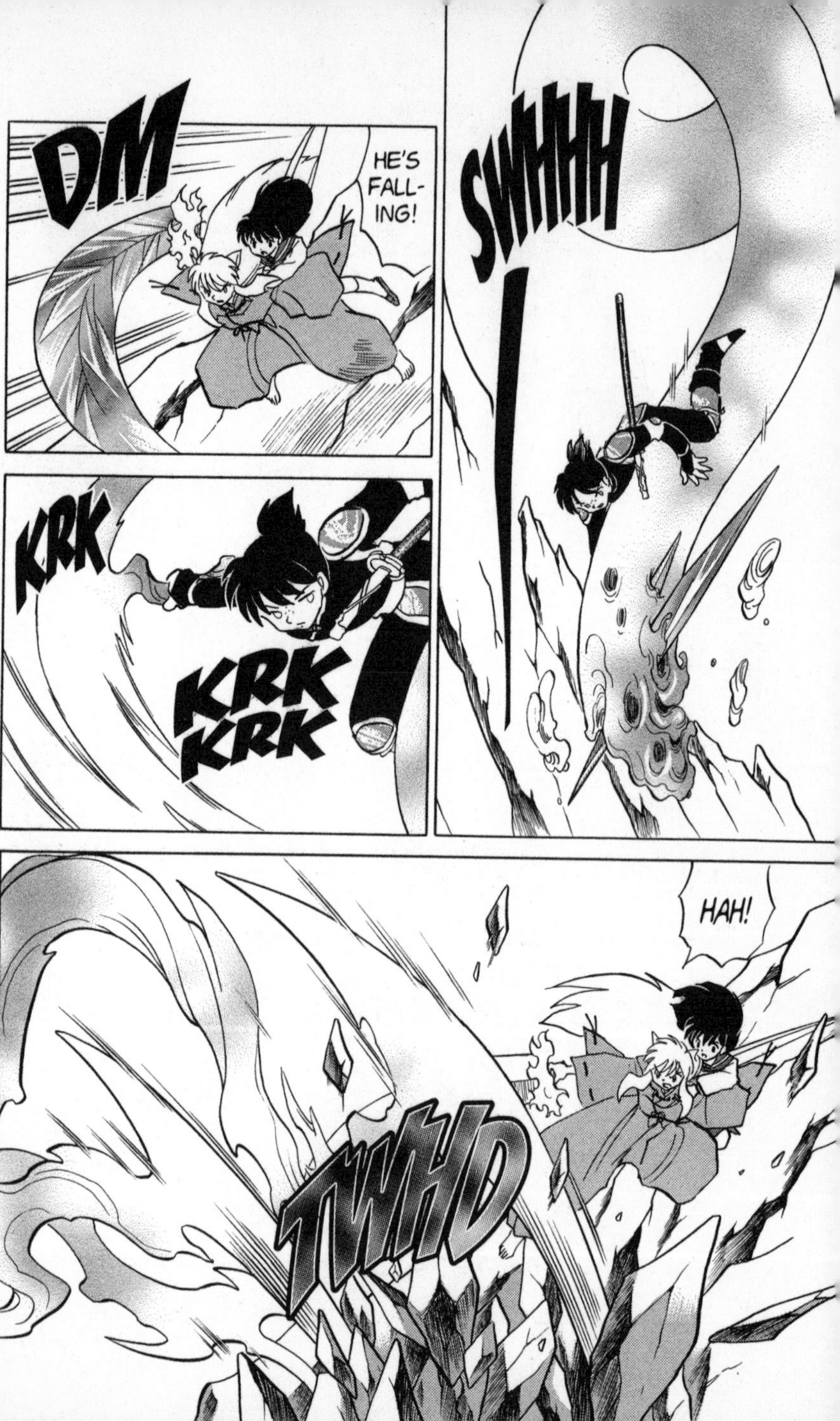
SWHHHH
DM
HE'S FALLING!
KRK
KRK KRK
HAH!
THWD

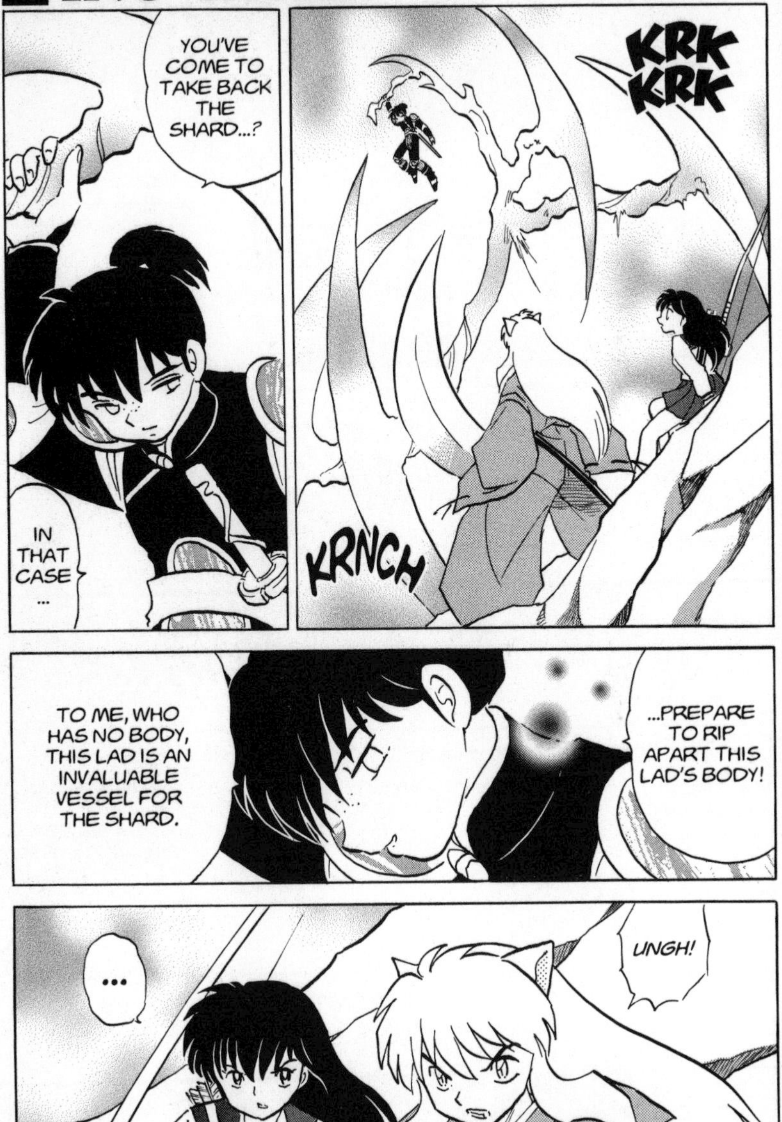
KRK KRK
KRNCH
YOU'VE COME TO TAKE BACK THE SHARD...?
IN THAT CASE...
...PREPARE TO RIP APART THIS LAD'S BODY!
TO ME, WHO HAS NO BODY, THIS LAD IS AN INVALUABLE VESSEL FOR THE SHARD.
UNGH!
...

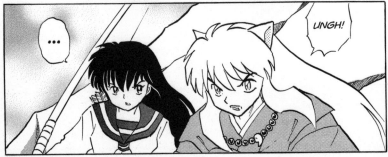

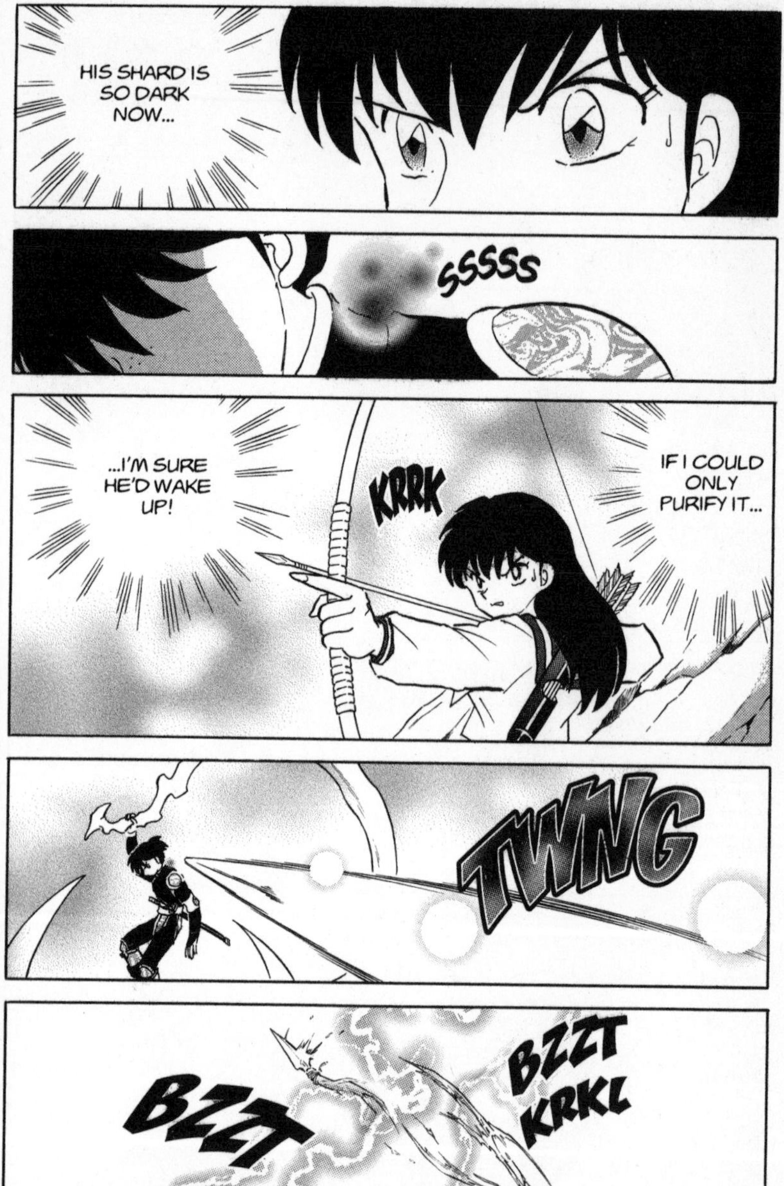
HIS SHARD IS SO DARK NOW...
SSSSS
IF I COULD ONLY PURIFY IT...
KRRK
...I'M SURE HE'D WAKE UP!
TWNG
BZZT
KRKL
BZZT

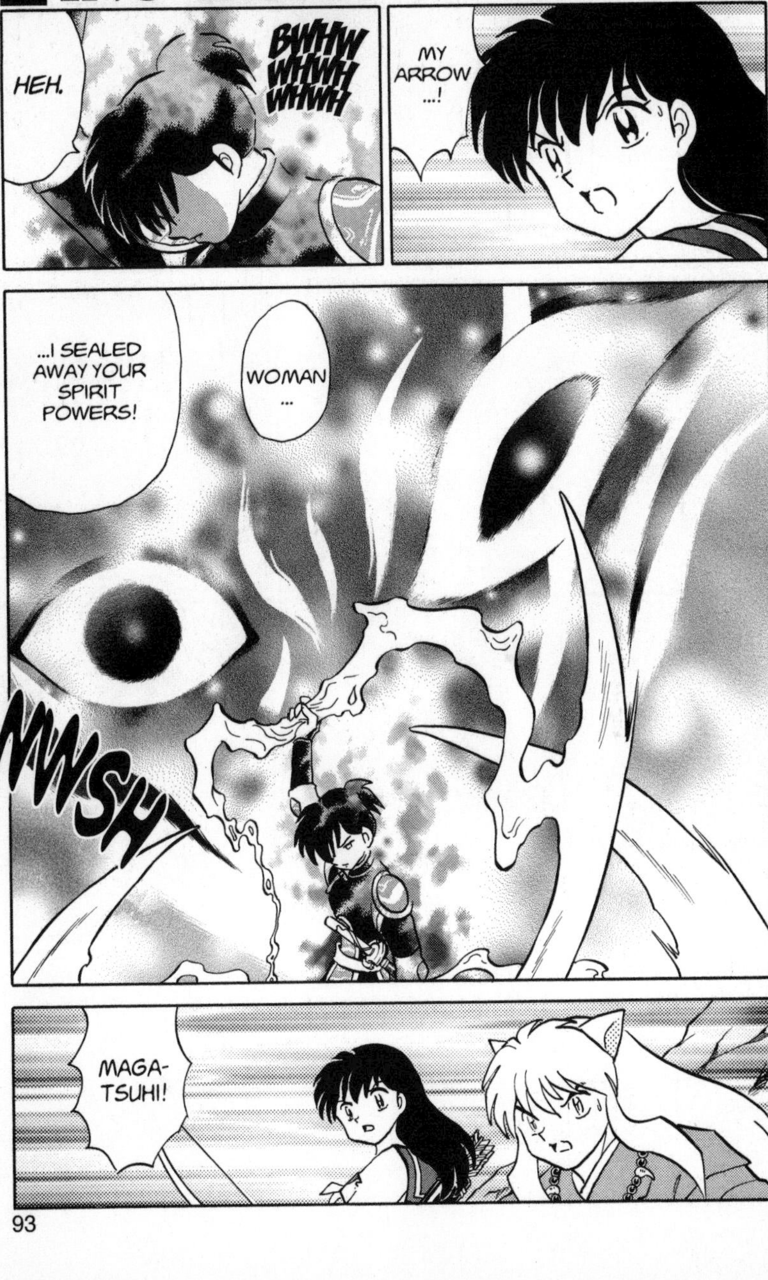
MY ARROW ...!
HEH.
BWHW WHWH WHWH
WOMAN ...
...I SEALED AWAY YOUR SPIRIT POWERS!
FWWSH
MAGA-TSUHI!

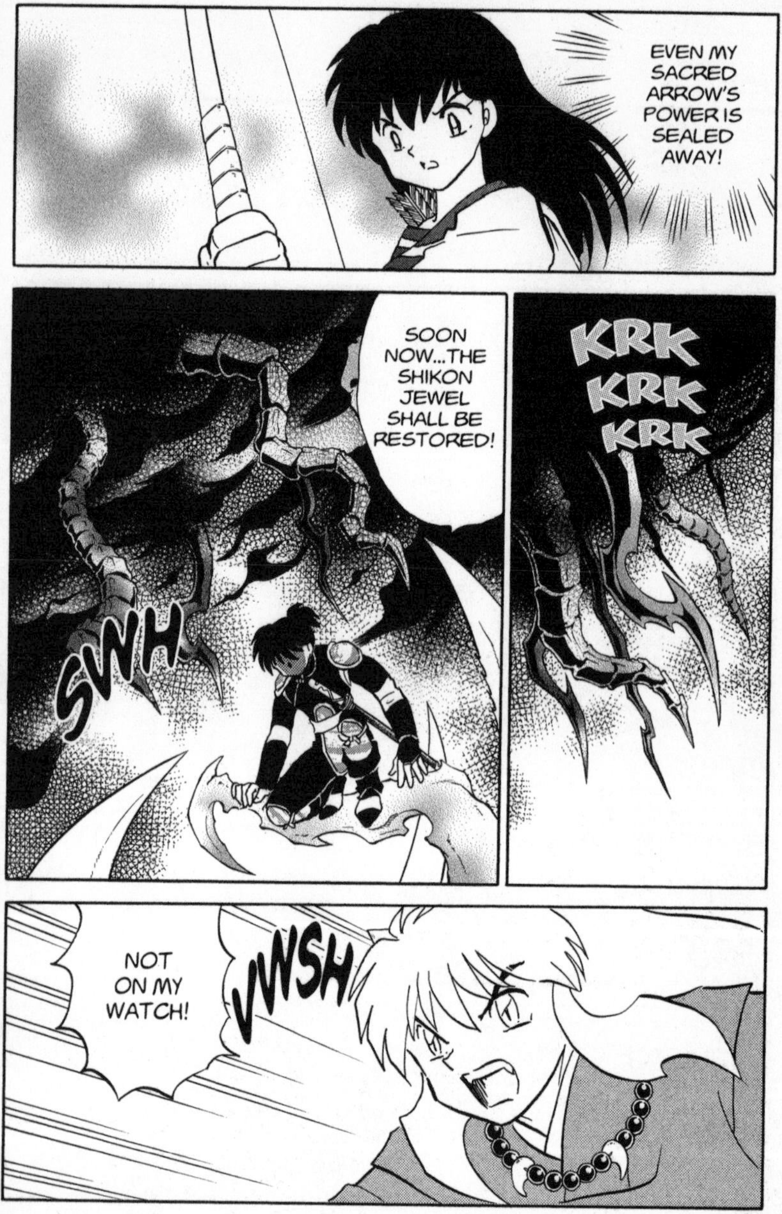
EVEN MY SACRED ARROW'S POWER IS SEALED AWAY!
KRK KRK KRK
SOON NOW...THE SHIKON JEWEL SHALL BE RESTORED!
SWH
VWSH
NOT ON MY WATCH!

SCROLL 6

AWAKENING

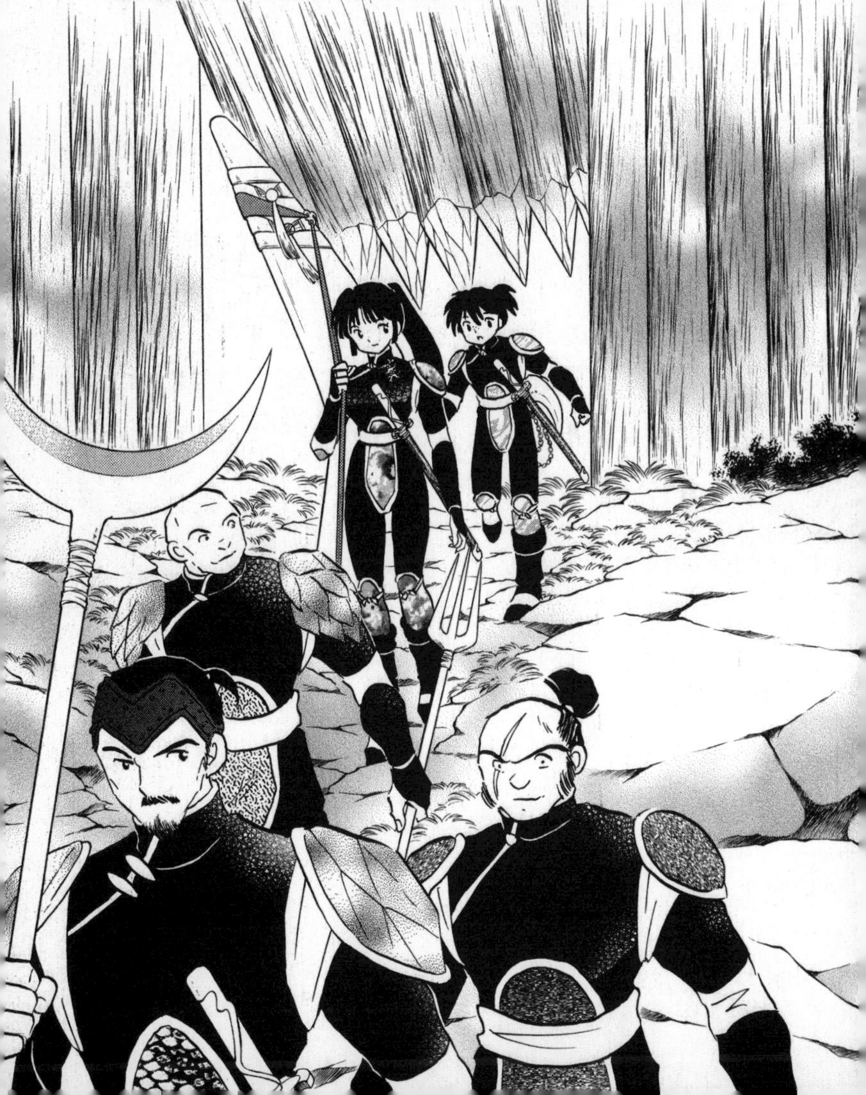

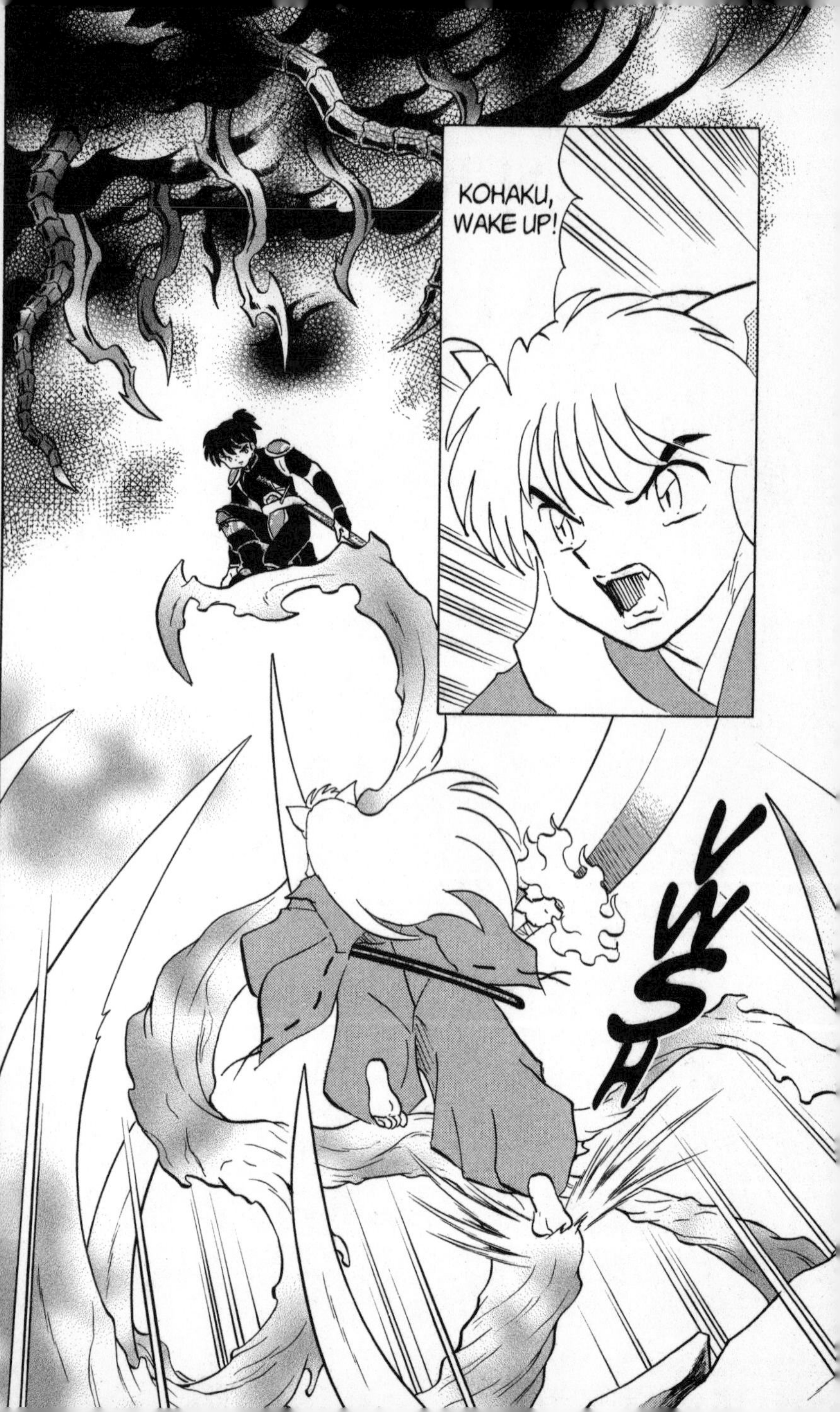
KOHAKU, WAKE UP!
VWSSH

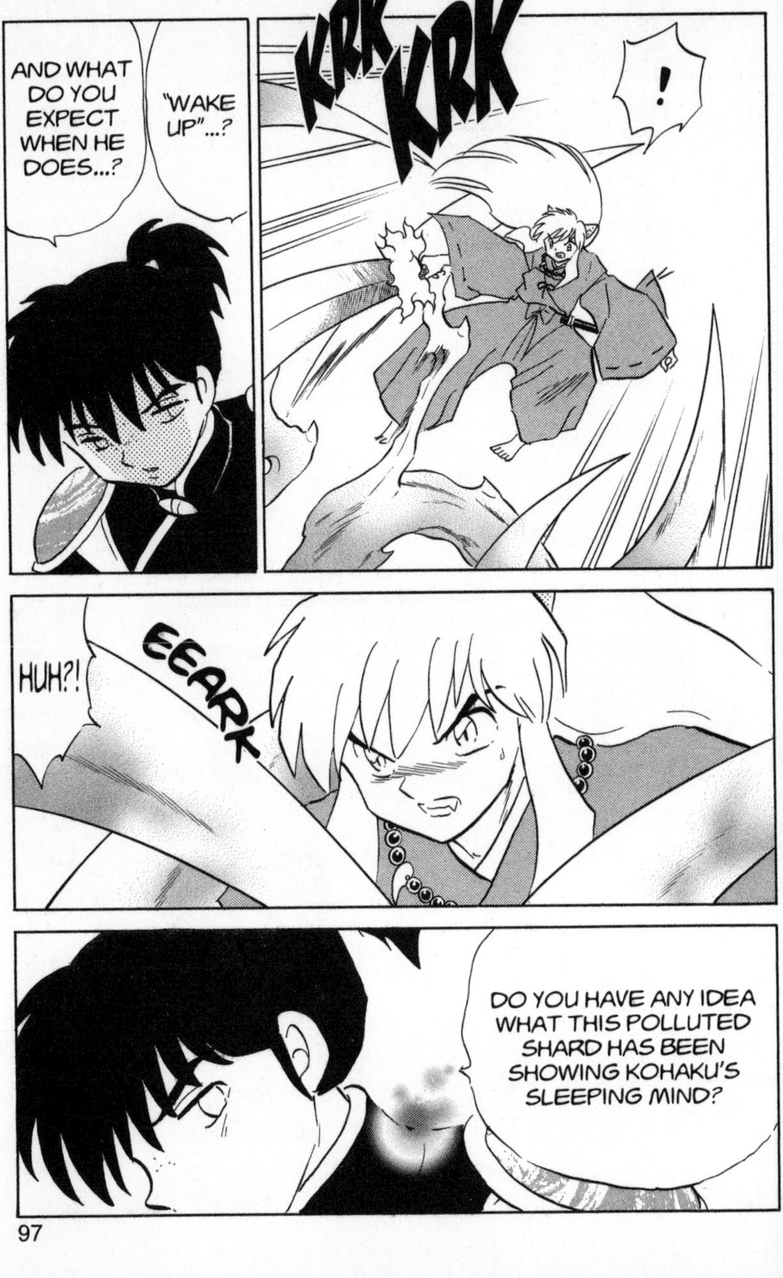
KRK KRK
!
"WAKE UP"...?
AND WHAT DO YOU EXPECT WHEN HE DOES...?
EEARK
HUH?!
DO YOU HAVE ANY IDEA WHAT THIS POLLUTED SHARD HAS BEEN SHOWING KOHAKU'S SLEEPING MIND?

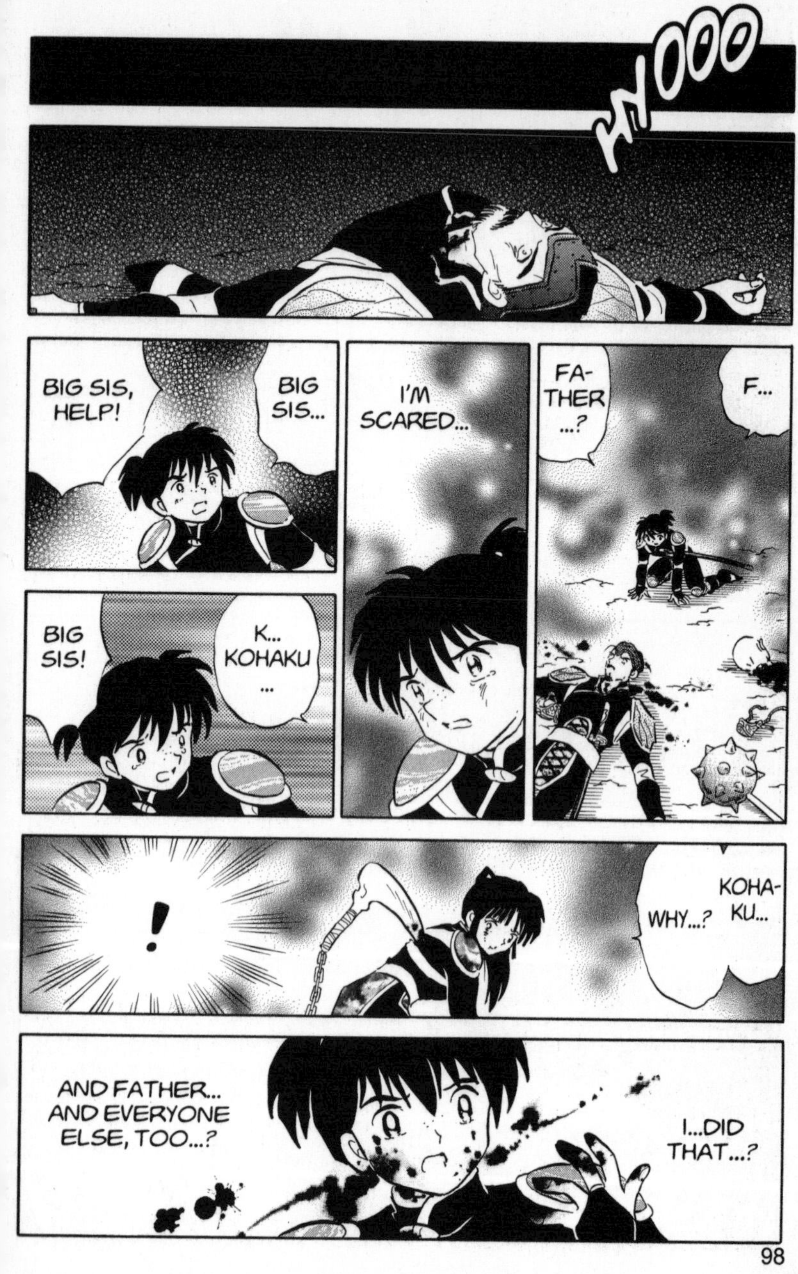
HYOOO
F...
FA-THER ...?
I'M SCARED...
BIG SIS...
BIG SIS, HELP!
K... KOHAKU ...
BIG SIS!
KOHA-KU...
WHY...?
!
I...DID THAT...?
AND FATHER... AND EVERYONE ELSE, TOO...?

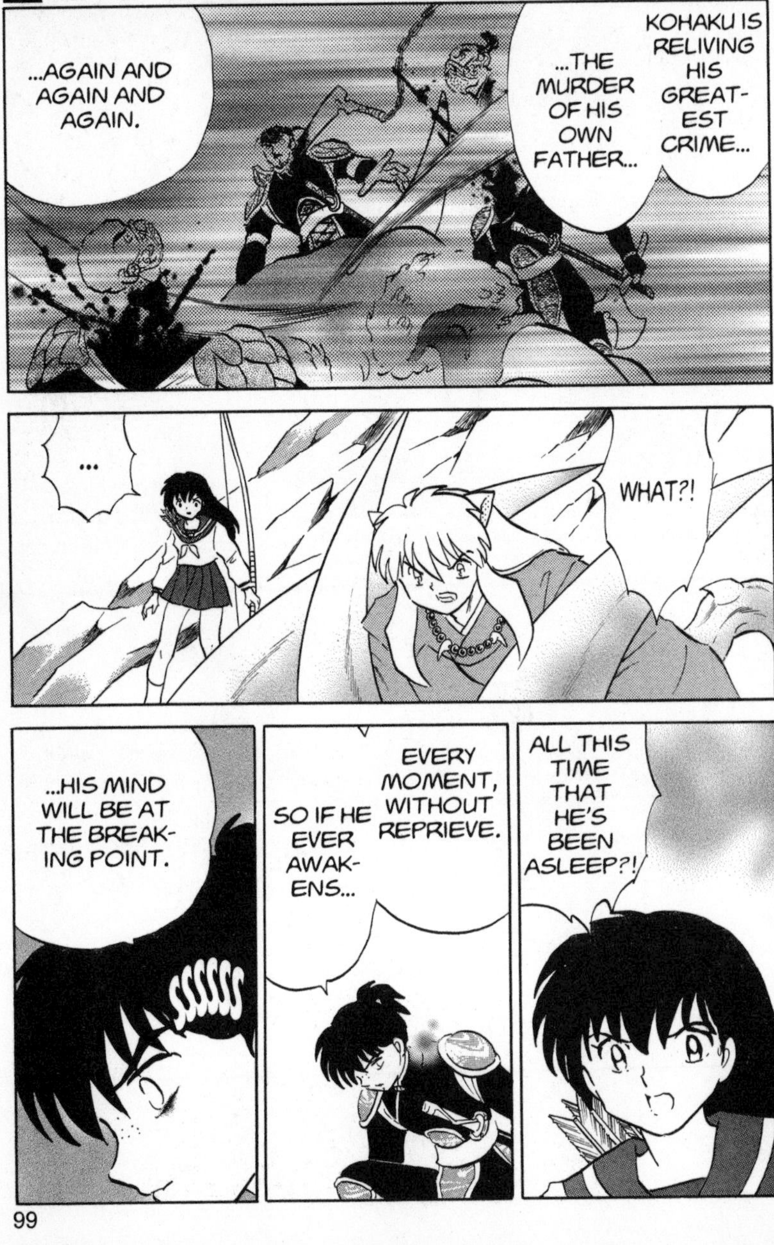
KOHAKU IS RELIVING HIS GREAT-EST CRIME...
...THE MURDER OF HIS OWN FATHER...
...AGAIN AND AGAIN AND AGAIN.
WHAT?!
...
ALL THIS TIME THAT HE'S BEEN ASLEEP?!
EVERY MOMENT, WITHOUT REPRIEVE.
SO IF HE EVER AWAK-ENS...
...HIS MIND WILL BE AT THE BREAK-ING POINT.

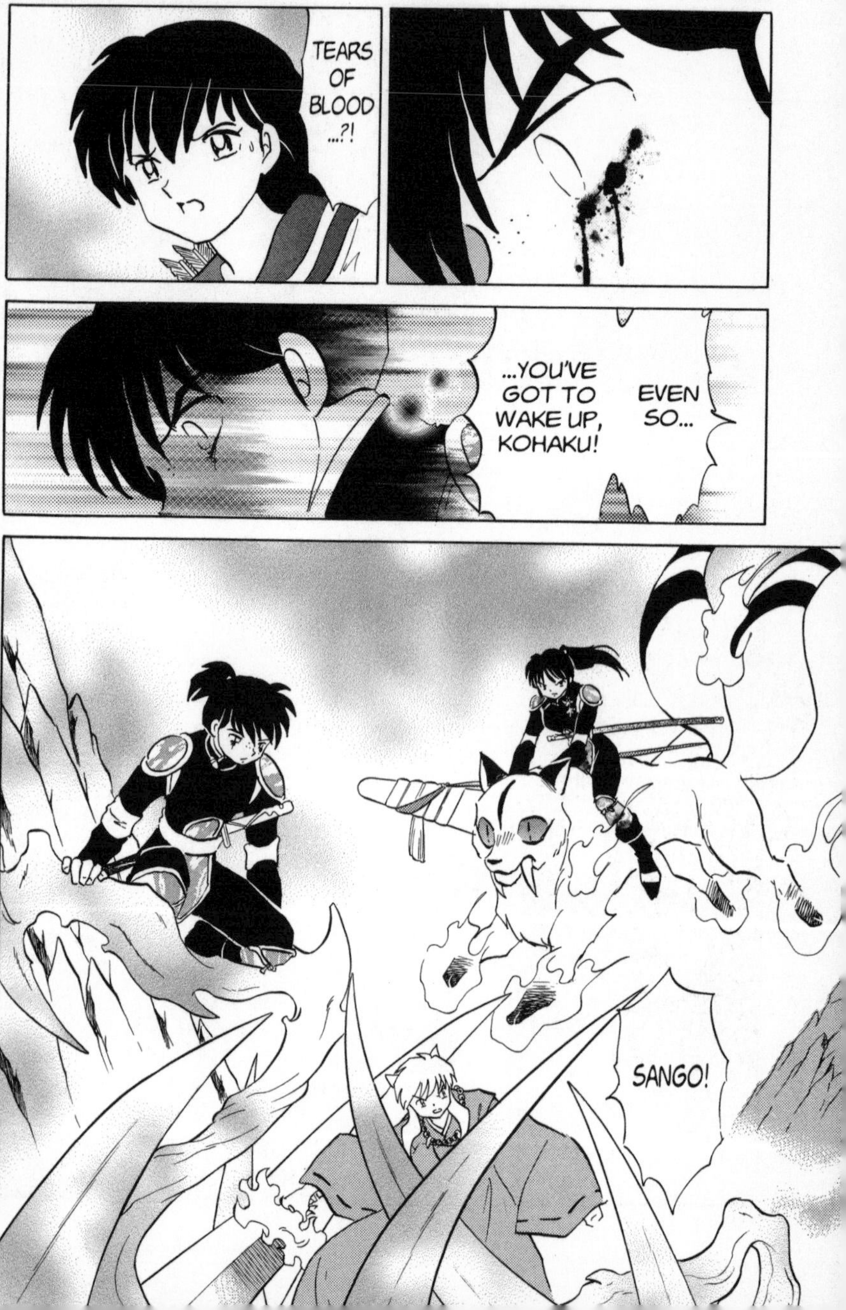
TEARS OF BLOOD ...?!
EVEN SO...
...YOU'VE GOT TO WAKE UP, KOHAKU!
SANGO!

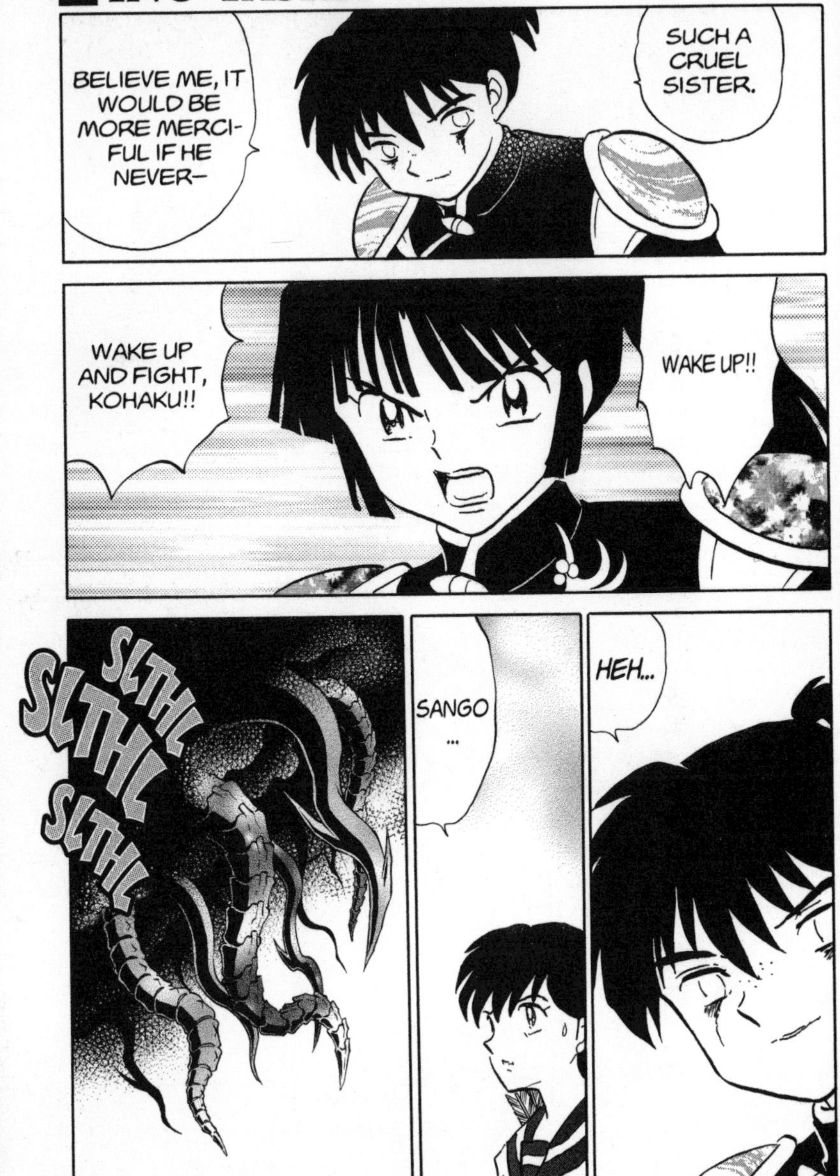
SUCH A CRUEL SISTER.
BELIEVE ME, IT WOULD BE MORE MERCI-FUL IF HE NEVER—
WAKE UP!!
WAKE UP AND FIGHT, KOHAKU!!
HEH...
SANGO ...
SLTHL SLTHL SLTHL

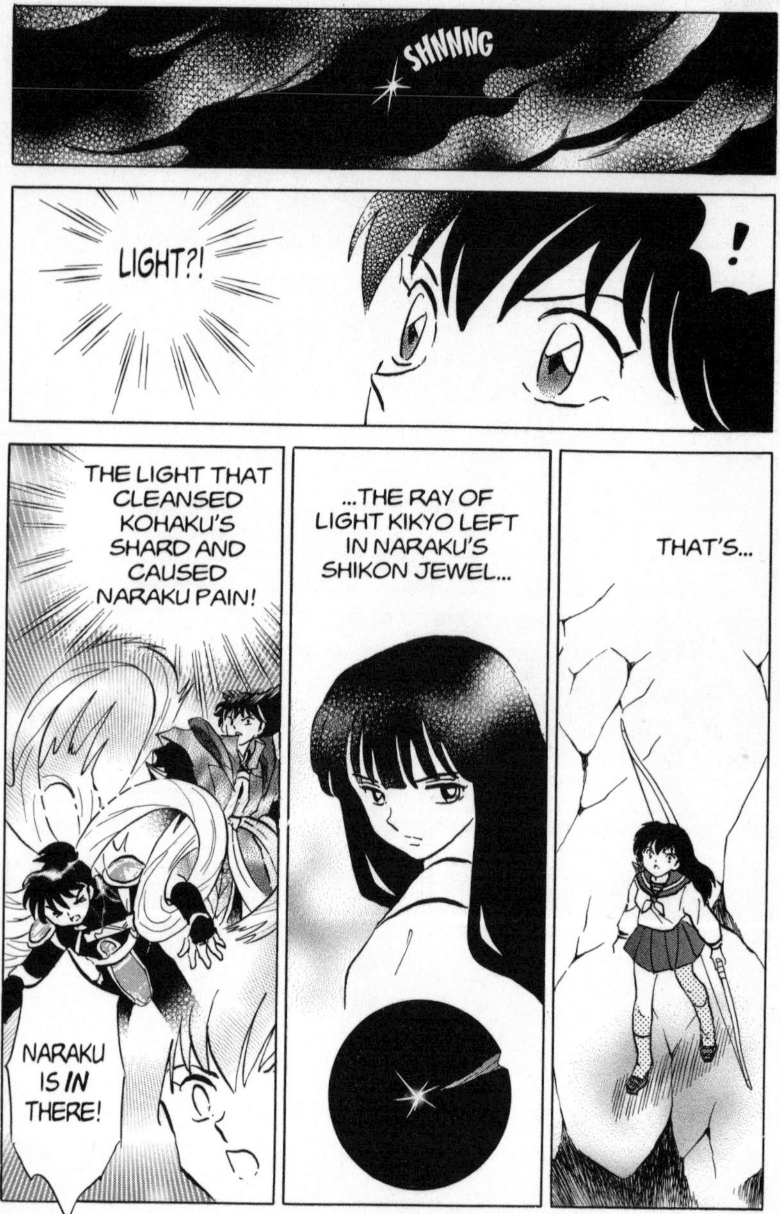
SHNNNG
!
LIGHT?!
THAT'S...
...THE RAY OF LIGHT KIKYO LEFT IN NARAKU'S SHIKON JEWEL...
THE LIGHT THAT CLEANSED KOHAKU'S SHARD AND CAUSED NARAKU PAIN!
NARAKU IS *IN* THERE!

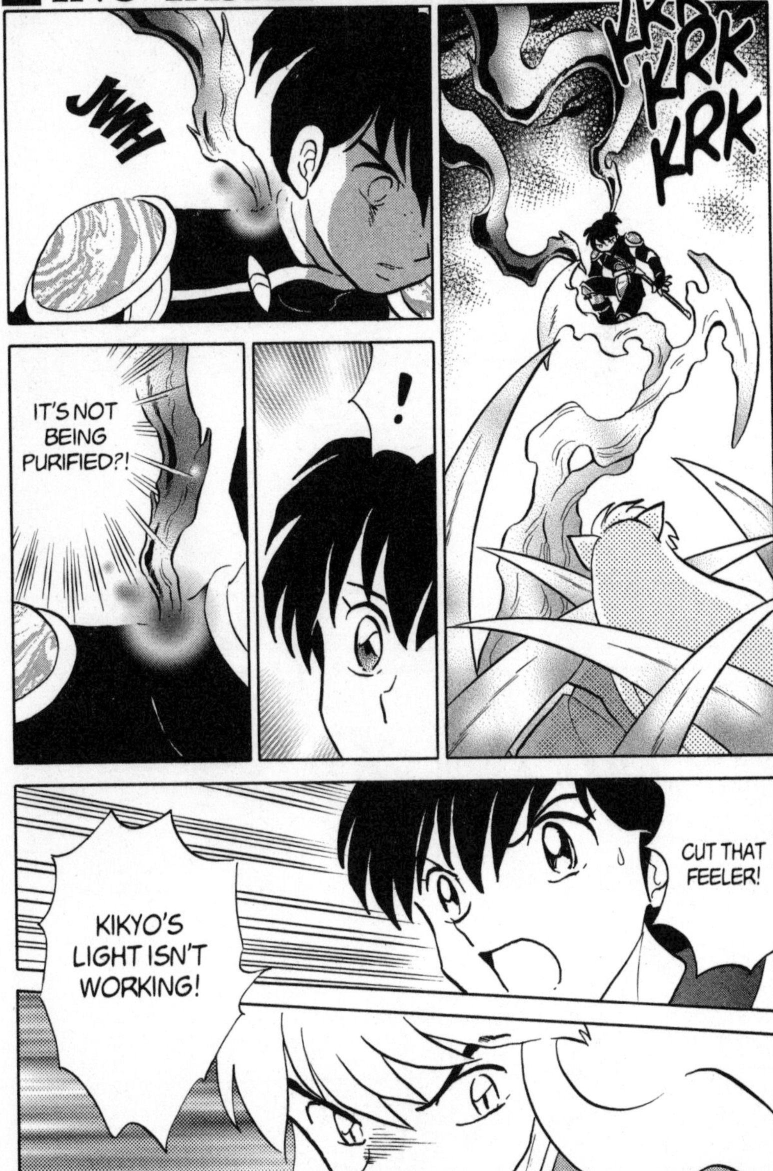
KRK KRK KRK
JWH
!
IT'S NOT BEING PURIFIED?!
CUT THAT FEELER!
KIKYO'S LIGHT ISN'T WORKING!

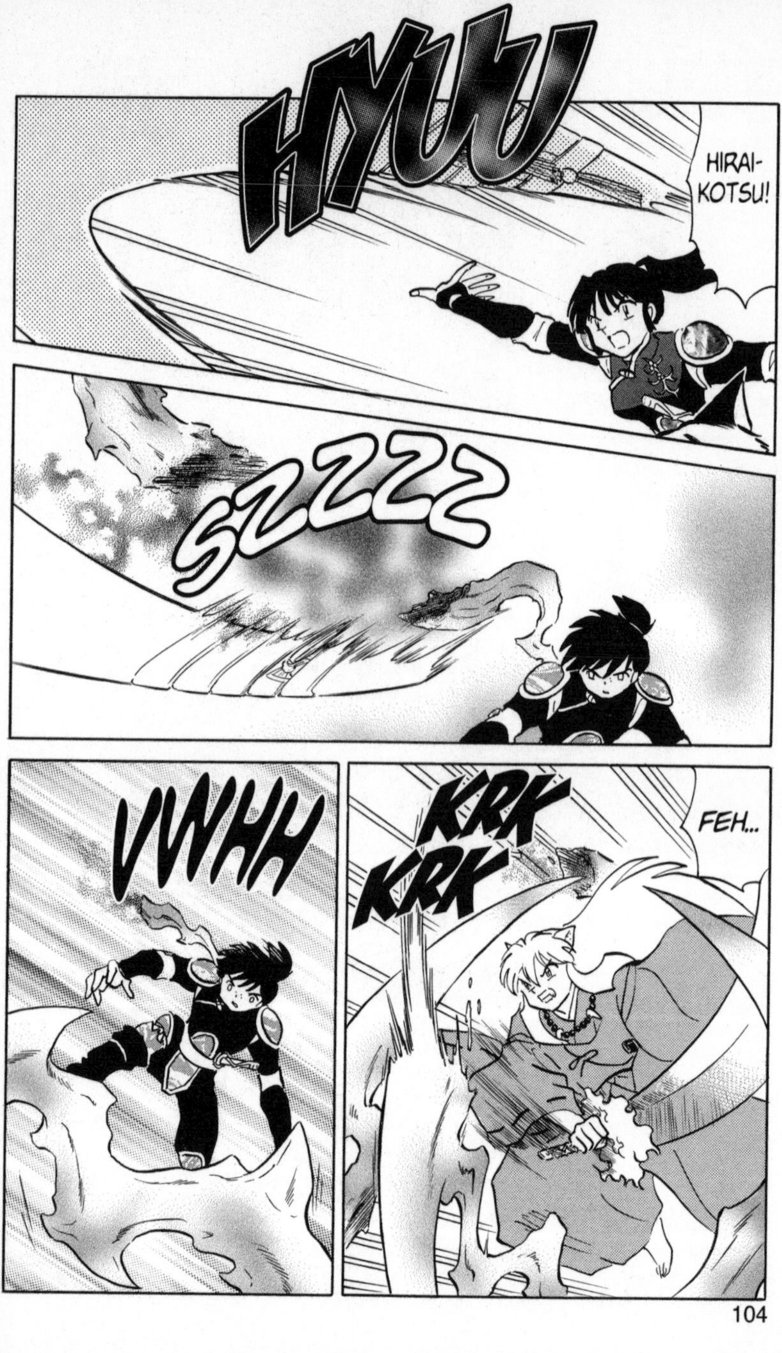
HYUU
HIRAI-KOTSU!
SZZZZ
KRK KRK
FEH...
VWHH

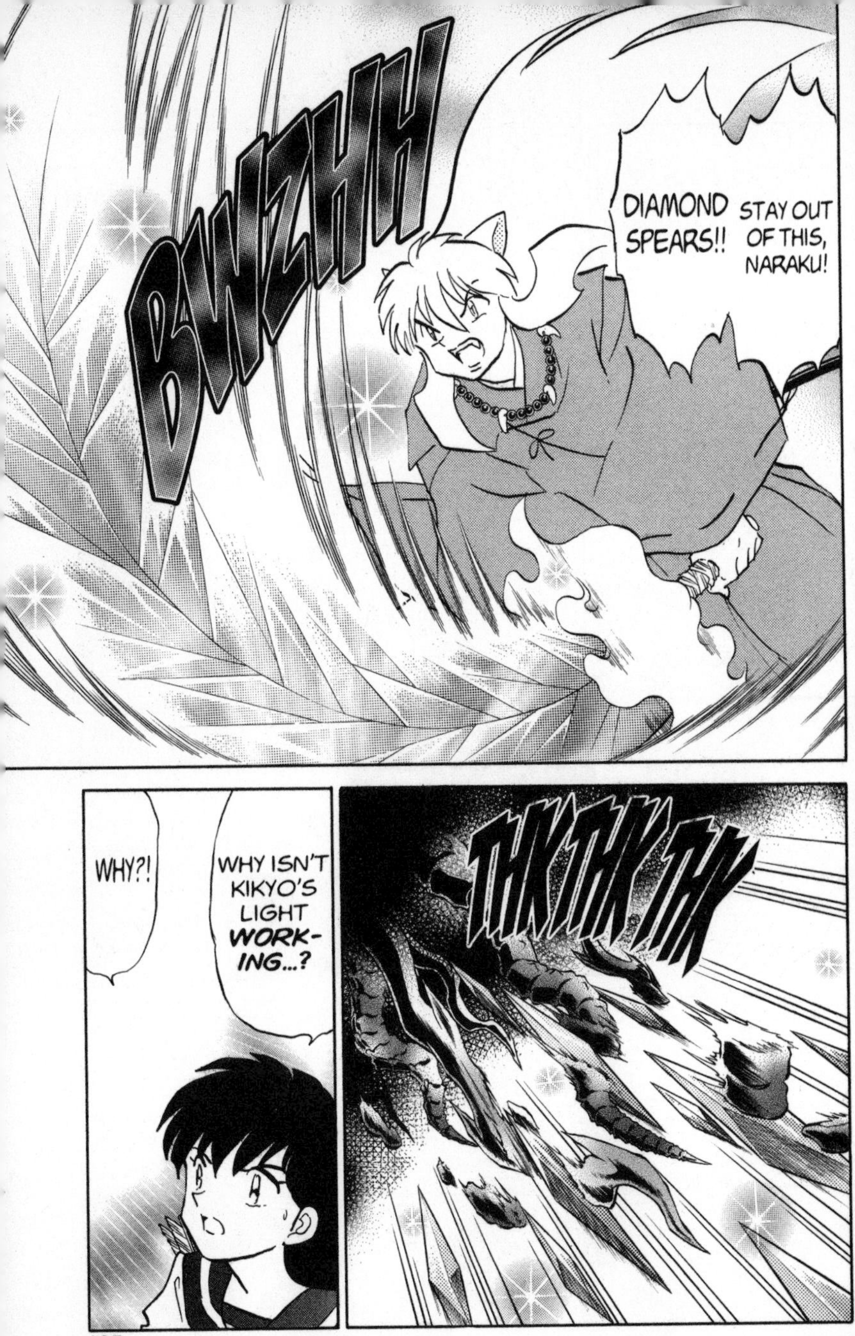
BWZHH
STAY OUT OF THIS, NARAKU!
DIAMOND SPEARS!!
THK THK THK THK
WHY ISN'T KIKYO'S LIGHT **WORKING...?**
WHY?!

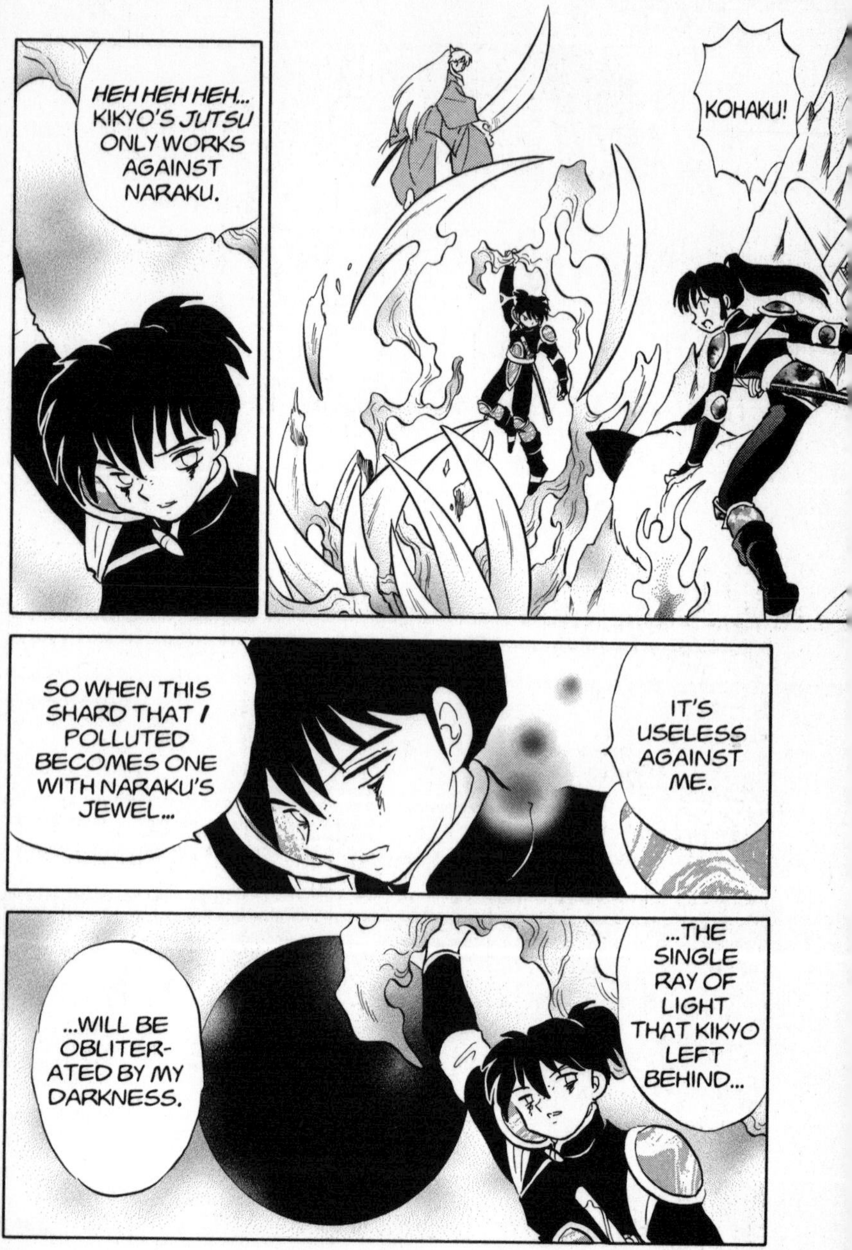
KOHAKU!
HEH HEH HEH... KIKYO'S JUTSU ONLY WORKS AGAINST NARAKU.
IT'S USELESS AGAINST ME.
SO WHEN THIS SHARD THAT I POLLUTED BECOMES ONE WITH NARAKU'S JEWEL...
...THE SINGLE RAY OF LIGHT THAT KIKYO LEFT BEHIND...
...WILL BE OBLITER-ATED BY MY DARKNESS.

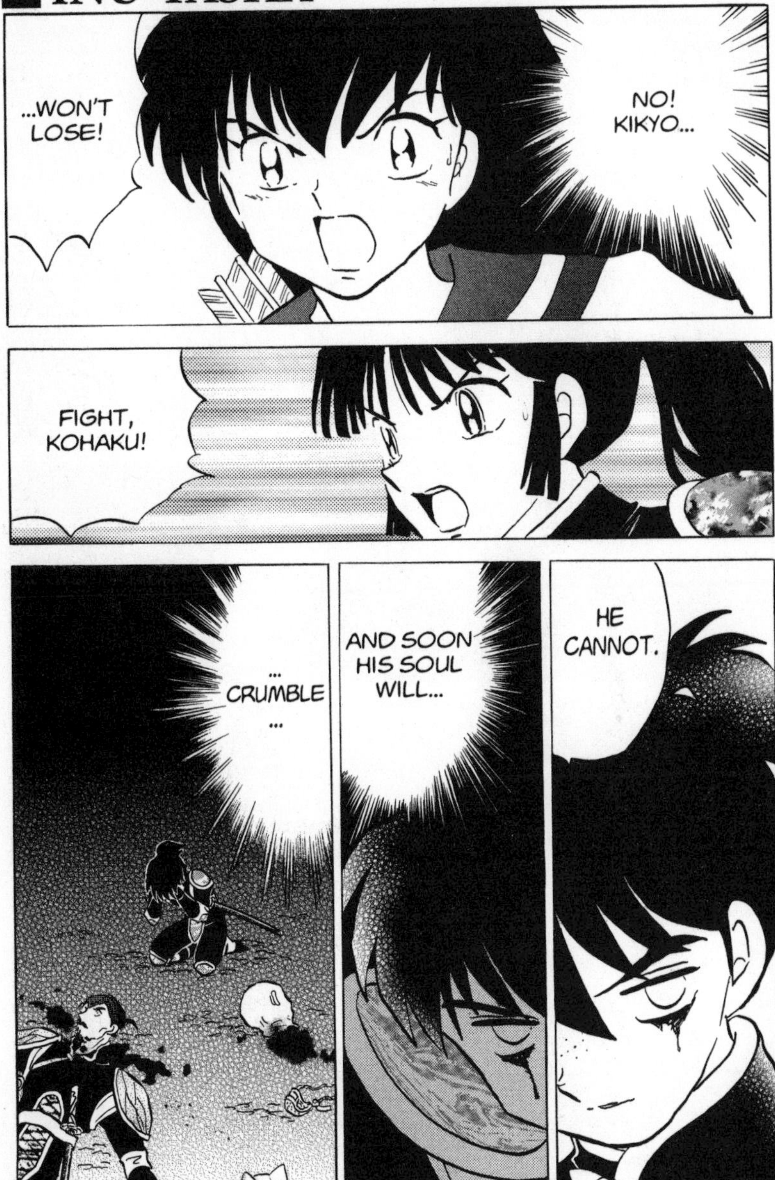
NO! KIKYO...
...WON'T LOSE!
FIGHT, KOHAKU!
HE CANNOT.
AND SOON HIS SOUL WILL...
... CRUMBLE ...

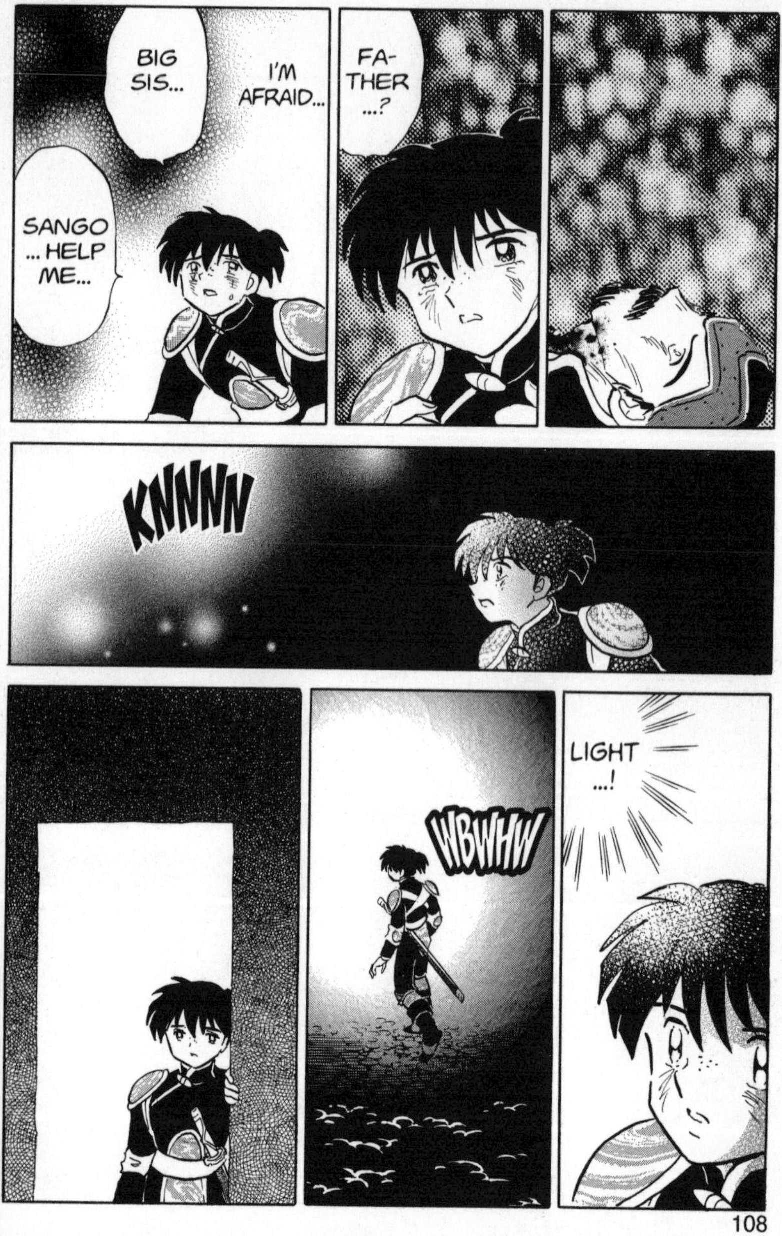
FA-
THER
...?
I'M
AFRAID...
BIG
SIS...
SANGO
... HELP
ME...
KNNNN
LIGHT
...!
WBWHW

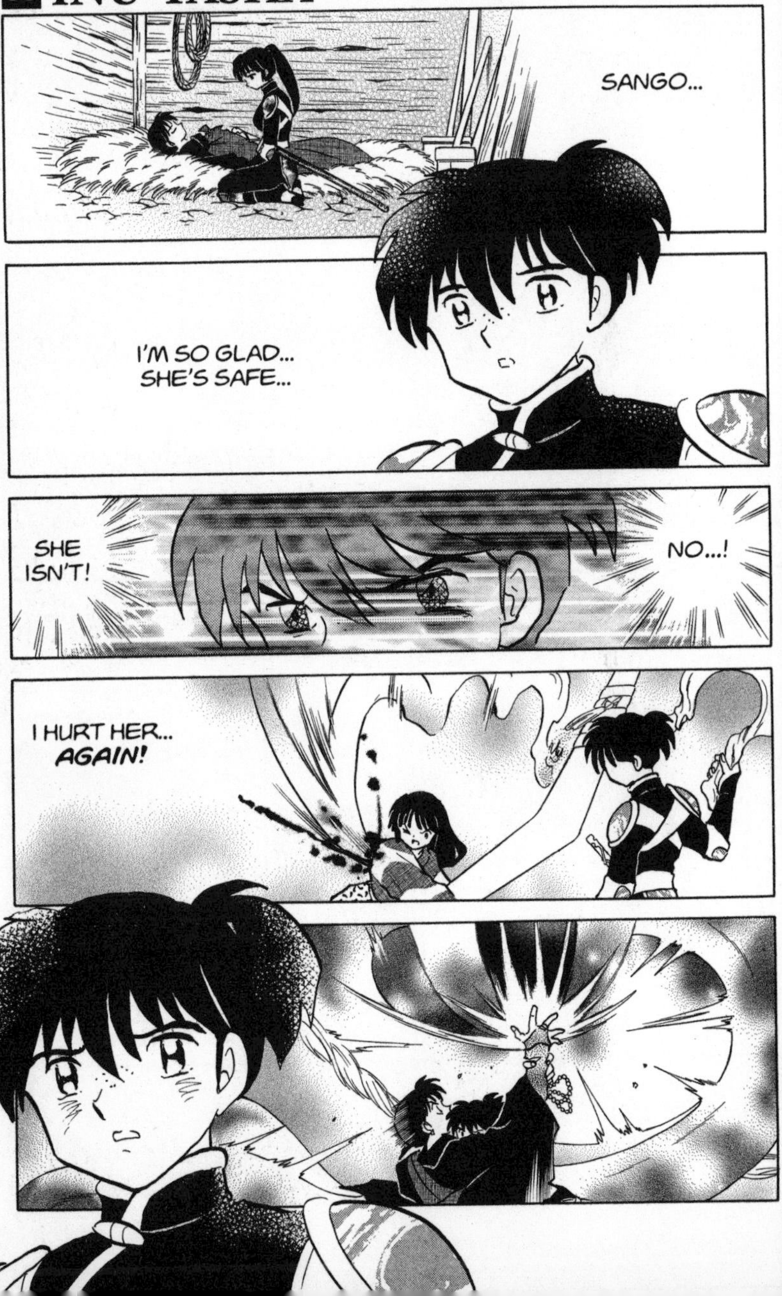
SANGO...
I'M SO GLAD... SHE'S SAFE...
NO...!
SHE ISN'T!
I HURT HER... AGAIN!

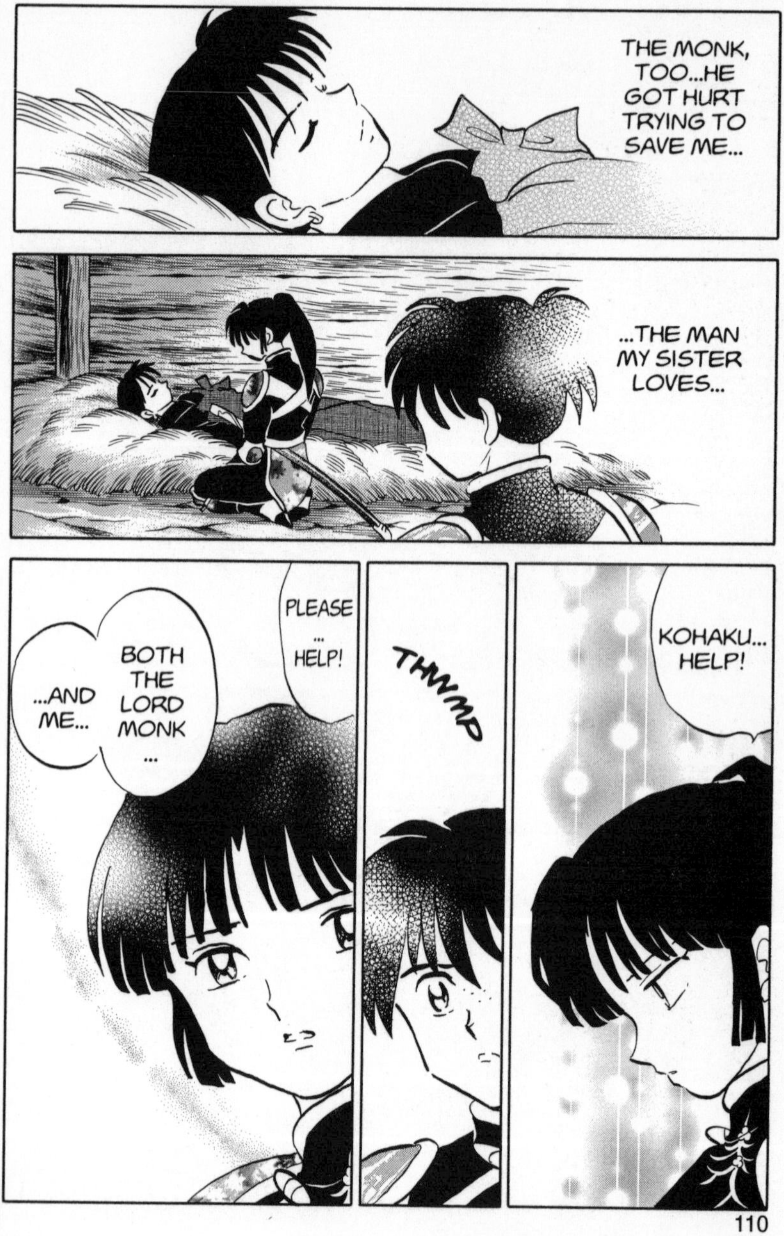
THE MONK, TOO...HE GOT HURT TRYING TO SAVE ME...
...THE MAN MY SISTER LOVES...
KOHAKU... HELP!
THWMP
PLEASE ... HELP!
BOTH THE LORD MONK ...
...AND ME...

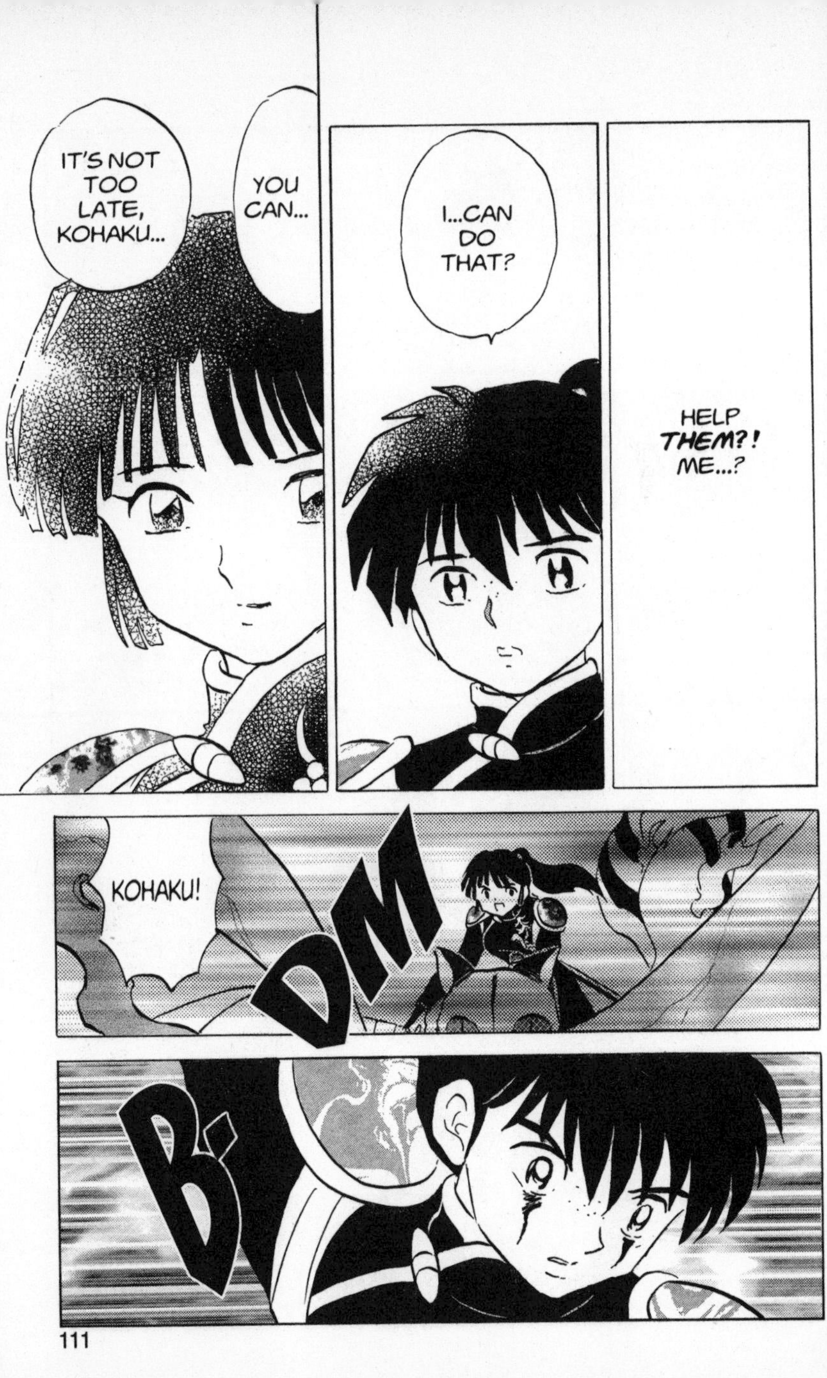
HELP THEM?! ME...?
I...CAN DO THAT?
YOU CAN...
IT'S NOT TOO LATE, KOHAKU...
KOHAKU!
DM
B

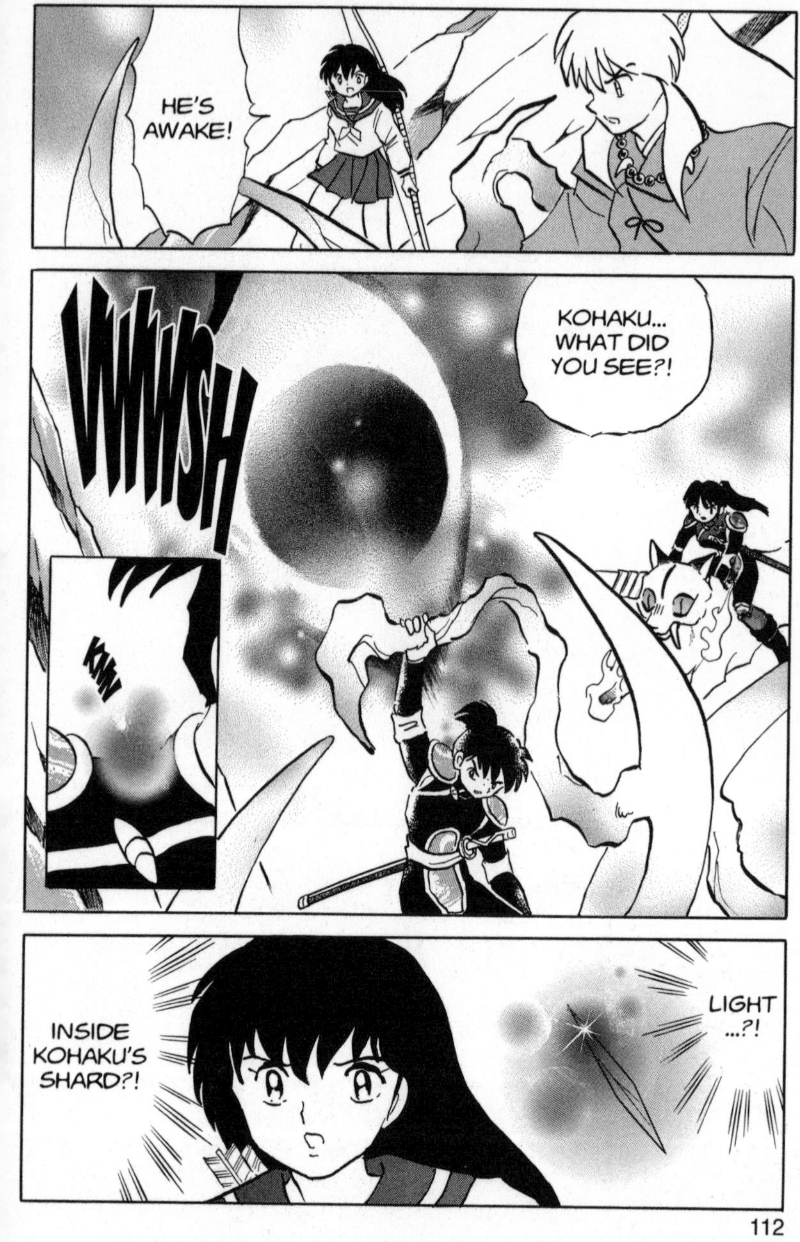
HE'S AWAKE!
KOHAKU... WHAT DID YOU SEE?!
VWWSH
KNN
LIGHT ...?!
INSIDE KOHAKU'S SHARD?!

SCROLL 7

RELEASE

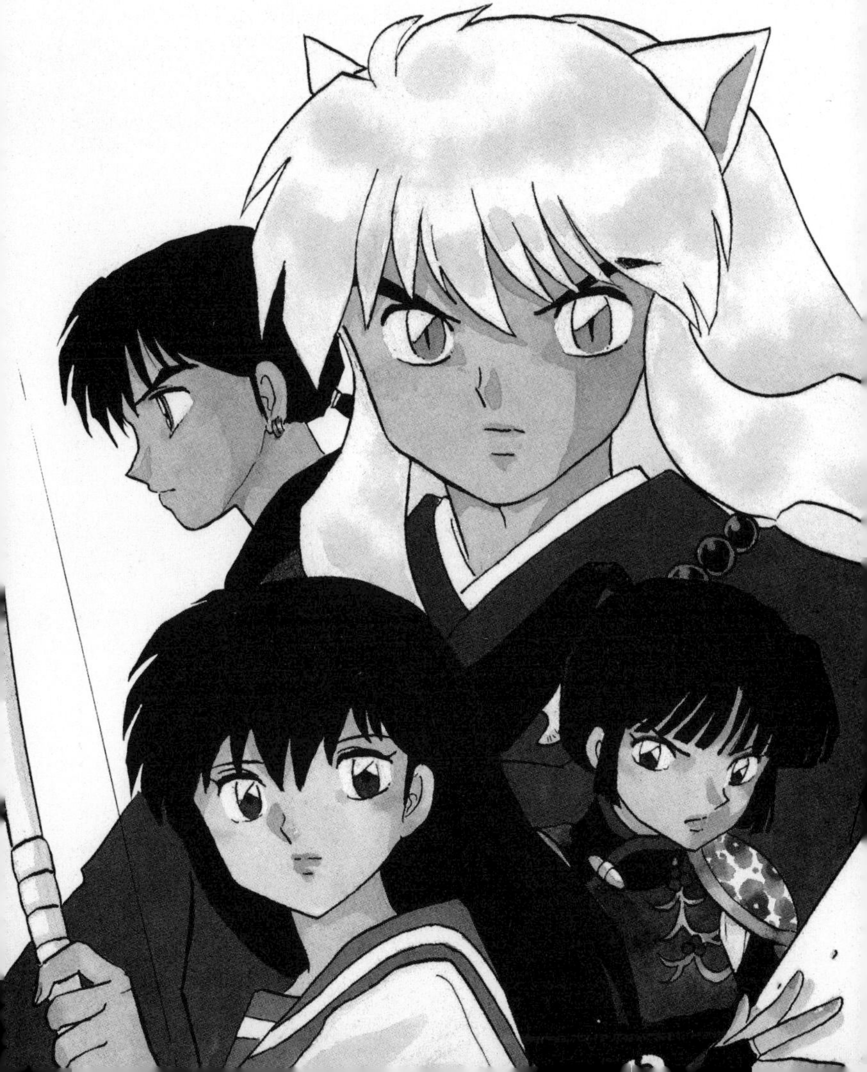

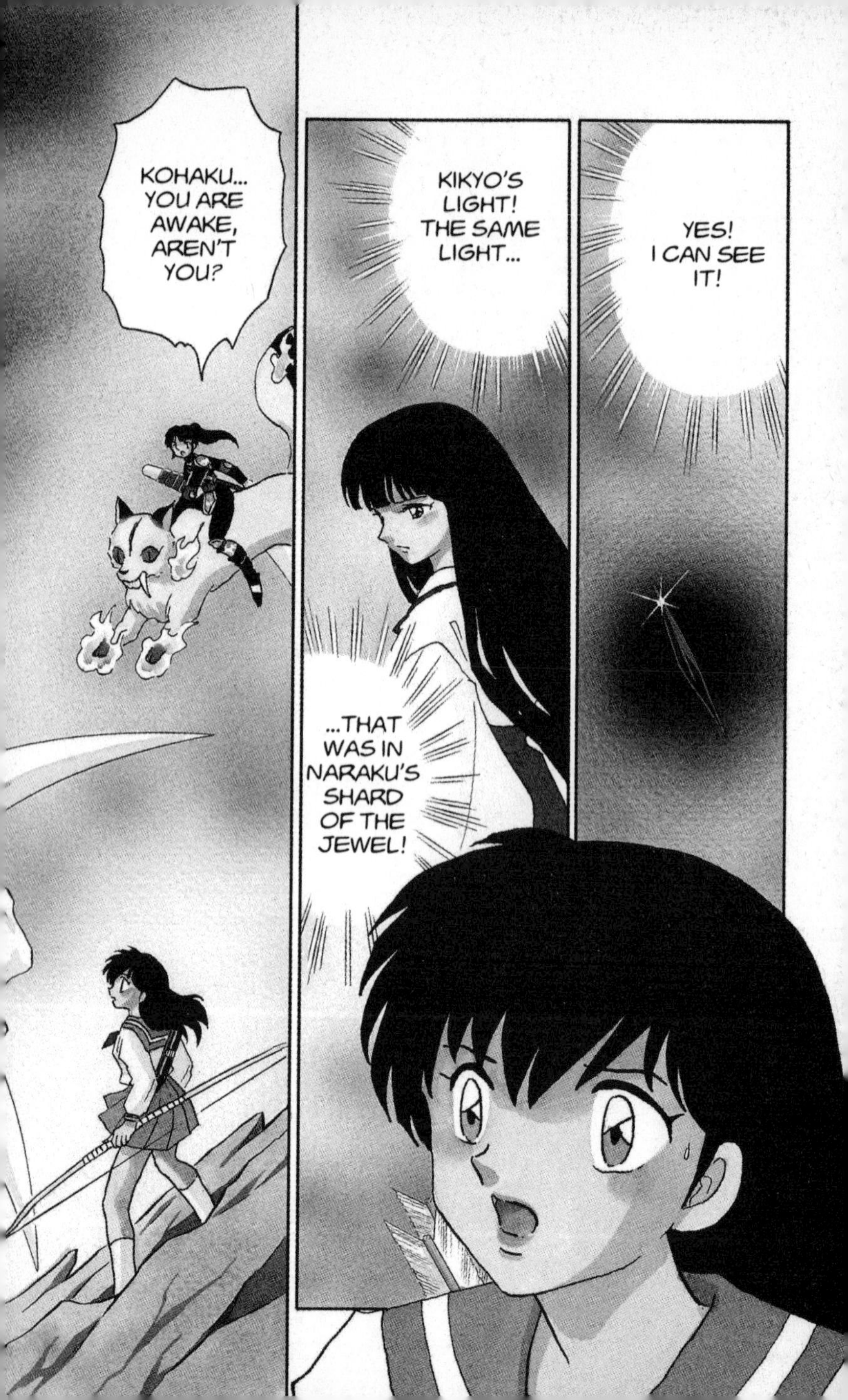
KIKYO'S LIGHT! THE SAME LIGHT...
...THAT WAS IN NARAKU'S SHARD OF THE JEWEL!
YES! I CAN SEE IT!
KOHAKU... YOU ARE AWAKE, AREN'T YOU?

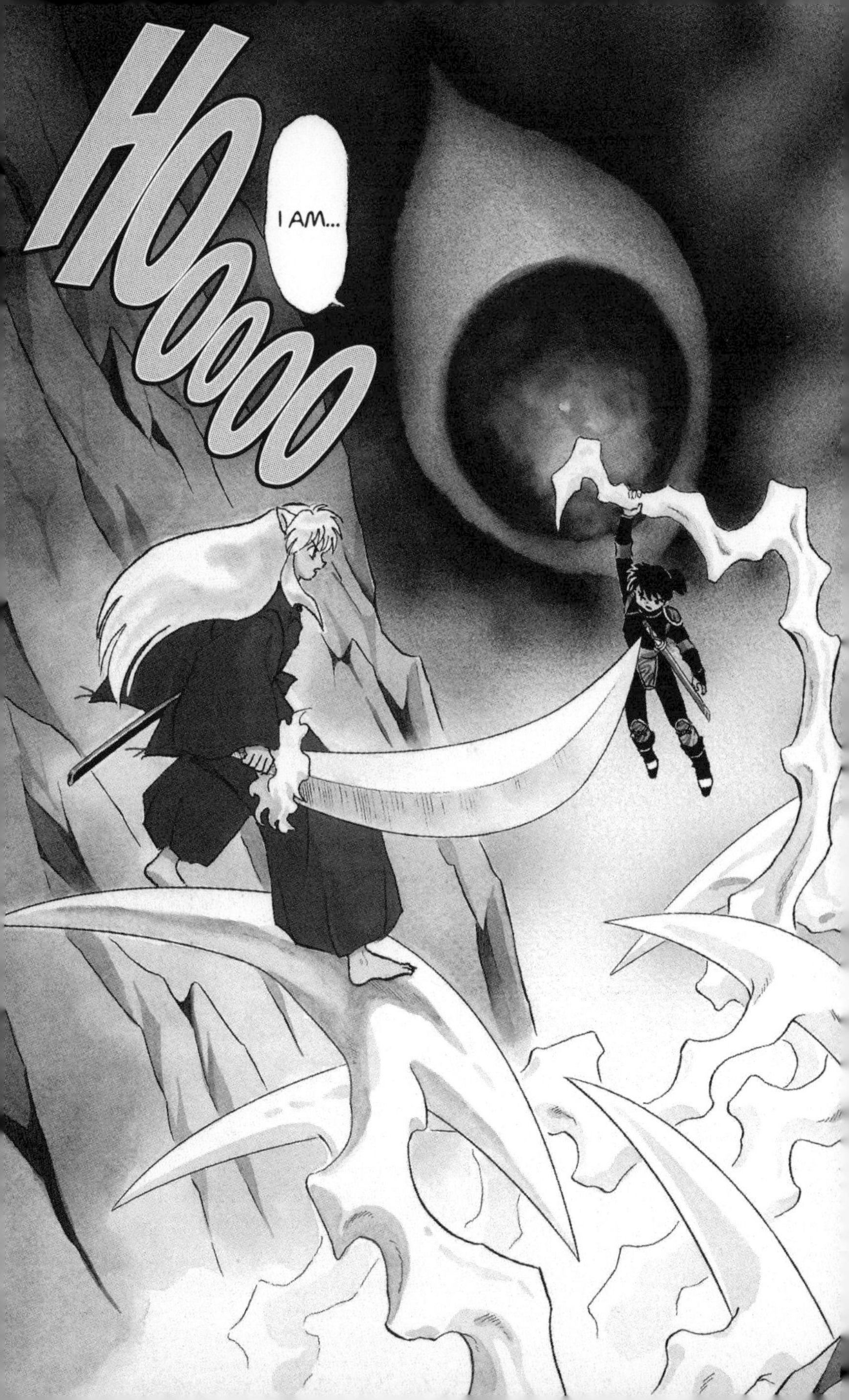
I AM...
HOOOOO

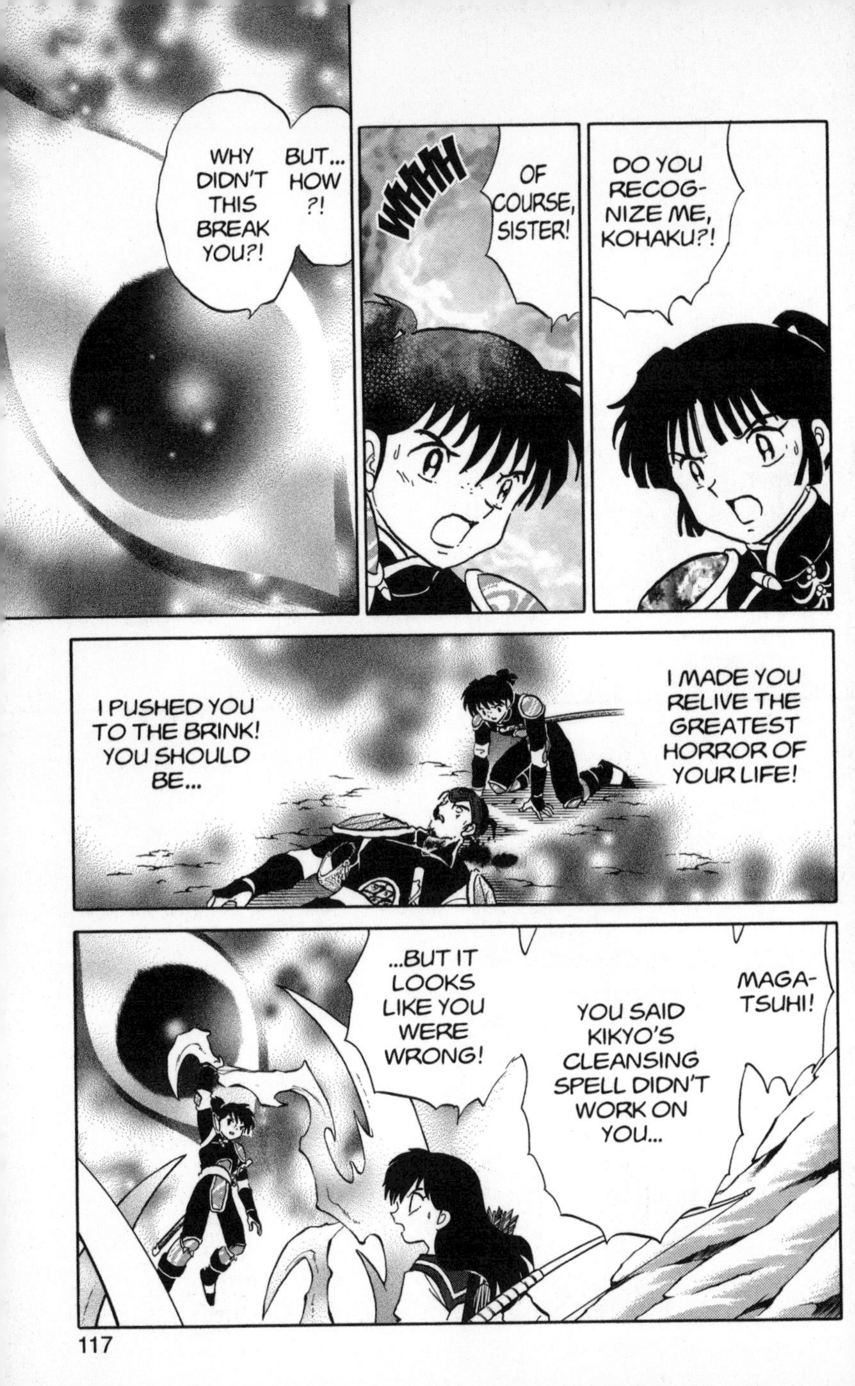
DO YOU RECOG-NIZE ME, KOHAKU?!
WHHH
OF COURSE, SISTER!
BUT... HOW ?!
WHY DIDN'T THIS BREAK YOU?!
I MADE YOU RELIVE THE GREATEST HORROR OF YOUR LIFE!
I PUSHED YOU TO THE BRINK! YOU SHOULD BE...
MAGA-TSUHI!
YOU SAID KIKYO'S CLEANSING SPELL DIDN'T WORK ON YOU...
...BUT IT LOOKS LIKE YOU WERE WRONG!

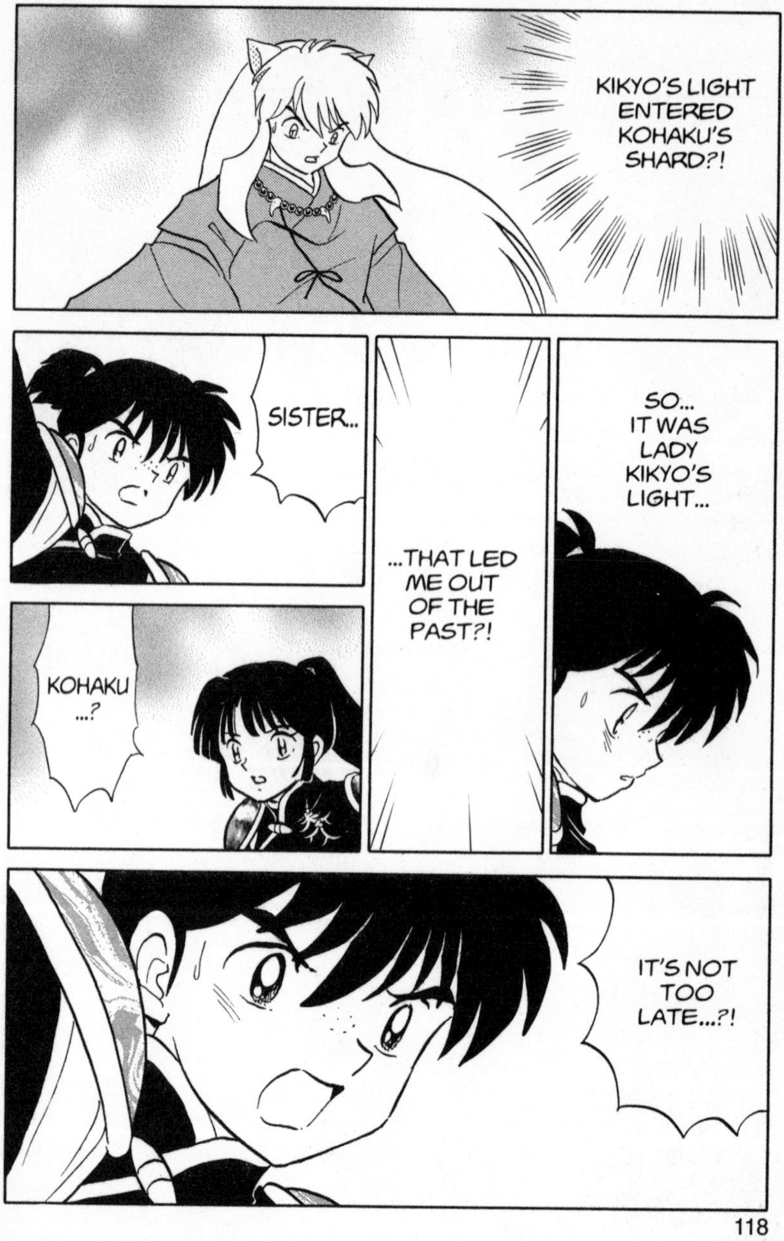
KIKYO'S LIGHT ENTERED KOHAKU'S SHARD?!
SO... IT WAS LADY KIKYO'S LIGHT...
...THAT LED ME OUT OF THE PAST?!
SISTER...
KOHAKU ...?
IT'S NOT TOO LATE...?!

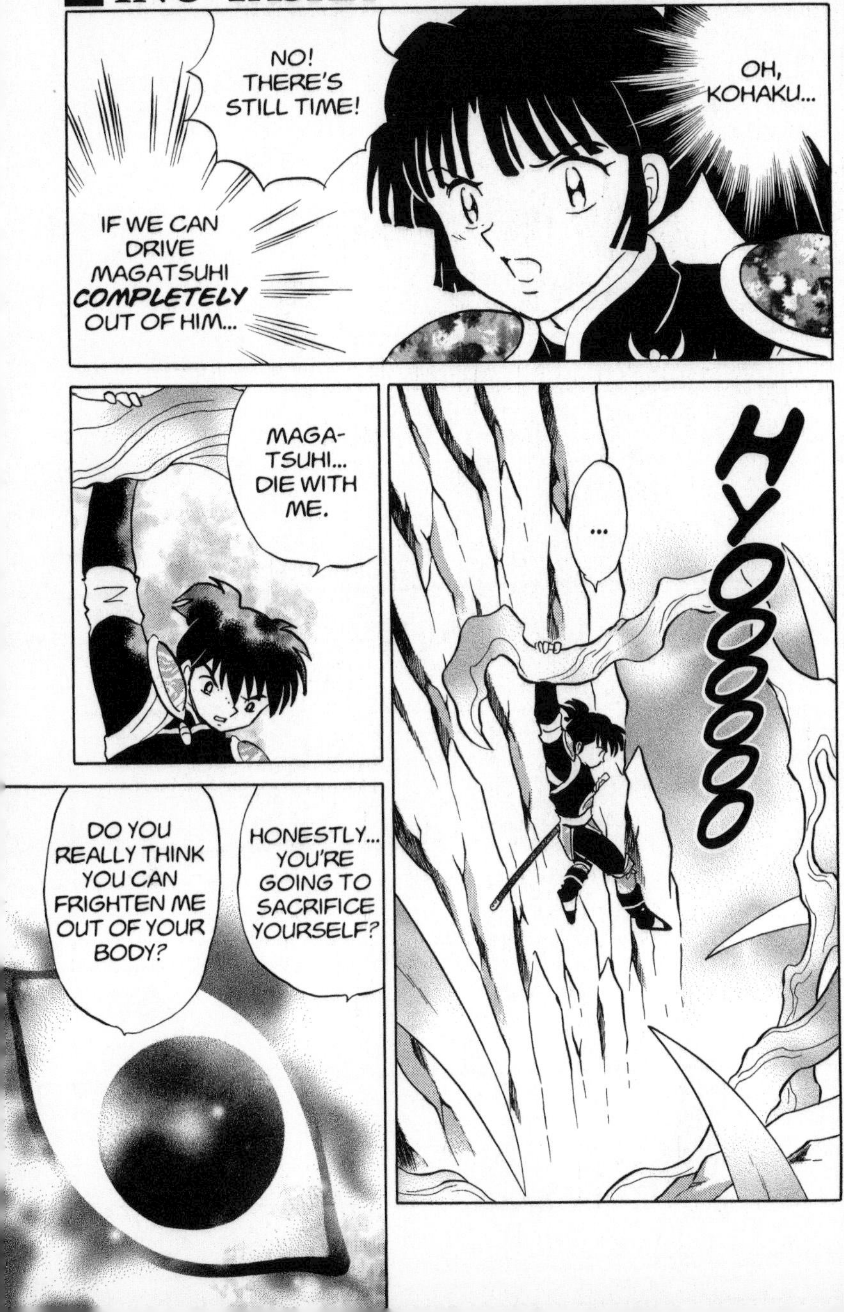
OH, KOHAKU...
NO! THERE'S STILL TIME!
IF WE CAN DRIVE MAGATSUHI COMPLETELY OUT OF HIM...
HYOOOOOO
...
MAGA-TSUHI... DIE WITH ME.
HONESTLY... YOU'RE GOING TO SACRIFICE YOURSELF?
DO YOU REALLY THINK YOU CAN FRIGHTEN ME OUT OF YOUR BODY?

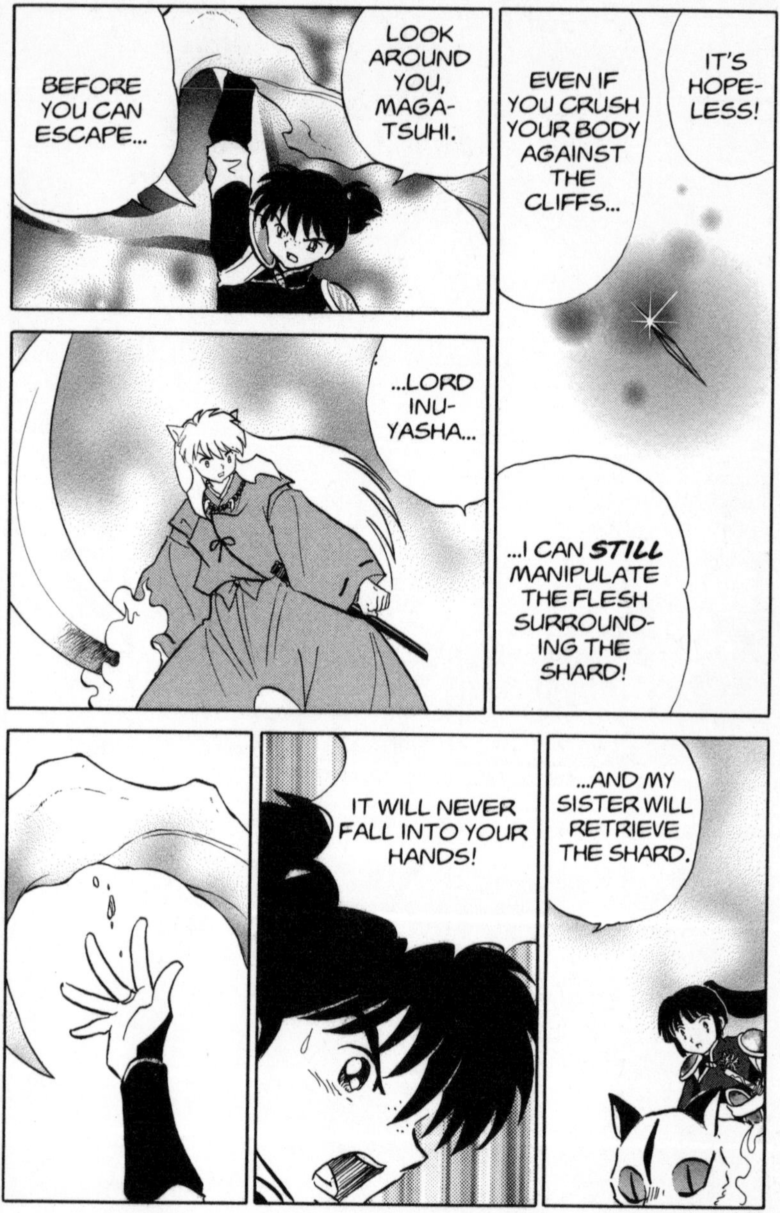
IT'S HOPE-LESS!
EVEN IF YOU CRUSH YOUR BODY AGAINST THE CLIFFS...
...I CAN **STILL** MANIPULATE THE FLESH SURROUND-ING THE SHARD!
LOOK AROUND YOU, MAGA-TSUHI.
BEFORE YOU CAN ESCAPE...
...LORD INU-YASHA...
...AND MY SISTER WILL RETRIEVE THE SHARD.
IT WILL NEVER FALL INTO YOUR HANDS!

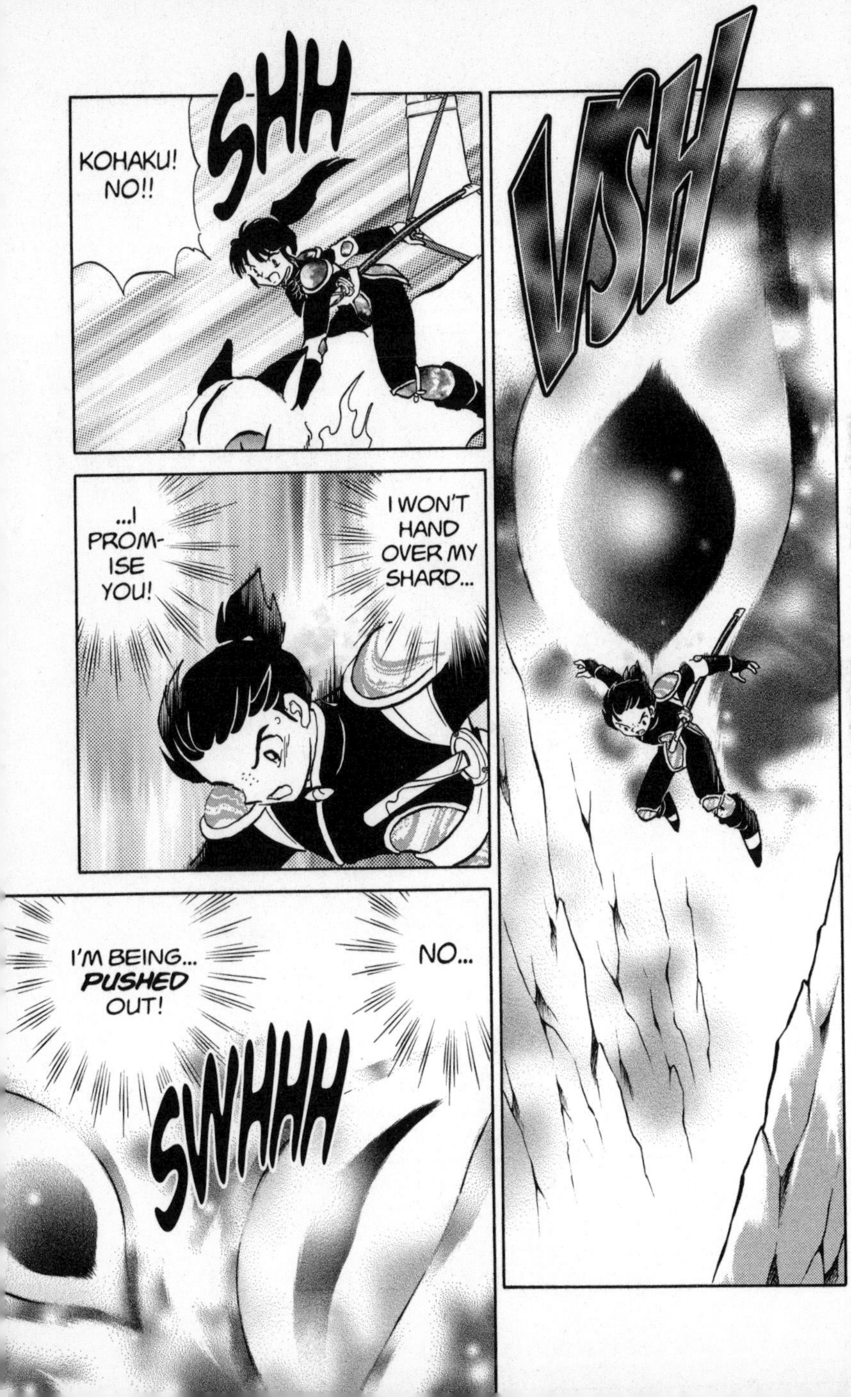
VSH
SHH
KOHAKU! NO!!
I WON'T HAND OVER MY SHARD...
...I PROMISE YOU!
NO...
I'M BEING... **PUSHED** OUT!
SWHHH

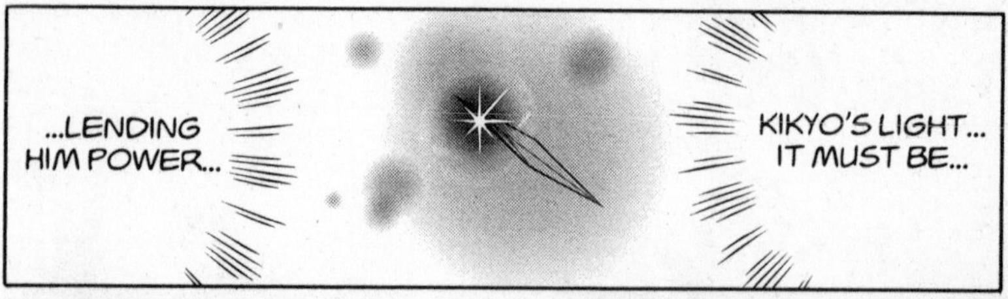
KIKYO'S LIGHT... IT MUST BE...
...LENDING HIM POWER...

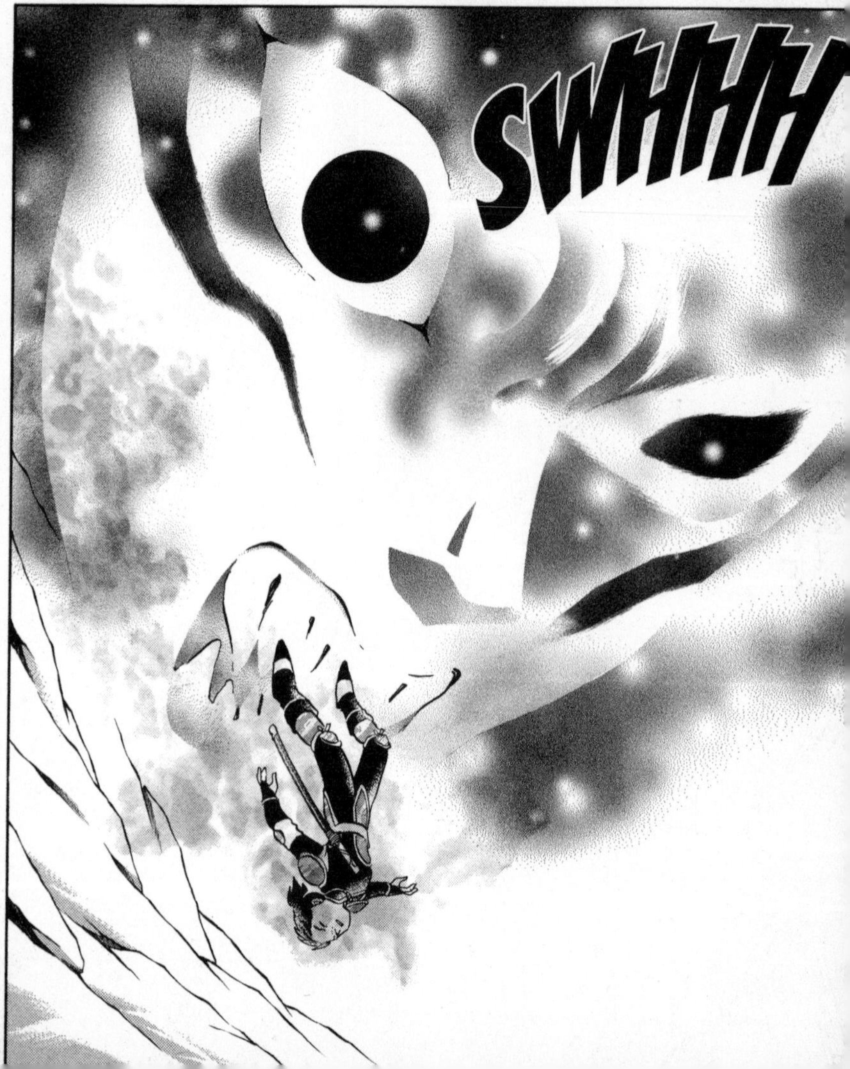
SWHHHH

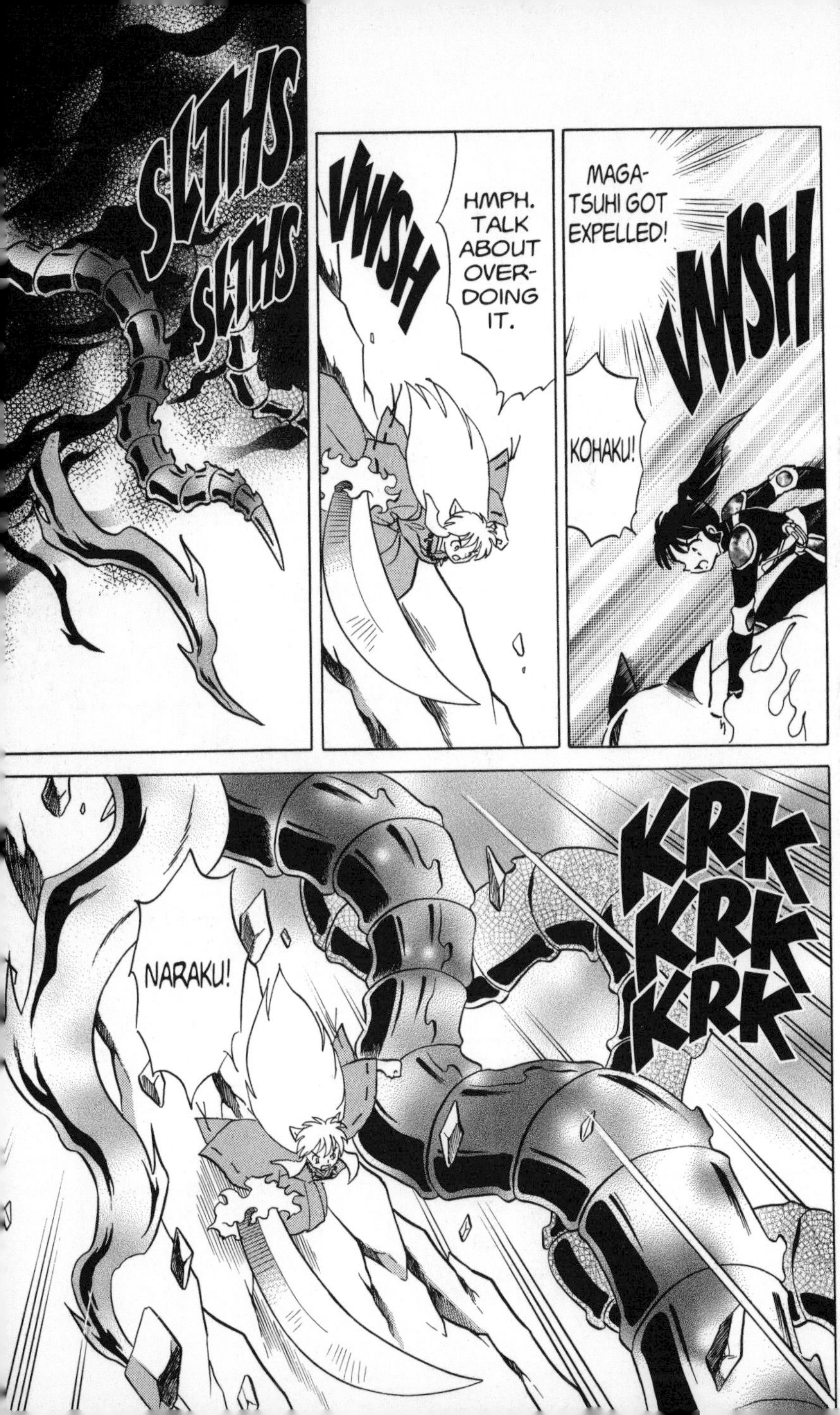
MAGA-TSUHI GOT EXPELLED!
VWISH
KOHAKU!
VWISH
HMPH. TALK ABOUT OVER-DOING IT.
SLTHS
SLTHS
KRK KRK KRK
NARAKU!

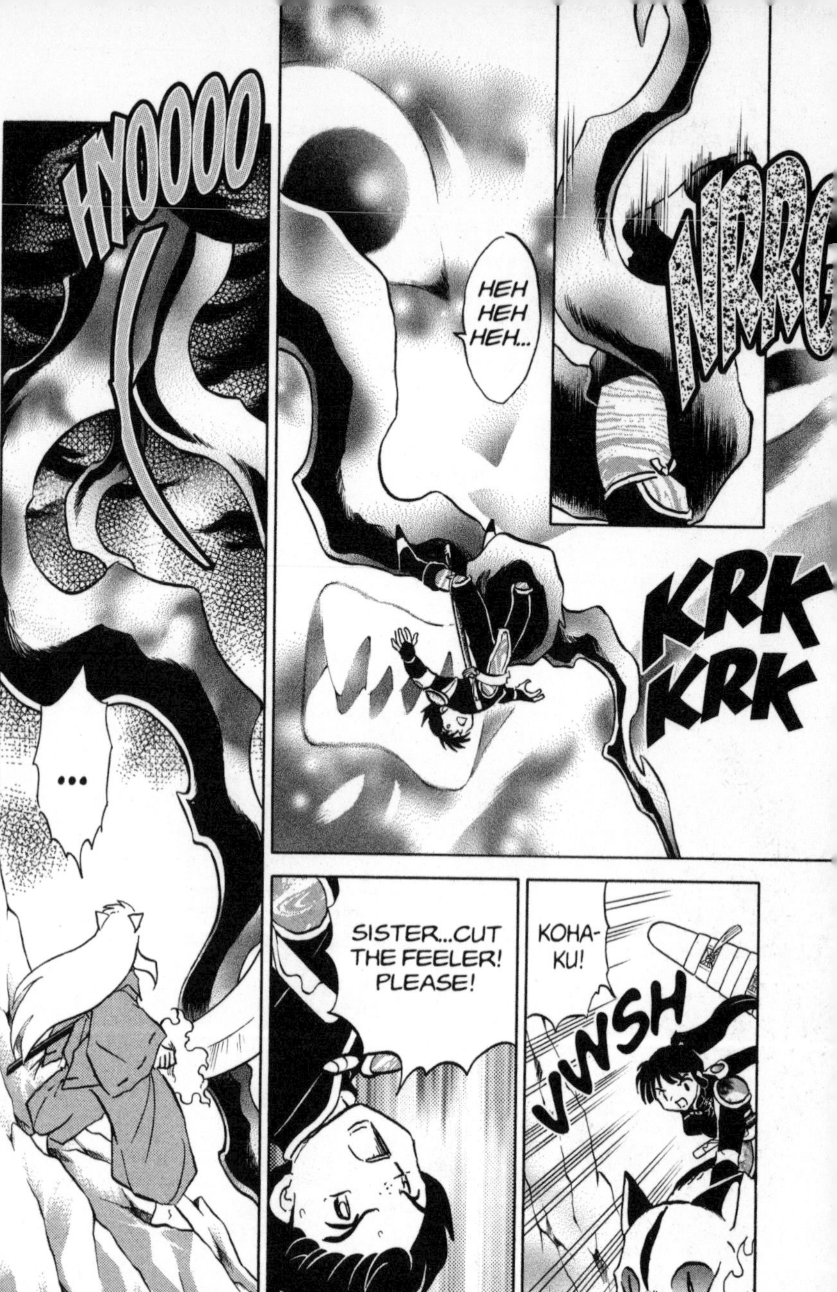
NRRG
HEH HEH HEH...
KRK KRK
KOHA-KU!
VWSH
SISTER...CUT THE FEELER! PLEASE!
HYOOOO
...

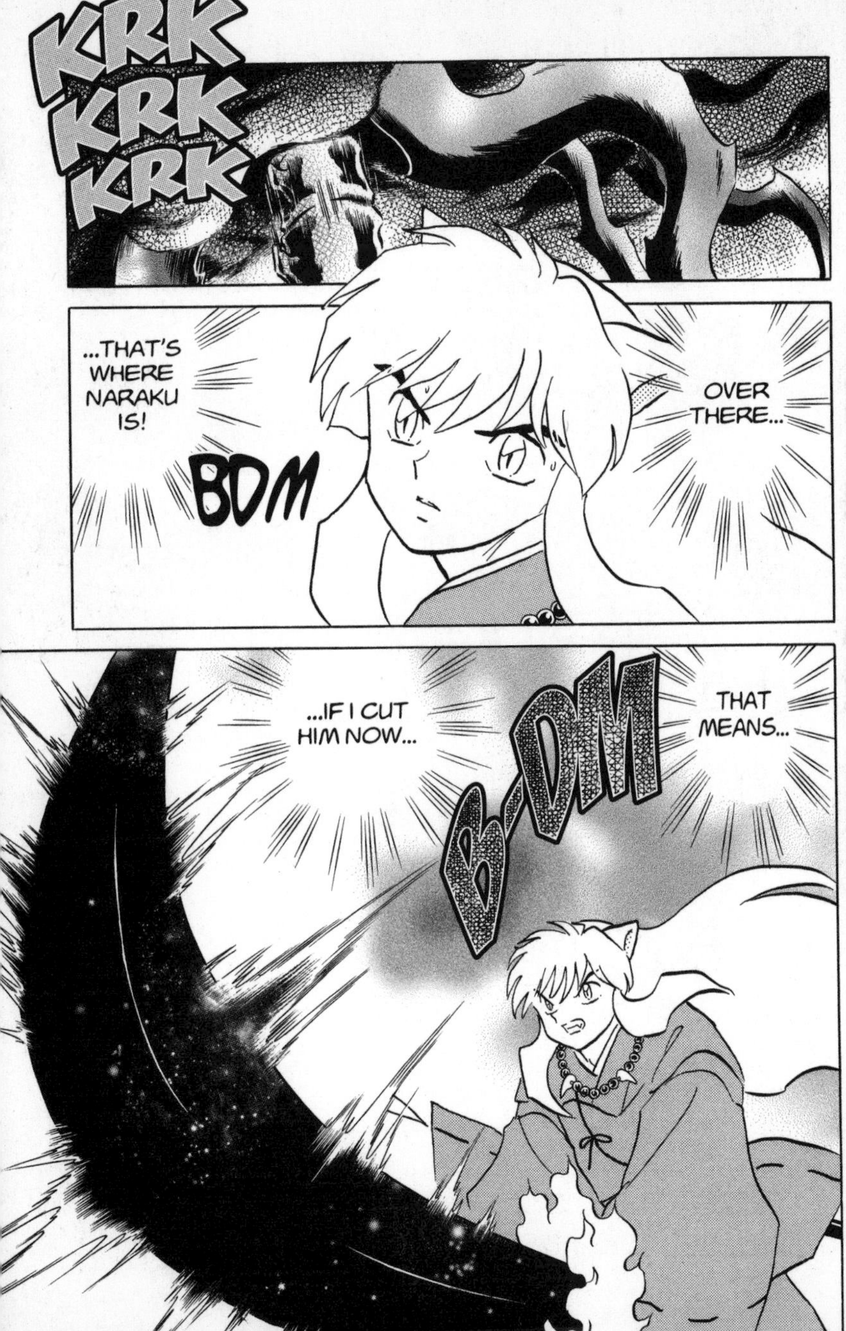
KRK KRK KRK
OVER THERE...
...THAT'S WHERE NARAKU IS!
BDM
THAT MEANS...
...IF I CUT HIM NOW...
B-DM

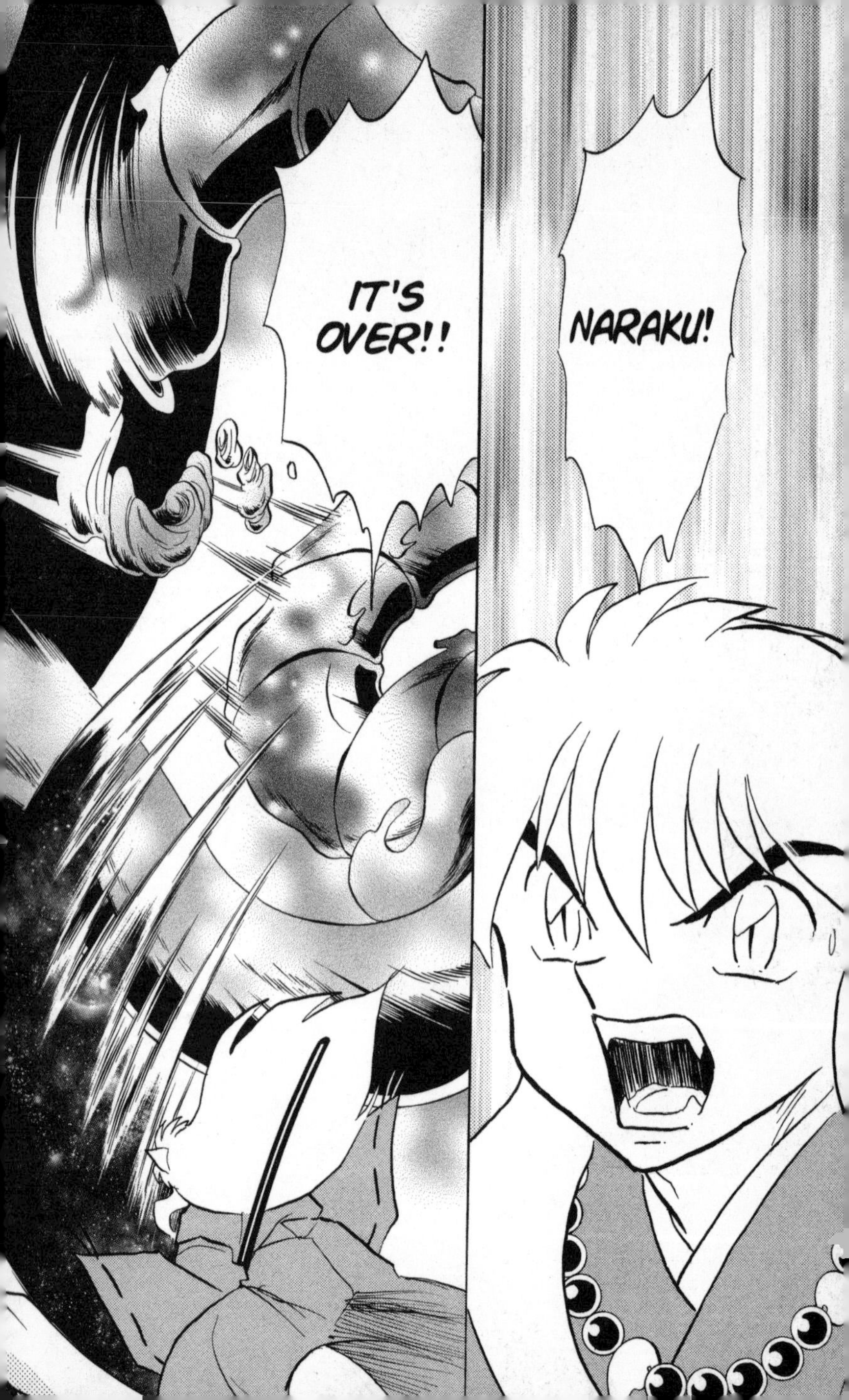
NARAKU!
IT'S OVER!!

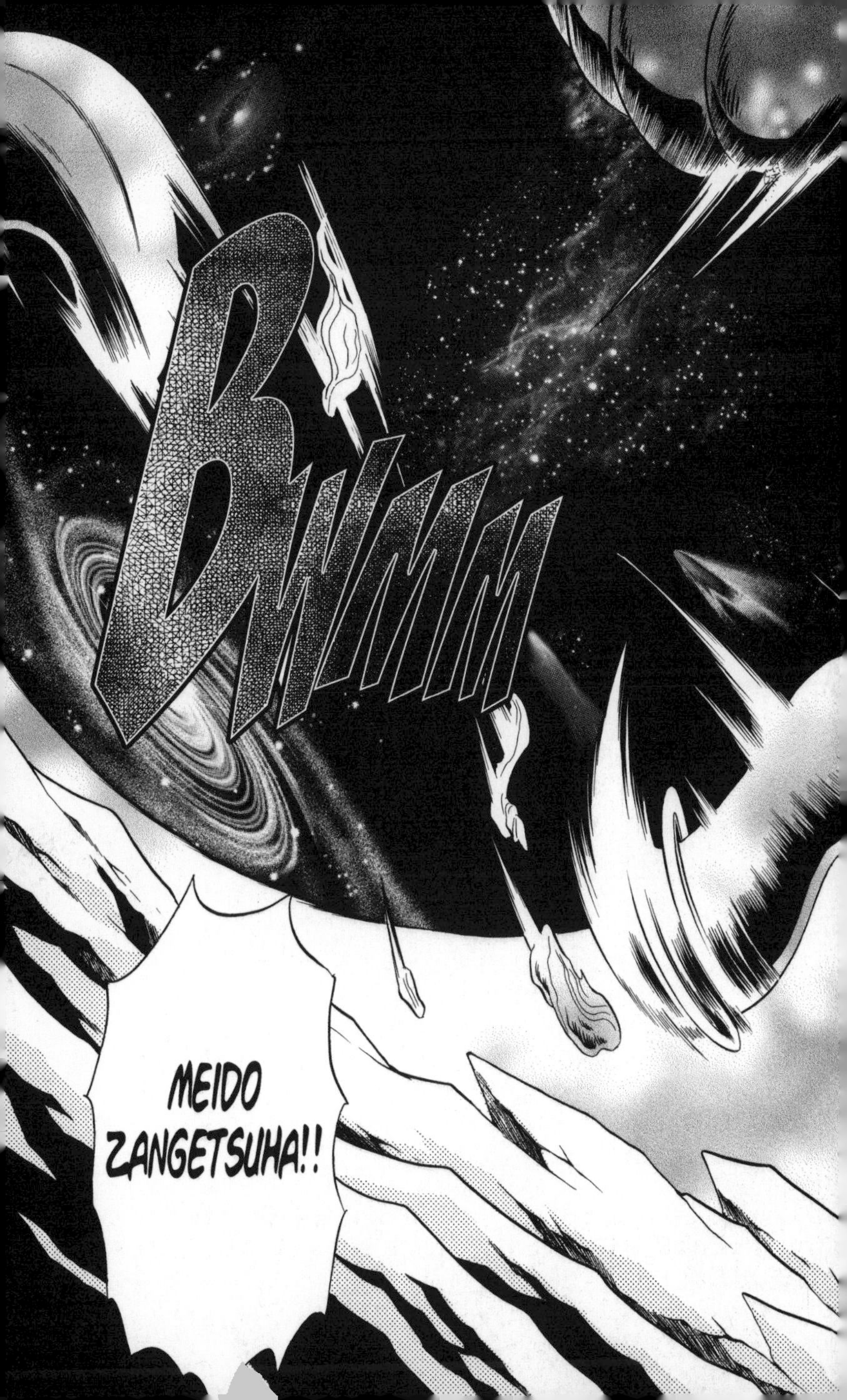
BWMM
MEIDO ZANGETSUHA!!

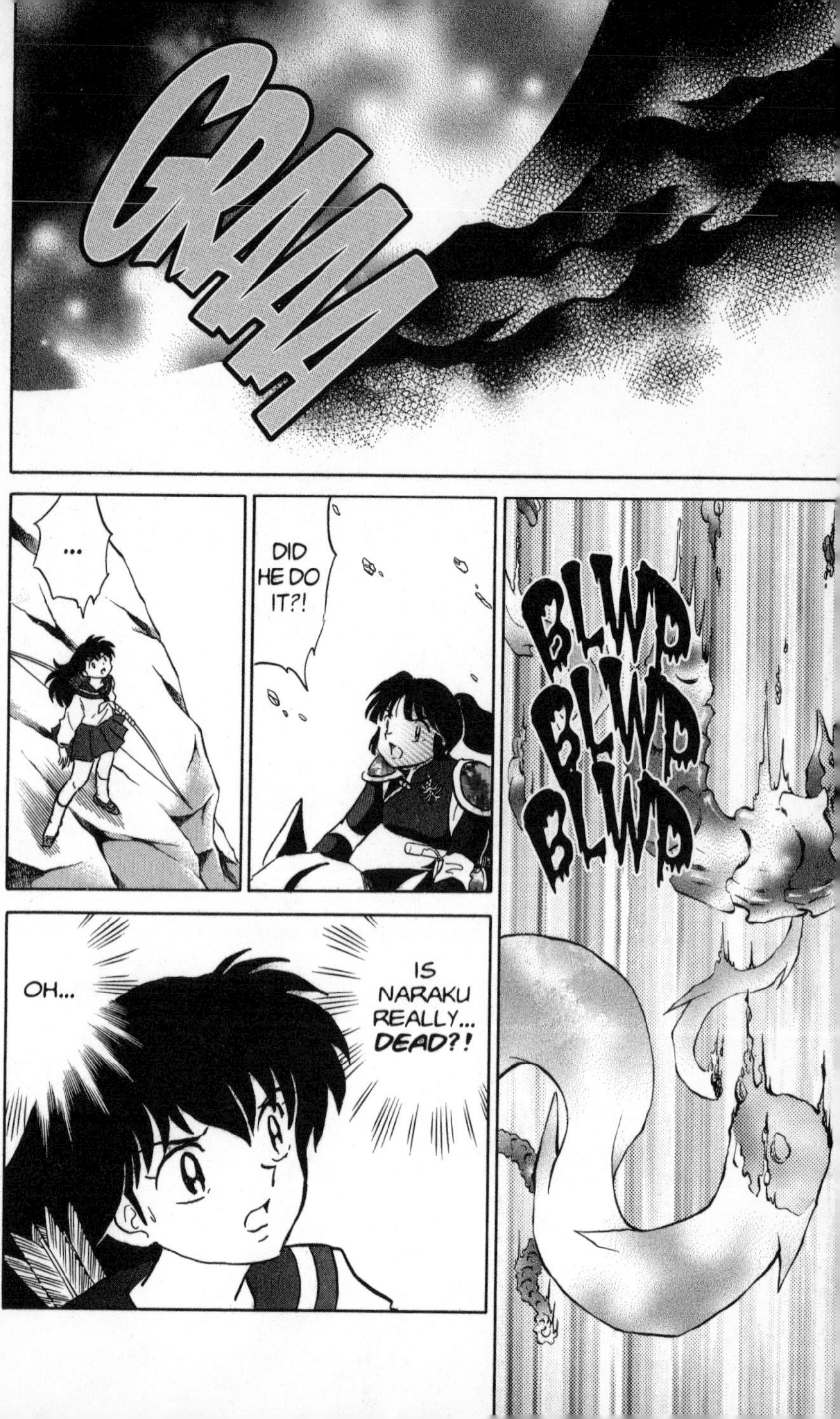
GRAAA
BLWP BLWP BLWP
DID HE DO IT?!
...
IS NARAKU REALLY... **DEAD?!**
OH...

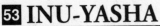

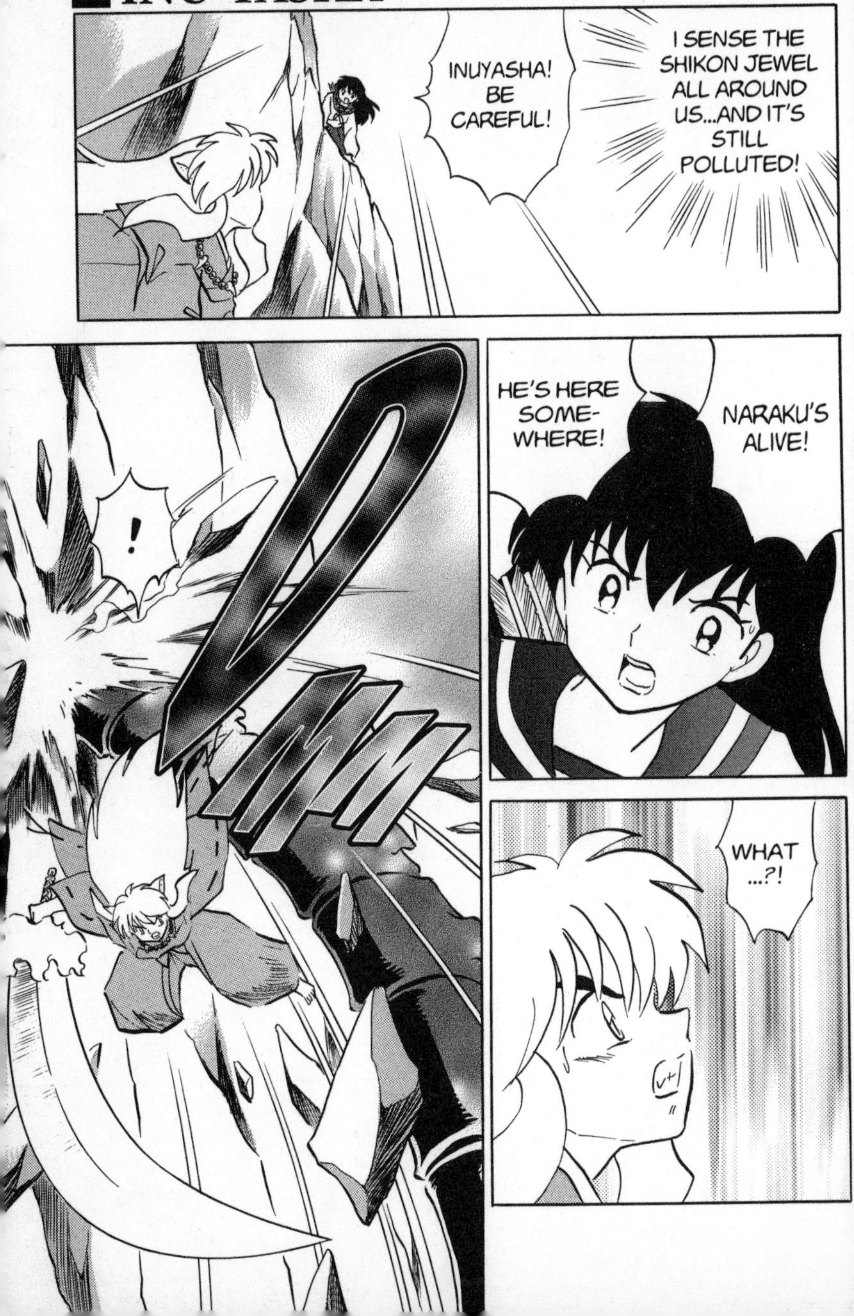
I SENSE THE SHIKON JEWEL ALL AROUND US...AND IT'S STILL POLLUTED!
INUYASHA! BE CAREFUL!
NARAKU'S ALIVE!
HE'S HERE SOME-WHERE!
WHAT ...?!
!
DOMM

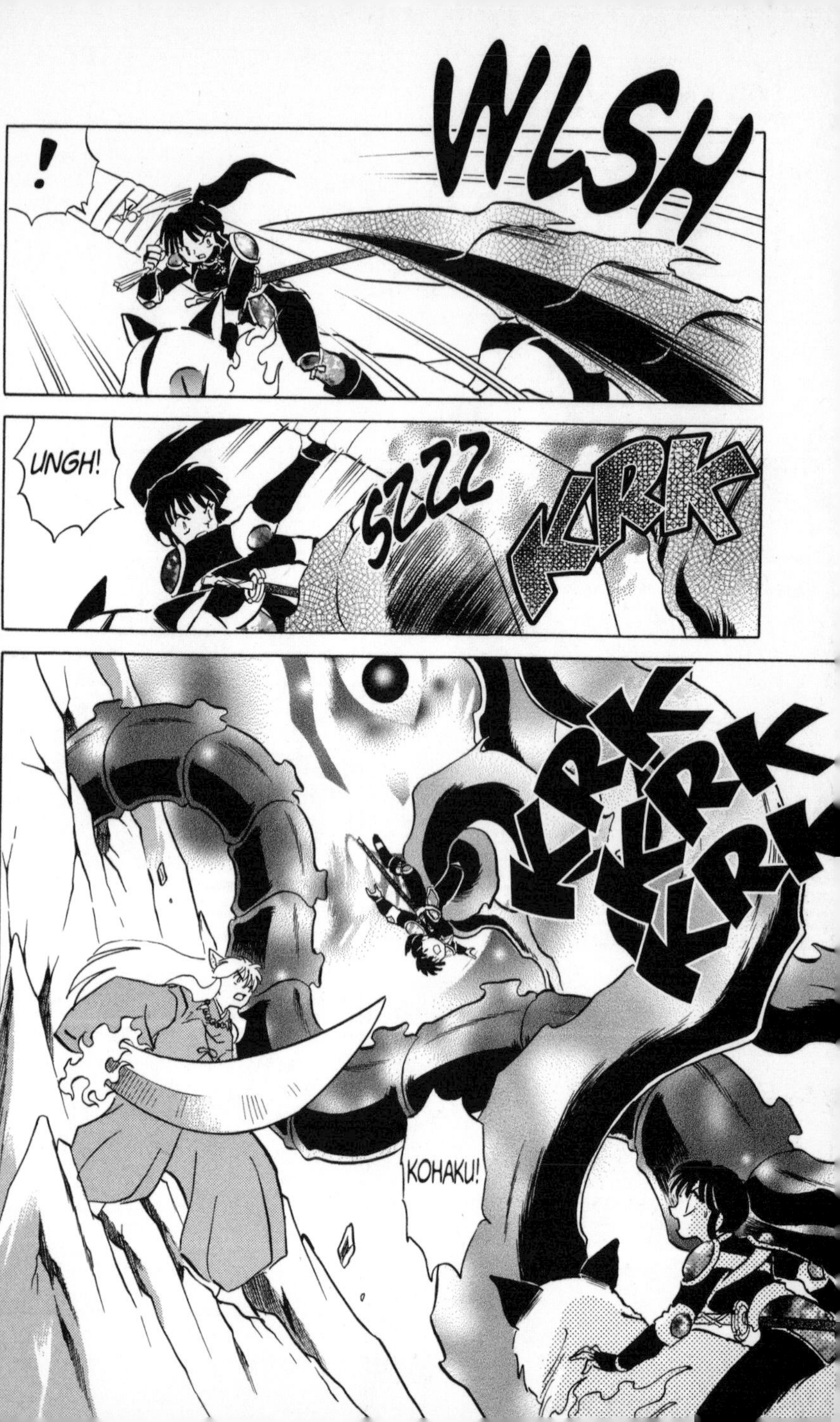
WLSH
!
KRK
SZZZ
UNGH!
KRK KRK KRK KRK
KOHAKU!

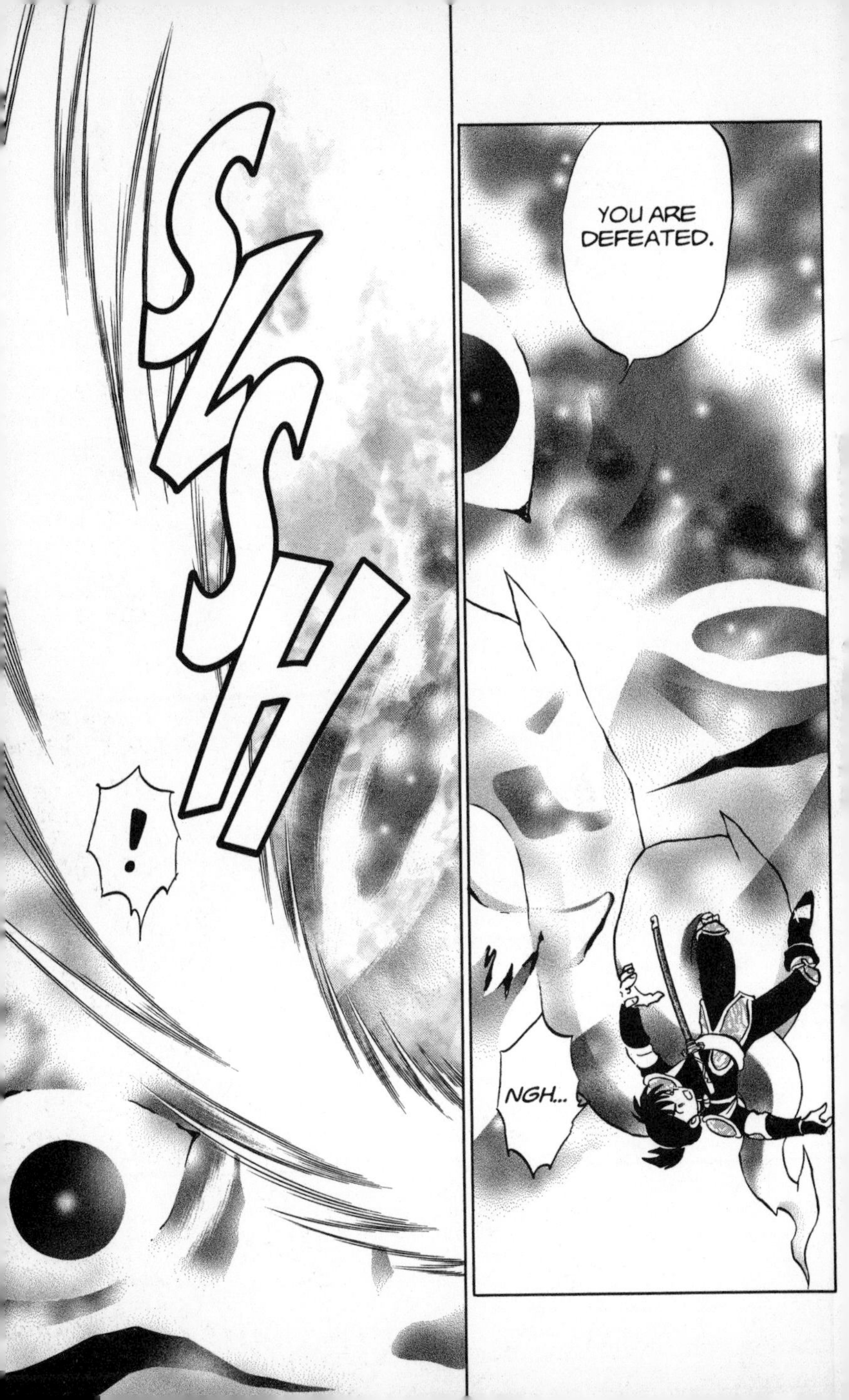
YOU ARE DEFEATED.
NGH...
SWSH
!

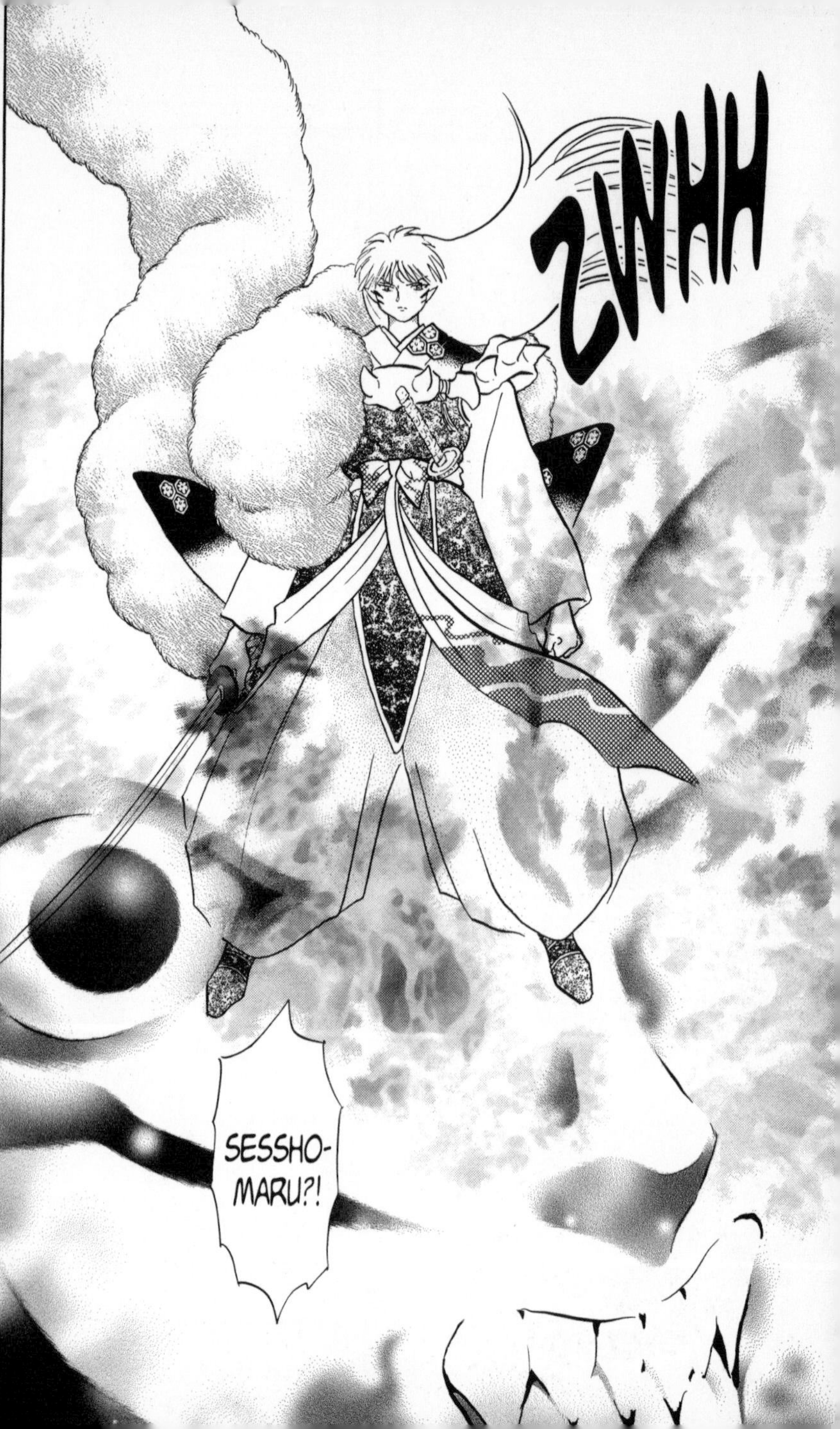
ZWHH
SESSHO-MARU?!

SCROLL 8
THE VANISHING POWERS

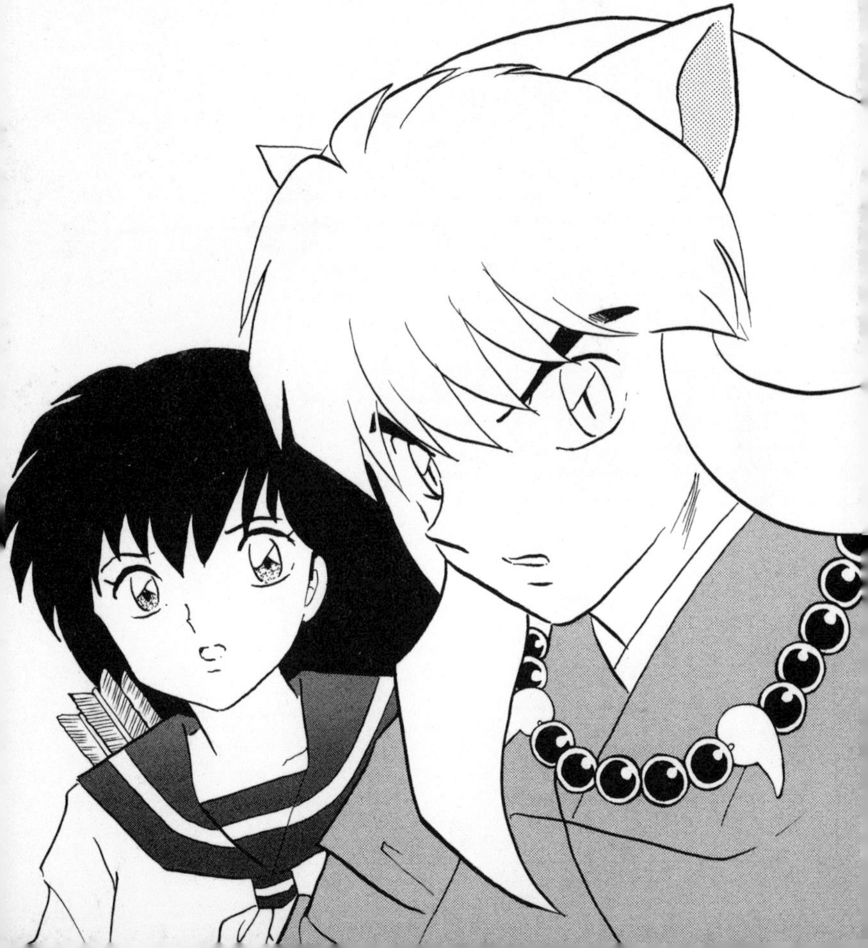

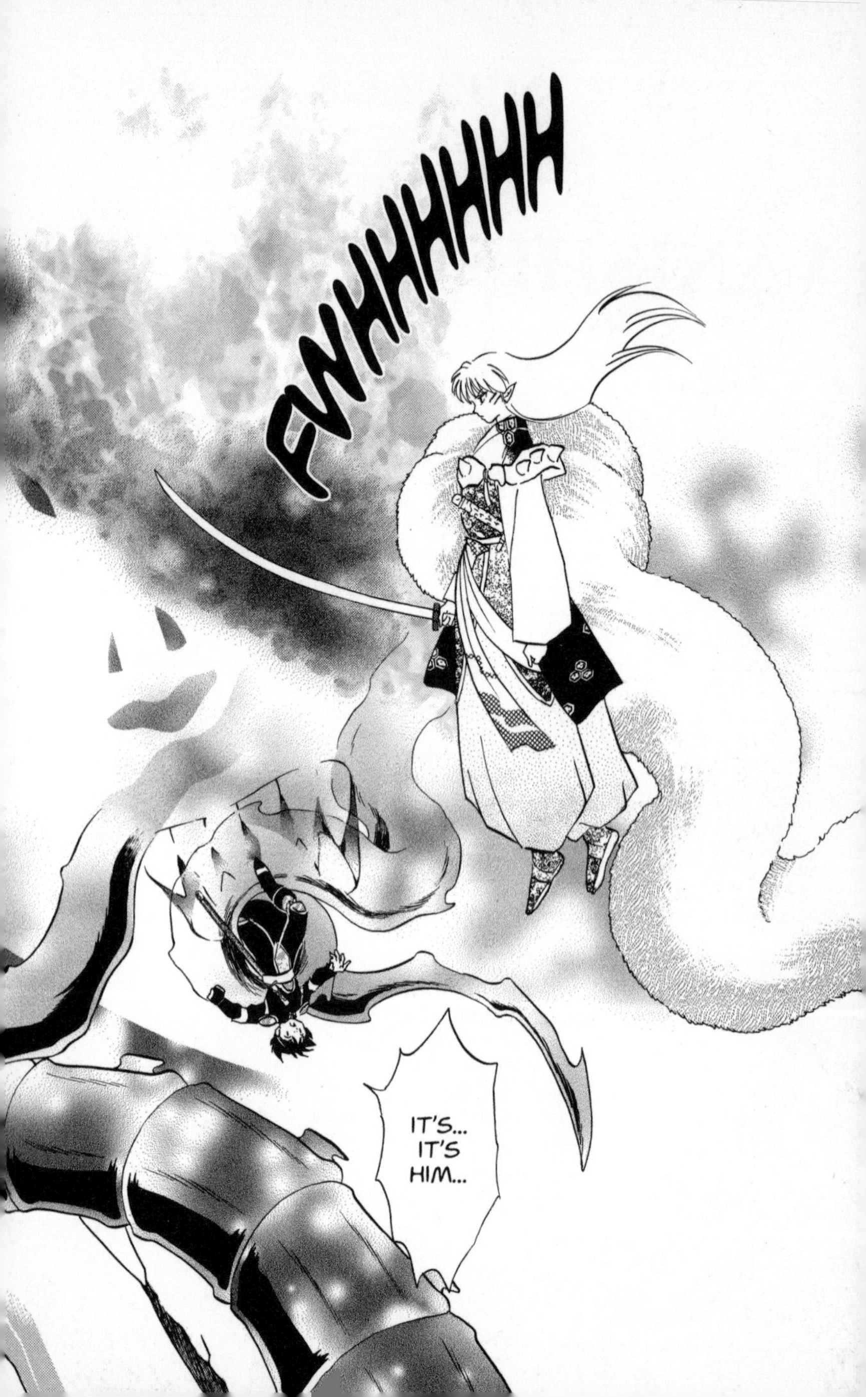
FWHHHHHH
IT'S... IT'S HIM...

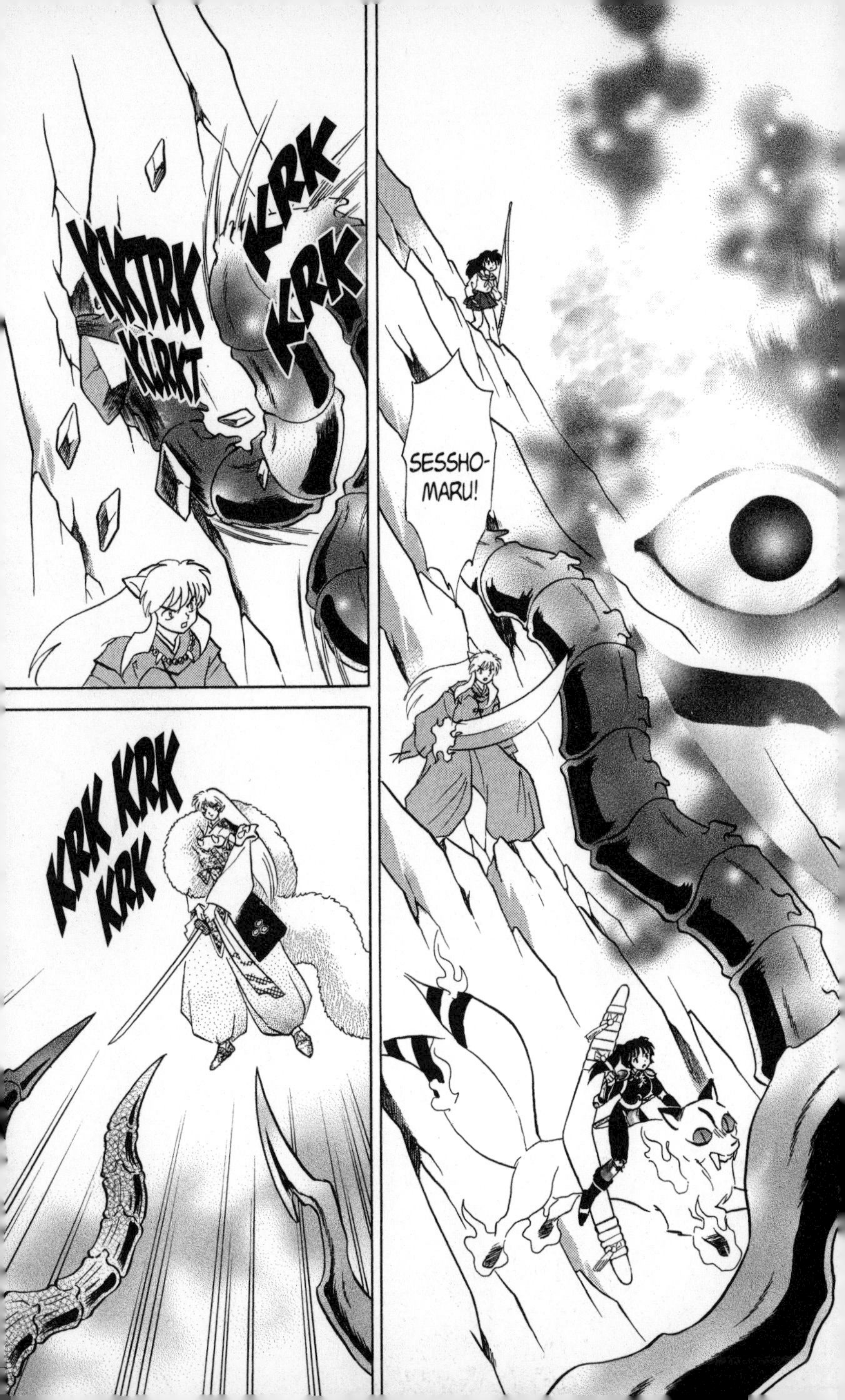
SESSHO-MARU!
KRK KRK
KKTRK KLRKT
KRK KRK KRK

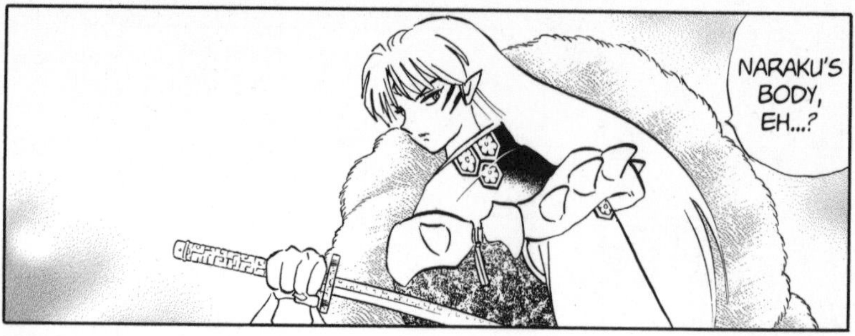
NARAKU'S BODY, EH...?

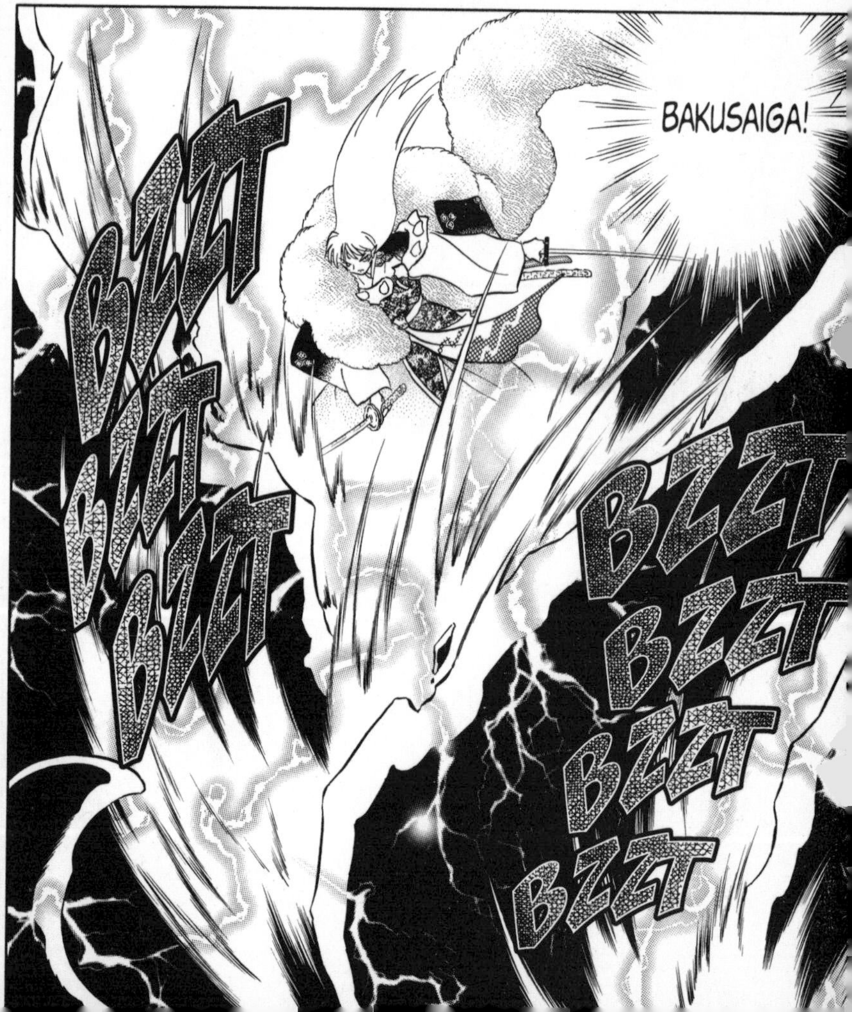
BAKUSAIGA!
BZZT BZZT BZZT BZZT
BZZT BZZT BZZT

BWP BWP

VWSH

KOHA-KU!

BZZT BZZT

WMP

!

WHOA...

BWP BWP

ANY PART OF HIS BODY THAT'S BEEN CUT BY BAKUSAIGA CAN NEVER BE RESTORED...

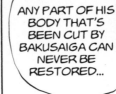

KOHA-KU!

SISTER!

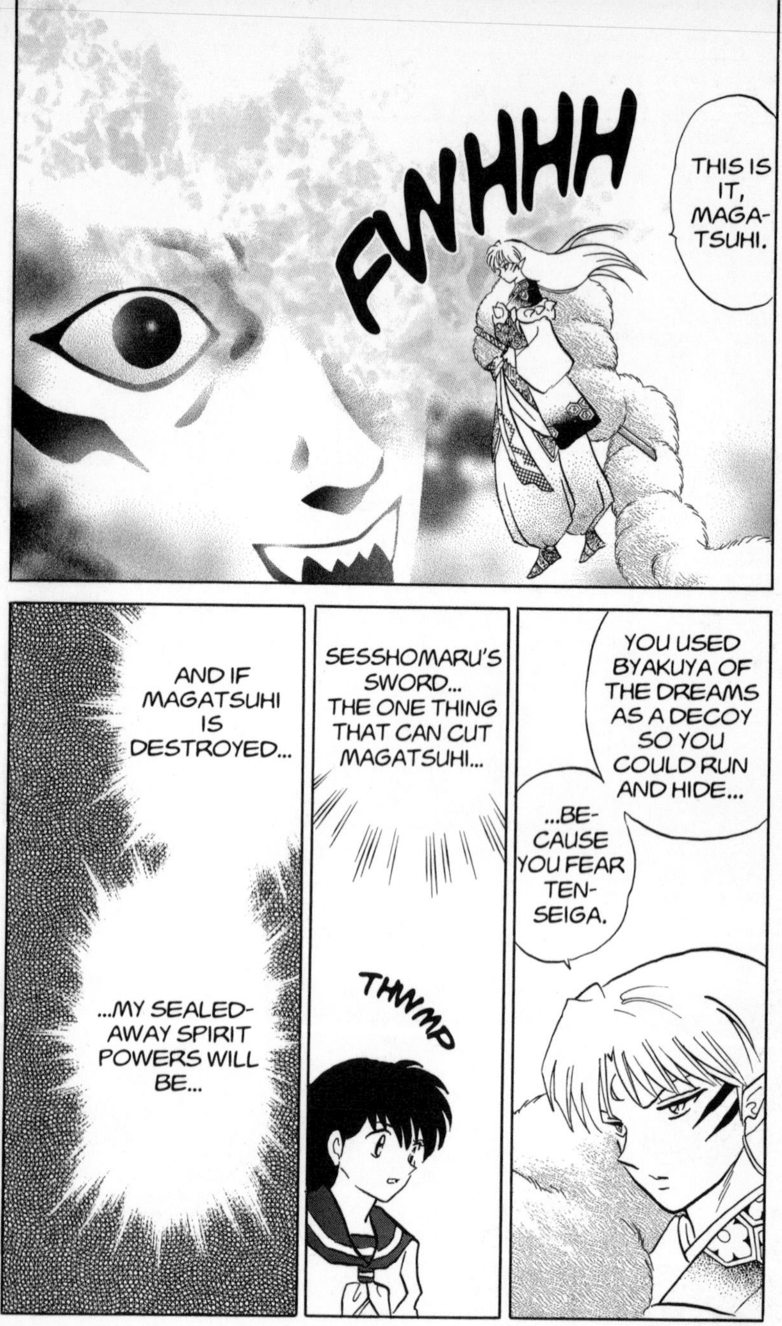
THIS IS IT, MAGATSUHI.
FWHHH
YOU USED BYAKUYA OF THE DREAMS AS A DECOY SO YOU COULD RUN AND HIDE...
...BECAUSE YOU FEAR TENSEIGA.
SESSHOMARU'S SWORD... THE ONE THING THAT CAN CUT MAGATSUHI...
THWMP
AND IF MAGATSUHI IS DESTROYED...
...MY SEALED-AWAY SPIRIT POWERS WILL BE...

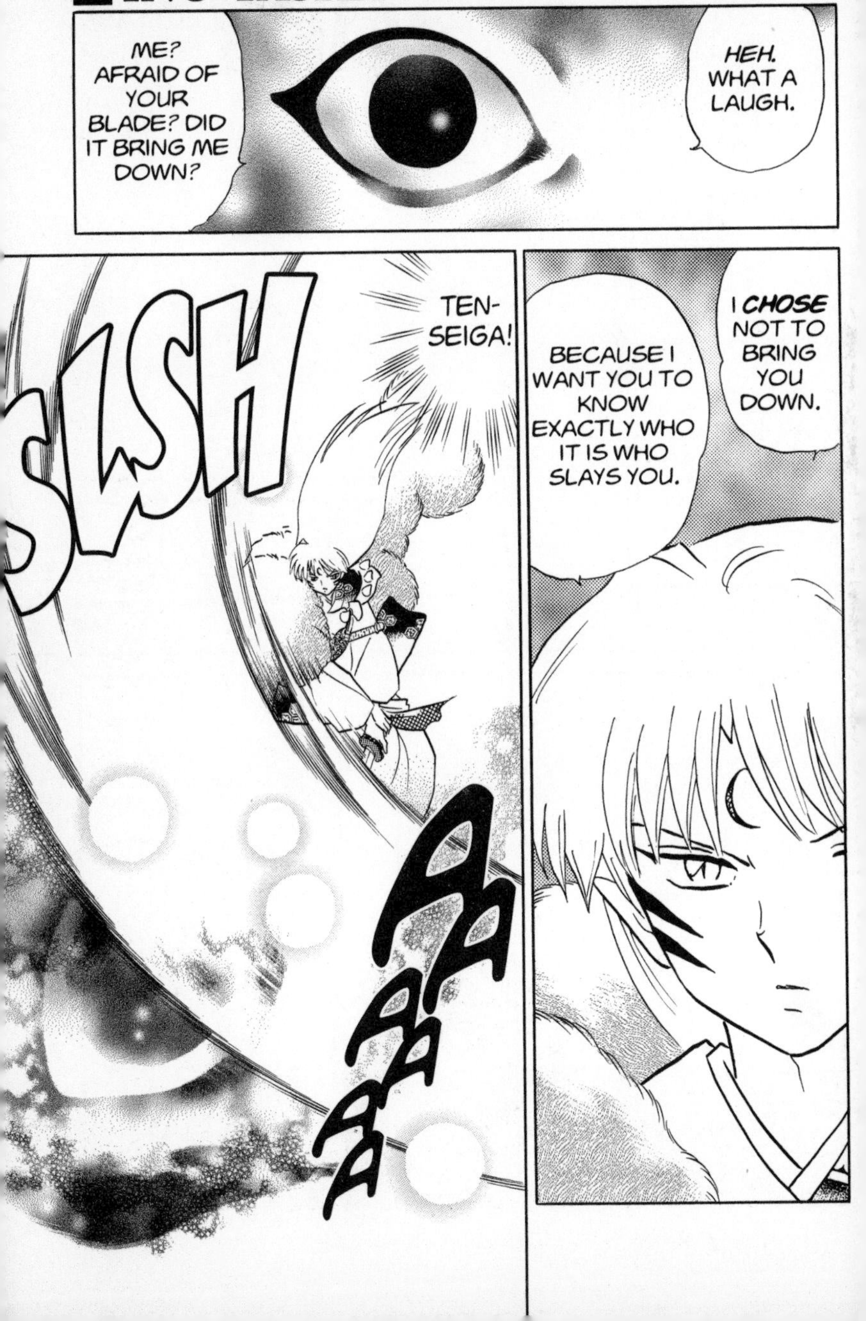
HEH. WHAT A LAUGH.
ME? AFRAID OF YOUR BLADE? DID IT BRING ME DOWN?
I *CHOSE* NOT TO BRING YOU DOWN.
BECAUSE I WANT YOU TO KNOW EXACTLY WHO IT IS WHO SLAYS YOU.
TEN-SEIGA!
SLSH

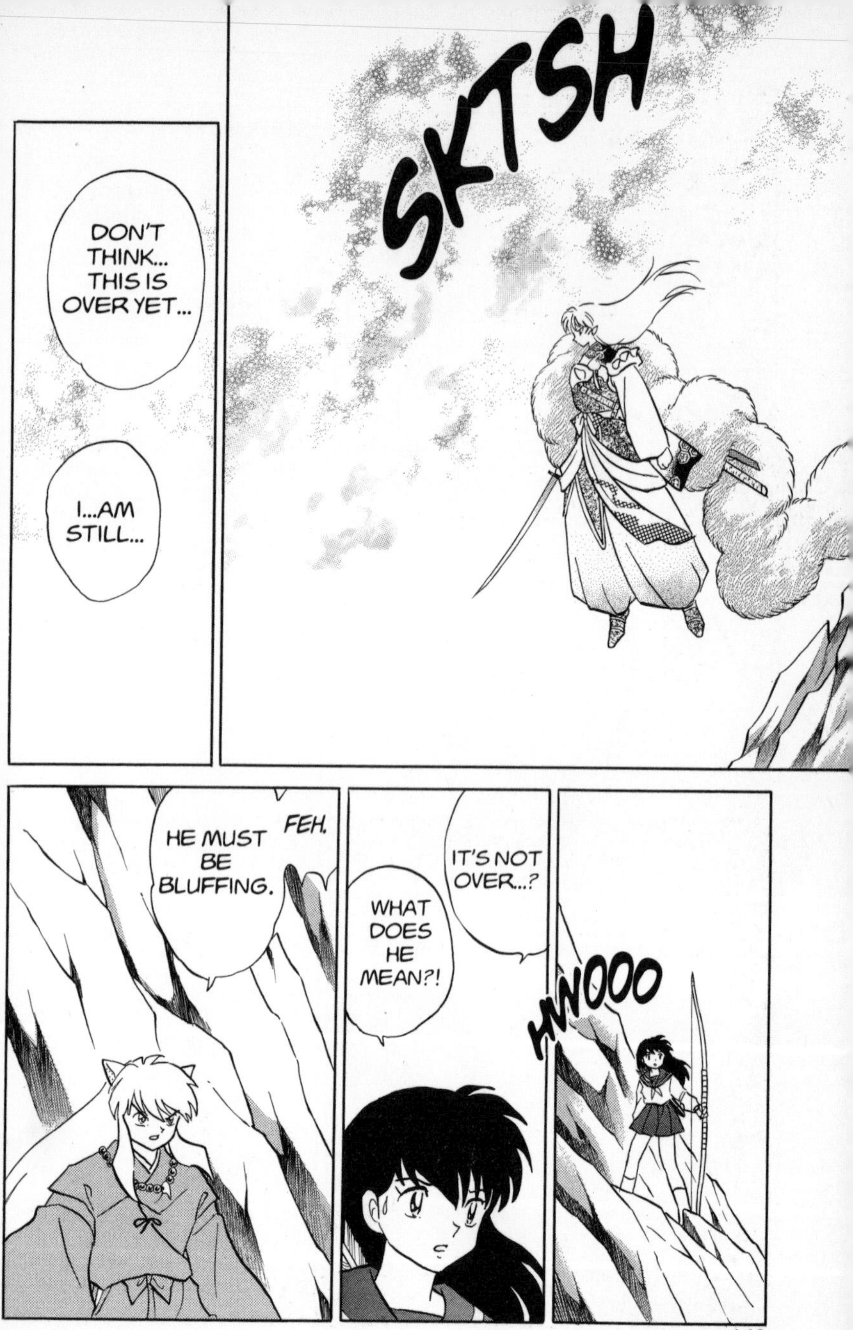
SKTSH
DON'T THINK... THIS IS OVER YET...
I...AM STILL...
HWOOO
IT'S NOT OVER...?
WHAT DOES HE MEAN?!
FEH.
HE MUST BE BLUFFING.

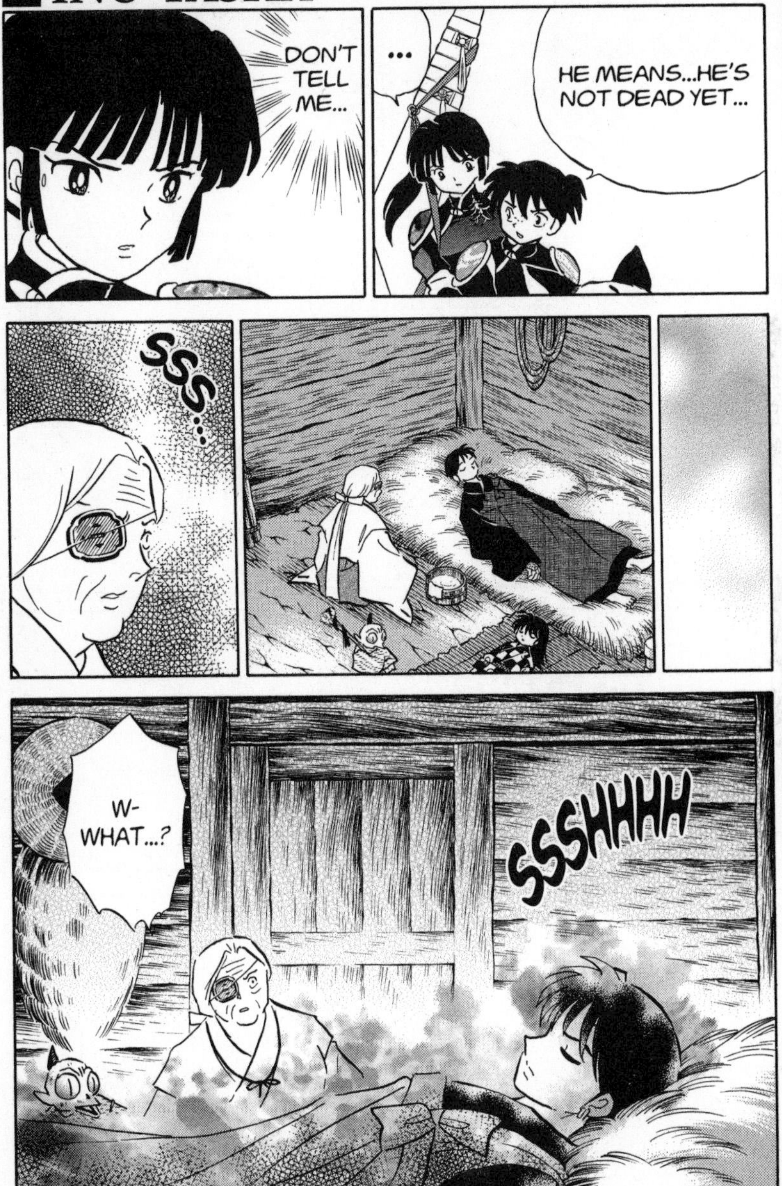
HE MEANS...HE'S NOT DEAD YET...
...
DON'T TELL ME...
SSS...
SSSHHHH
W-WHAT...?

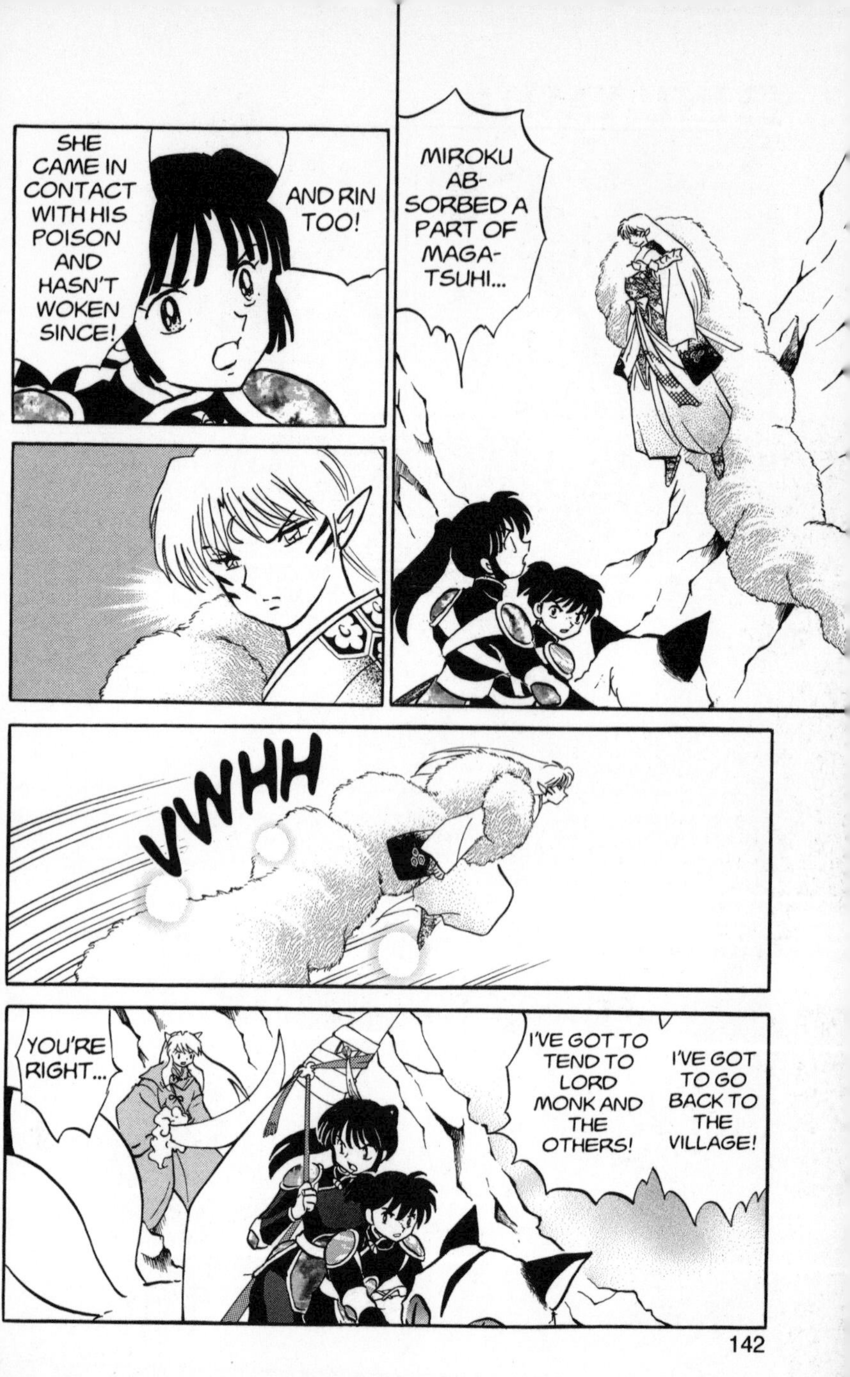
MIROKU ABSORBED A PART OF MAGATSUHI...
SHE CAME IN CONTACT WITH HIS POISON AND HASN'T WOKEN SINCE!
AND RIN TOO!
VWHH
I'VE GOT TO GO BACK TO THE VILLAGE!
I'VE GOT TO TEND TO LORD MONK AND THE OTHERS!
YOU'RE RIGHT...

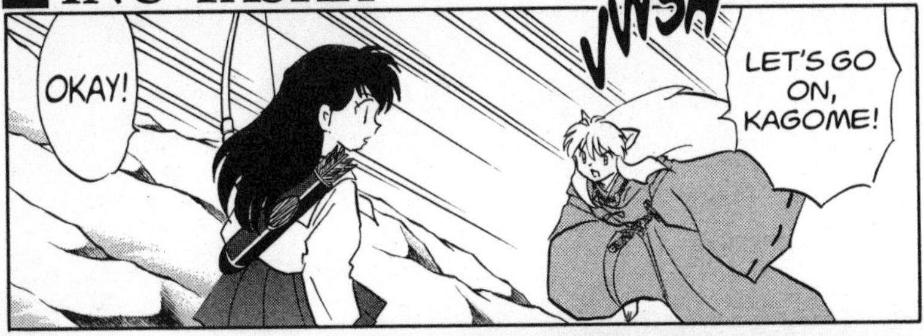
VWSH
LET'S GO ON, KAGOME!
OKAY!

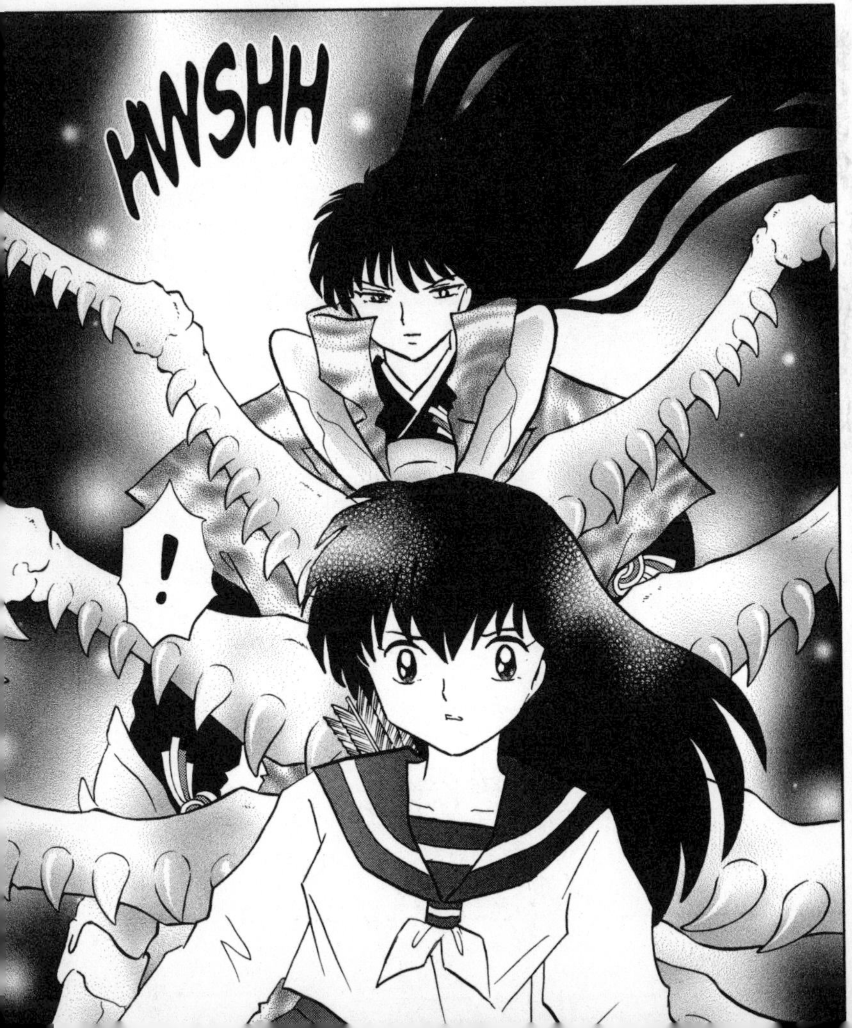
HWSHH
!

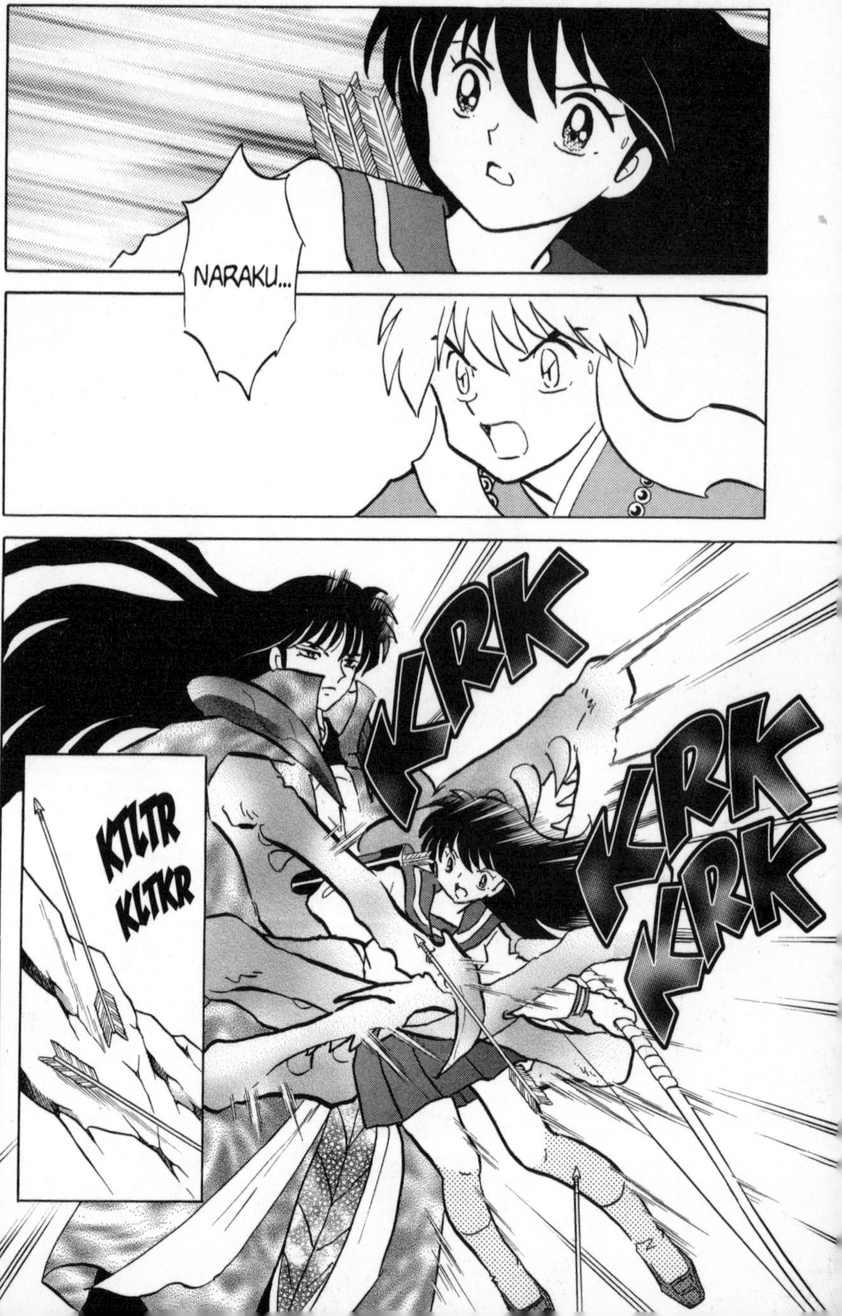
NARAKU...
KRK
KRK
KRK
KTLTR
KLTKR

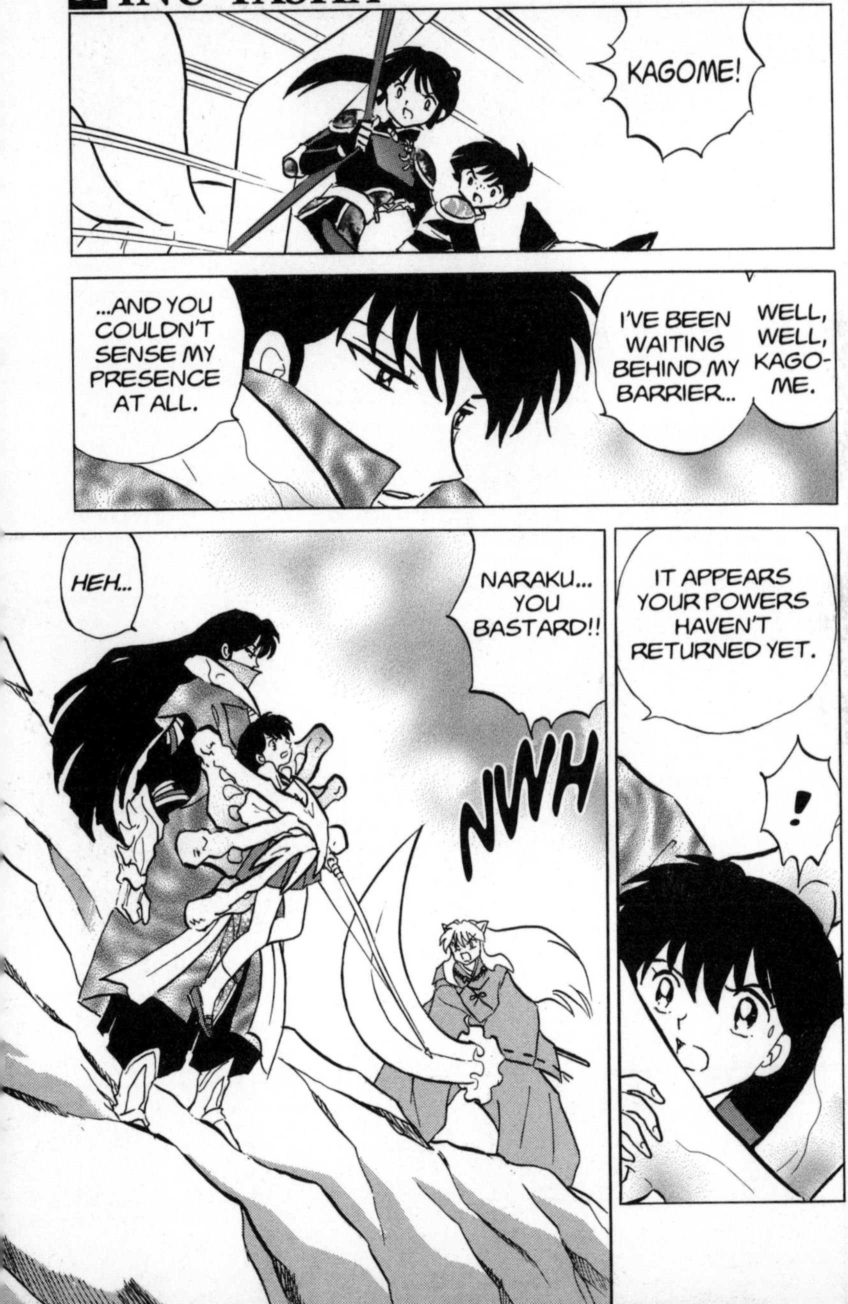
KAGOME!
WELL, WELL, KAGOME.
I'VE BEEN WAITING BEHIND MY BARRIER...
...AND YOU COULDN'T SENSE MY PRESENCE AT ALL.
IT APPEARS YOUR POWERS HAVEN'T RETURNED YET.
!
NARAKU... YOU BASTARD!!
HEH...
NWH

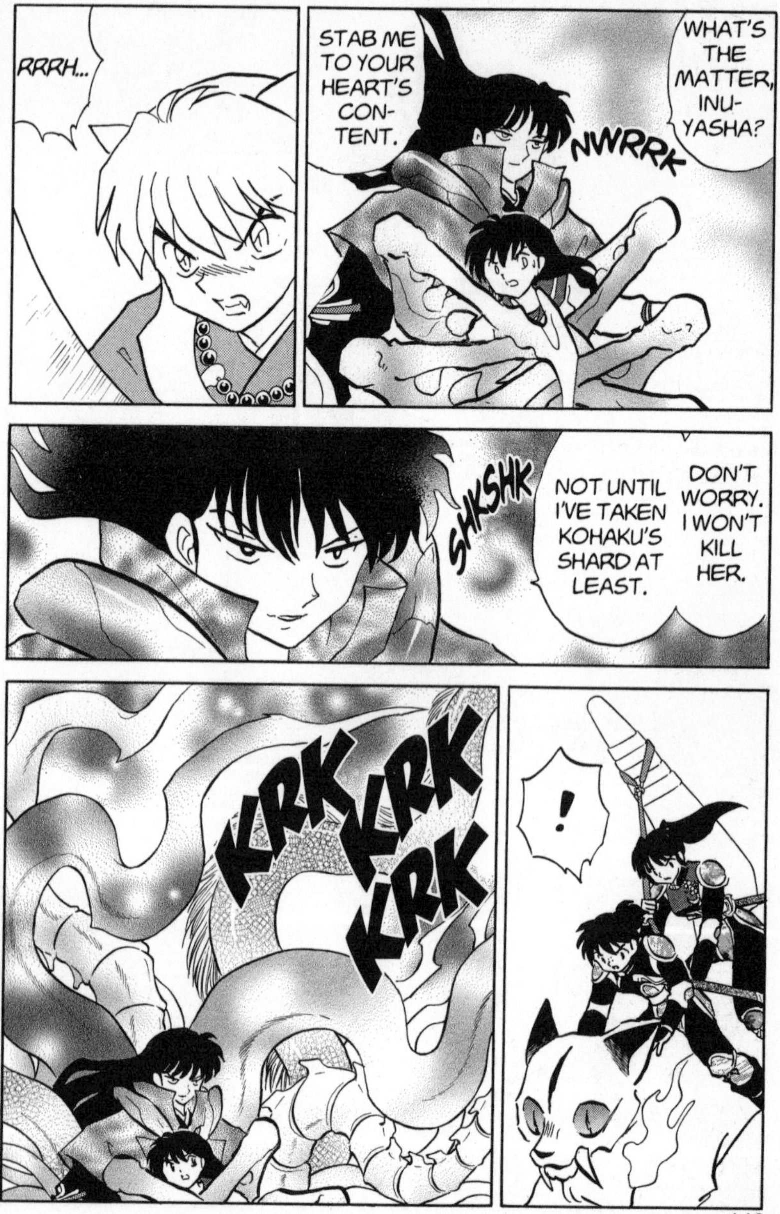
WHAT'S THE MATTER, INU-YASHA?
STAB ME TO YOUR HEART'S CON-TENT.
NWRRK
RRRH...
DON'T WORRY. I WON'T KILL HER.
NOT UNTIL I'VE TAKEN KOHAKU'S SHARD AT LEAST.
SHKSHK
!
KRK KRK KRK

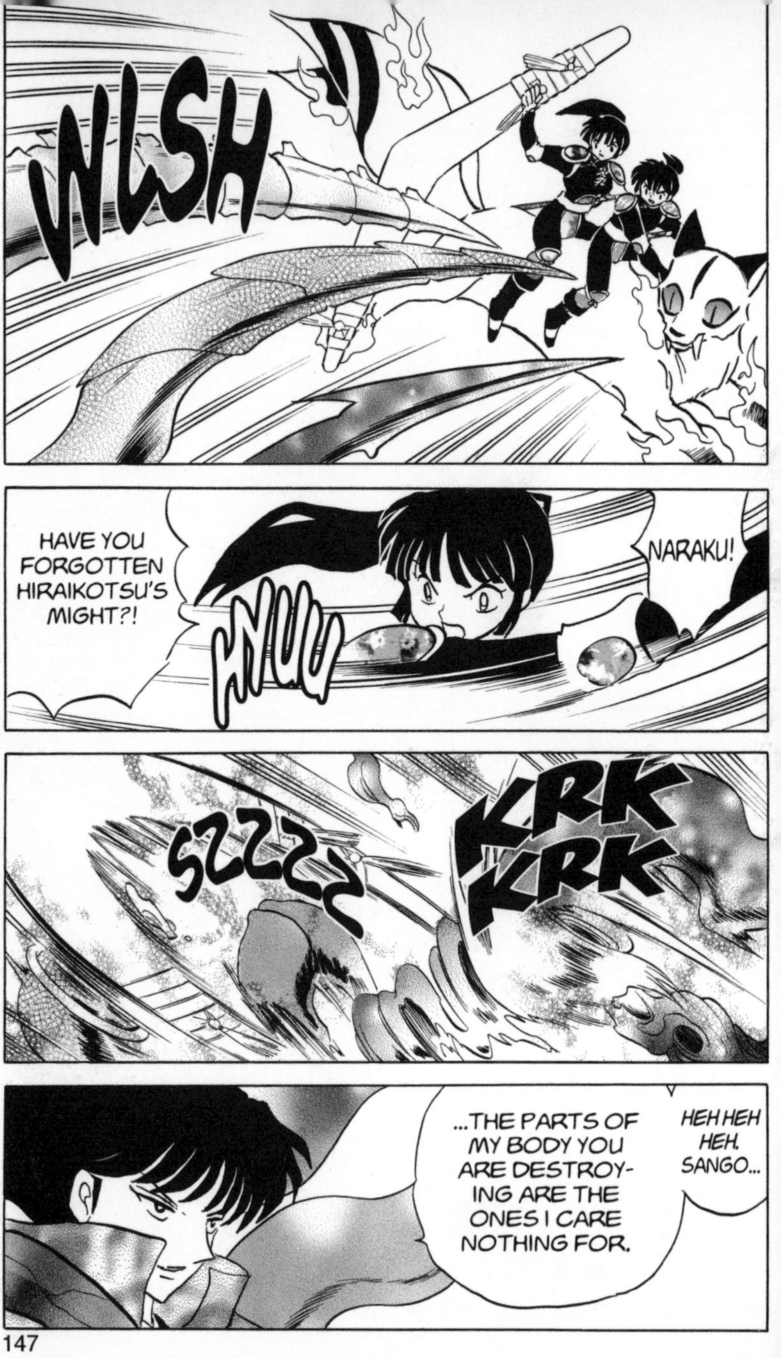
WLSH
NARAKU!
HAVE YOU FORGOTTEN HIRAIKOTSU'S MIGHT?!
KRK KRK
SZZZZ
HEH HEH HEH. SANGO...
...THE PARTS OF MY BODY YOU ARE DESTROY-ING ARE THE ONES I CARE NOTHING FOR.

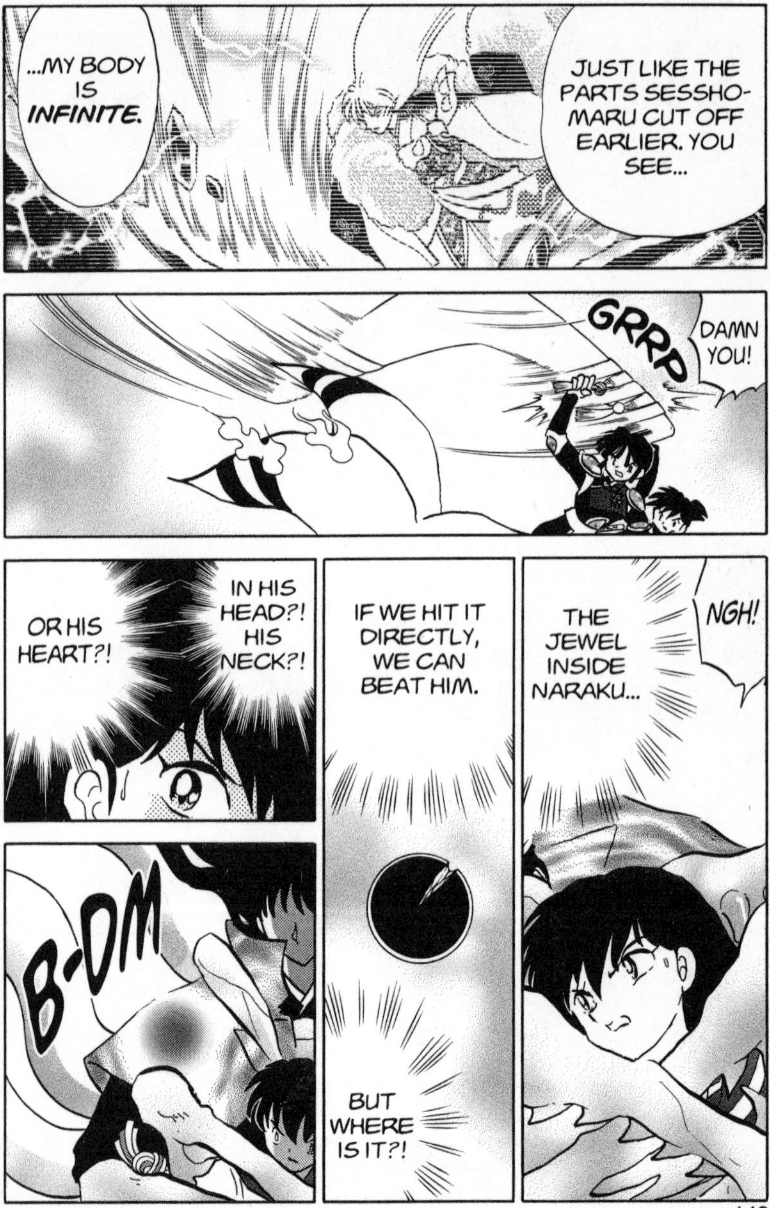

JUST LIKE THE PARTS SESSHO-MARU CUT OFF EARLIER. YOU SEE...
...MY BODY IS *INFINITE.*
DAMN YOU!
GRRP
NGH!
THE JEWEL INSIDE NARAKU...
IF WE HIT IT DIRECTLY, WE CAN BEAT HIM.
BUT WHERE IS IT?!
IN HIS HEAD?! HIS NECK?!
OR HIS HEART?!
B-DM

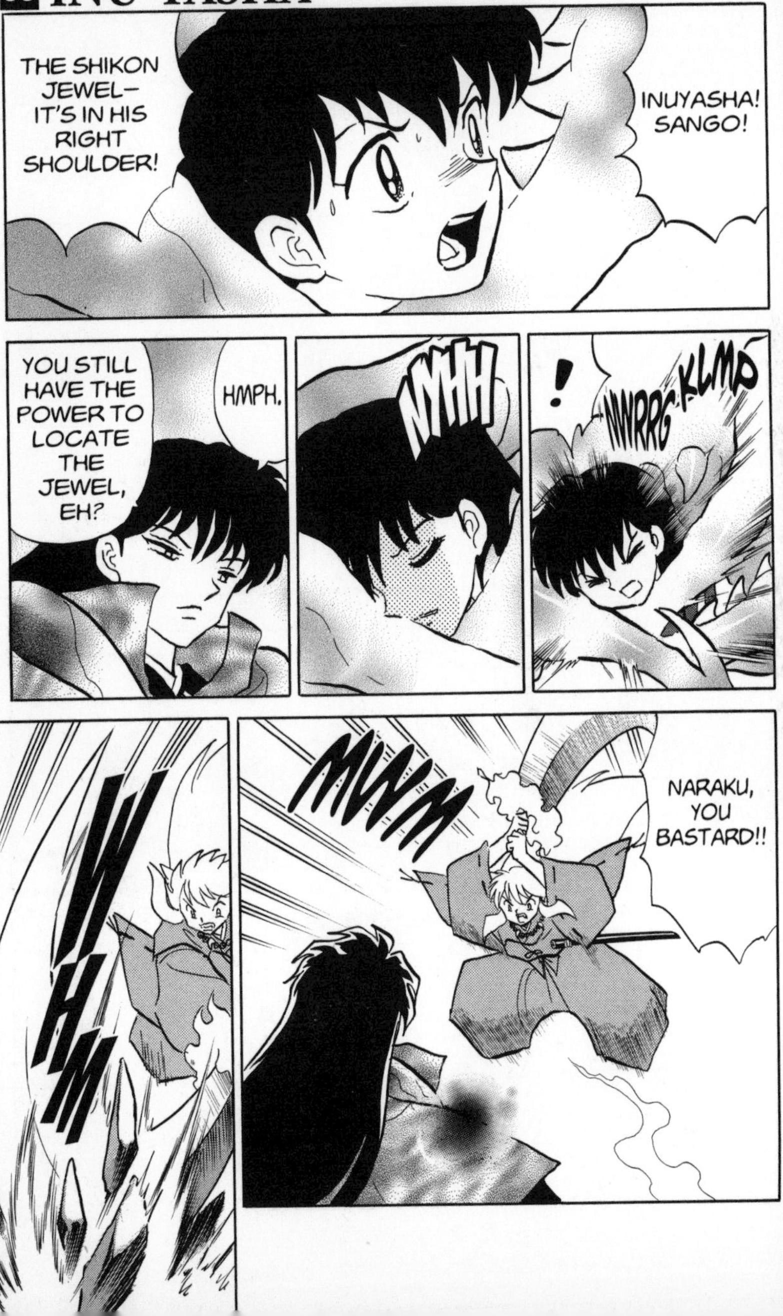
INUYASHA! SANGO!
THE SHIKON JEWEL— IT'S IN HIS RIGHT SHOULDER!
!
KLMP
NNRRG
NYHH
HMPH.
YOU STILL HAVE THE POWER TO LOCATE THE JEWEL, EH?
NARAKU, YOU BASTARD!!

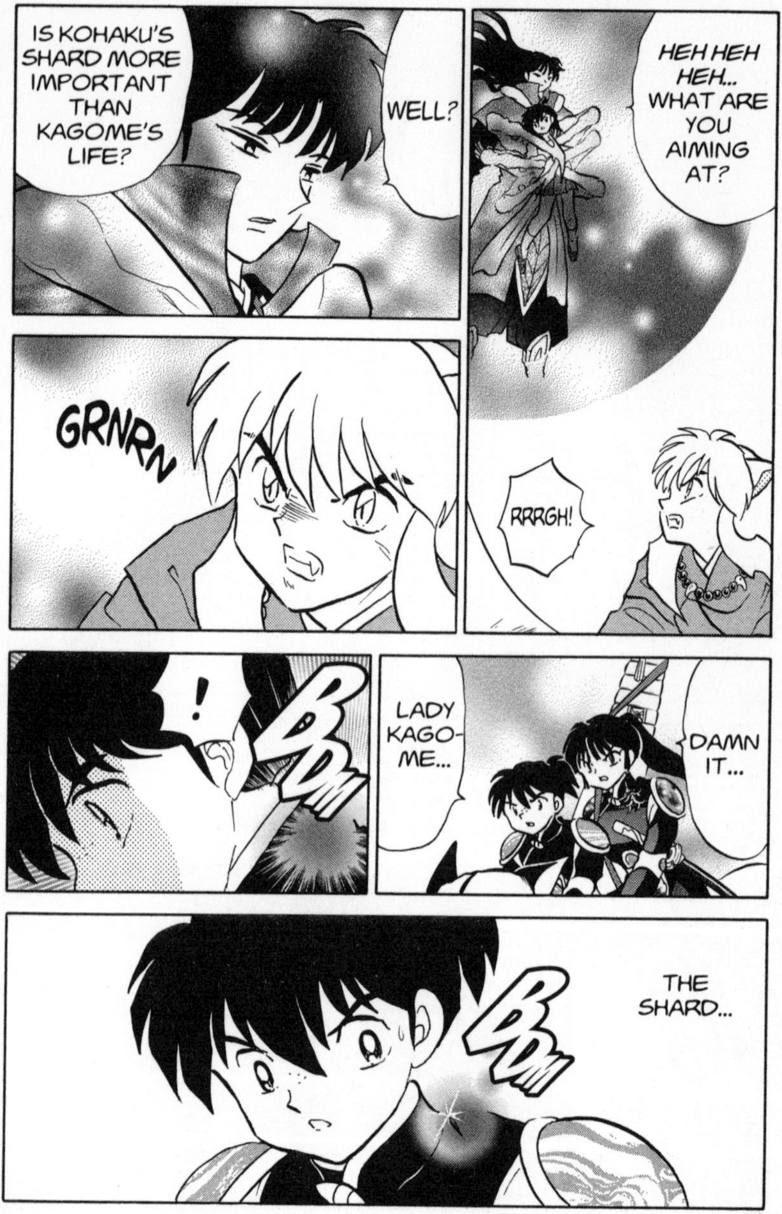
HEH HEH HEH... WHAT ARE YOU AIMING AT?
RRRGH!
IS KOHAKU'S SHARD MORE IMPORTANT THAN KAGOME'S LIFE?
WELL?
GRNRN
DAMN IT...
LADY KAGOME...
!
BDM
THE SHARD...
BDM

SCROLL 9

A LIFE ONCE LOST

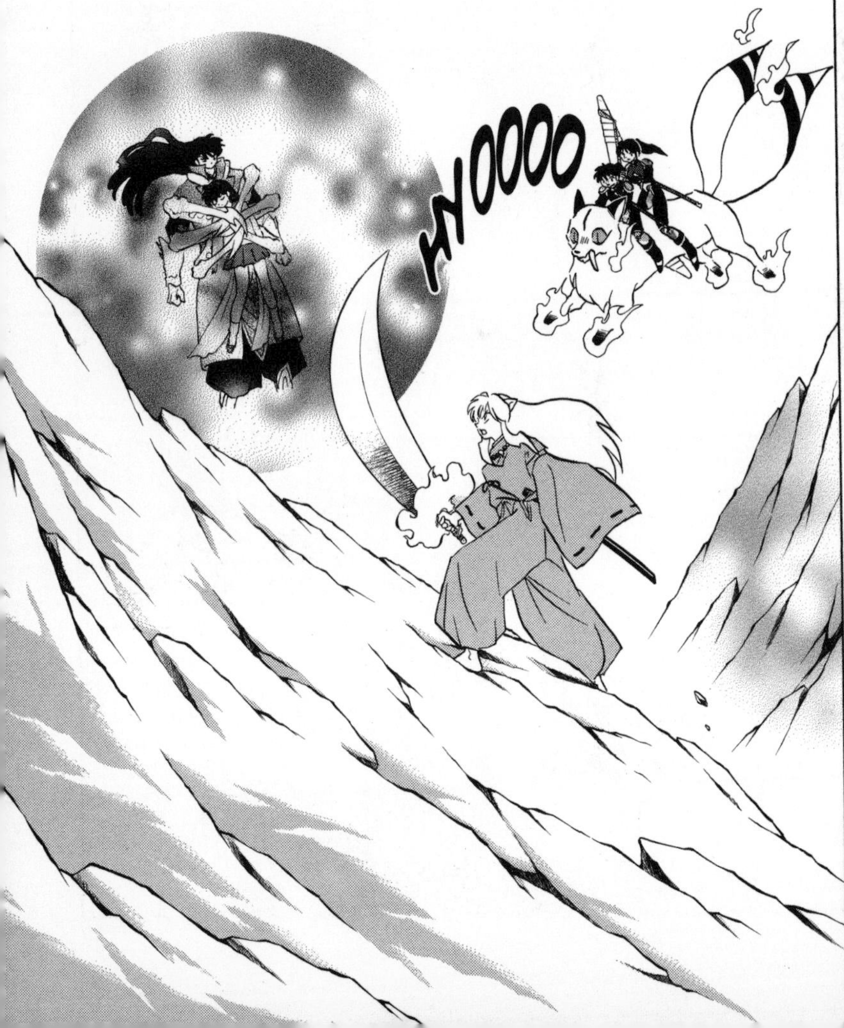
HYOOOO

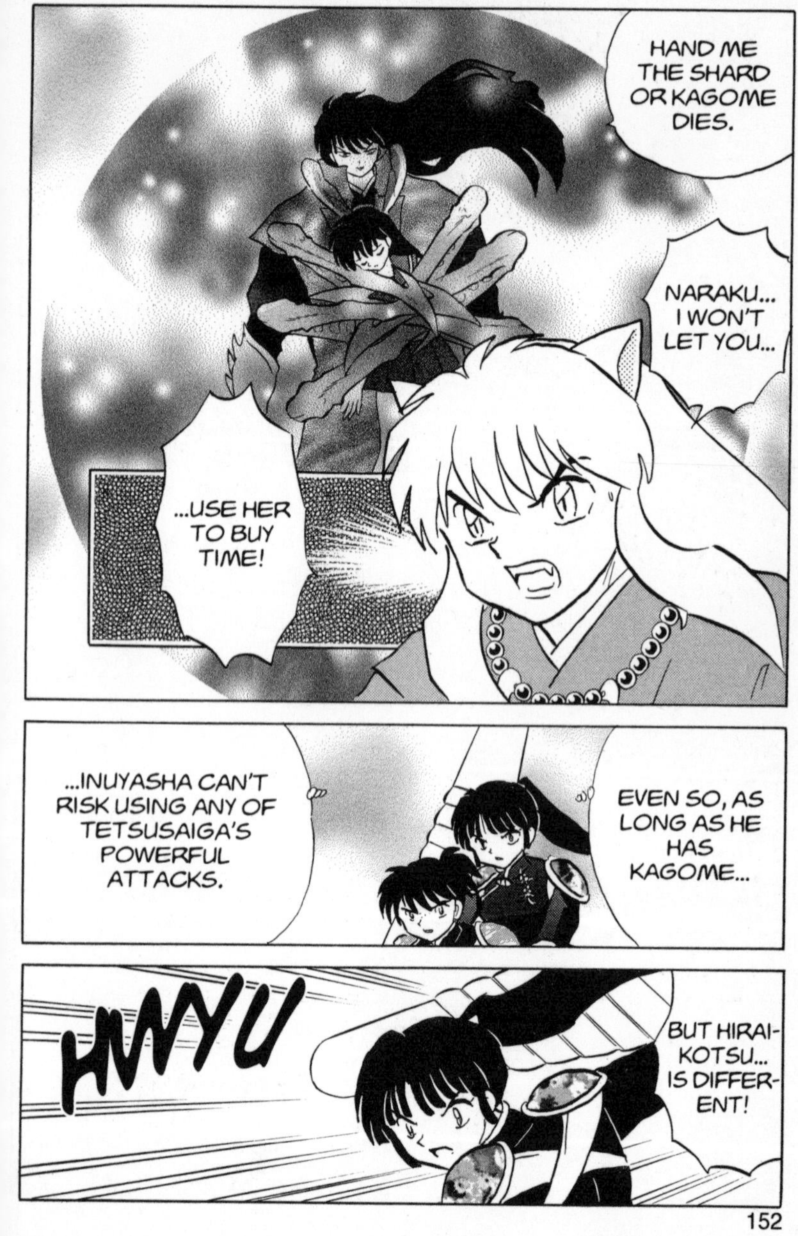
HAND ME THE SHARD OR KAGOME DIES.
NARAKU... I WON'T LET YOU...
...USE HER TO BUY TIME!
EVEN SO, AS LONG AS HE HAS KAGOME...
...INUYASHA CAN'T RISK USING ANY OF TETSUSAIGA'S POWERFUL ATTACKS.
BUT HIRAI-KOTSU... IS DIFFER-ENT!
HWYU

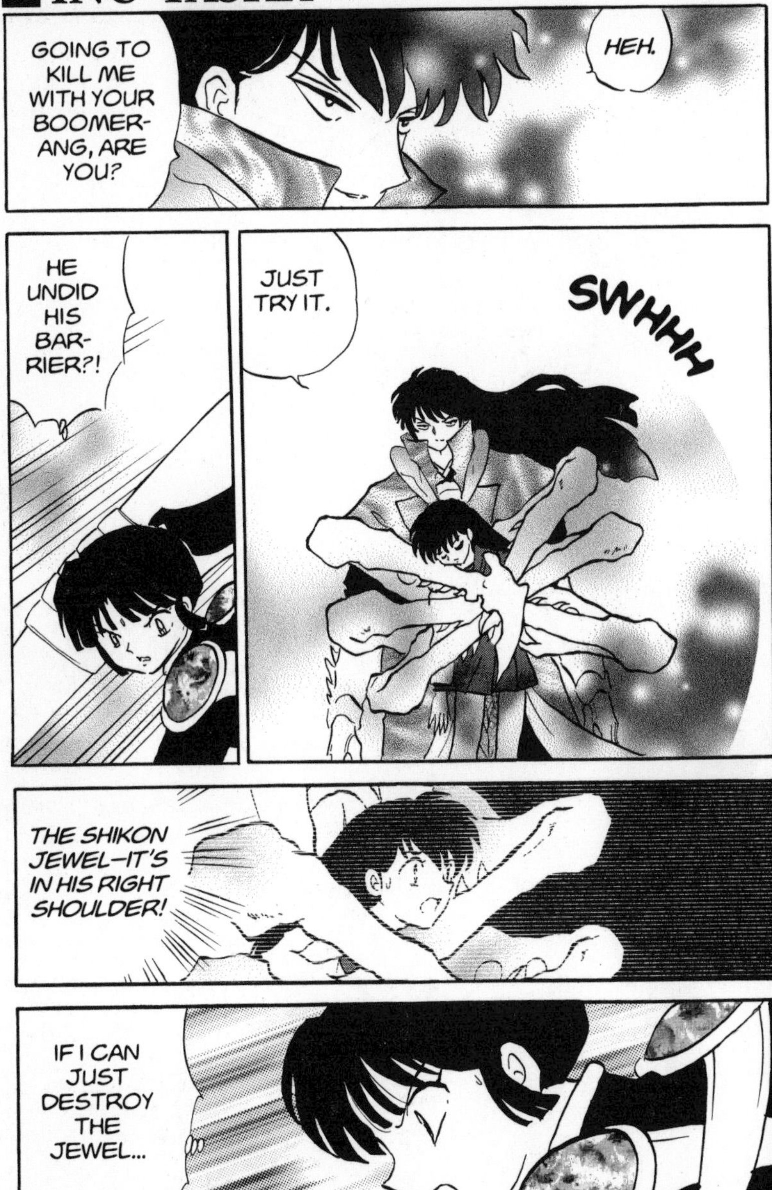
HEH.
GOING TO KILL ME WITH YOUR BOOMER-ANG, ARE YOU?
JUST TRY IT.
SWHHH
HE UNDID HIS BAR-RIER?!
THE SHIKON JEWEL–IT'S IN HIS RIGHT SHOULDER!
IF I CAN JUST DESTROY THE JEWEL...

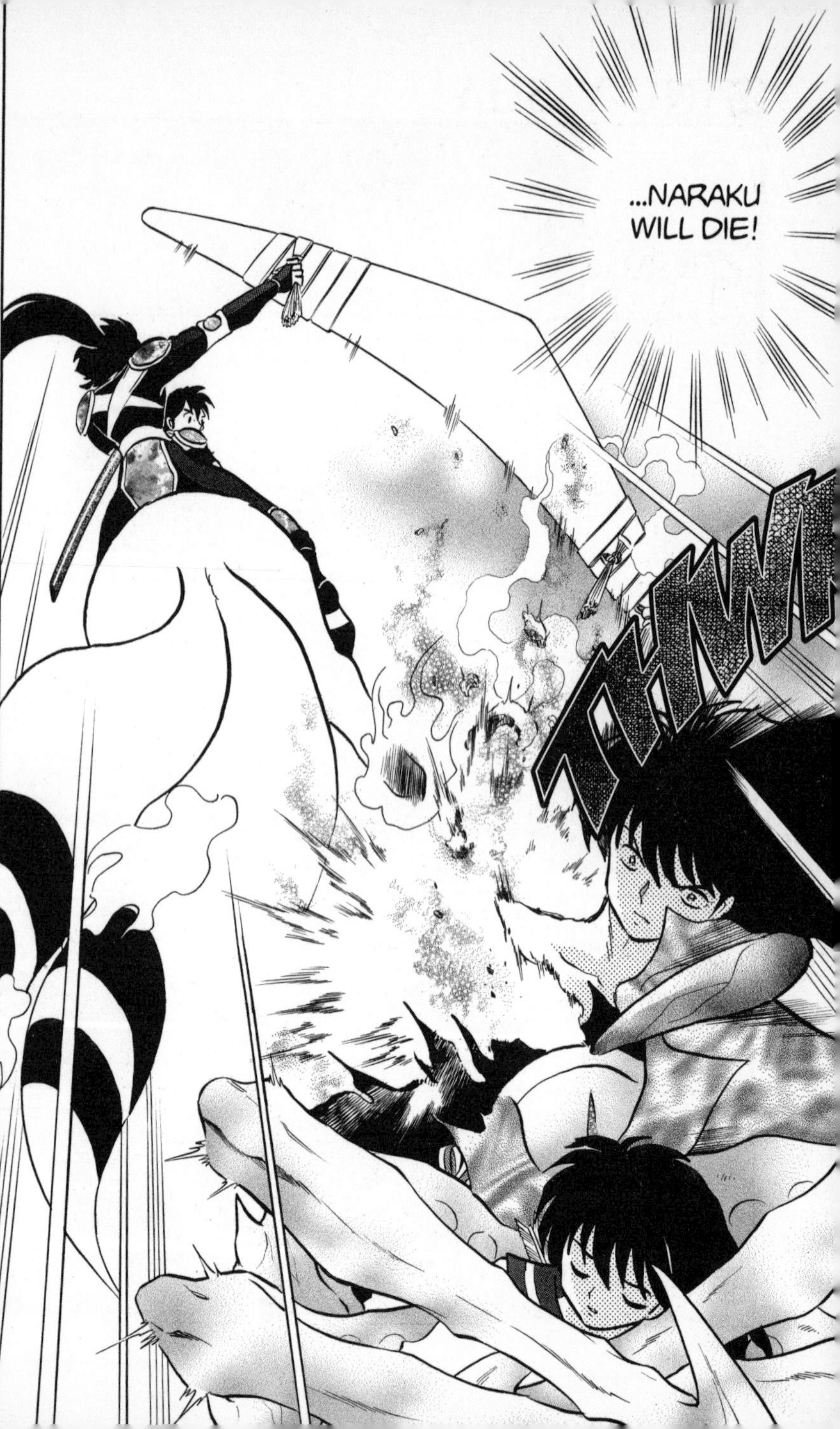
...NARAKU
WILL DIE!

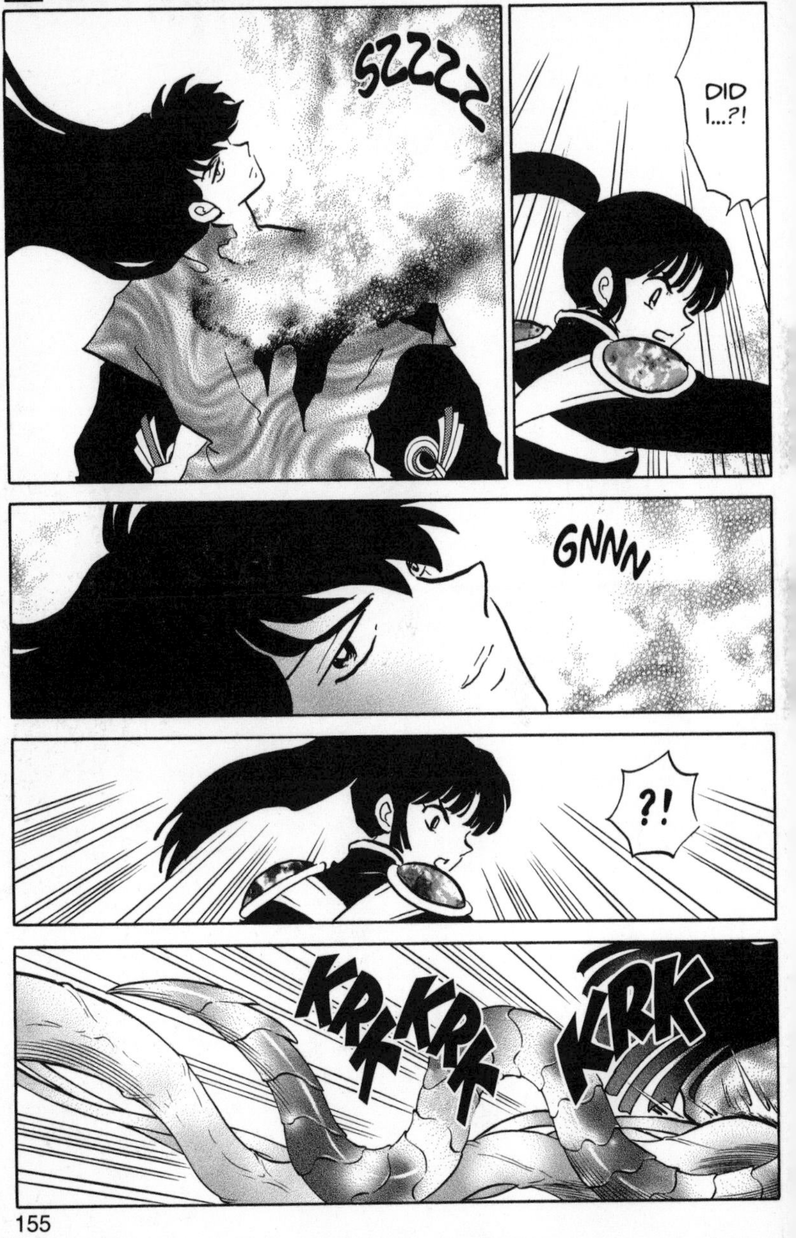
DID I...?!
SZZZZ
GNNN
?!
KRK
KRK KRK

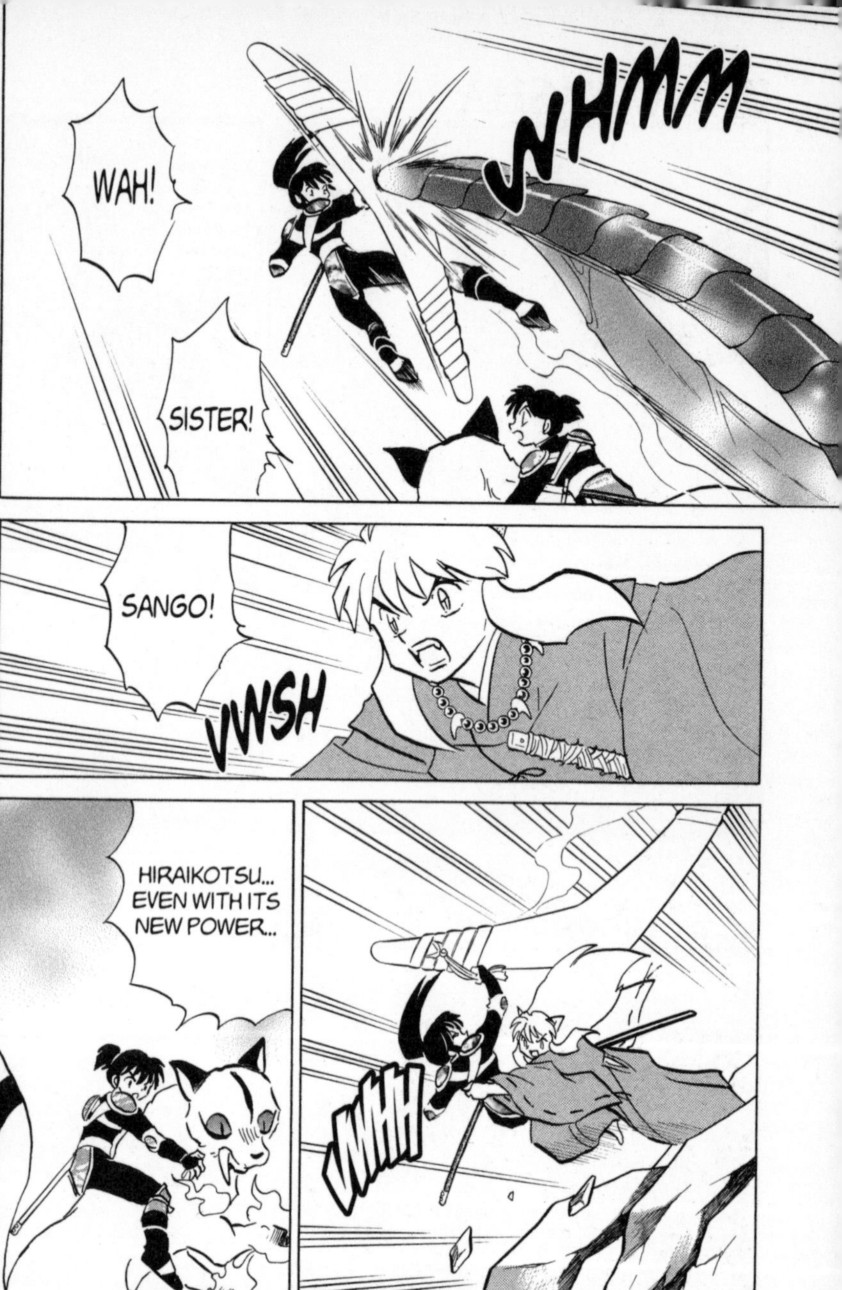
WHMM
WAH!
SISTER!
SANGO!
VWSH
VWHH
HIRAIKOTSU... EVEN WITH ITS NEW POWER...

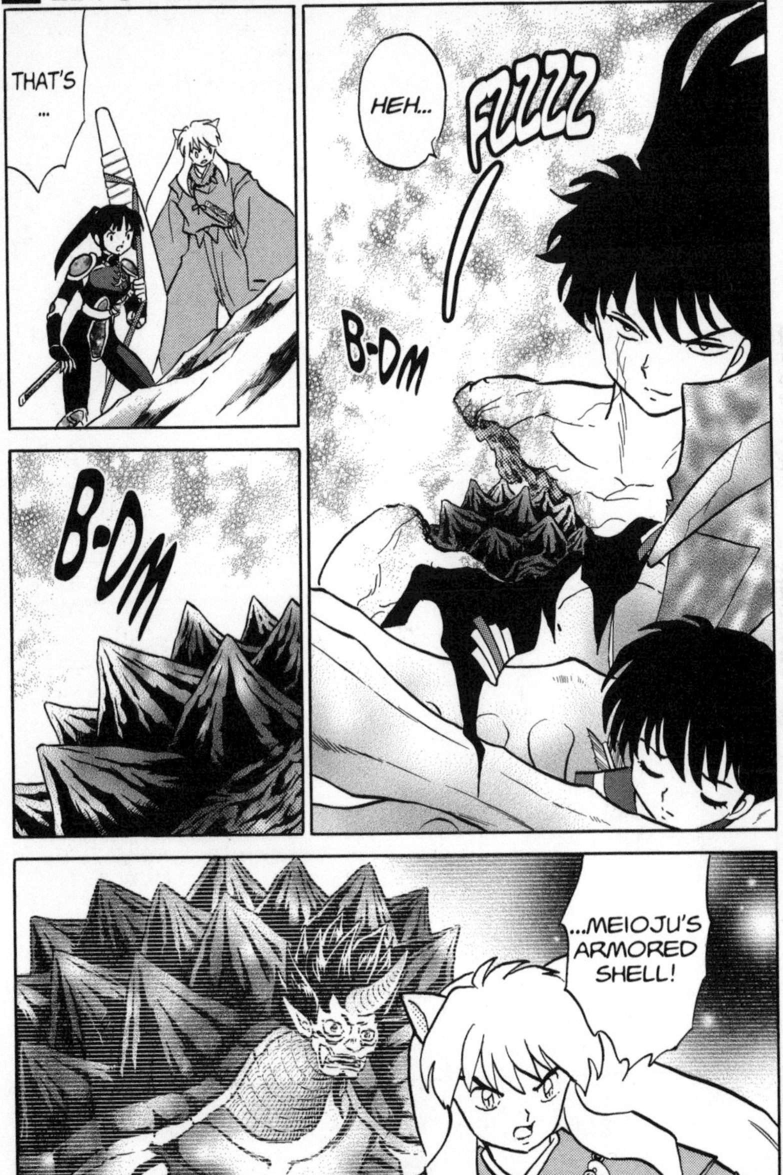
HEH...
FZZZZ
B-DM
THAT'S ...
B-DM
...MEIOJU'S ARMORED SHELL!

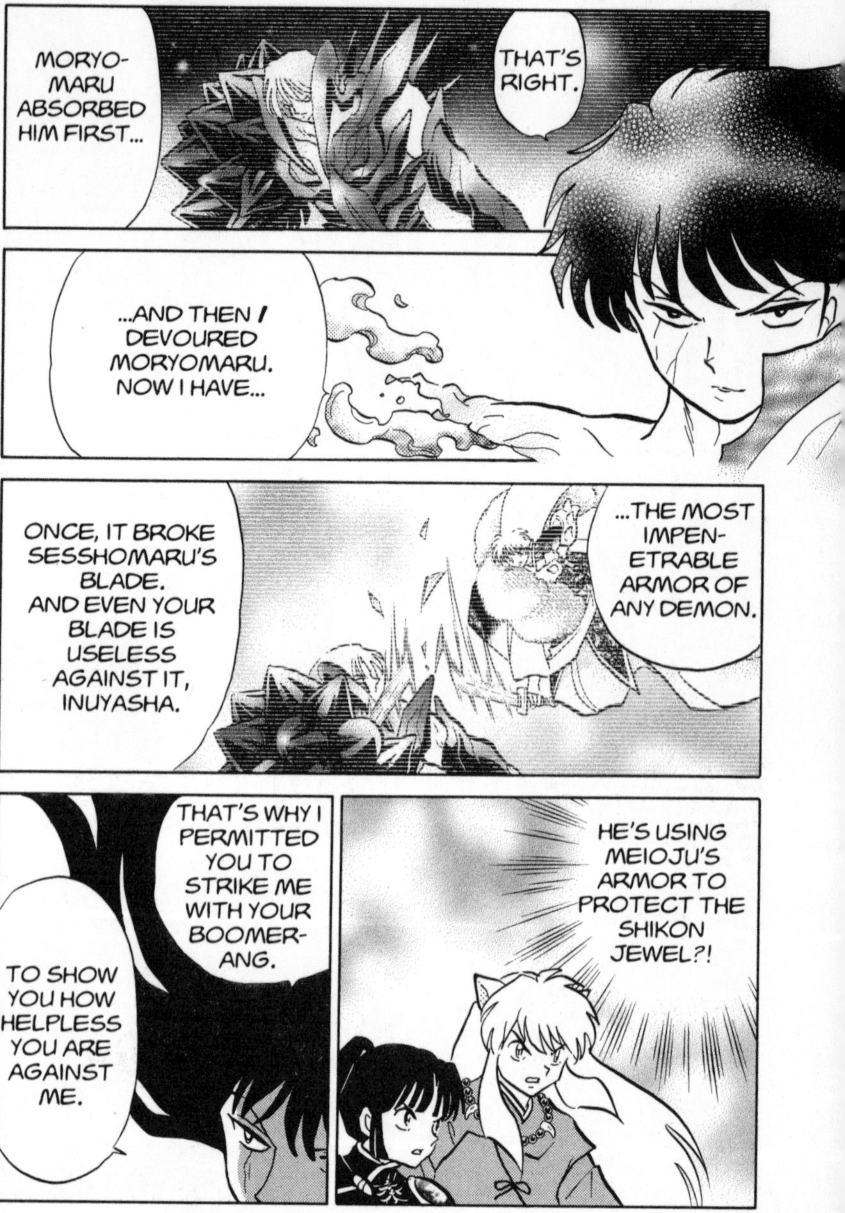
THAT'S RIGHT.
MORYO-MARU ABSORBED HIM FIRST...
...AND THEN I DEVOURED MORYOMARU. NOW I HAVE...
...THE MOST IMPEN-ETRABLE ARMOR OF ANY DEMON.
ONCE, IT BROKE SESSHOMARU'S BLADE. AND EVEN YOUR BLADE IS USELESS AGAINST IT, INUYASHA.
HE'S USING MEIOJU'S ARMOR TO PROTECT THE SHIKON JEWEL?!
THAT'S WHY I PERMITTED YOU TO STRIKE ME WITH YOUR BOOMER-ANG.
TO SHOW YOU HOW HELPLESS YOU ARE AGAINST ME.

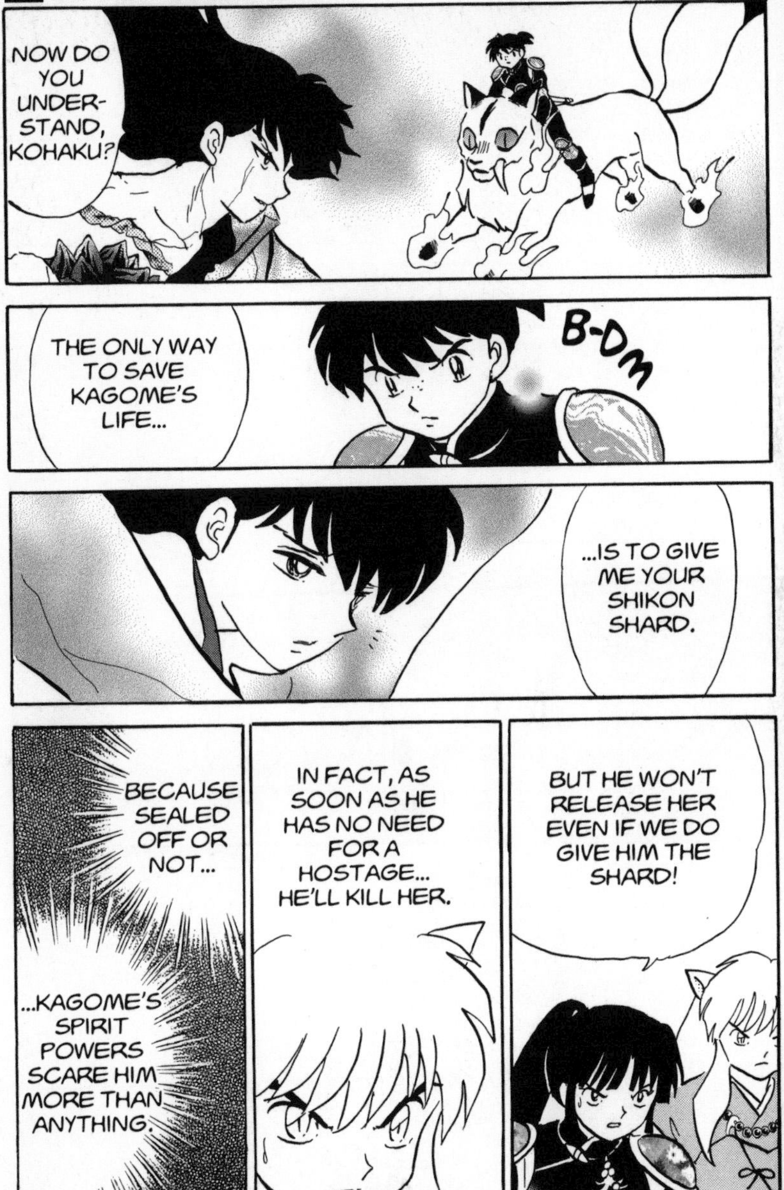
NOW DO YOU UNDER-STAND, KOHAKU?
B-DM
THE ONLY WAY TO SAVE KAGOME'S LIFE...
...IS TO GIVE ME YOUR SHIKON SHARD.
BUT HE WON'T RELEASE HER EVEN IF WE DO GIVE HIM THE SHARD!
IN FACT, AS SOON AS HE HAS NO NEED FOR A HOSTAGE... HE'LL KILL HER.
BECAUSE SEALED OFF OR NOT...
...KAGOME'S SPIRIT POWERS SCARE HIM MORE THAN ANYTHING.

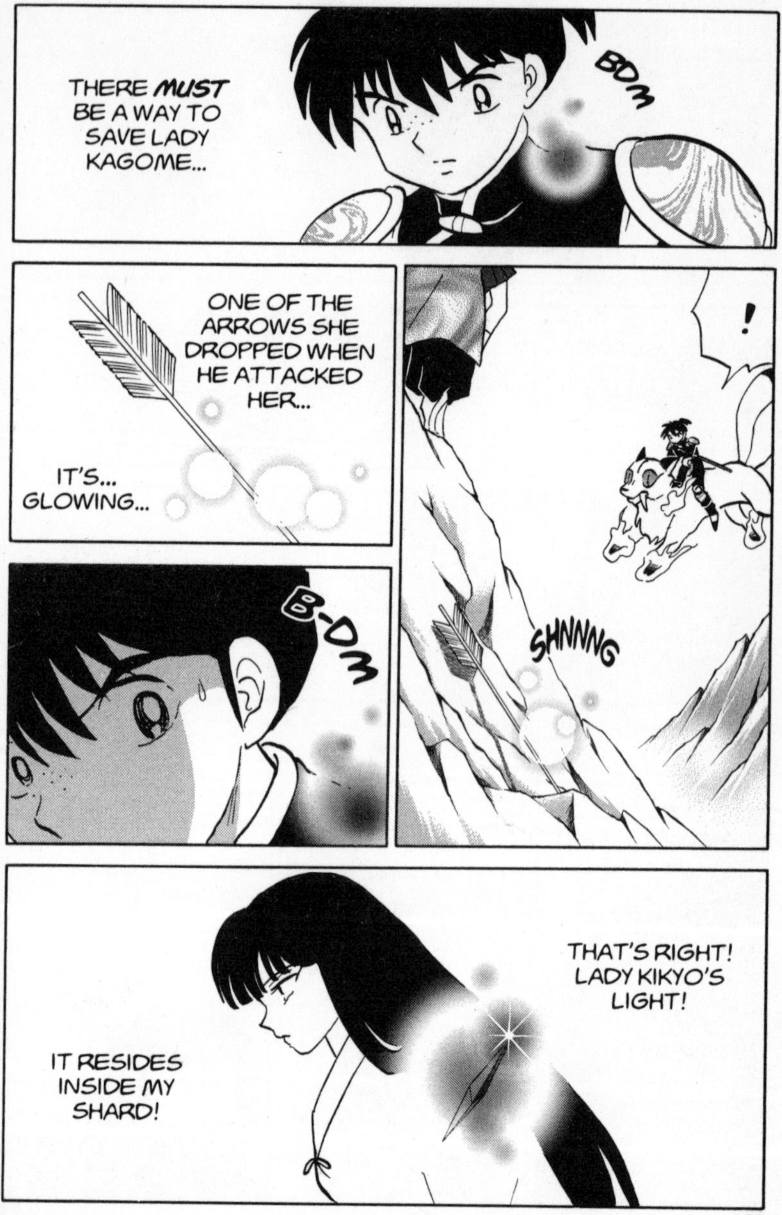
BDM
THERE MUST BE A WAY TO SAVE LADY KAGOME...
!
SHNNNG
ONE OF THE ARROWS SHE DROPPED WHEN HE ATTACKED HER...
IT'S... GLOWING...
B-DM
THAT'S RIGHT! LADY KIKYO'S LIGHT!
IT RESIDES INSIDE MY SHARD!

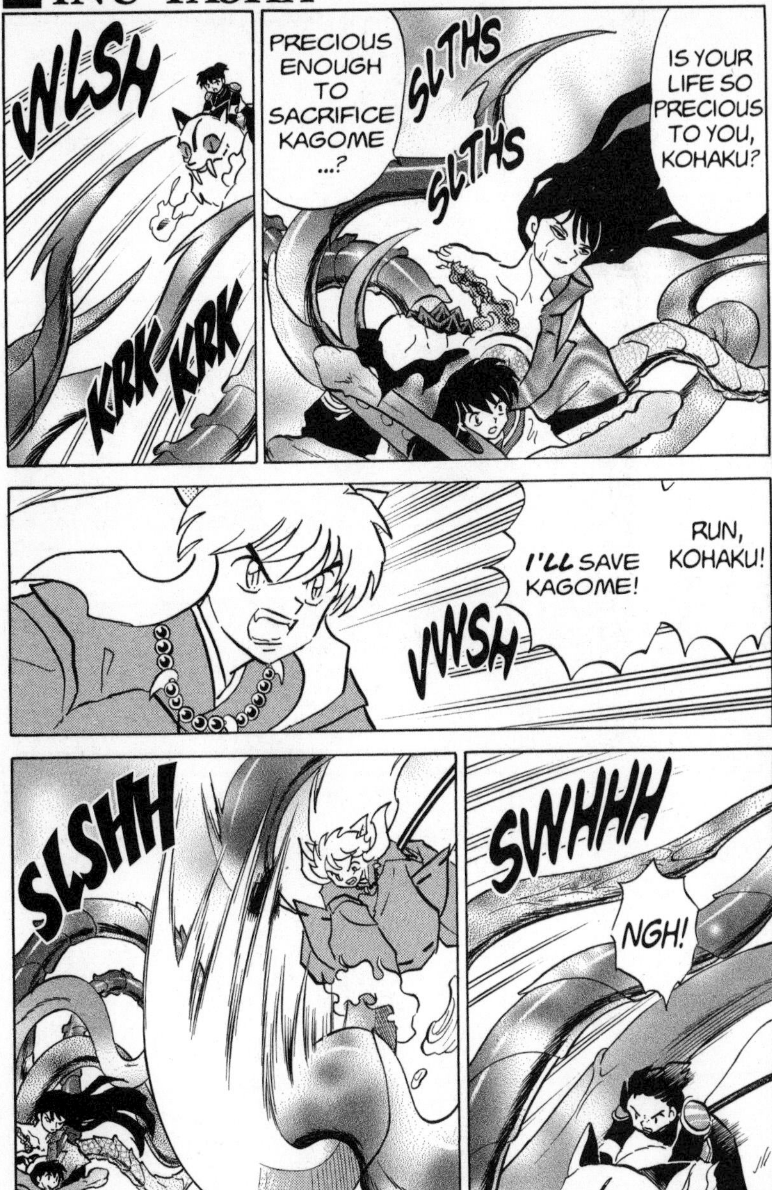
IS YOUR LIFE SO PRECIOUS TO YOU, KOHAKU?
SLTHS
SLTHS
PRECIOUS ENOUGH TO SACRIFICE KAGOME ...?
WLSH
KRK KRK
RUN, KOHAKU!
I'LL SAVE KAGOME!
VWSH
SWHHH
NGH!
SLSHH

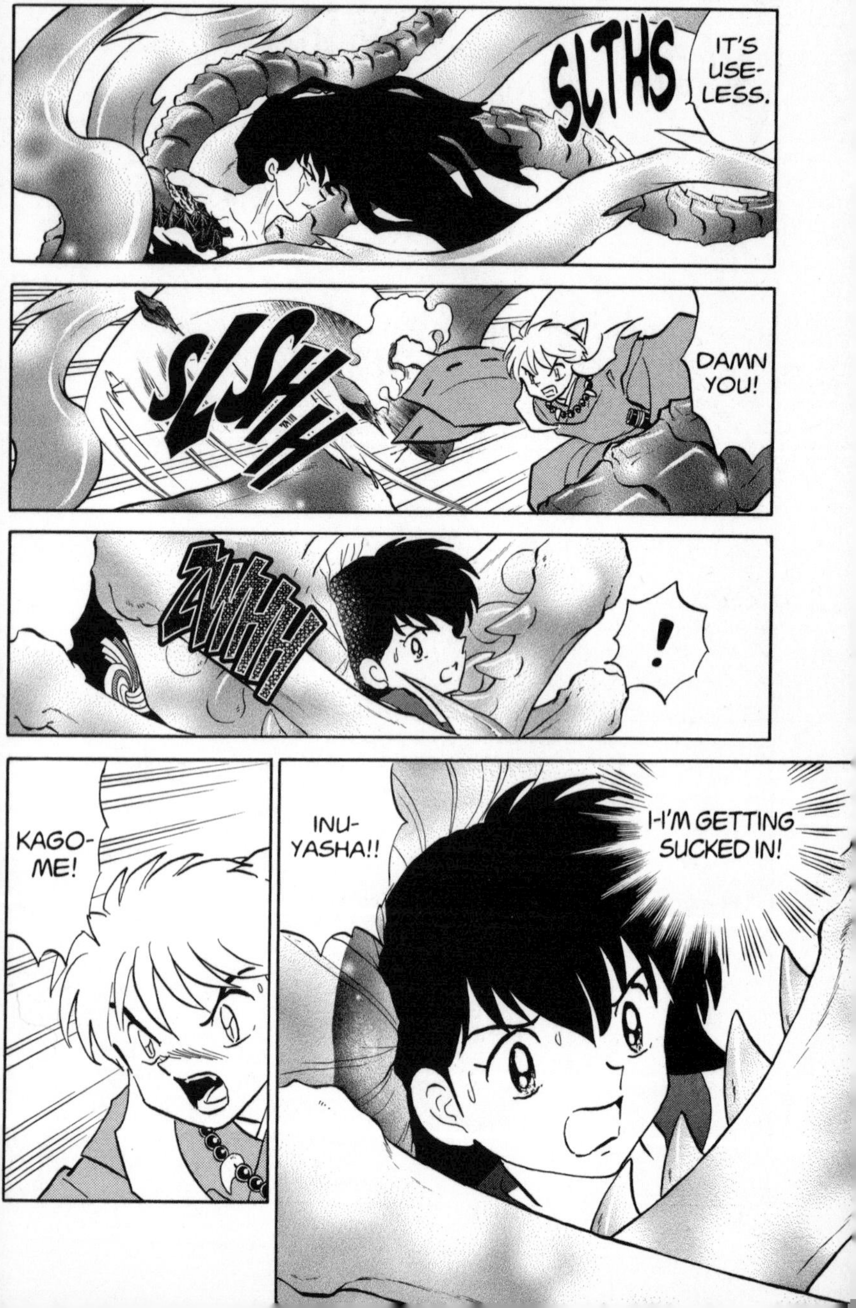
IT'S USE-LESS.
SLTHS
DAMN YOU!
SLSHH
!
ZWHH
I-I'M GETTING SUCKED IN!
INU-YASHA!!
KAGO-ME!

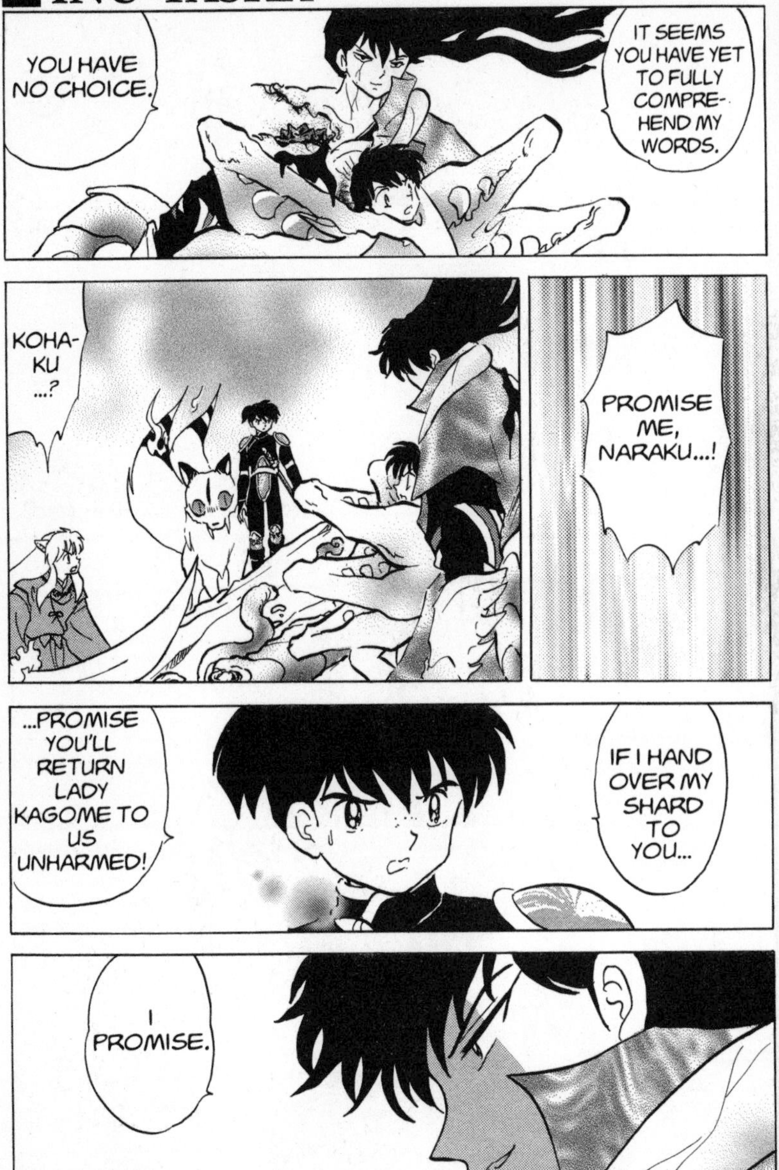
IT SEEMS YOU HAVE YET TO FULLY COMPREHEND MY WORDS.
YOU HAVE NO CHOICE.
PROMISE ME, NARAKU...!
KOHAKU ...?
IF I HAND OVER MY SHARD TO YOU...
...PROMISE YOU'LL RETURN LADY KAGOME TO US UNHARMED!
I PROMISE.

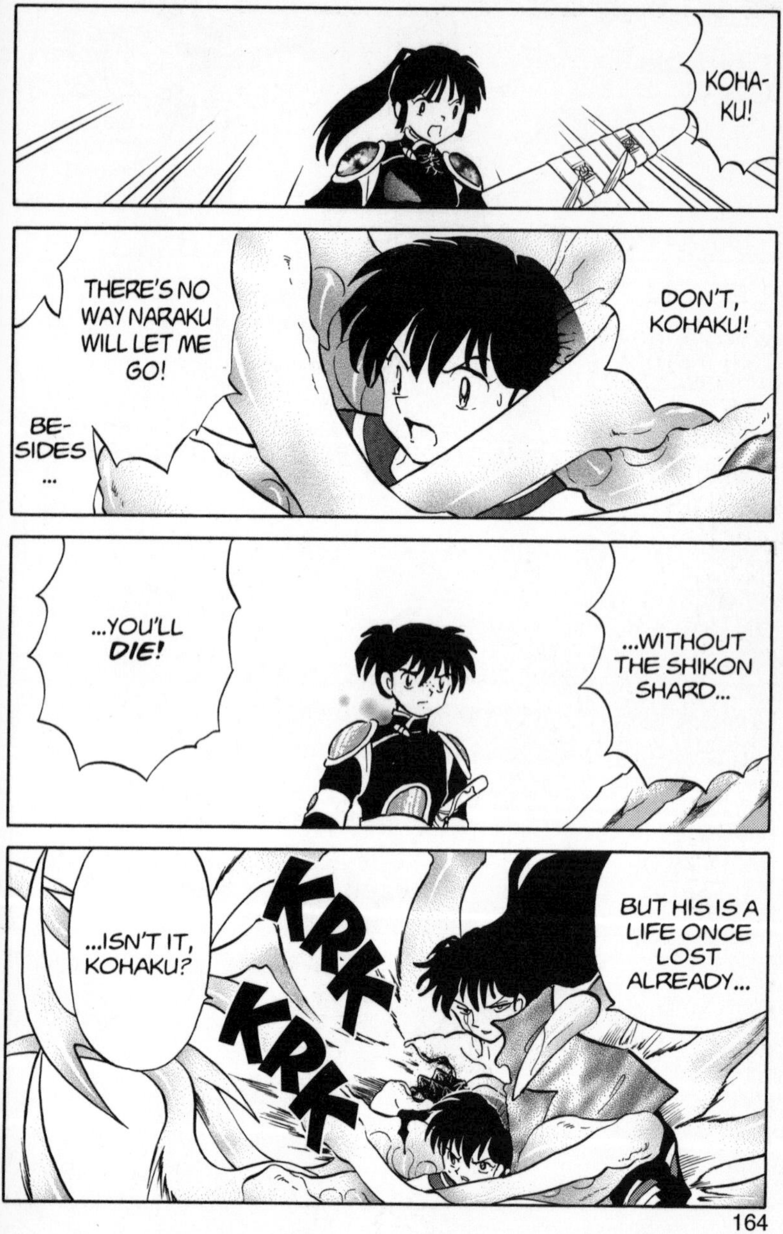
KOHA-KU!
DON'T, KOHAKU!
THERE'S NO WAY NARAKU WILL LET ME GO!
BE-SIDES...
...WITHOUT THE SHIKON SHARD...
...YOU'LL DIE!
BUT HIS IS A LIFE ONCE LOST ALREADY...
KRK KRK
...ISN'T IT, KOHAKU?

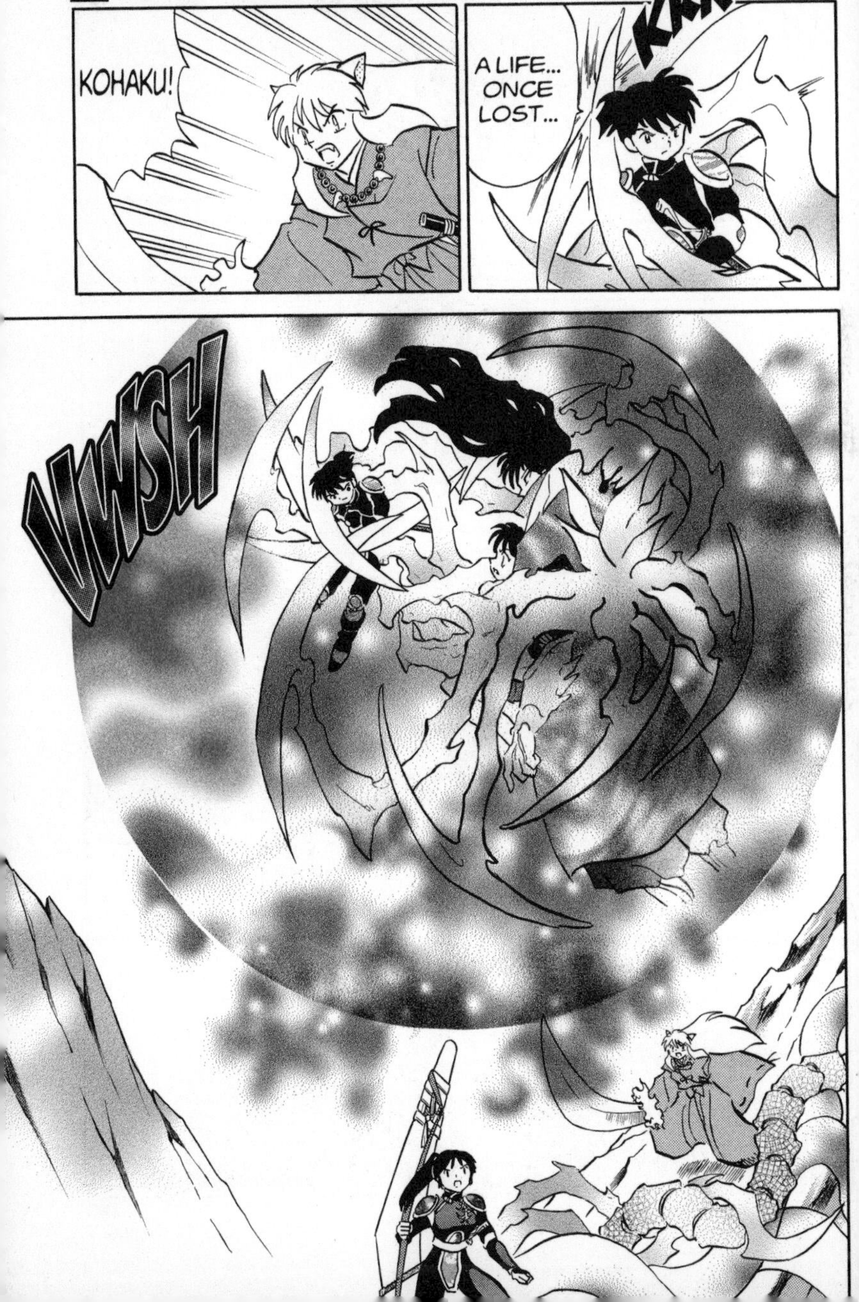
KRK
A LIFE... ONCE LOST...
KOHAKU!
VWSH

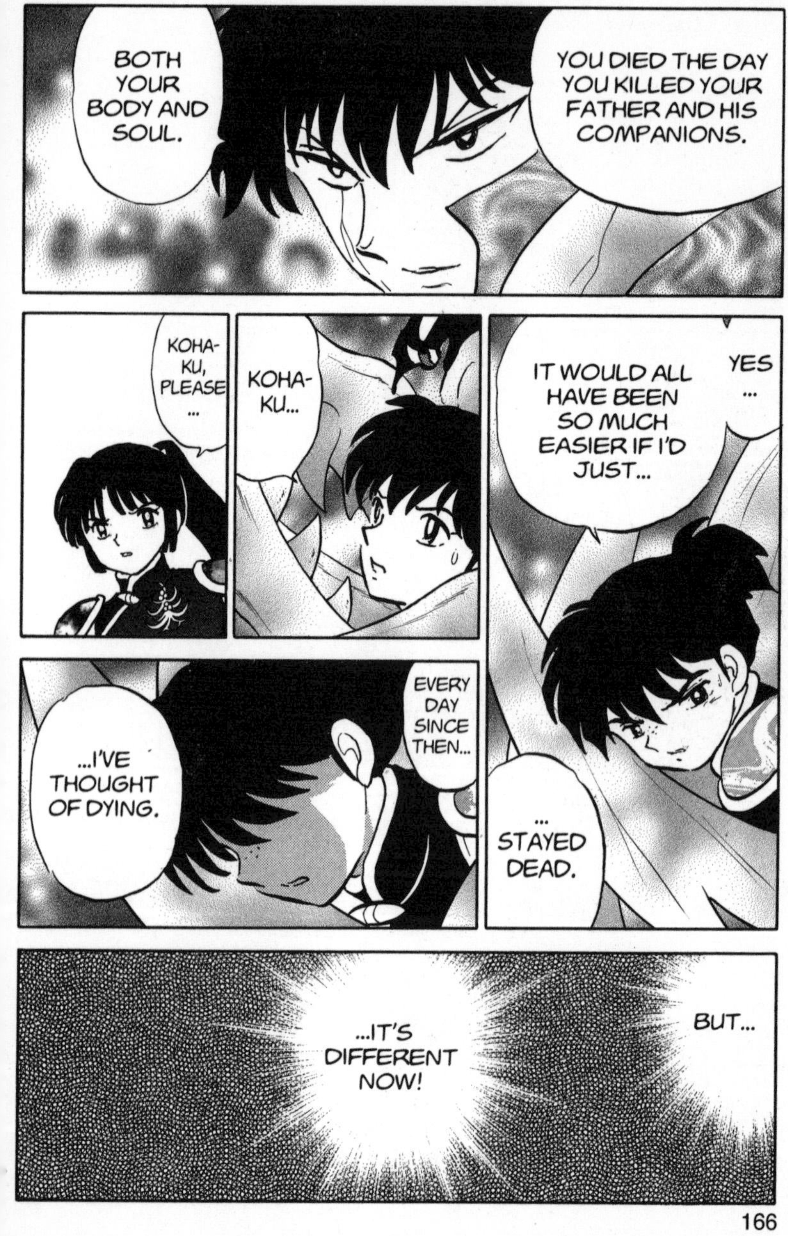
YOU DIED THE DAY YOU KILLED YOUR FATHER AND HIS COMPANIONS.
BOTH YOUR BODY AND SOUL.
YES ...
IT WOULD ALL HAVE BEEN SO MUCH EASIER IF I'D JUST...
... STAYED DEAD.
KOHA-KU...
KOHA-KU, PLEASE ...
EVERY DAY SINCE THEN...
...I'VE THOUGHT OF DYING.
BUT...
...IT'S DIFFERENT NOW!

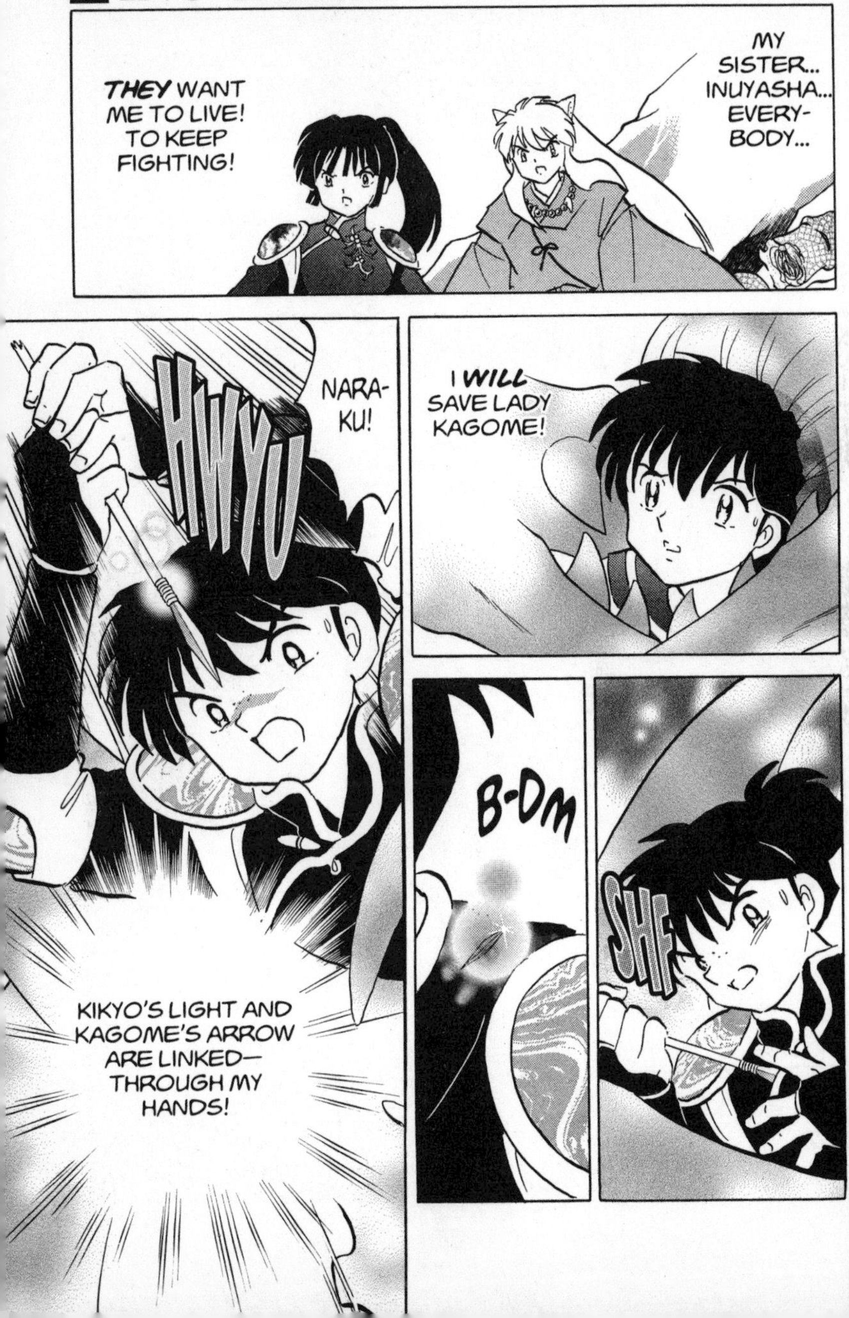
MY SISTER... INUYASHA... EVERY-BODY...
THEY WANT ME TO LIVE! TO KEEP FIGHTING!
I *WILL* SAVE LADY KAGOME!
SHF
B-DM
NARA-KU!
HWYU
KIKYO'S LIGHT AND KAGOME'S ARROW ARE LINKED— THROUGH MY HANDS!

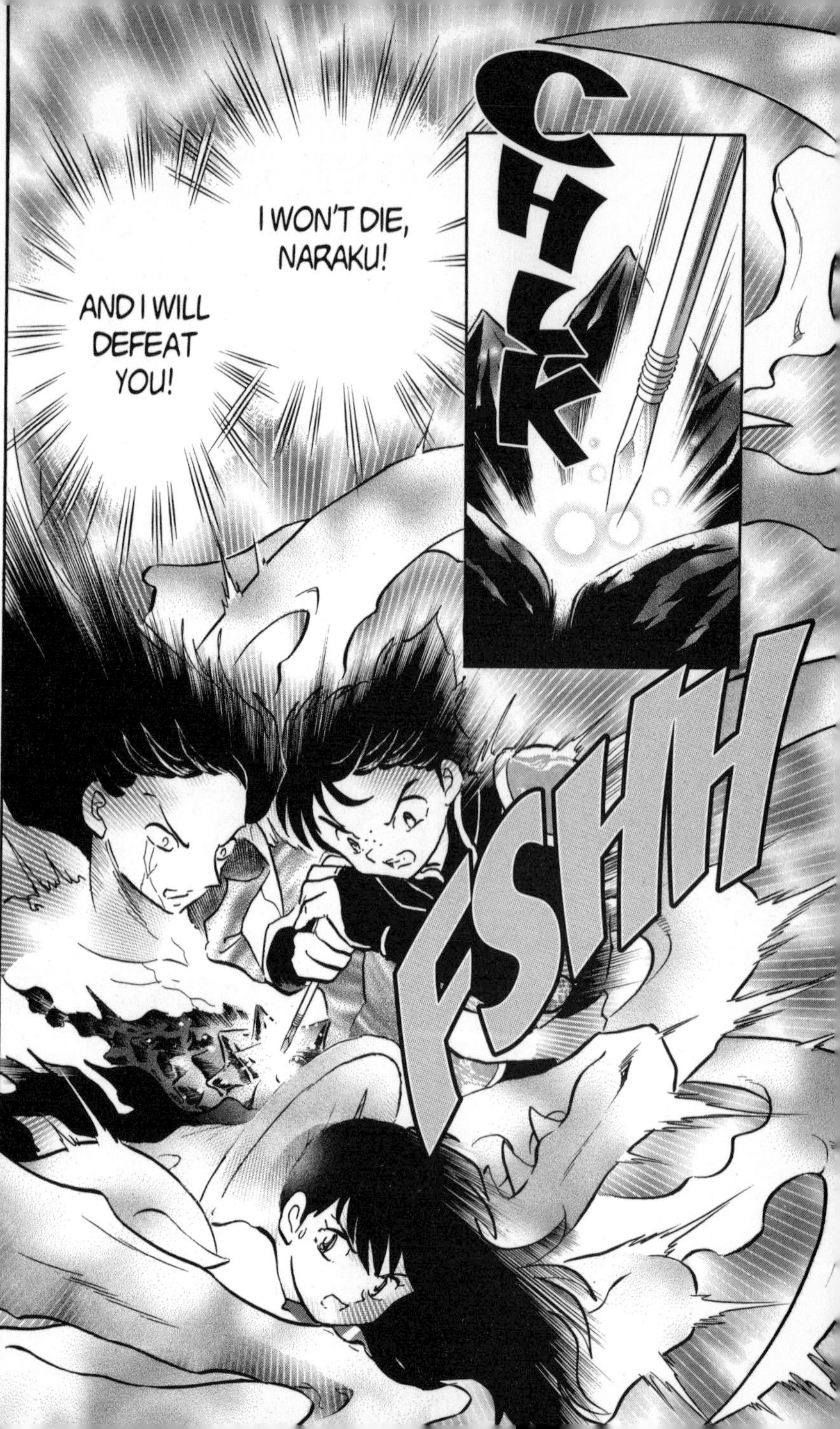
CHKK
I WON'T DIE, NARAKU!
AND I WILL DEFEAT YOU!
FSHH

SCROLL 10

FROM HERE ON OUT

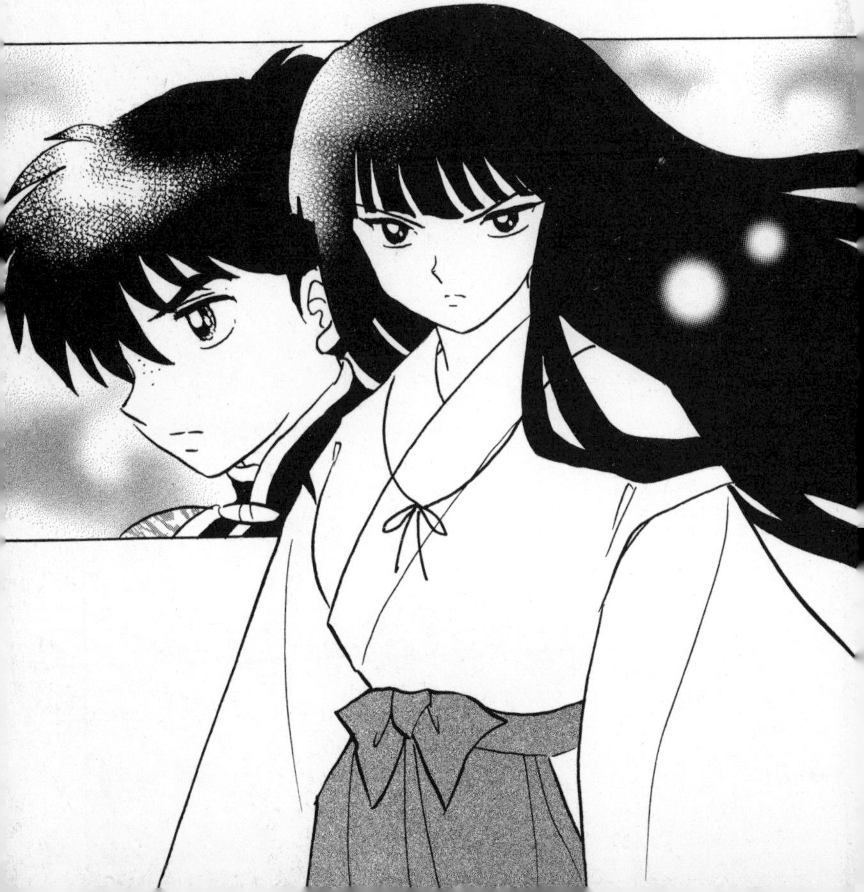

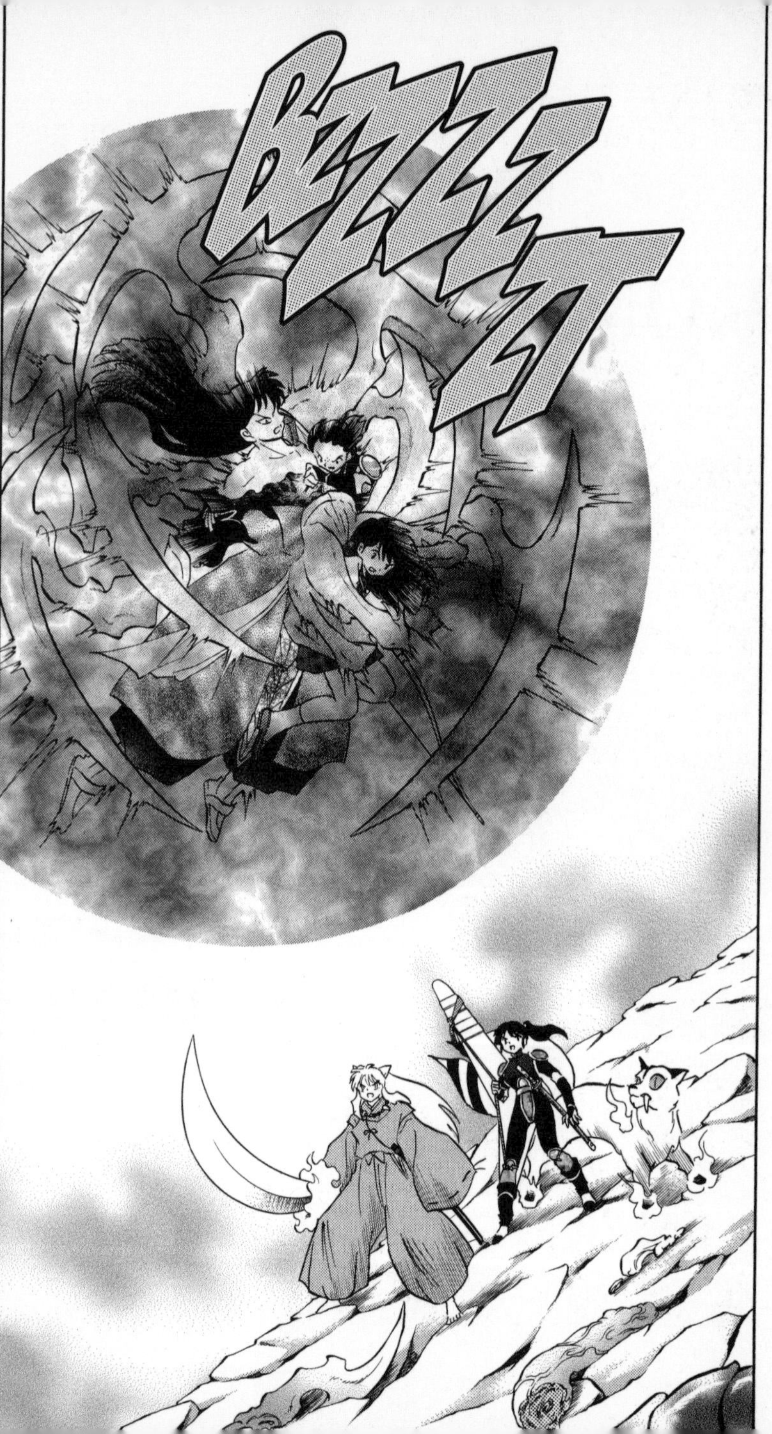
BZZZZT

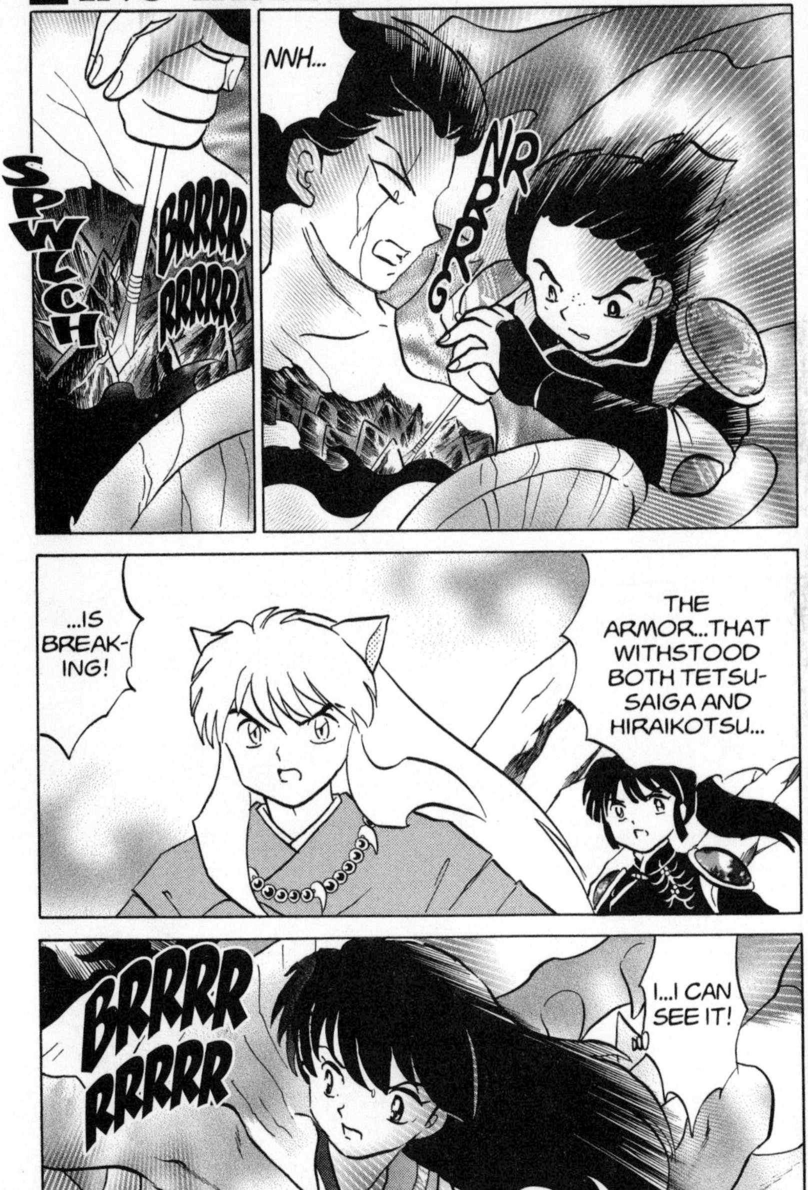
NNH...
NRRRG
SPWLCH
BRRRR
RRRRR
THE ARMOR...THAT WITHSTOOD BOTH TETSU-SAIGA AND HIRAIKOTSU...
...IS BREAKING!
I...I CAN SEE IT!
BRRRR
RRRRR

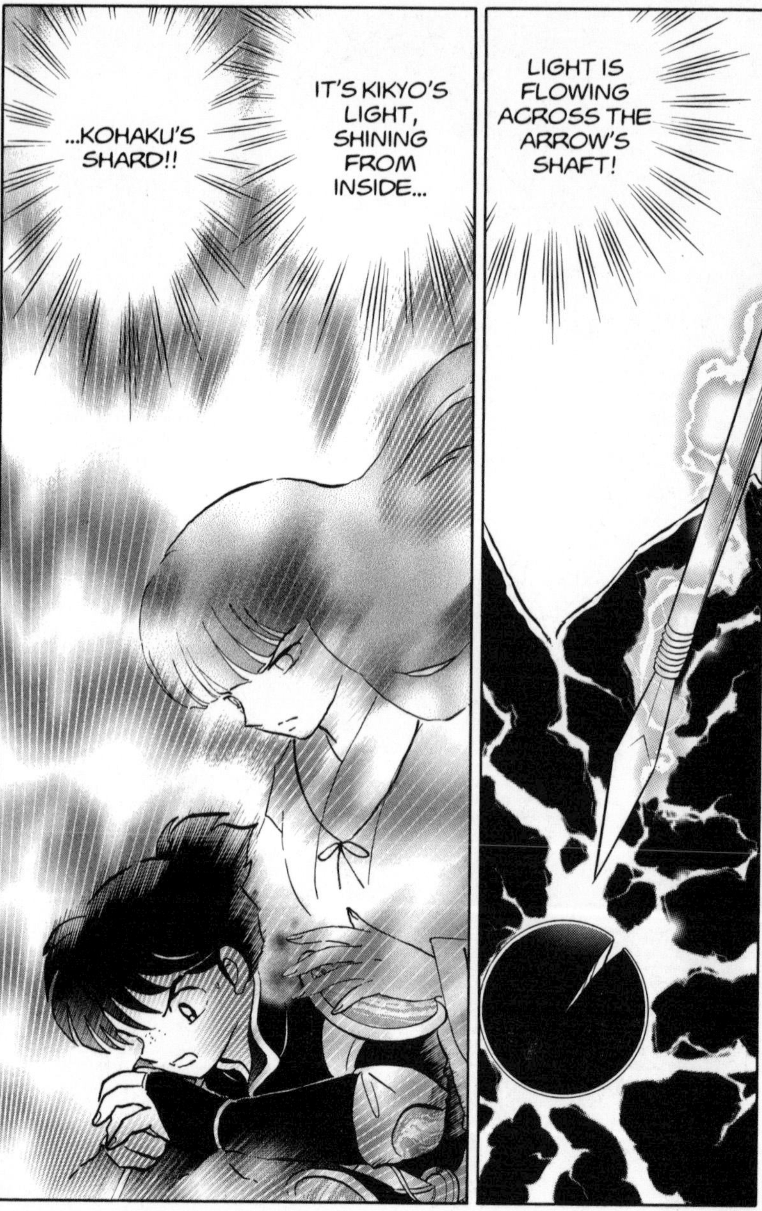
LIGHT IS FLOWING ACROSS THE ARROW'S SHAFT!
IT'S KIKYO'S LIGHT, SHINING FROM INSIDE...
...KOHAKU'S SHARD!!

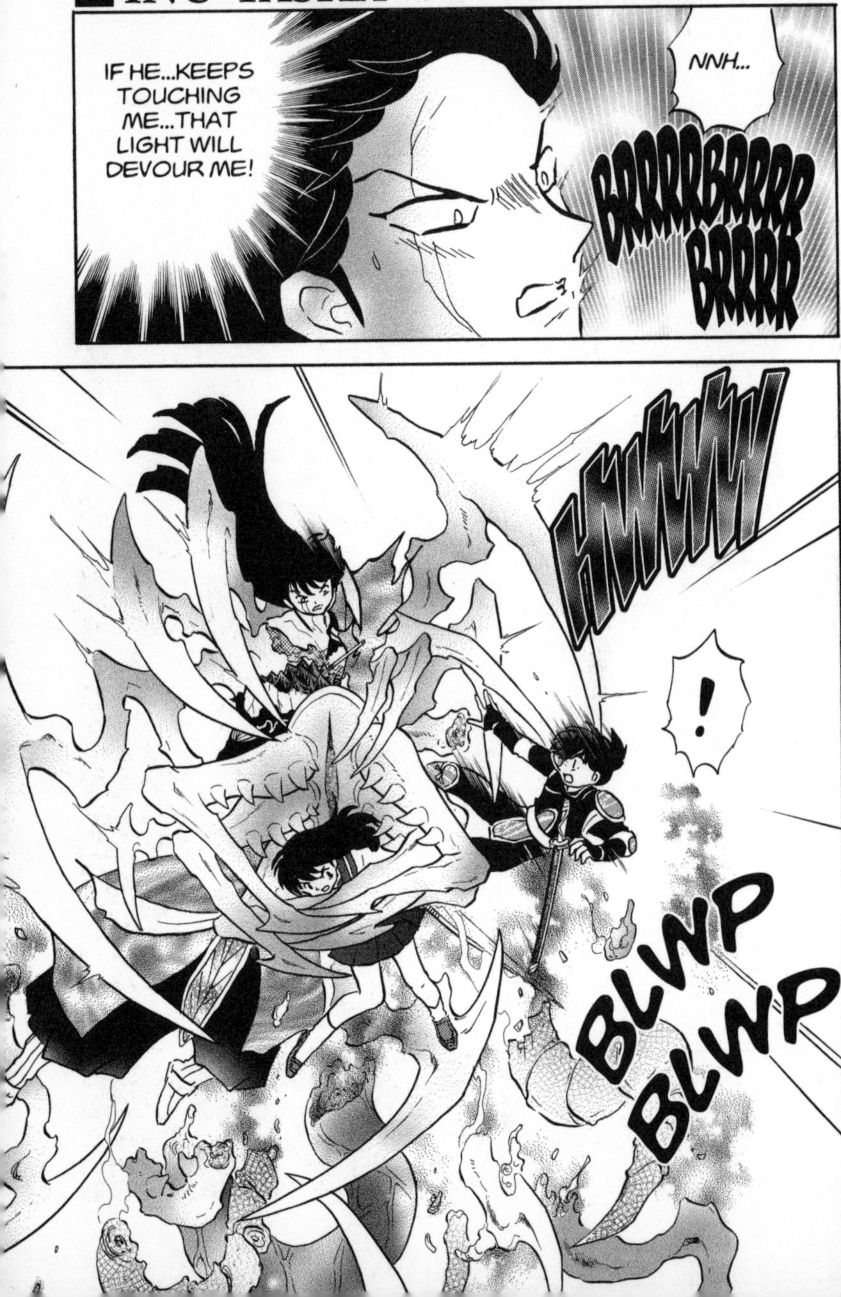
NNH...
BRRRRBRRRR
BRRRR
IF HE...KEEPS TOUCHING ME...THAT LIGHT WILL DEVOUR ME!
HWWWWW
!
BLWP
BLWP

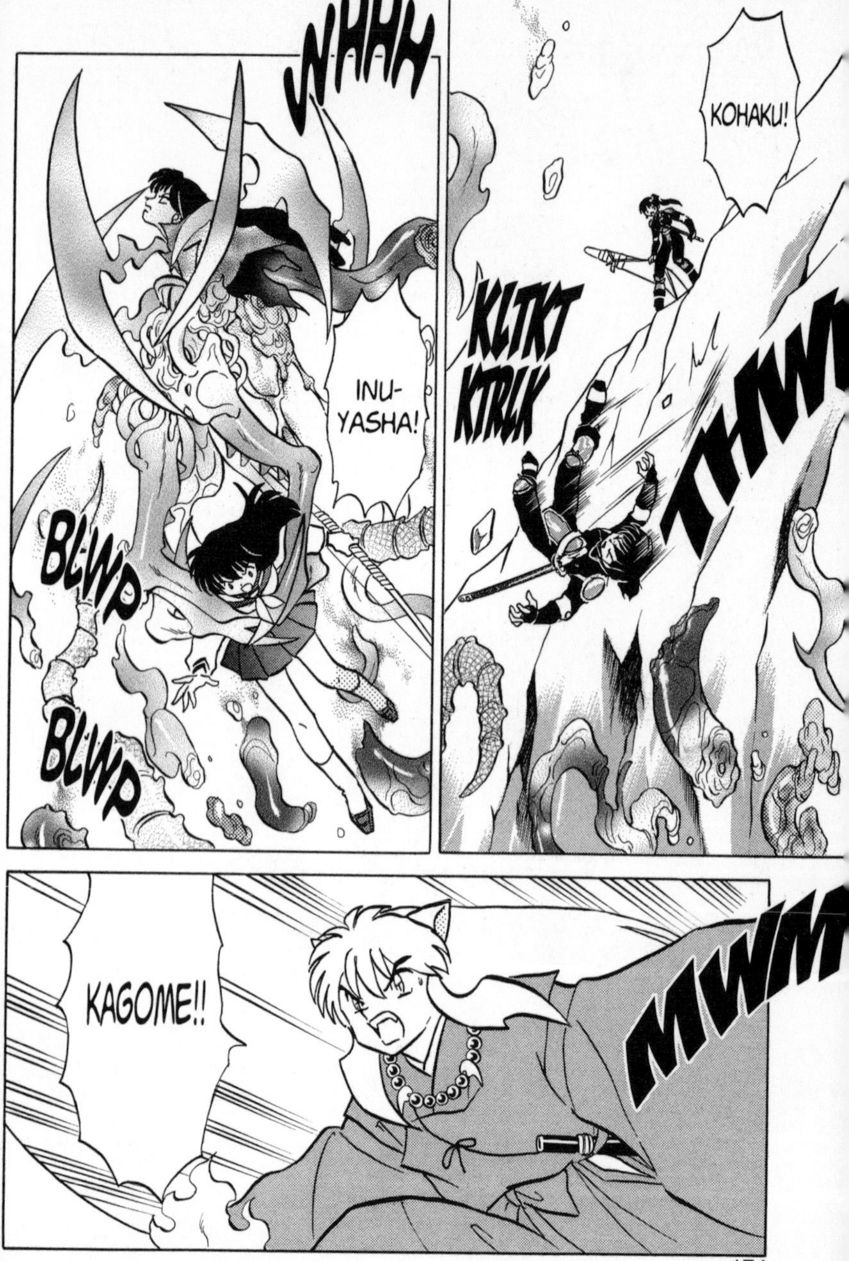
KOHAKU!
KLTKT KTRLK
WHHH
INU-YASHA!
BLWP
BLWP
KAGOME!!

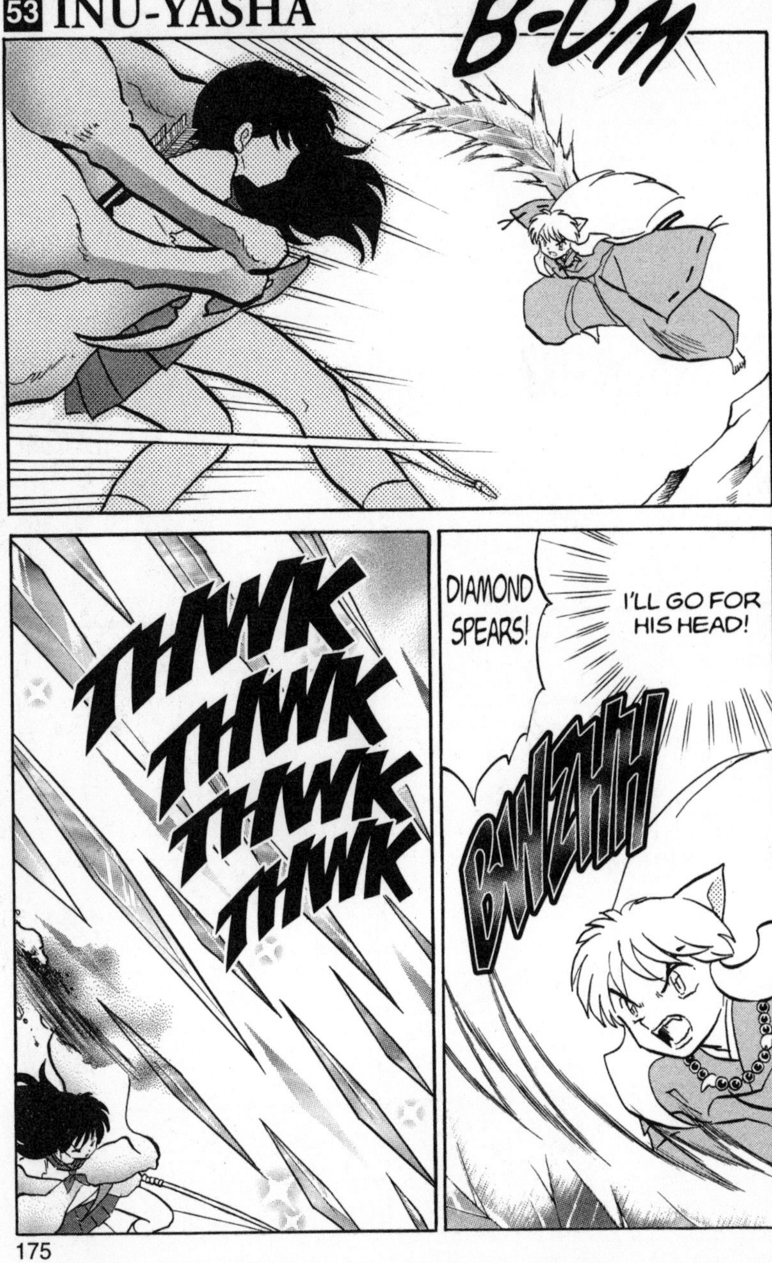
B-DM
I'LL GO FOR HIS HEAD!
DIAMOND SPEARS!
BWZHH
THWK
THWK
THWK
THWK

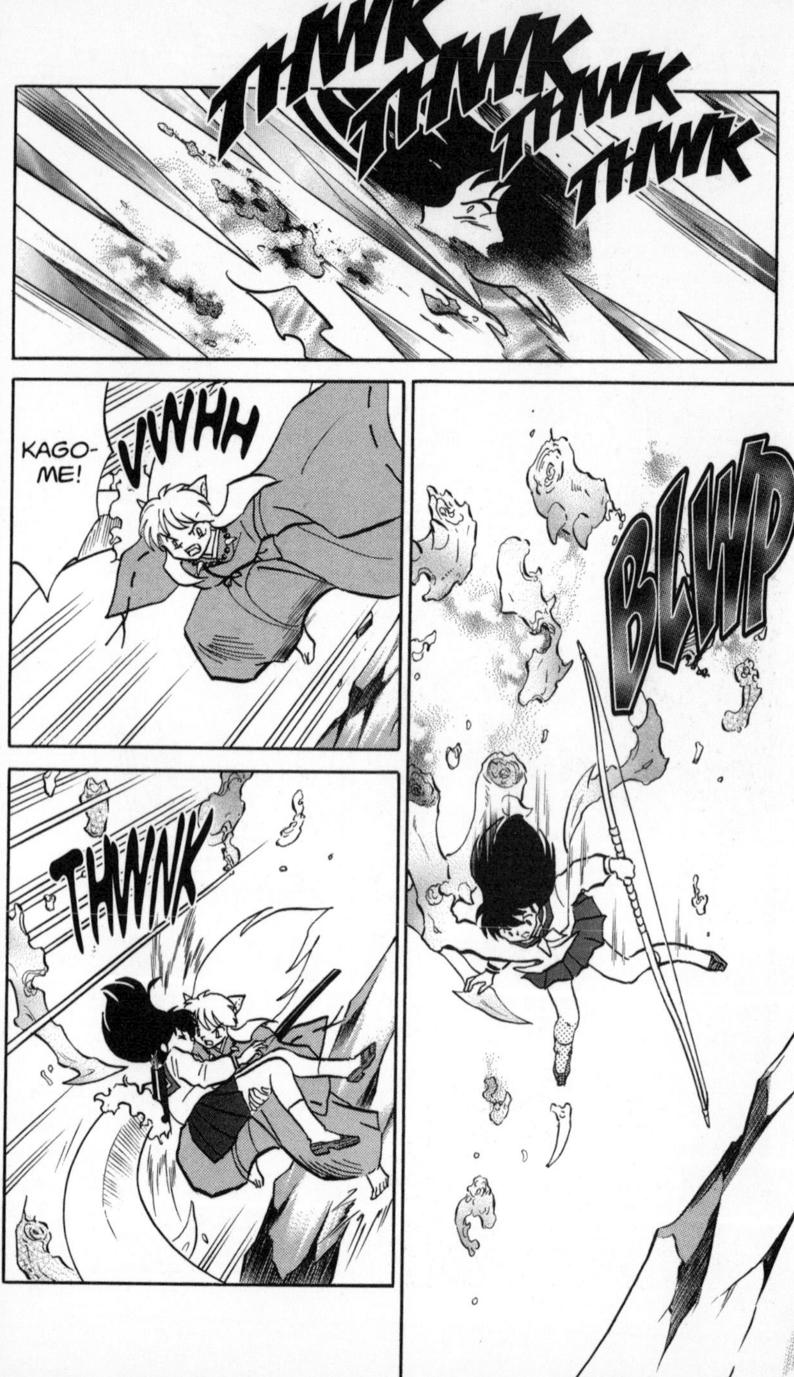
THWK
THWK
THWK
THWK
BLWP
KAGO-
ME!
VWHH
THWNK

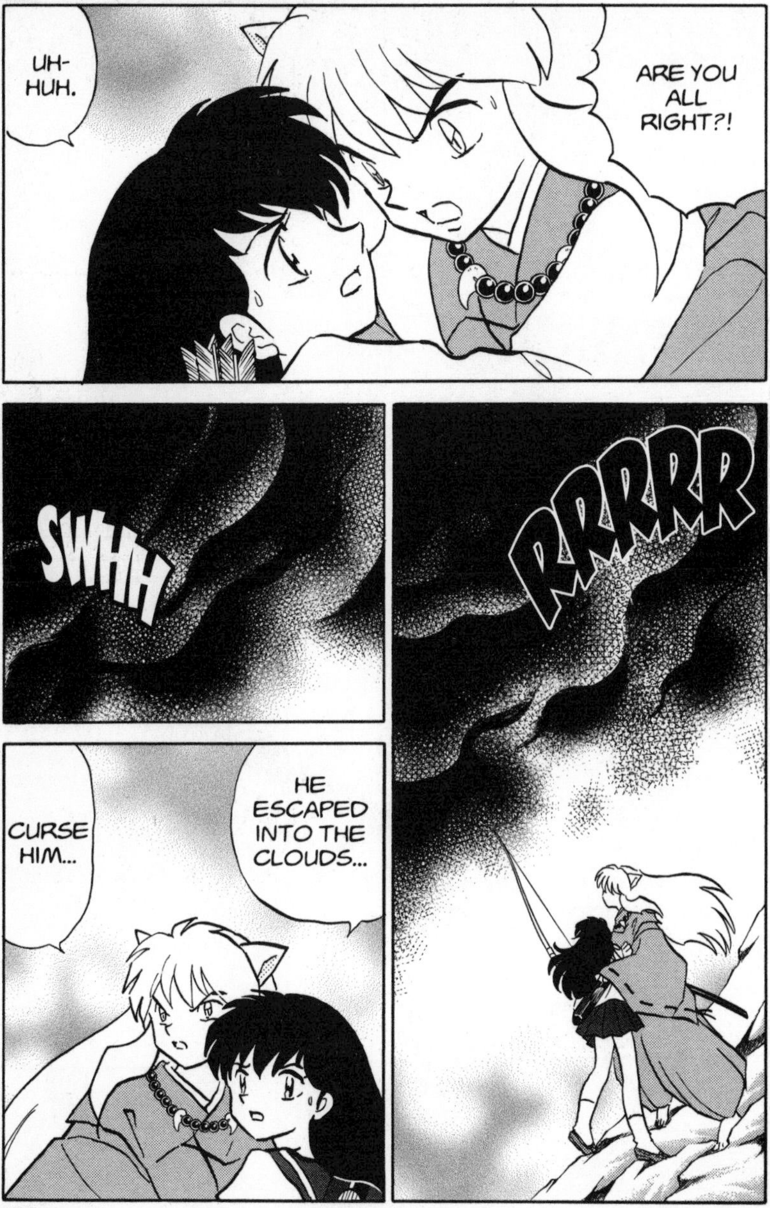
ARE YOU ALL RIGHT?!
UH-HUH.
RRRRR
SWHH
HE ESCAPED INTO THE CLOUDS...
CURSE HIM...

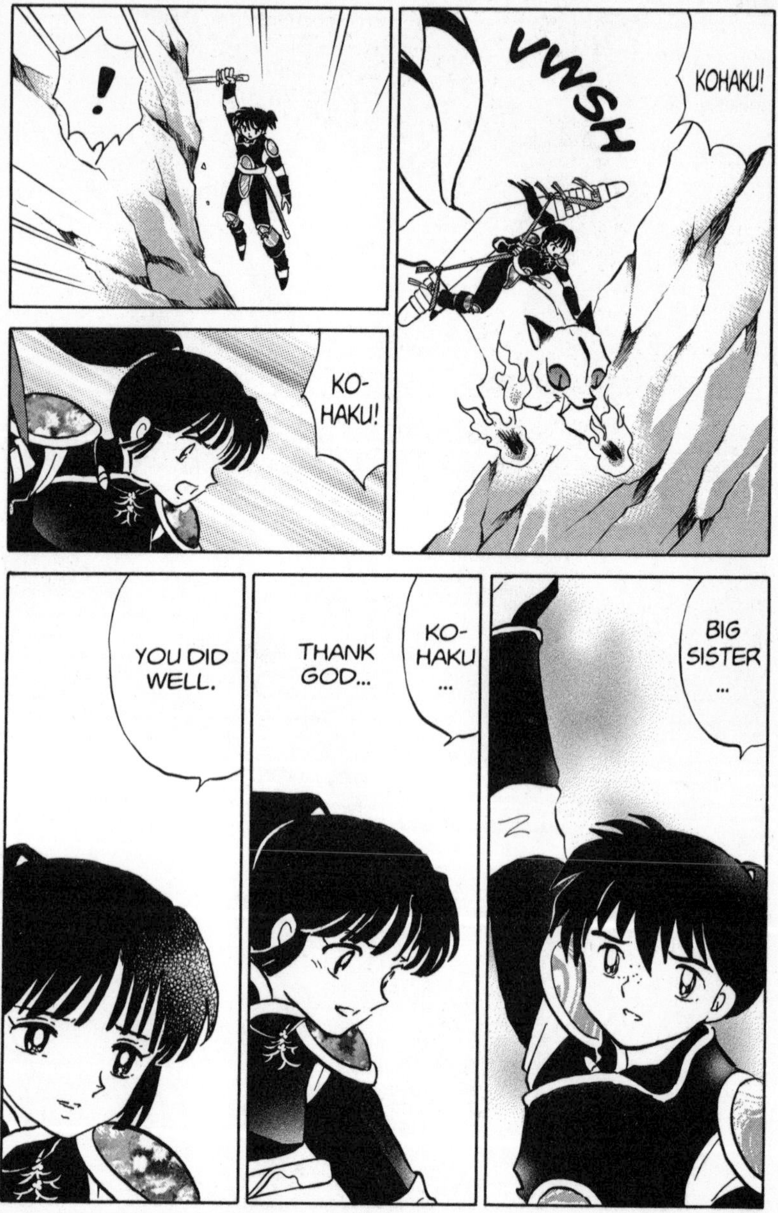
VWSH
KOHAKU!
!
KO-HAKU!
BIG SISTER...
KO-HAKU...
THANK GOD...
YOU DID WELL.

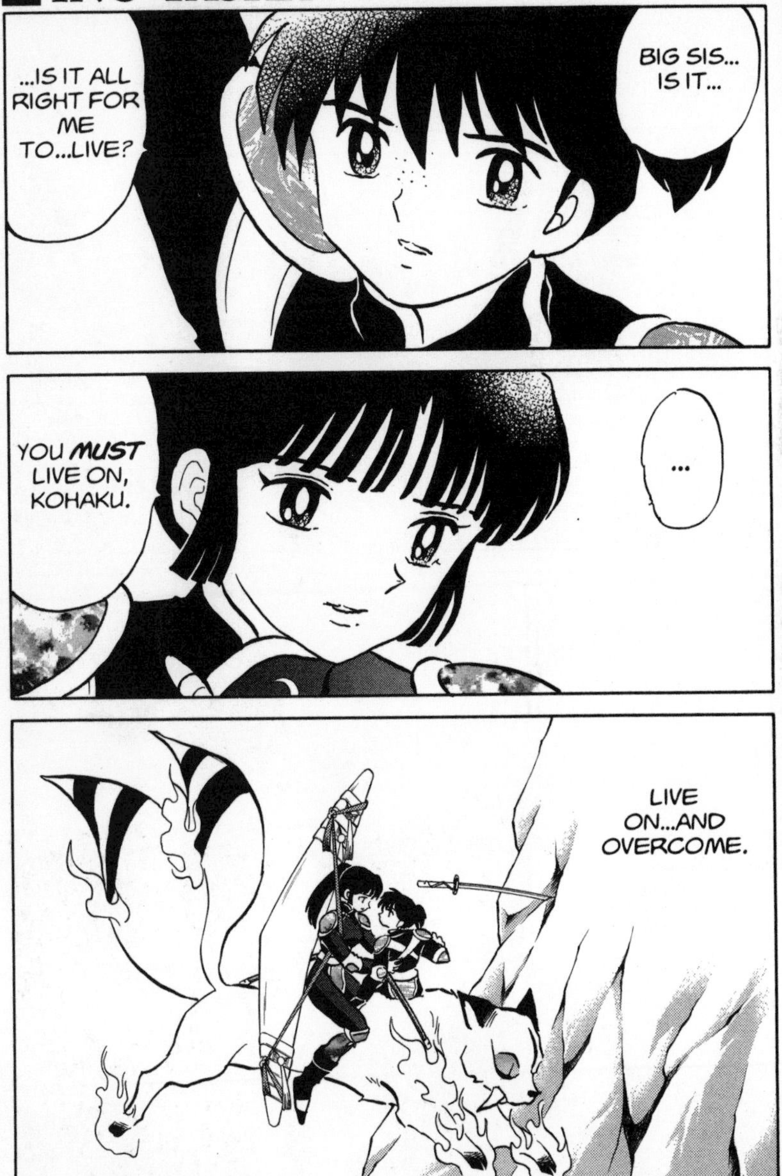
BIG SIS... IS IT...
...IS IT ALL RIGHT FOR ME TO...LIVE?
...
YOU *MUST* LIVE ON, KOHAKU.
LIVE ON...AND OVERCOME.

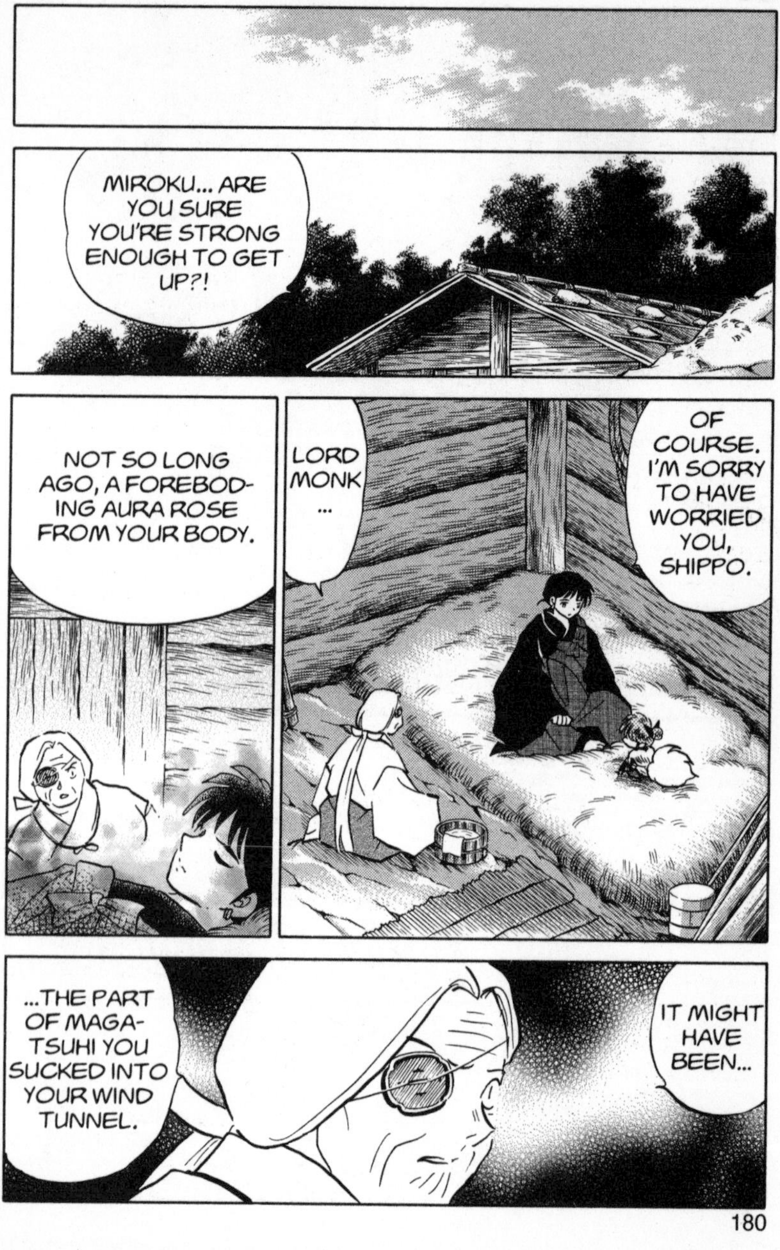
MIROKU... ARE YOU SURE YOU'RE STRONG ENOUGH TO GET UP?!
OF COURSE. I'M SORRY TO HAVE WORRIED YOU, SHIPPO.
LORD MONK ...
NOT SO LONG AGO, A FOREBOD-ING AURA ROSE FROM YOUR BODY.
IT MIGHT HAVE BEEN...
...THE PART OF MAGA-TSUHI YOU SUCKED INTO YOUR WIND TUNNEL.

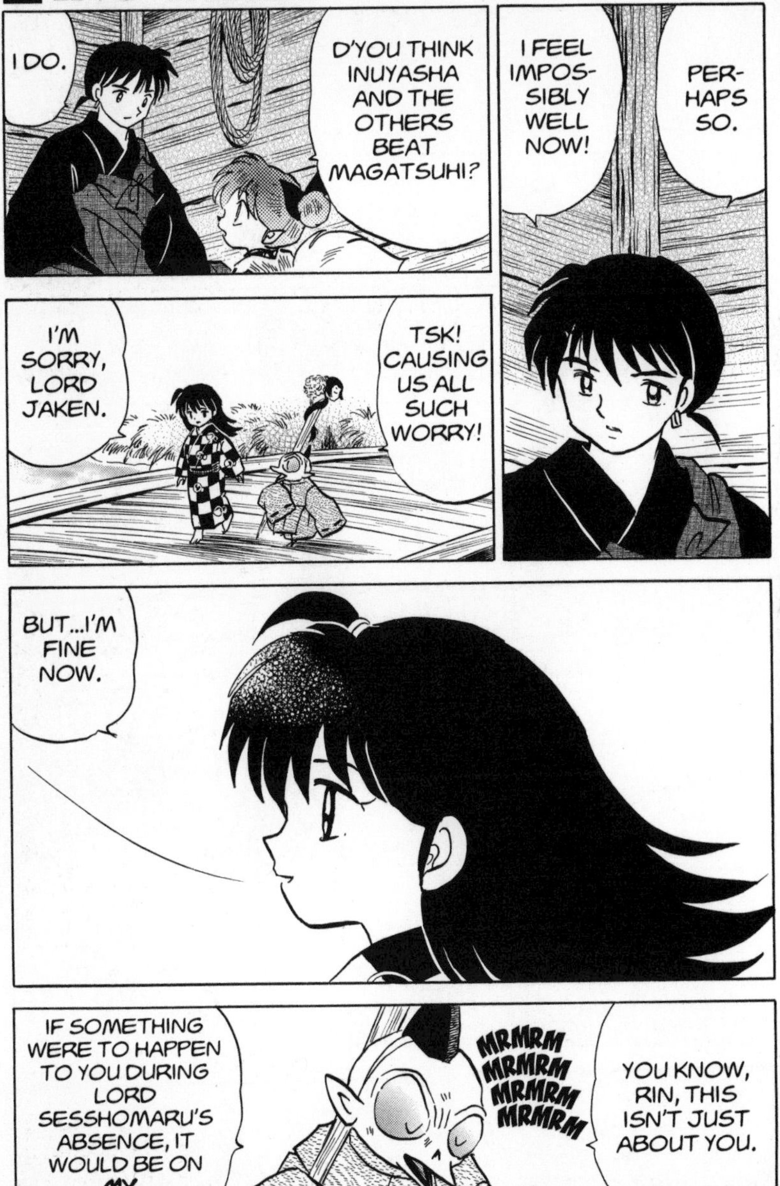
PERHAPS SO.
I FEEL IMPOSSIBLY WELL NOW!
D'YOU THINK INUYASHA AND THE OTHERS BEAT MAGATSUHI?
I DO.
TSK! CAUSING US ALL SUCH WORRY!
I'M SORRY, LORD JAKEN.
BUT...I'M FINE NOW.
YOU KNOW, RIN, THIS ISN'T JUST ABOUT YOU.
MRMRM MRMRM MRMRM MRMRM
IF SOMETHING WERE TO HAPPEN TO YOU DURING LORD SESSHOMARU'S ABSENCE, IT WOULD BE ON *MY*...

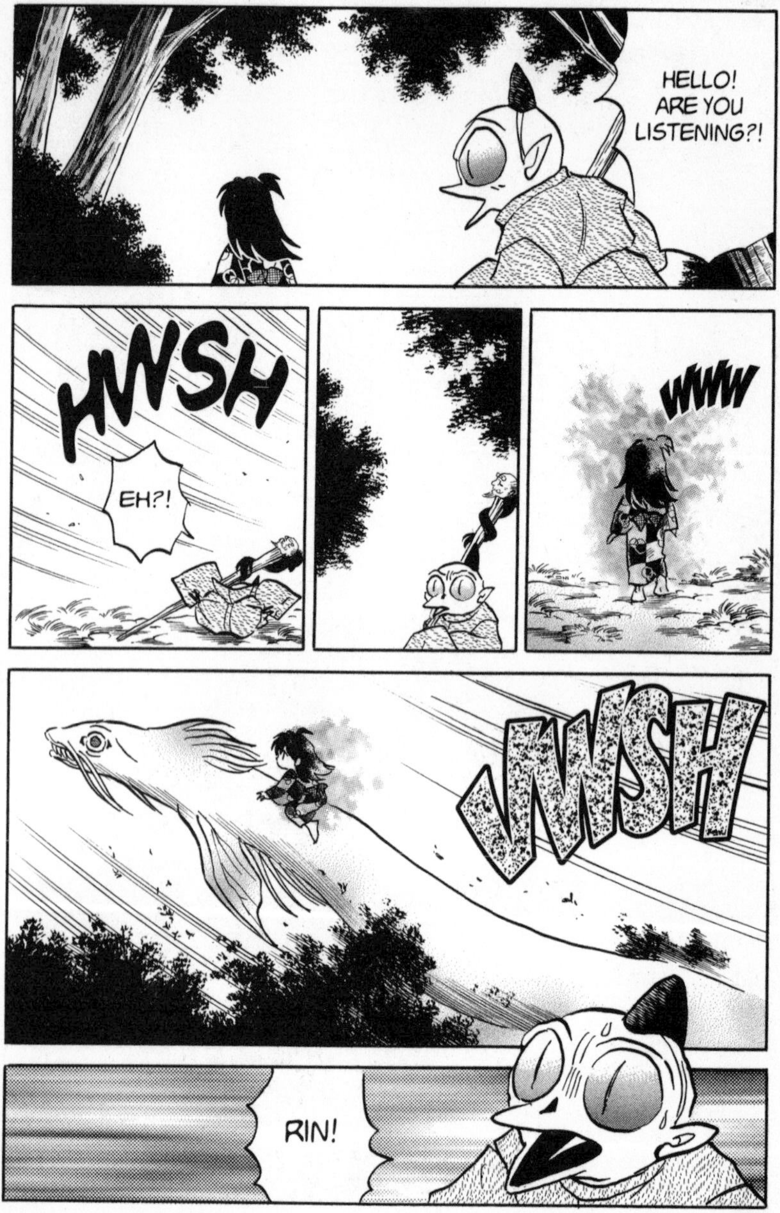
HELLO! ARE YOU LISTENING?!
WWW
HWSH
EH?!
WWSH
RIN!

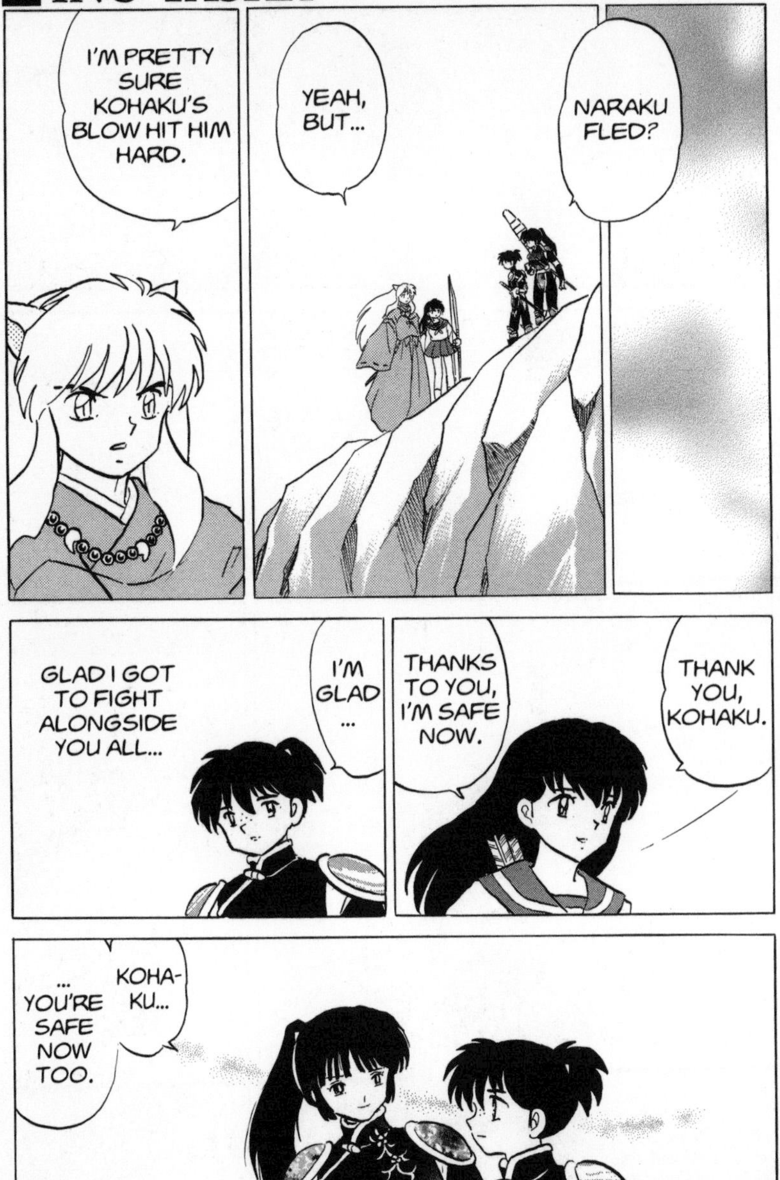
NARAKU FLED?
YEAH, BUT...
I'M PRETTY SURE KOHAKU'S BLOW HIT HIM HARD.
THANK YOU, KOHAKU.
THANKS TO YOU, I'M SAFE NOW.
I'M GLAD ...
GLAD I GOT TO FIGHT ALONGSIDE YOU ALL...
KOHA-KU...
... YOU'RE SAFE NOW TOO.

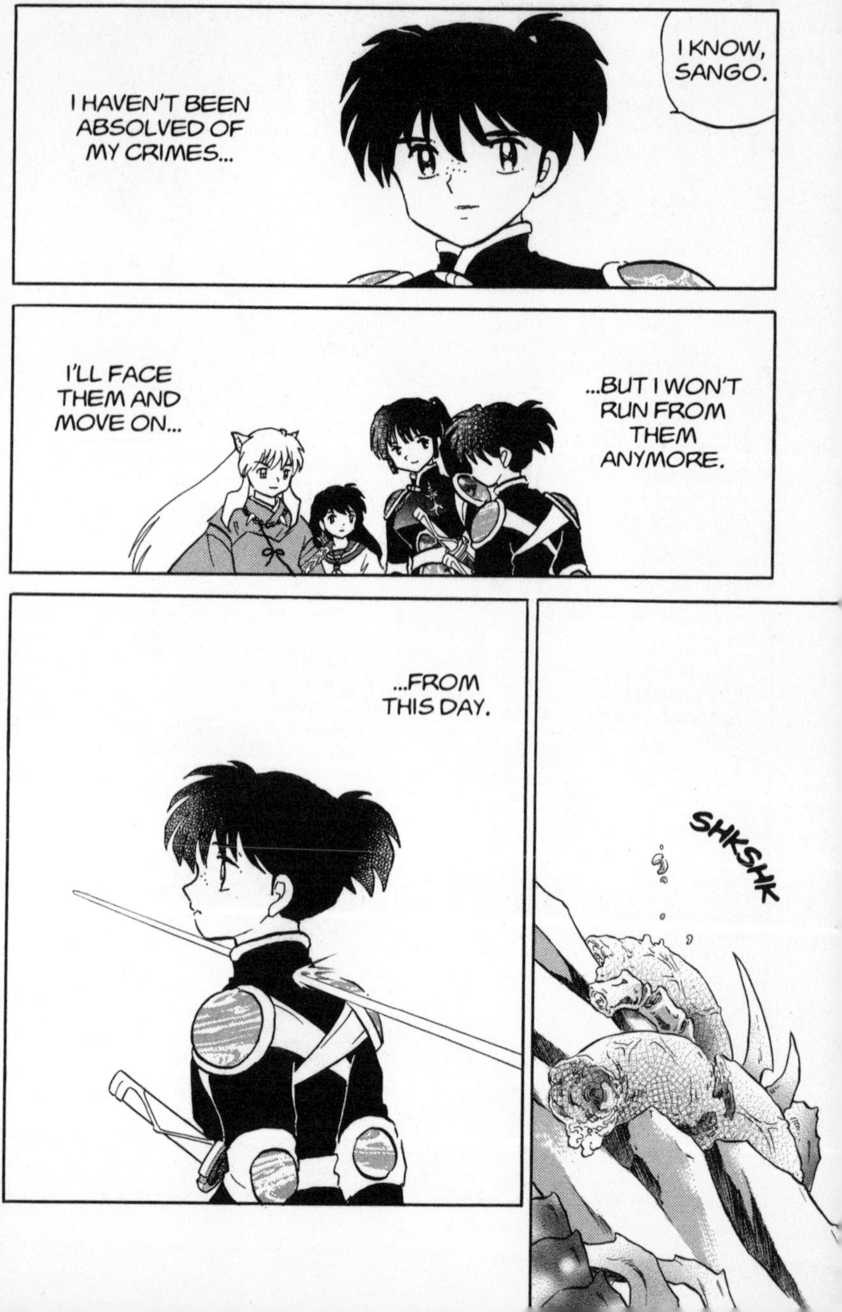
I KNOW, SANGO.
I HAVEN'T BEEN ABSOLVED OF MY CRIMES...
...BUT I WON'T RUN FROM THEM ANYMORE.
I'LL FACE THEM AND MOVE ON...
SHKSHK
...FROM THIS DAY.

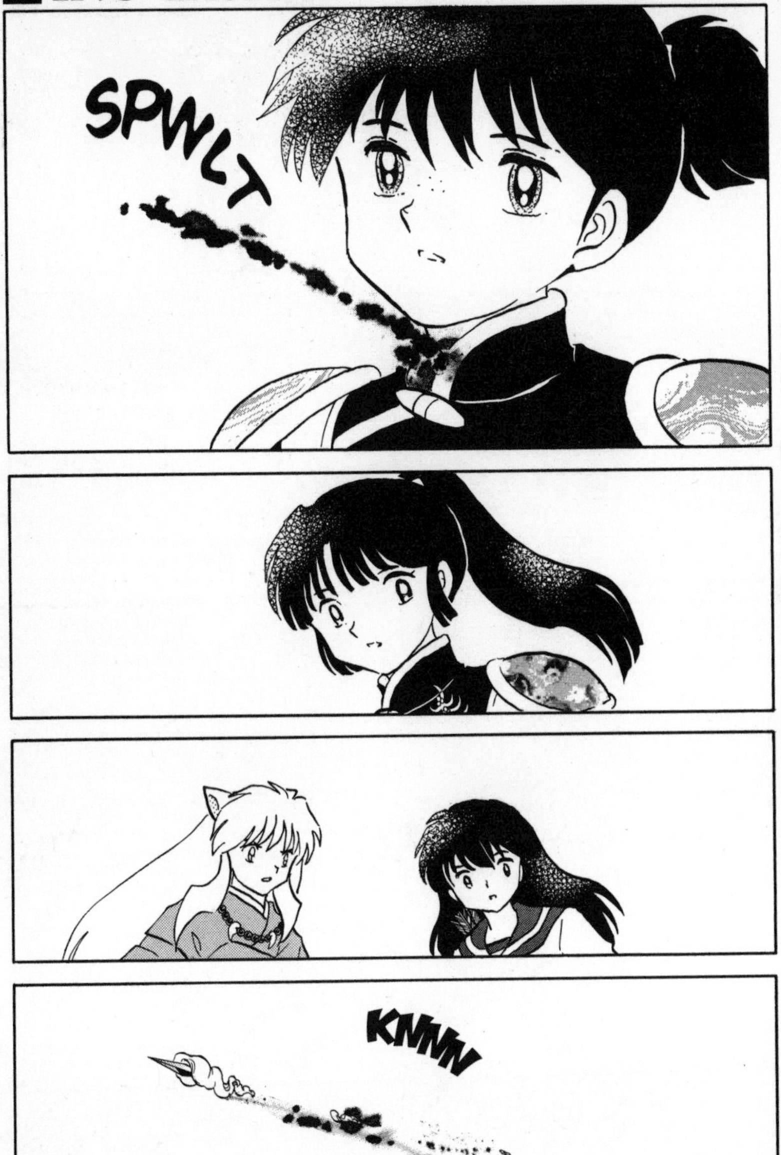
SPWLT
KNNNN

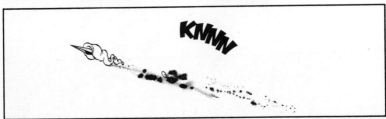

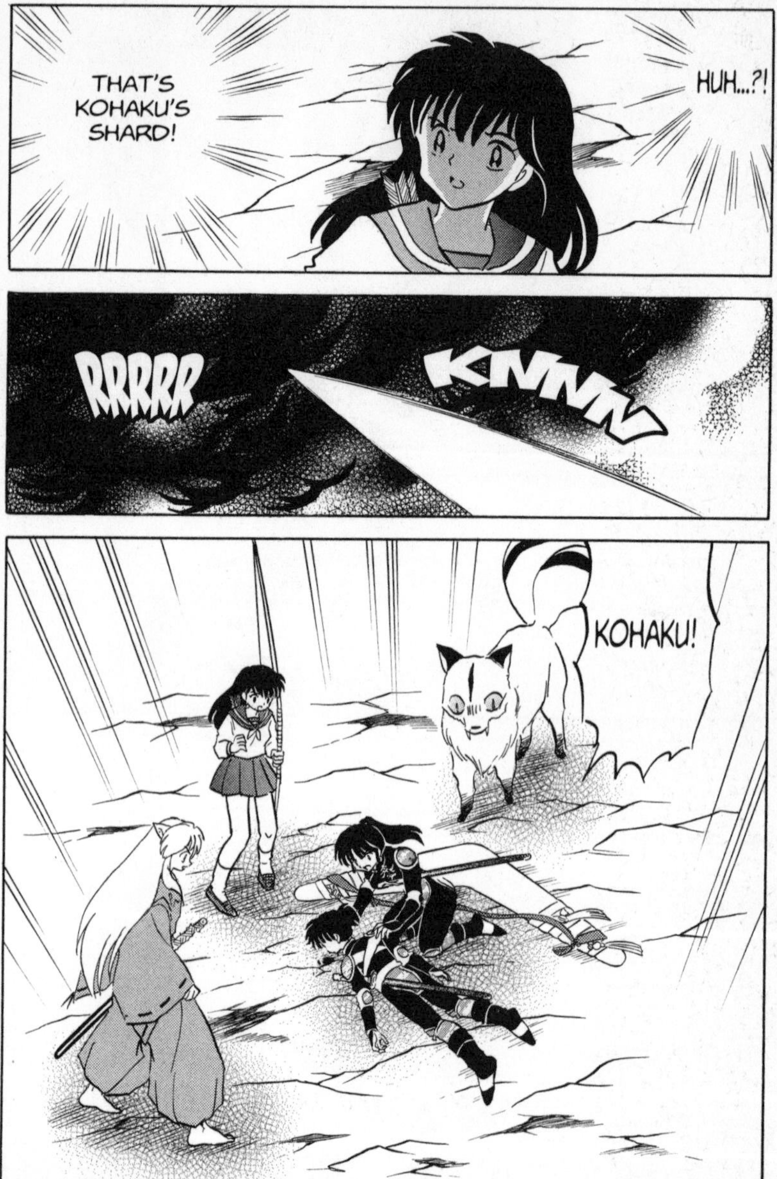
HUH...?!
THAT'S KOHAKU'S SHARD!
KNNN
RRRRR
KOHAKU!

TO BE CONTINUED...

INUYASHA

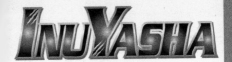

INUYASHA

VOL. 53

Shonen Sunday Edition

Story and Art by

RUMIKO TAKAHASHI

Original Japanese edition "INUYASHA"
published by SHOGAKUKAN Inc.

English Adaptation by Gerard Jones

Translation/Mari Morimoto
Touch-up Art & Lettering/Bill Schuch
Cover & Interior Graphic Design/Yuki Ameda
Editor/Annette Roman

VP, Production/Alvin Lu
VP, Sales & Product Marketing/Gonzalo Ferreyra
VP, Creative/Linda Espinosa
Publisher/Hyoe Narita

Printed in the U.S.A.

Published by VIZ Media, LLC
P.O. Box 77010
San Francisco, CA 94107

10 9 8 7 6 5 4 3 2 1
First printing, October 2010

RATED T+ FOR OLDER TEEN

PARENTAL ADVISORY
INUYASHA is rated T+ for Older Teen and is recommended for ages 16 and up. This volume contains violence.

ratings.viz.com

viz media

SHONEN SUNDAY

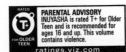

www.viz.com WWW.SHONENSUNDAY.COM

INUYASHA

action
VIZ media
INUYASHA
Story and Art by
RUMIKO TAKAHASHI
Vol. 1

Read the action from the start with the original manga series

action
INUYASHA
ANI-MANGA
CREATED BY
RUMIKO TAKAHASHI
1

Full color adaptation of the popular TV series

The Art of
INUYASHA
Original Illustrations by
Rumiko Takahashi

Art book with cel art, paintings, character profiles and more

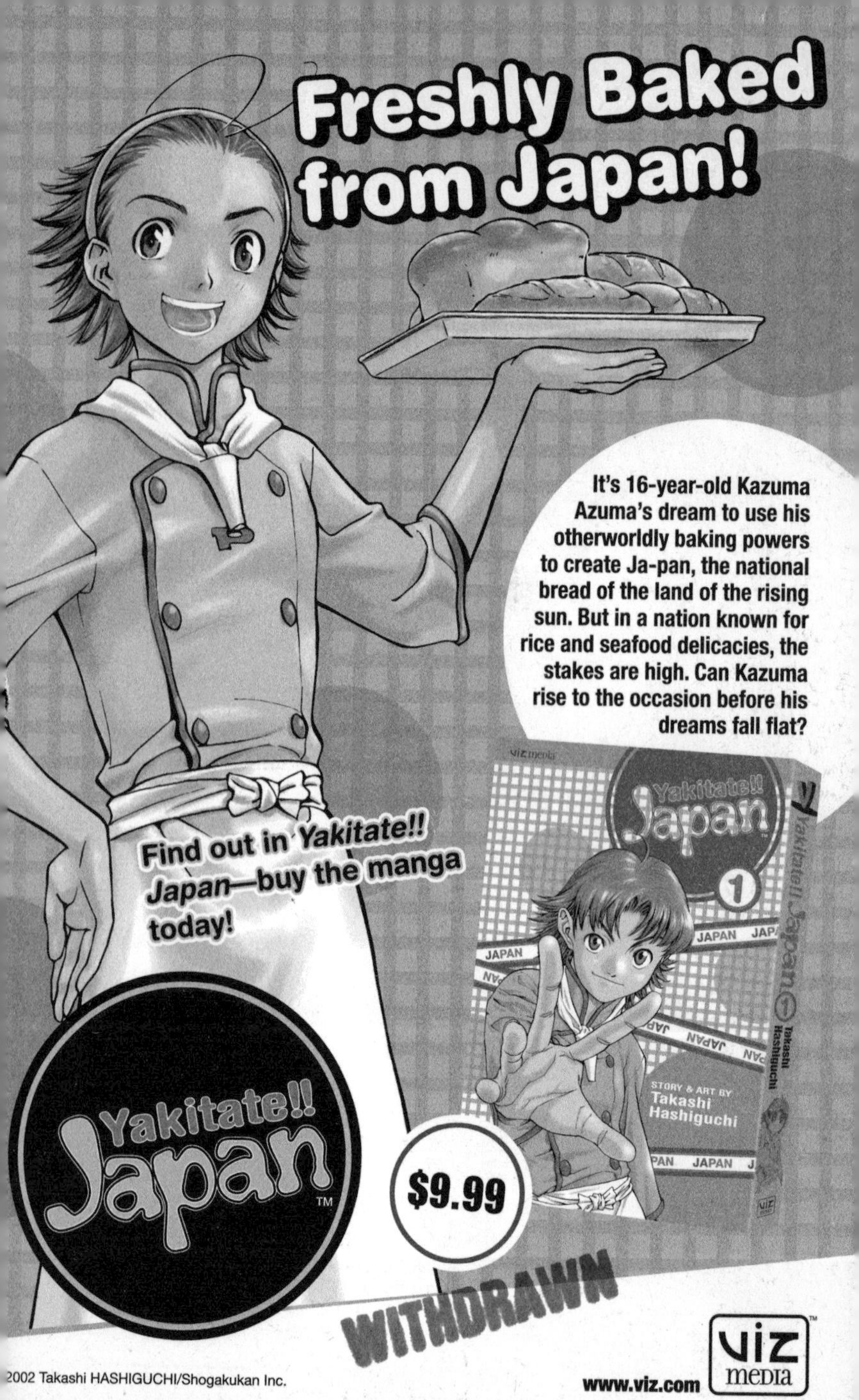
Freshly Baked from Japan!
It's 16-year-old Kazuma Azuma's dream to use his otherworldly baking powers to create Ja-pan, the national bread of the land of the rising sun. But in a nation known for rice and seafood delicacies, the stakes are high. Can Kazuma rise to the occasion before his dreams fall flat?
Find out in Yakitate!! Japan—buy the manga today!
Yakitate!! Japan TM
$9.99
viz media
Yakitate!! Japan
1
JAPAN
STORY & ART BY
Takashi Hashiguchi
Yakitate!! Japan 1 Takashi Hashiguchi